AINSLIE'S COMPLETE HOYLE

Other Books by Tom Ainslie

The Complete Horseplayer

Ainslie's Complete Guide to Thoroughbred Racing

Handicappers Handbook

Ainslie on Jockeys

AINSLIE'S COMPLETE HOYLE

BY

TOM AINSLIE

ILLUSTRATIONS BY JILL SCHWARTZ

BARNES
&NOBLE
BOOKS
NEW YORK

This edition specially printed for
Barnes and Noble Books by Simon & Schuster, Inc.

2003 Barnes & Noble Books

ISBN 0-7607-4159-X

Printed and bound in the United States of America

03 04 05 06 07 08 MC 9 8 7 6 5 4 3 2 1

Contents

PART TWO: RUMMY AND ITS RELATIVES

PART FOUR: THE BEST GAMES OF SOLITAIRE

PART FIVE: CARDS FOR CHILDREN—AND WITH 'EM

BOOK TWO: BOARD AND TABLE GAMES

PART ONE: RACES AND CHASES

PART TWO: WAR GAMES

PART THREE: DICE GAMES

PART FOUR: TILE GAMES

PART FIVE: MANCALA GAMES

PART SIX: GAMES OF LOGIC

PART SEVEN: WORD GAMES

PART EIGHT: GAMES OF SIMULATION

BOOK THREE: GAMBLING-CASINO GAMES

BOOK FOUR: GAMES FOR CLUB CAR AND TAVERN

Introduction

Edmond Hoyle's first published work was probably *A Short Treatise on the Game of Whist,* which appeared in 1742, when its author was a ripe 70. The booklet became an instantaneous success. Hoyle had previously acquired a considerable reputation as an instructor of card games, with which polite British society was absolutely obsessed.

Before he died at 97, Hoyle augmented his Whist prescriptions with advice about Chess, Backgammon, Quadrille and Piquet. On each subject, his published word exerted the force of law. It still does. To settle arguments, one opens any volume that bears Hoyle's name, finds the desired rule and is forthwith entitled to announce the verdict with absolute authority: "According to Hoyle . . ."

In our own time, experts as substantial as Ely Culbertson (*Culbertson's Hoyle*) and Albert H. Morehead (*The New Complete Hoyle*) have elected to ride the old master's coattails when coining titles for their own compendious texts. The no less consequential John Scarne deplores this. Pointing out that modern manuals contain none of Hoyle's writings and deal mainly with games unknown in Hoyle's day, he has suggested that "the practice of giving titles such as *The Revised Hoyle, The Up-to-Date Hoyle* and even *Poker According to Hoyle* seems to me comparable to titling an engineering book *Fulton on Diesel Engines,* or one on atomic energy *The Revised Aristotle.*"

One might as well complain that Noah Webster gets a by-line on dictionaries that he did not compile, or that Peter Mark Roget continues with top billing on many a modern thesaurus, although dead for more than a century. Like Webster and Roget, Hoyle is a special case, a godlike figure. Hardly anyone concedes that he is gone. The general assumption is that he issues periodic revisions of his rules and, indeed, is not only available for consultation but perfectly capable of walking through the door and smiting down anyone who bids out of turn.

Accordingly, this book is a Hoyle. Expanding the tradition of most of its predecessors, it attempts to instruct the reader in the play of any game that (a) uses cards, counters or dice and (b) is genuinely popular in any substantial area of the Western world. Included are numerous games that have become obsolete—and even are forgotten—in some regions, yet continue to command loyalty elsewhere. Our guiding principle is that there is no such thing as a bad yet popular game. Any pastime interesting enough to divert large numbers of human adults is worth looking into. If on some rainy afternoon the reader riffles through these pages and discovers the fascinations of Klab or Pitch, it will have all been worthwhile.

With the same thought in mind, we have included an unusually extensive section dealing with games of Solitaire. And we have not neglected certain so-called children's games that not only deserve adult attention but get it in many parts of the world.

Card games are the most numerous of the recreations to be explored here, but are by no means the whole story. We also cover the gamut of board and table games, with new and unprecedented emphasis on the amazing games of simulation and strategy to which computers have given rise. As we shall show, some of the commercially developed sports and war and investment games are as interesting as any board or card games in history. They already enjoy rather wide vogue, as the prosperity of manufacturers attests, but they have never been dealt with by Hoyle before. Which makes this book a great leap forward for them and the old man alike.

There is more to the book than that. Betting propositions for bar and club car occupy a section of their own. And casino gambling is also covered thoroughly. In short, if you are curious about a sedentary game, or some aspect of such a game, the chances are enormous that you will find answers here. Moreover, you will usually find enough detail to help you play that game at a reasonably competent level.

Obviously, a work of this kind cannot substitute for the specialized texts that form the literature of great games like Bridge, Chess, Poker and Backgammon. Rather than make so vain an attempt, we shall refer our reader to the best books in those well-tilled fields, contenting ourselves with just enough procedural and tactical advice to hold Mr. Hoyle's franchise.

Thanks to him, then, for getting us off to such a splendid start more than two hundred years ago. Thanks also to a contemporary figure, my editor, Norman Monath. Himself a world expert in the development, analysis and teaching of games, he has managed this project with great patience and thoughtfulness. Henry Kuck helped mightily with the research, and Patricia Miller, an extraordinarily discerning copy editor, rescued me from numerous errors. Thanks to them both.

T.A.

BOOK ONE

THE CARD GAMES

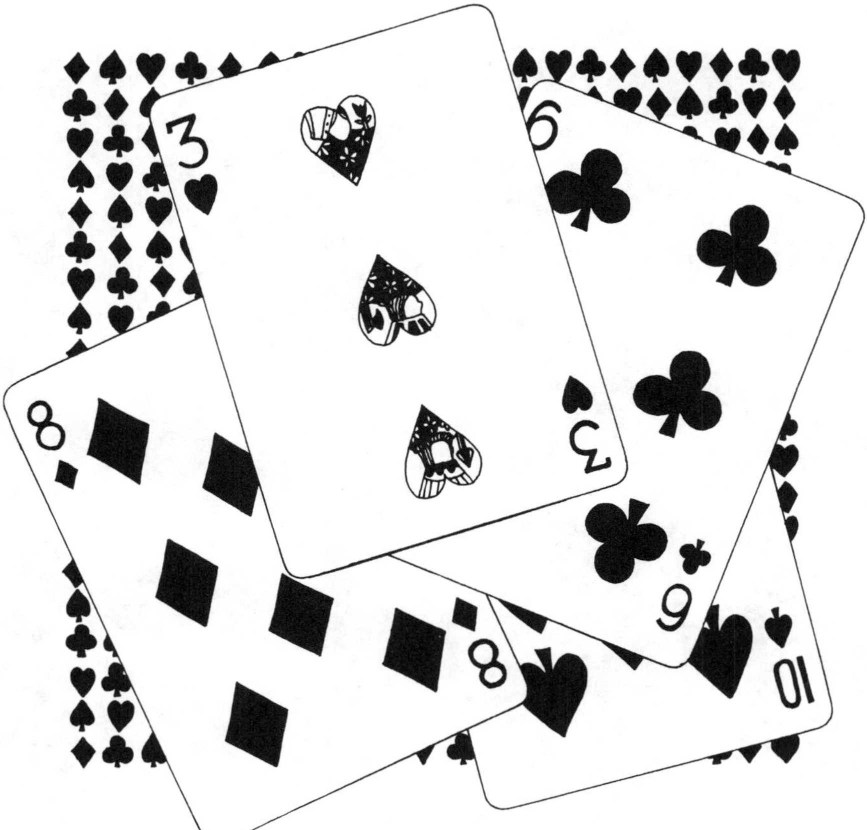

PART ONE

Games of Trick and Trump

Among recreations discussed by Charles Cotton in *The Compleat Gamester* (1673) was the card game known variously as Triumph, Trump, Ruff and Honors, Slam, Whisk and, most recently, Whist. Cotton was an established authority on the uses of human leisure. He was a good friend of Izaak Walton (some say his adopted son) and added a treatise to the fifth edition of Izaak's historic *The Compleat Angler*. His disdain of Whist was definitive.

Whist was a game of skill in an epoch when persons of social importance had neither the need nor the desire to expose their abilities to tests. Their mental and moral superiority was inherited. Moreover, it was said to be entrenched by divine decree, and was permanently beyond challenge. In the feudal sanctuaries where Charles Cotton's blooded clientele made sport, the big game was Hazard, a linear ancestor of Craps. Hazard pitted one against fate, a harmlessly playful god who imposed no penalties beyond those the gambler was willing to pay. When Cotton fibbed to his readers that "every child hath a competent knowledge" of Whist, he was prostrating himself for the Hazard crowd, reminding them that games of skill were for farmers, kitchen workers, weavers, eccentric clergymen, university grinds and other unfashionable types beyond the pale.

The world changes rapidly. Less than 70 years after Cotton's book, Edmond Hoyle wrote his all-time best seller, *A Short Treatise on the Game of Whist.* Society—high and otherwise—was now ready for Hoyle and skill. The Industrial Revolution was beginning. Feudal tradition was on its last legs. Philosophers of science and reason called attention to the challenges and opportunities of freedom, thereby approving the competitive appetites of merchants, traders and workers who aspired to a new order of things.

Games had always imitated life. Man's choice of games had always revealed his basic concerns. He was now interested most of all in demonstrating his wit, his shrewdness, his masterful cool. Whist allowed him to prove his mettle in competition with other men. If he won, the game served as verification of his superiority. If he lost, it was only a game—but a stimulating one suited to the mood of the times.

It appears that literary pirates profited more abundantly from Hoyle's work than did the author himself. Hardly was the first edition of his *Treatise* available when clever forgeries flooded the market. The pirates stole each new edition of Hoyle's booklet, and each edition of his later works. The public hungered for Hoyle's advice.

Whist became the game of choice not only in Great Britain but throughout Europe. It held sway without serious competition until late in the nineteenth century, when it was supplanted by a variant known first as Biritch or Russian Whist and later as Bridge or Bridge Whist. The essential innovation was the use of an exposed hand (dummy) during the play of the cards. Early in the present century, Auction Bridge, with its added feature of allowing each player to bid for the right to choose the trump suit, became supreme.

And then, in 1925, Commodore Harold S. Vanderbilt with some friends and chance acquaintances changed the scoring system, producing a better game, which has swept the world. Contract Bridge is unquestionably the most popular of all card games that combine the taking of tricks and the element of a trump suit—just as Chess is the foremost board game and Poker the leader among card games in which the showdown (comparison of hands) is decisive. Furthermore, Contract Bridge is the most highly organized of all card games. In the United States, at least 200,000 activists can boast that they have earned "master points" in tournaments of the American

Contract Bridge League. No count exists of the number of persons who play the game regularly, even if not at the tournament level. The popularity and longevity of instructional columns written for newspaper syndication by Bridge experts plus the sales volume achieved by playing-card manufacturers indicate that the game has tens of millions of adherents.

The Whist family has by now survived more than two centuries of preeminence among intellectual card games. As we shall see, other groups of games also feature bidding and the trumping of tricks, but Bridge and its cousins come first.

1 CONTRACT BRIDGE

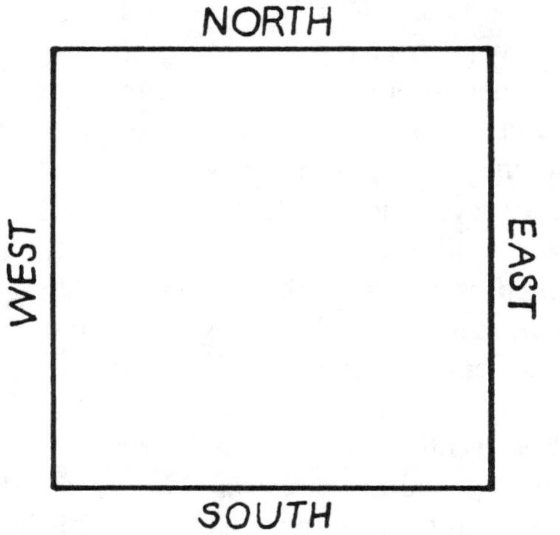

The compass points designate the positions occupied by the players at a Bridge table. In the vast instructional literature of the game, and in the notations used for official records of bidding and play, the compass points become a convenient means of referring to a hand, or to the human being who plays the hand. In all Bridge games, North and South are partners against East and West.

The Deck

A regular 52-card deck. Cards rank downward from the ace in the familiar order: A, K, Q, J, 10, 9, 8, 7, 6, 5, 4, 3, 2.

Cuts and Shuffles

If the partnerships have not been prearranged, a deck of cards is spread face down. Each player draws and exposes one card. The holder of the highest card becomes the first dealer and gets first choice of seats. The holder of the next-highest card becomes dealer's partner. If the session involves more than four players (but fewer than the eight needed for two tables of Bridge), the holders of the third- and fourth-highest cards play as partners. The others wait for the first match to end. The match may be best two rubbers of three or out of consideration for those waiting, one rubber, sudden death. If only one player is waiting, the losing team draws cards and the one drawing the lower card yields his place. If two are waiting, they replace the losing team. If three are waiting, a draw of cards determines the new partnership.

In games between predetermined partnerships, the draw determines the first dealer. By agreement, the opponent who draws the higher of his team's two cards may be required to serve as second dealer, taking the seat at the first dealer's left.

Before the first deal, the player to dealer's left shuffles the deck. The dealer then presents it to the player at his right, who divides the deck into two stacks of more-or-less equal height by cutting the cards. Etiquette demands that this be done with a minimum of flourish and, at all costs, without exposing cards. The player simply picks a stack of cards off the top of the deck and deposits it promptly and neatly alongside the other cards. The dealer then finishes the ritual by reassembling the deck, placing what formerly was the bottom portion on top.

Before each hand, dealer's partner shuffles a second deck of cards, which he then places to his own right. After play of the hand, the shuffled deck is ready for the next dealer, whose partner proceeds to shuffle the other deck. As usual, the cut is performed by the player at dealer's right.

The Deal

Clockwise, one by one, face down, until all cards have been distributed and each player has thirteen. At the completion of each hand, the dealership moves clockwise, from the latest dealer to the player at his left.

The Auction

The dealer looks at his hand (without exposing any of his cards) and evaluates its worth by applying one of the methods to be described later. He then may *pass*, indicating that he does not consider his hand strong enough to launch the bidding. Or he may offer a bid, signifying his belief that he and his partner can win six tricks (*book*) plus the number mentioned in the bid. The bid also shows whether the bidder proposes to play the hand in a trump suit, and if so which one. Thus, a bid of one heart offers to win seven tricks (the "book" of six tricks plus the "odd" single trick signified in the bid) with hearts as trump. A bid of one no-trump also commits the bidder to win seven tricks, but without using a trump suit.

The bidding proceeds in the game's usual clockwise rotation. If dealer has declined to bid (saying "Pass" or "No bid"), the player to his left then decides whether to open the bidding or not, and announces his decision. If dealer bid, the second player may pass, or may *double* the opening bid, or may *overcall.*

Double: The player who says "Double" or "I double" commits an act of defiance that increases the points at stake in the hand, unless someone else cancels the double by entering a new bid. The double demonstrates belief that the bidder's situation is not as secure as might otherwise be assumed. In retaliation, a *redouble* doubles a double. If allowed to stand without a superseding bid, it quadruples many of the rewards and penalties of play.

Overcall: As the word implies, this is a bid that exceeds the previous bid.

Each new bid must be higher than any previous bid.

The lowest possible bid is one club. For bidding purposes, the suits rank upward from clubs to diamonds (the two *minor suits*) to hearts to spades (the two *major suits*) and finally to no-trump, which outranks any suit bid that names no greater number of tricks. Thus, a bid of one spade legitimately overcalls a bid of one club or one diamond or one heart. And a bid of two clubs overcalls a bid of one no-trump or, for that matter, any other one-bid.

An auction might proceed as follows:

SOUTH	WEST	NORTH	EAST
1 Club	Pass	1 No-Trump	2 Hearts
3 Spades	Pass	4 Spades	Double
Redouble	Pass	Pass	Pass

South opened by announcing readiness to win seven tricks with clubs as trump. After West passed, South's partner responded to the opening bid with a higher offer of his own. The significance of both bids was apparent—or should have been—to the opponents. No secret bidding systems are permitted. Partners who use unorthodox or unfamiliar bidding codes are required to explain them before the game begins.

East having overcalled with two hearts, South could have recovered with two spades, a higher bid. His call of three spades indicated unusual strength and was intended to encourage all-out optimism in his partner. However, North thought it best to end the bidding at four spades. Whereupon the stubborn East doubled and the confident South redoubled.

The auction closed with South as *declarer.* That is, he had been the first member of his partnership to bid the suit that finally became trump. As declarer, South would play the hand. To avoid penalty, he would have to win ten of the thirteen tricks. Moreover, the redoubling of the contract meant that the final result would be expensive for the losing side.

Note that neither East's double nor South's redouble would have remained in force had a member of either team offered a bid higher than the one that had been doubled. But nobody did, and the auction —like all Bridge auctions—ended when the last bid (or double or redouble) was followed by three consecutive passes.

Note also that if dealer had not opened the bidding when he did, and if all three of the other players had then passed in turn, the cards would have been thrown in as *passed out.* No scoring would have been possible, no auction or play having occurred. The deal would have moved clockwise to the next in order, West.

THE PLAY

The player at declarer's left makes the *opening lead,* placing whatever card he considers appropriate in the middle of the table, face up. Declarer's partner, the *dummy,* now places his own hand face up on his side of the table, arranging the cards in columns, each containing one suit. In orderly games, the trump suit is placed in the column at the dummy's right, and the cards of each suit are arranged in value sequence—the highest at the top, lowest at the bottom of the exposed column of cards.

The declarer plays his own hand and the dummy hand. His object

is to win no fewer than the number of tricks for which his side has contracted.

The object of the defense is to *set,* or defeat, the contract by winning sufficient tricks of its own.

Beginning with the opening lead, play is clockwise. Each trick consists of one card from each player. The winner of a trick leads to the next trick (plays the first card). When dummy wins a trick, declarer must lead to the next trick with a card from dummy.

The suit of the first card played to a trick determines the suit in which the trick is played. Each player is required to follow suit if he can. If he has no card in the suit, he can play a card of any other suit, including trump. But he may play trump only in such circumstances, or if the trick is being played in trump.

A trick containing no trump cards is won by the highest card of the suit in which the trick is being played.

A trick containing trump cards is won by the highest trump.

One member of each team collects the tricks won by the team. The tricks are kept face down, separate from one another. Any player may turn over the last trick and look at its cards if neither he nor his partner has yet played to the next trick.

Play ends after all thirteen tricks have been played.

Scoring

The players designate one of their number as scorekeeper. Or each team may have its own scorekeeper. The scoring sheet provides one column for "We"—the recorder's own partnership—and another for "They"—the opposition. Certain values are tabulated below the center line, others above it. The procedures are not as complicated as they usually seem to beginners. They depend on proper use of a few numerical formulas, plus understanding of the following terminology.

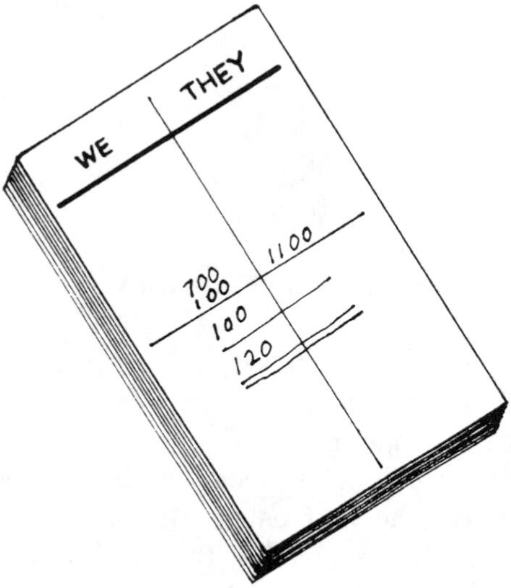

Below the Line: When the declarer makes or surpasses the number of tricks called for in his contract, *the value of the contract itself* is recorded below the line. Any extra credits, such as might be earned by winning extra tricks, are recorded above the line. The below-the-line score is known sometimes as the *trick score.*

Here is the numerical formula for scoring below the line:

	Odd Tricks Bid and Made						
	1	2	3	4	5	6	7
Major Suits (Spades and Hearts)	30	60	90	120	150	180	210
Minor Suits (Diamonds and Clubs)	20	40	60	80	100	120	140
No-Trump	40	70	100	130	160	190	220

Double the score if contract was doubled.
Quadruple the score if contract was redoubled.

Game: When a partnership earns 100 or more points below the line, it has won a *game*. Note that a successful bid of five is therefore necessary to make game in the two minor suits; a bid of four is a *game bid* in the major suits, and game can be scored in no-trump by bidding and making three. After a side scores sufficient points for game, the scorekeeper draws a new horizontal line beneath the tally and enters the next game's trick scores below this new line. Points scored below the line by the partnership that loses a game are credited in the accounting at the end of the session, but do not otherwise apply to the scoring. Each game begins with a below-line score of zero for each side.

Vulnerable: After it wins its first game of a particular *rubber,* a partnership is *vulnerable,* which increases some of the rewards and penalties recorded above the line. We shall now itemize these bonus situations.

Overtricks: These are tricks won in excess of the basic contract. Each such trick is scored above the line according to the following formula:

Minor Suits	20
Major Suits and No-Trump	30

Bonuses increase dramatically if the contract is doubled or redoubled. Regardless of the contract's denomination, each overtrick scored by a declarer when doubled and not vulnerable is worth 100 points. When doubled and vulnerable, the overtrick earns 200 points. Should the contract be redoubled, each overtrick scores 200 points not vulnerable and 400 vulnerable.

Double Bonus: When declarer makes a doubled or redoubled contract, his side scores 50 points above the line, regardless of any other bonuses he may earn in the process.

Honors: Each suit contains five honors—ace down through ten. If any player holds four of these five honors in a trump suit, his team gets 100 points above the line. This is why the score above the line often is known as the *honor score.* If a player holds all five honors, his side scores 150 above the line. In contracts at no-trump, if a player holds all four aces, his side scores 150.

Little Slam: When the bid is six and the declarer is under contract to win all but one of the thirteen tricks, his side is trying for a *little slam,* or *small slam.* If he makes it, his side scores a bonus of 500 above the line if not vulnerable or 750 if vulnerable.

Grand Slam: Whoever bids and makes seven odd tricks—winning every trick in the hand—scores a bonus of 1,000 above the line if his side is not vulnerable, 1,500 when vulnerable.

Penalties: If the defense sets the contract, declarer *goes down.* Declarer's partnership may suffer heavy penalties. These are not deducted from the score on the declarer's side, but are recorded above the line on the defenders' side. Triumphant defenders earn points at the following rate for each undertrick charged against declarer:

	Not Vulnerable	*Vulnerable*
Contract Undoubled	50	100
Contract Doubled		
First Undertrick	100	200
Each Additional	200	300
Contract Redoubled		
First Undertrick	200	400
Each Additional	400	600

Rubber: The first side to bid and make two games wins the rubber. If the opponents have not won a game during the rubber, the victors score 700 above the line. Otherwise the bonus is 500. For winning the only game of an unfinished rubber, the bonus is 300. And for making the only partial score in an unfinished rubber that saw neither side winning a game, the bonus is 50. It is possible to win the rubber but come out on the short end of the over-all competition. Prizes are awarded for total points rather than rubbers. Thus, the score on page 12 shows that "They" finished the rubber with a winning margin of 80 points, although they had not won a game. This demonstrates the value of good defensive play.

Individual Scoring

The average neighborly bridge game is a *set game* in which the partnerships remain unchanged throughout the evening. Where the competitive spirit is differently disposed, or more than four players are involved, it is customary to use a system of *back scoring*, which identifies the individuals who fared best. In such games, partnerships rotate according to the sequences established by cuts and draws or other arrangements. By evening's end, every player has been the partner of every other for at least one rubber. Hardships of that kind having been evenly distributed, skill is decisive. The person with the highest score is therefore entitled to a certain amount of deference.

To keep the scores, the winning margin is computed at the end of each rubber and is divided by 100. Each winning partner is credited with the resultant number at the rate of 1 point per 100, plus another point if the remainder is 50 or more. In short, a winning margin of 630 earns each winner 6 points. A margin of 660 would be worth 7 points. The losers are charged with their losing margins. After the next and subsequent rubbers, each of which is played by different partnerships, the scores are adjusted to new net figures. Thus, if one player earned 10 points in the first rubber and lost 6 in the second, his net score would now be 4. Needless to say, net scores in minus quantities are not unusual.

Bases of Bidding

Because tricks won but not bid earn far fewer points than tricks bid *and* won, and because the rules inflict heavy punishment on players who bid too high and are set too often or too severely, bidding is crucial. Persons with the faculty known as "card sense" have relatively little trouble acquiring competence in the actual play of the hand. But bidding is another problem entirely. For this reason, Bridge literature devotes more space to bidding than to play, and the new Bridge theories that abound at every season of the year are concerned invariably and exclusively with bidding techniques, striving to make them more precise.

Fundamental to every system of bidding is the evaluation of the hand. For most players, and in most situations, this is a fairly cut-and-dried process. Serious difficulty does not usually arise until the player needs to communicate, through his bidding, the precise shape and substance of the hand.

Evaluation is comparatively easy because of the *point-count method* developed and popularized by Charles Goren.

Point Count:	Ace	= 4
	King	= 3
	Queen	= 2
	Jack	= 1

Accordingly, the deck contains 40 high-card points. It has been demonstrated that a partnership should usually have an aggregate of 26 points to make a game in a major suit, 29 in a minor. A little slam is within reach if the two hands add up to 33, and 37 is usually needed for a grand slam.

Suit Distribution: In considering whether to open with a suit bid, players elaborate the basic point count with standard values reflecting the imbalance (and extra potential playing strength) of the hand:

A void suit is worth 3
A singleton is worth 2
A doubleton is worth 1

A hand containing all four aces is credited with 1 extra point. But an aceless hand loses 1.

To earn full credit, honors must be adequately guarded. Thus, a singleton king—less likely to win a trick than if accompanied by a sacrificial smaller card in the same suit—is reduced from 3 to 2. To be worth its full 2, the queen must be accompanied by two small cards. Unless the jack is protected by two small cards, it loses its point value.

After a player opens with a suit bid, his partner must assess his own hand in terms of its potential strength as a dummy in the proposed trump suit:

A void is worth 5
A singleton is worth 3
A doubleton is worth 1

Furthermore, an honor in the proposed trump suit gains 1 extra point when the player evaluates his hand as a dummy. Thus, the king is worth 4, the queen 3 and the jack 2. In the unusual event that the player holds two honors in the proposed trump suit, he must not give them extra credit if to do so would raise their combined worth above 4.

The player deducts 1 point if he holds three or fewer cards in the proposed trump suit.

If his partner supports the proposed trump by responding at some stage with a bid of his own in the same suit, the opening bidder adds new values to his own hand:

1 extra point for the fifth trump card
2 extra points for the sixth and each additional trump card

Except for the matter of properly guarded honors, distributional values are not considered in assessing the worth of hands for purposes of no-trump bidding. Only high-card points are counted.

Standard Bidding Techniques

Under the tutelage of Charles Goren, countless Bridge fans practice a common-sense system of bidding that has served them well for years. It also served Goren and his peers well in international competition, which the United States dominated for decades. What finally toppled us and, in fact, has made us a third-rate power in the Bridge world was bidding of a more accurate character than is possible under our own familiar procedures. European and Asian experts now toy with any U.S. teams that have not mastered one or another of the new bidding systems.

If precision were their only new feature, the foreign systems would have long since become dominant in American Bridge. Unfortunately, they have almost no application to the more-or-less casual games played by nonexperts. They are too intricate for anything but tournament play. Indeed, the average country-club shark is extremely fortunate if he can understand some of the newer methods, much less use them with his regular partners.

Championship Bridge has accordingly become an even more rarefied activity than it used to be. Until recently, after all, the Bridge fan could at least understand the meaning of the bids reported in the daily Bridge column or in the news of international competitions. But now it is all Greek. For that reason, the overwhelming majority of sociable Bridge players continues to depend on the common-sense system of bidding promulgated by Goren.

In this book we also conform to those realities, offering the fundamentals of bidding as presently understood by the kinds of players with whom the reader is most likely to collide.

Opening in No-Trump: If the hand is balanced (a suit distribution of 4-3-3-3 or 4-4-3-2) and contains not less than 16 or more than 18 high-card points, with no valueless doubleton, it is worth an opening bid of one no-trump.

If the hand contains 22 to 24 points and is balanced, with no unprotected honors, the player opens with two no-trump.

And a phenomenal hand worth 25 to 27 high-card points can win a no-trump game all alone. So it warrants an opening bid of game—three no-trump.

Responding to a No-Trump Opening Bid: Because he knows the procedures just explained, the opening bidder's partner knows the combined point value of the two hands to within 2 points. If his own hand is balanced or otherwise amenable to no-trump play, the potential dummy simply counts points and responds logically to an opening bid of one no-trump:

With 8 or 9 the bid is 2 NT
With 10 to 14 the bid is 3 NT
With 15 or 16 the bid is 4 NT
With 17 or 18 the bid is 5 NT
With 19 or 20 the bid is 6 NT
With 21 or more the bid is 7 NT

If the hand is sufficiently unbalanced to suggest that it can be played effectively in a suit contract, with the opening bidder's balanced hand as dummy, the response is made in a trump suit.

If the opening no-trump bid was at the level of two or higher, logic continues to prevail. For example, in reply to two no-trump, the partner with a balanced hand and 3 to 8 points will bid three no-trump. With 9 points or more, he would try for slam by whatever conventional means he and partner employ in such circumstances (*see below*). Similarly, if opening bid was three no-trump and partner is satisfied to see the hand played in no-trump, he will suggest slam when he holds 6 points or more.

Opening in a Suit: Under the Goren system, an opening bid is considered mandatory if high-card plus distributional points total 14 or more. A count of 13 points makes opening optional—likely if the potential trump suit is strong, and less likely if the hand lacks a five-card suit.

The Biddable Suit: To offer a suit bid, the player must have a biddable suit in his hand. At a minimum, this requires four cards including queen–jack or better. A five-card suit is considered biddable if headed by the queen or the jack–ten.

A suit is *rebiddable*—the opening bidder may bid in the suit again even when the partner has not supported the suit—if it contains five cards headed by not less than two honors, or if it contains any six cards.

Choosing the Suit: Bid the longer suit first. If two are of the same length, bid the higher-ranking suit unless the two contain four cards each and one of the suits is clubs—in which case the customary bid is one club.

Opening at Two in a Suit: In ordinary American bidding, an opening bid of two signifies great strength. Some experts recommend a two-bid if the hand contains 25 points and a good five-card suit, or 23 and a good six-card suit, or 21 and a good seven-card suit. Others suggest that a more practical approach is to count the sure tricks in the hand. If they total nine and the proposed trump will be a major suit, or ten for a minor suit, it is safe to open the bidding at the level of two. Note that nine in a major or ten in a minor are but one trick short of enough for game.

Opening at Three or Four in a Suit: When the player's hand contains a notably long suit but is weak in high cards and seems unlikely to be much use for defensive purposes, it is customary to consider offering a *preemptive* bid at the level of three or four. The purpose of such a move is to disrupt communications between the opponents, preventing them from achieving a likely game contract.

The criteria for making such a bid are *not more than* 9 points when not vulnerable and not more than 10 when vulnerable. The potential trump suit should be long enough to assure the player of missing his contract by no more than two tricks when vulnerable, three when not vulnerable. No help from partner is anticipated. A typical hand for this kind of bidding is likely to contain eight trumps or more, with little or no honor strength in the anemic side suits.

Responding to a Suit Bid of One: If partner has opened the bidding at the level of one and the other team has kept mum, your only clues to the situation are (a) the strength of your own hand and (b) the certain knowledge that partner's hand contains not less than 13 points. With any strength, your duty is to keep the bidding open until partner has had a chance to describe his holdings more completely. For all you know, he has 19 or 20 points in his fist. Despite your measly 6, your team might be in position to take a game.

In considering the response to an opening bid of one, it is necessary to remember several customs that have taken on the force of rules. Violations or misunderstandings of these practices can ruin a game of Bridge. Here are the rules:

1. If responder's hand is strong enough to have justified an opening bid on his part, he knows that he and partner are almost certain to have enough strength for a game contract. The formula: *Opening bid opposite opening bid equals game* works whenever the partners are deft enough to land in the proper trump suit or, if more appropriate, in no-trump.

2. If responder bids in a suit other than that named by his partner, the response is *forcing* for one round. That is, opening bidder must bid at least once more, keeping the auction alive.

3. Responder may not bid in a new suit at the level of two unless he has at least 10 points.

4. With a below-average hand (fewer than 10 points), responder's objective should be to raise partner's opening bid to the level of two. If this is not practical because responder lacks adequate support for partner's suit, responder sees about naming a new suit at the level of one. But if his hand contains fewer than 6 points, he passes.

5. With 19 or more points and strong support for partner's suit, or a strong suit of his own, responder is required to proclaim his

strength by *jumping* in a new suit. That is, he bids a new suit at a level one trick higher than necessary—bidding three, for example, when two would suffice to keep the bidding open.

6. Adequate trump support consists of three cards including one honor, or four cards without an honor. If partner rebids the suit, a player is on firm ground if he decides to support the suit with a bid of his own while holding only two cards including an honor, or three cards without an honor.

Having committed those principles to mind, the player will find that the problem of responding to an opening bid is quite simple:

Raise partner to two in his own suit with 7 to 10 points and trump support.

Raise partner to three in his own suit with at least four trumps and 13 to 16 points.

Raise to four with 9 or fewer high-card points, at least five trump cards and a singleton or void side suit.

Respond with one no-trump if holding 6 to 9 points in high cards, no particular support for partner's suit, and either a balanced hand or one in which the long suit would have to be bid at the level of two (for which a hand as weak as this does not qualify). For example, after partner opens with one spade:

♠ A x ♡ x x x ◇ K J x x ♣ x x x x

The hand is worth 7 dummy points in spades (*see page 16*). Trump support will be adequate if partner rebids the suit, but is not inspiring at this stage. The hand is too weak for a bid of two diamonds, but is too strong for a mere pass. The proper call is one no-trump.

Balanced hands with high-point counts of 13 to 15 and no unguarded honors justify responses of two no-trump.

With 16 to 18 points and a balanced hand without unguarded honors, the answer is three no-trump.

Responding to a Suit Bid of Two: The powerful opening bid at the level of two is a *forcing* bid. The responder is required to keep the bidding open until the partnership has reached game. If responder's hand is poor (6 points or less), he bids two no-trump. With 8 or 9 and a balanced hand, he bids three no-trump. Otherwise, he raises partner's suit (with adequate trump support) or names his own best suit.

Responding to a Suit Bid of Three or Four: Because the preemptive opening bid signifies weakness, responder should have a powerful hand to raise. If the opening bid is at the level of four in a major suit, the only reasons to raise are (a) competitive bidding by the other team or (b) sufficient high-card strength in responder's hand to assure a slam.

Free Bid: If responder's right-hand opponent inserts an overcall in reply to the opening bid, a bid by responder now signifies greater strength than it would without the overcall. For one thing, the overcall assures the opening bidder of another chance to be heard, and his partner is under no pressure to keep the bidding open for him. To name a new suit at the level of one in these circumstances, responder should have a solid 9 points. To justify a bid at the level of two, 12 points are needed. If he has less, he can indicate as much at his next turn. If he wants to offer a *free raise*—supporting partner's suit after an overcall—he should have at least 9 points.

Rebidding: Having interpreted his partner's response, the opening bidder usually knows whether the combined strength of the two hands is likely to be within firing range of game. His second bid, known as the *rebid,* communicates this appraisal to the responder, and prepares the team for whatever additional action may be indicated.

If partner named a new suit or responded with a jump bid (one higher than necessary to keep the bidding alive), the opening bidder is obliged to rebid, even with a hand of minimum values.

If partner responded with one no-trump, opener usually passes with fewer than 18 points, realizing that game is probably out of the question. With unbalanced distribution, such as a six-card suit, opener may rebid the suit at the level of two. With more points, opener may jump directly to game in his suit or in no-trump (depending on distribution), or, with 22 points or more, may invite slam bidding by offering a jump rebid in a *new* suit. This jump rebid is forcing to game—the partner must keep bidding until game is reached.

If responder offered only a single raise (which means a raise in the opener's suit), opener is under no compulsion to keep the bidding alive unless he has at least 17 points. The nature of the rebid will depend on whether he has a rebiddable suit or can name another suit at the level of one.

If responder named a new suit, opener signifies minimum values by rebidding one no-trump with a balanced hand, or supports responder's suit with a single raise (indicating adequate trump support). Or he may rebid his own suit, or name a new suit, provided that this would not push the bidding beyond the level of two should responder decide to support the opener's *original* suit. For example, if the opening bid was in diamonds and response was in spades, opener would not exaggerate the worth of his minimum hand by going to two hearts, which would require responder to say three diamonds if he wanted to show support for the first suit mentioned in the bidding.

With a somewhat better hand worth 16 to 19 points, opener replies more vigorously to a response that names a new suit. With four cards in responder's suit, the rebid may jump a step in that suit, indicating that game is within reach if responder has a couple of extra points. Or, with a strong suit of his own, opener may offer a jump bid in that denomination.

With a hand of 20 points or better, the rebid in reply to responder's mention of a new suit should show that game is certain and slam possible. This is done by jumping in a third suit (Goren calls this rebid the *jump shift,* an apt term).

Slam Bidding: When it becomes evident that the combined strength of the two hands is 33 points or more, and that the trump suit is strong and well supported, the partners check to see whether they control all suits sufficiently to prevent the enemy from winning two tricks.

If the contract is to be played in a suit, the partners often employ the *Blackwood Convention,* a series of artificial bids that show whether the two hands have all the aces and kings. To invoke this convention, one of the partners simply bids four no-trump. The other player is obliged to reply with five clubs if he holds no aces or all four aces, five diamonds with one ace, five hearts with two aces or five spades with three. The next step may be a direct bid of slam, or the player may bid five no-trump, which means that he wants to know where the kings are. Partner's responses at the level of six give this information (he bids six no-trump if he has all four kings).

In other situations, the partners name their aces simply by bidding the suits in which they hold the aces. Because slam strength (or thereabouts) has been demonstrated and a trump suit found in the first two or three calls, the naming of other suits is unmistakably the *cue bidding* that identifies aces.

Defensive Bidding

The other side has opened the bidding. Your partner has passed or has not yet had an opportunity to be heard. If your hand measures up, you may be able to prevent the opponents from bidding—and making—the decisive game of the rubber. You may even be able to capture the initiative and make a partial game of your own. And occasions arise in which you and partner *can* make game even though the other side opened the auction.

Overcall: A defensive bid after the other side has opened, the simple overcall may be inserted for the purpose of telling one's own partner what suit to lead to the first trick. This can be dangerous. If opponents are not too sure of their own offensive strength, they may solve their problem by doubling your overcall, forcing you to play a doomed contract under hazardous terms.

Accordingly, the overcall is approached much like a preemptive bid. The overcaller's suit should be long and fairly solid. He should be able to guarantee winning within two tricks of the bid if vulnerable and within three tricks if not.

Sometimes you find yourself with a hand that would warrant an opening bid of one no-trump—16 to 18 points and balanced distribution, including a guarded honor in opponents' suit. An overcall of one no-trump signifies this, and usually puts an end to the other side's pretensions.

A jump overcall—naming a new suit at a level higher than necessary to keep the bidding alive—is a preemptive bid. It should not be used unless the bidder is positive of his ability to hold losses to the usual minimums required in preemptive bidding.

Takeout Double: A simple overcall is not forcing on partner. Where a player has a genuinely strong hand, and wants to hear from partner, he may decide to use the *takeout double,* which requires partner to "take out" the auction into a new suit. To differentiate the takeout double from the traditional "business" double, which is used to inflict penalties, the ground rules are strict. The double must be made at the player's first opportunity to double; the player's partner must not have offered a bid; and the doubled bid must have named a suit at a level no higher than three.

By doubling for takeout, the player signifies that his hand is strong enough to warrant an opening bid of its own, and that the hand probably features a kind of distribution likely to offer excellent support in any trump suit the partner names.

Doubler's partner is obliged to respond. The chances are large that his hand is below average in point-count strength. After all, everybody at the table cannot have a good hand. All partner need do, however, is name his longest suit. And if he happens to have a good hand (as might occur when the opening bidder holds minimum values and opening bidder's partner has a handful of blanks), he should jump in his best suit, calling for a game contract.

Defensive Cue Bid: If North opens with one spade and East overcalls with two spades, East announces that his own hand is good enough to have opened the bidding at the level of two. Moreover, he either is void in spades or has the ace—in short, he can control the suit in the first round of play. His bid is forcing on his partner, who must keep the auction going until a game contract is reached.

Other Bidding Systems

Among tournament competitors of the top rank, highly systematized bidding has largely supplanted the natural approach described above. The new methods permit important communication at lower bidding levels, mainly through the use of conventionalized one-club and two-club bids to indicate special forms of strength. The forcing two-bid of yore is no longer in wide use among champions, who find bids of two more effective when used as indications of weakness. Also, the double raise (jump) is not often regarded as forcing. While the details of such methods are far beyond the scope of this book, the reader should have some idea of what his companions mean when they use some of the better-established terms in the complex world of "scientific" bidding. Accordingly, here are brief glimpses at important bidding systems more widely employed in tournament halls than in living rooms.

Bulldog: A pioneering departure which permits an opening bid of one no-trump with 12 to 14 points when not vulnerable, 17 to 19 when vulnerable. Psychic opening bids allowed with only 7 points, but opener must pass any response other than three clubs or two no-trump. The latter response means 20 to 23 points, and the other indicates confidence that the partnership will win no fewer than nine tricks. Opening bid at two level means weakness.

Canapé: Popular in France and incorporated in many of the newer European systems (especially the trail-blazing Italian ones), this method features the naming of shorter biddable suits before the longer ones.

Kaplan-Sheinwold: A one no-trump opening always a weak 12 to 14, whether vulnerable or not. No four-card major may be used for opening bid. A one no-trump rebid means balanced hand and 15 to 17 points. Jump bids usually announce weakness. Devised by the New York masters or Edgar Kaplan and Alfred Sheinwold.

Little Major: A staggeringly complicated system invented by Terence Reese and Jeremy Flint, the renowned Britons, in an effort to counteract the artificial systems played by Italian masters. Opening bid of one club means a good heart suit; one diamond means either a spade suit or a good balanced hand; one heart means either great strength or pronounced weakness, depending on whether the opener rebids or passes on the next round. From these artificial beginnings, the system proceeds into a welter of conventions that any serious student of the game will find most provocative.

Neapolitan: One of the chief Italian methods, in which a one-club opening bid means not less than 17 points or strong distribution and is forcing for one round. Responder bids artificially to show controls (a king counting as one control and an ace as two). Thus one diamond means 5 points or less and two controls or less, and one heart announces the same poor situation with respect to controls but promises 6 points or more. A one-spade response indicates three controls, one no-trump four, two clubs five, two diamonds six and two no-trump seven or more. Responses of two hearts and two spades identify six-card suits headed by two honors. Subsequent rounds of bidding are equally artificial and no less precise in their meanings.

Precision: In 1969 and 1970, inexperienced players representing Taiwan finished second in the world Bridge championships, using an ingenious bidding system devised by C. C. Wei, a China-born citizen of the United States. As if this were not sufficient to make the Precision method an international sensation, a team of obscure Americans won the American Contract Bridge League's National Knockout Team championship in 1970 after only two weeks of instruction and practice with Wei and his method. Moreover, the upstarts repeated that triumph in 1971. As in other departures from established bidding practice, the Precision system utilizes an artificial opening bid of one club. In this case, the bid proclaims a hand of not less than 16 points and is forcing. An opening bid of one diamond indicates 11 to 15 points with at least four diamonds. To open with one heart or one spade means at least five cards in the particular major suit and 11 to 15 points. With 13 to 15 points and a balanced hand, the proper opening bid is one no-trump. Responses are equally precise and are made at extremely low levels of bidding. For example, the player who responds to a one-club opening bid with one heart or one spade declares a five-card suit, at least 8 points and insistence on reaching a game contract if a suit fit is found. More details on this and other bidding systems will be found in books listed under Recommended Readings on page 46.

Roman: Most of the responses and rebids in this prime Italian method reveal distribution rather than high-card strength. The one-club opening means either 12 to 16 points or, depending on subsequent bids, 21 to 25. Hands of 17 to 20 points are opened with one no-trump. Opening bids of one diamond, one heart or one spade are forcing, usually indicating a suit of at least four cards. A response in the next-higher suit (or one no-trump in answer to one spade) means fewer than 9 points. Shorter suits are bid before longer ones, as in the Canapé method.

Roth-Stone: A fascinating system that provides considerable latitude yet sometimes requires greater high-card strength than natural bidding demands in comparable situations. Many opportunities for psychic opening bids when holding as few as 3 points while seated in first or second position and not vulnerable. Indeed, responder is obliged to *assume* that the bid was psychic in such circumstances. A positive response from him therefore suggests great power. The system was developed by the U.S. stars Alvin Roth and Tobias Stone.

Schenken: The celebrated Howard Schenken's highly refined method depends on an artificial opening bid of one club, indicating not less than 17 points. A response of one diamond means weakness. All others show at least 9 points and are forcing to game. Opening bids of one spade, one heart or one diamond announce mediocre hands of not more than 16 points and call for natural bidding thereafter. With one foot in the mainstream of modern international play and the other in tradition, this system (known as "The Big Club") is a splendid opportunity for the venturesome student of the game.

Bidding Conventions

By agreement between partners and, in due course, among bridge players at large, certain bids have assumed special, artificial meanings in specific situations. For most of the *conventions*, suitable situations seldom arise except in tournament play. Some, however, are familiar to addicts of social Bridge and are essential to even the most casual player's repertoire. Bridge law requires that each partnership declare and, if necessary, describe its conventions before play begins. The following material offers inklings of some of the more widely used conventions, fuller descriptions of which are obtainable in books listed later under Recommended Reading.

Asking Bids: Numerous conventions enable a player to discover whether his partner holds the crucial control cards needed for a slam contract. One such convention has been abstracted from the Roman system. After partners have agreed on their suit, a nonjump bid in a previously unnamed suit asks the partner for an artificial reply naming his controls in the suit. Thus if the bidding has reached the level of three and hearts have been agreed upon, a bid of four clubs would inquire about partner's controls. His reply of four diamonds would mean no controls. One step higher (four hearts) would signify a king, the next step (four spades) an ace, and four no-trump would mean ace–king or ace–queen. In other bidding systems, an exaggerated jump bid is an asking bid, especially in a situation in which slam seems likely. For example, if a bid of three in a new suit were a jump shift exhibiting slam power, a bid of four in that suit would be unnecessarily strong at that phase of the bidding and, in addition to signifying the power, would ask partner about controls.

Astro: A complex and difficult system of overcalling an opening bid of one no-trump. Overcall of two clubs means a hand featuring hearts and another suit, whereas two diamonds means spades and another suit. Overcaller's partner is faced with a profusion of alternatives depending on his own distribution and strength. Although regarded as a set of conventions, Astro is copious enough to qualify as a defensive bidding system.

Blackwood: The famous Indiana master, Easley Blackwood, devised this now-standard method of ascertaining the number of aces in two slam-bound hands (*see page 23*).

Brozel: Lucille Brown and Bernard Zeller devised this means of adding precision to overcalls. After an opening one no-trump bid, a double indicates a hand with one long suit. If partner is interested, he simply bids two clubs and then passes the doubler's next bid.

Two-suited hands are announced by overcalls at the level of two. Thus two clubs shows hearts and clubs, two diamonds means hearts and diamonds, two hearts means both major suits, two spades shows spades and a minor and two no-trump means both minors. If opening bid was not in no-trump, a jump overcall at the level of three declares a three-suited hand with a singleton or void in the opener's suit. An ordinary overcall at a lower level means a hand in which the strong suits are (a) the one bid by the overcaller and (b) the next higher suit as yet unbid in the particular auction. An overcall of two spades means spades and either minor suit.

Culbertson Four–Five No-Trump. A four no-trump bid promises either three aces or two aces and a king of a suit already bid by the partnership. A reply of five no-trump indicates either two aces or one ace plus the kings of all suits previously bid by the partnership (provided, of course, that the suits were genuinely bid and were not used artificially). If partner has no aces, his reply is five of the lowest suit previously (and genuinely) bid by the team. Holding one ace, his reply is in the ace's own suit—at the level of five if possible, but at the level of six if a lower bid might be misunderstood to mean a lack of aces.

Drury: If a player passes and his partner opens the bidding in a major suit, a response of two clubs asks for more information. A conventional rebid of two diamonds shows that the opening bid was based on a weak holding. If opener's partner continues with two in the opener's suit he shows strong support. With only moderate support, he would not have used the two-club response but would simply have supported the opening bid.

Fishbein: An ingenious takeout call concocted by Harry Fishbein for combat against a preemptive opening bid. If opener says three diamonds, an overcall of three hearts (the next-higher suit) requires partner to bid his best suit. Has the effect of a takeout double, without the risk.

Gambling Three No-Trump: When partners use the normal two-club opening bid to signify a powerful hand, a three no-trump opening bid may be used conventionally to announce a long, powerful suit without side strength. A response of four clubs asks opener to name the suit and play the hand at the level of four.

Gerber: Where Blackwood is used in reaching suit slams, Gerber is useful in determining whether the partners have enough aces to warrant a slam in no-trump. With a strong but marginal hand, response to an opening of one or two no-trump is four clubs, which asks partner to use John S. Gerber's conventional replies: four diamonds means none or four aces, four hearts means one, four spades means two and four no-trump three. If the four-club bidder then calls five clubs, he asks partner to indicate kings by bidding at the five level. Any bid other than five clubs is intended as a "sign-off"—an attempt to terminate the bidding.

Jacoby Transfer: America's most versatile card player and instructor, Oswald Jacoby, devised an intelligent means of arriving at a subgame contract in a major suit after a one no-trump opening. If responder wants to see the game played in hearts or spades at the level of two, he bids two diamonds or two hearts (the next lower suit). By convention, the opening bidder dutifully replies in the desired suit and, unless opponents interfere, becomes declarer—an advantage, inasmuch as his hand is the stronger. Occasionally, this convention can be used to approach a game contract. Responder simply raises partner's bid to three, indicating that an extra value or two will justify the next step.

Landy: Alvin Landy originated the conventional use of a two-club overcall as a request to partner to name his best major suit in face of the opponent's opening one no-trump bid.

Lightner: One of the early frontiersmen of Contract Bridge, Theodore Lightner devised a means of defeating slam contracts while increasing the rewards of doing so. When a user of this convention doubles an opponent's slam bid, he not only seeks extra points, but directs his partner to make an unusual lead to the first trick. That is, partner is obliged to lead a card in a suit that he might otherwise by-pass. If he does so, doubler pounces, takes the trick and—perhaps—proceeds to set the contract.

Michaels Cue Bid: When opponent opens the bidding, an overcall in opener's suit is used as a takeout double and, in the Michaels convention, to show a two-suited hand. If opener bid a minor suit, the cue bid means strength in both majors. If opener bid a major, the cue bid promises strength in the unbid major and a minor.

Relays: Many of the newer systems enable the responder to explore the opening bidder's hand simply by making the lowest possible call of his own. For example, if opening bid is one diamond, the response of one heart is entirely conventional, asking the opener for further particulars.

Ripstra: When opponent opens with one no-trump, an overcall in a minor suit means a three-suit hand with not more than one card in the unbid minor.

Roman Blackwood: In response to the conventional four no-trump, five clubs means no ace or three of them; five diamonds means one or four; five hearts means two aces of the same color; five spades means one of the two mixtures—A ♡ and A ♣ or A ♠ and A ◇.

Roman Gerber: Conventional four clubs asks for aces. A response of four diamonds means three or none, four hearts means four or one and four spades means two. To ask for kings, the proper call is the lowest possible one—for example, four spades after a response of four hearts. Partner then proceeds according to the basic system, using the lowest possible reply (other than no-trump) to indicate none or three kings, the next-higher reply for one or four, and so forth.

Roman Jump Overcall: In the almost unbelievably precise Roman system, jump overcalls represent hands with two long suits. The suits are always the one named in the bid and the next-higher one. If opener bids one diamond, an overcall of two hearts means a hand with strength in hearts and spades. Suit named in the opening bid is always excluded. Therefore, if opener bid one heart, a call of three diamonds would mean strength in diamonds and spades.

Roman Two Diamonds: Another bonbon borrowed from the Roman system for use as a convention. An opening bid of two diamonds indicates a three-suit hand with from 17 to 20 points and either 4-4-4-1 or 5-4-4-0 distribution. With a good hand, responder bids two no-trump. Opener then names his short suit and responder names his own best suit, leading to an easy trump fit at an appropriate level.

Short Club: So familiar and natural that it seldom causes the complications to which most actual conventions give rise, this permits opening bidder to call one club with a three-card suit. Responder is then able to name his own best suit at the lowest level. A necessity in systems that require five-card major suits for opening bids, but a convenience in natural bidding as well.

Stayman: Sam Stayman originated this standard convention, in which responder to an opening bid of one no-trump can ask partner to name his best major suit. The conventional bid is two clubs. Opener who lacks a decent four-card major suit replies two diamonds. A variation called *Double-Barreled Stayman* uses the two-club response for middling hands and two diamonds for stronger ones, forcing to game.

Texas: Just as the Jacoby convention (*see above*) enables the stronger hand to play small suit contracts after an opening bid of one no-trump, this one uses similar means on occasions when a game contract is intended. When responder has a long major suit, he replies to the opening bid with a bid at the level of four in the suit that ranks just below his strong one. The opener then bids game in the desired suit and plays the hand.

Two-Club Opening: Many modern methods use a conventional opening bid of two clubs to show a powerful hand and oblige the partner to continue the auction to game. (*See Weak Two-Bid, below.*)

Unusual No-Trump: With distribution such as 6-5-1-1 or 5-5-2-1, and with the strength in the minor suits, this device of Alvin Roth's is extremely useful. To ask partner to name his own best minor and perhaps capture the bidding initiative, the player simply interrupts opponents' bidding with an unusual no-trump call of his own. What makes the bid "unusual" is that it generally occurs at a time when bids of the kind are seldom heard. For example:

SOUTH	WEST	NORTH	EAST
1 Spade	2 Clubs	2 Spades	Pass
Pass	2 No-Trump		

West's overcall of two clubs is an orthodox showing of club length. North's modest raise and South's relieved pass suggest that the East-West team may have at least a partial game if they can find a suit. The two no-trump bid asks that the effort be made, showing East that the suit should be a minor. Those who have difficulty appreciating that two no-trump is "unusual" at this juncture of an auction should consider that a player with a legitimate no-trump hand would probably have indicated as much at his first opportunity —when West bid two clubs.

Weak Jump Overcall: A bid of preemptive intent, injected after opponents have opened. For example, South opens with one spade and West overcalls with three diamonds. An effective disrupter, this convention is widely used. Overcaller should have no more than 9 points and a long suit of at least six cards.

Weak No-Trump: It is convenient to be able to bid one no-trump with 13 points. Many players do this conventionally when not vulnerable, using the more severe standard when vulnerable.

Weak Two-Bid: If the partnership uses two clubs as a strong forcing bid, opening calls in other suits signify a point count of 7 to 11, with a strong six-card suit, as in ordinary preemptive bidding.

Play by Declarer

As in other card games that involve trump suits and the taking of tricks, skillful Bridge demands knowledge of the game's probabilities, trained powers of analysis and a functioning memory. To the newcomer, good Bridge players seem to have X-ray eyes: they know exactly which cards remain in one's hand after the early tricks have been played. This ability is more easily acquired by persons of natural talent than by others, but anyone motivated to do so can learn through study and experience to play the normal run of Bridge hands extremely well.

A sample hand may give the reader some of the flavor of what happens. Imagine yourself as South, with this holding:

♠ K Q 10 7 4
♡ A 5 2
◇ Q 4
♣ K J 9

West opens the bidding with one diamond. North (your partner) passes and so does East. Your bid is one spade. West stays in his suit with two diamonds, indicating a hand not much better than minimum. North now pipes up with three spades, showing good trump support, a bit of side strength, and willingness to accept a game contract if you have a good hand. You bid four spades and everyone passes, making you declarer.

West's opening lead:

K ◇

As soon as the card hits the table, North displays the dummy:

♠ J 9 8 3
♡ K Q 8
◇ 10 6 2
♣ A 10 5

You study it in relation to your own hand:

♠ K Q 10 7 4
♡ A 5 2
◇ Q 4
♣ K J 9

Clearly enough, you must lose a trick to the A ♠, and two more to the A ◇ and K ◇. You are otherwise secure in trump, impregnable in hearts and able to *ruff* (play trump cards on) any diamond tricks after the first two losing ones. Your only problem is clubs. Your ace and king are winners. But the probabilities are slight that the enemy queen will fall to one of them. After all, the opponents have seven clubs. One of them *might* be holding the queen doubleton, but you cannot count on it.

At this point, the average player decides to try a *finesse* (*described below*), in which his chances of avoiding the loss of a club trick (and the game contract) become approximately 50–50. But the better player takes steps to assure himself of positive protection against the loss—if such a happy outcome is possible at all. In this case it is.

Follow the play of the hand, and South's reasoning:

West takes the first two tricks with the K ♢ and A ♢. When he leads a third diamond, East ruffs with the 2 ♠ and South overruffs, winning the trick with the 4 ♠.

South Reasons: My side had only five diamonds. East had only two. West therefore had six.

South now leads a trump, winning the trick. On the next spade trick, West plays the ace and comes back with another trump.

South Now Knows: West started with three trump and six diamonds. East started with one trump and two diamonds. East's length is extreme in hearts and/or clubs. Chances are that East has the Q ♣.

To narrow the possibilities and acquire a more precise portrait of the enemy hands, South plays his three winning heart tricks. When West follows suit to each of these, it is clear enough that he has only one club in his hand!

South Observes: West cannot have more than one club. It is known that he started with three spades, three hearts and six diamonds, which make a total of twelve.

If West had a singleton Q ♣, the next play would be elegant indeed: South would simply drop it with his ace and claim the rest of the tricks. But the four hands at the table now actually look like this:

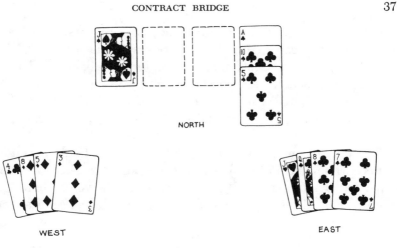

South leads his 9 ♣, takes it in dummy with the A ♣ and claims the rest of the tricks. East's Q ♣ is doomed. If South leads the 10 ♣ from dummy and East does not put the Q ♣ on it, South will take it with the J ♣ and then lead the K ♣. East's play now is immaterial, because the K ♣ and Q ♠ capture the final two tricks, securing the game contract.

South's observations are routine among good players. They call it "counting the hand." The process begins during the bidding, when distributional factors often are disclosed. With experience, counting becomes second nature.

The Finesse: As South, you hold only two hearts, the ace and the queen. Lead is in dummy, which also has only two hearts, the five and the three. To make your contract, you must take both tricks. If you have counted the hand, you may know that East holds the king and that you have nothing to fear. If he plays the king to the first trick, you will win with the ace, taking the other trick with the queen. On the other hand, if he ducks the first trick, you will win with the queen, taking the final trick with the ace.

But if you have been unable to count the hand, and no other stratagem presents itself, you have no choice but to *finesse.* That is, you lead your small card from dummy and if East follows with another small card, you play the queen, hoping that it can win the trick.

The play of finesses has been analyzed exhaustively by numerous experts. The distributional patterns are recognizable. Each calls for a particular sequence of plays. The subject is covered thoroughly in the specialized texts to which the reader will be referred at the end of this chapter.

Distributional Probabilities: Declarer sometimes wonders whether to play the ace and king and hope that the queen will fall harmlessly from an opponent's hand during those first two tricks in the suit. Or should he finesse against the queen? Where card-counting fails, probabilities sometimes help.

Cards Held in Suit	*Distribution*	*Percent of Time*
8	5–3	47
	4–4	33
	6–2	17
	7–1	3
7	4–3	62
	5–2	31
	6–1	7
6	4–2	49
	3–3	36
	5–1	15
	6–0	1
5	3–2	68
	4–1	28
	5–0	4
4	3–1	50
	2–2	41
	4–0	10
3	2–1	78
	3–0	22
2	1–1	52
	2–0	48

These probabilities surprise the unwary. For example, if you and partner hold nine spades between you, would you not assume that the most likely distribution would find two of the missing spades in each of the other hands? Mathematics proves otherwise. The odds are almost exactly even that the four adverse tickets will be divided 3–1. That is, three will be in one of the opponent's hands and one in the other.

One of the opponents will be entirely without spades almost 10 percent of the times that you and partner hold nine in the suit. And the logical 2–2 division occurs only 4 times in 10.

As a general rule, it is wise to expect that when the opponents hold an even number of cards in a suit, the division between them will be uneven. As Bridge players say, the suit will not usually *break*. But when the partners hold an odd number of cards, the division tends to be as close to even as possible.

Defensive Play

By means of certain conventional sequences of play, the defensive partners are permitted to signal each other about distributional factors that may help them to defeat the contract.

High-Low: By tossing an unnecessarily high card onto a trick that he cannot win and playing a lower card to the next trick of the same suit, a defensive player asks his partner to lead that suit as soon as possible. The most common use of this so-called *echo,* or *come-on,* is when the signaling player holds a doubleton in the suit and hopes to ruff the third trick. Possession of a guarded honor also occasions the high-low, as in a strong trump holding of three or more cards. Trump echoes are played exactly like others, with the signaler tossing in a higher-than-necessary card at the first opportunity and following with a smaller card. By extension of this logic, if a player discards a noticeably high card from a side suit on a losing trick in another suit, he asks partner for a lead in the discarded suit.

Suit-Preference Signal: When leading a card for partner to ruff, a defensive player may indicate his choice of a suit for partner's return lead. If the card he leads is relatively high—a seven or more—he suggests that partner return a card in the higher of the two remaining side suits. If he chooses a lower card, he indicates preference for the lower of the two suits.

Opening Leads: The first card played to the first trick of the hand is known as the opening lead. More often than not, the leader's partner can tell much about leader's hand by remembering the bidding, rechecking his own hand, inspecting the dummy, and associating all this with the meaning contained in the lead itself. After decades of theory and practice, the Bridge world agrees on the principles of the opening lead. The choice of card is usually cut-and-dried.

In defending against no-trump contracts, the usual lead is the fourth-highest card in player's longest and strongest suit. This play permits partner to determine how many winning cards the declarer holds in the suit. Assume that the lead is a four. Obviously, ten higher cards exist in the suit. But three of those higher cards are, by definition, in leader's hand. Therefore, seven are distributed among dummy, leader's partner and declarer. Since the partner can see his own hand and dummy, he has no difficulty computing the number of higher tickets in declarer's hand. The arithmetical basis is simple. The thirteen cards in a suit range from the two through the king (which ranks thirteen) and ace (fourteen). To determine the number of cards higher than a given card, subtract its number from fourteen. But, since the given card is identified as fourth highest in leader's hand, we know that three of the higher cards are in that hand. So we subtract its number not from fourteen but from eleven. The so-called *Rule of Eleven* is universal in Bridge.

Sometimes the opening leader chooses something other than the fourth-highest card in his longest and strongest suit. Examples:

When three honors are held in a suit, the customary lead is the higher of two or highest of three adjoining honors—except that the king is led when ace–king are held. Thus, lead the card underlined:

$\underline{K}$ Q J
A $\underline{Q}$ J
A $\underline{J}$ 10
K $\underline{J}$ 10
$\underline{K}$ Q 9
A $\underline{K}$ Q

Still, from A-K-10-x-x, the fourth highest is the most usual lead, and likewise from something like A-Q-10-x.

When partner leads an ace against a no-trump contract, the player is expected to drop his highest card of the suit—unless dummy's layout indicates that tricks might be sacrificed by this maneuver. The purpose, of course, is to enable opening leader to win numerous tricks in the suit. If his partner were to win the second trick with the king and were unable to lead a lower card of the same suit back to the opening leader, the suit might be *blocked.* Opening leader might never get the lead again and might win no more tricks in the suit.

An extremely useful opening lead is in the suit bid by partner. If opening leader holds only two cards in the suit, he signals by leading the higher of the two to the first trick and dropping the lower on the second trick. From three cards headed by an honor, he leads the lowest. From three cards including touching honors, such as Q-J-x, the highest card is led.

In defending against trump contracts, leads from short suits are more usual. Not seeking to establish long suits, as in defending against no-trump contracts, player's first consideration is likely to be safety. That is, he tries to do whatever he thinks may bother the declarer without unnecessary risk. If his partner has participated in the auction, he has more to go on in choosing the lead.

Adjoining honors are handled much as at no-trump, the higher being the preferred opening lead.

The higher card is also chosen from a doubleton. The middle card and then the higher and finally the lower are played from a holding such as 9-7-5.

When partner has doubled the contract for penalties, the best opening lead may be in trump, to deplete declarer's already dubious strength.

Contract Bridge Law

The word "law" is rather ponderous when used to describe the rules of a card game. But the American Contract Bridge League is not afflicted with false modesty about its own importance or that of the pastime that it superintends so effectively throughout the Western Hemisphere. Tomorrow the world. Meanwhile, rules are called laws. Whoever wants a copy of those scriptures can obtain them for $2 from the ACBL, 125 Greenwich Ave., Greenwich, Conn. 06830. Here are rules most likely to apply to situations at the average home table.

Shuffle: Should be done thoroughly, in full view and to everyone's satisfaction. Nobody may shuffle except the designated player and, if he pleases, the dealer.

Cut: Compulsory. No portion of the cut pack may contain fewer than four cards. No player other than dealer's right-hand opponent may cut.

Deal: Dealer may correct his dealing errors provided that he does so immediately and without objection from other players. Otherwise, cards must be reshuffled and dealer must deal again. If a player deals out of turn, the correct dealer can reclaim the deal before the last card is dealt. Otherwise the deal stands and the correct dealer loses his turn on that round.

Penalty Cards: As a result of various irregularities described below, a card may be designated a penalty card. It must be played at the first permissible opportunity. If a defender has two or more penalty cards, declarer may select the one to be played. Declarer may require a defender to lead a suit in which his partner has a penalty card, or declarer may forbid a lead in that suit. However, if that happens, the penalty card may be picked up and regarded as a penalty card no longer. Failure to play a penalty card involves no penalty, but declarer may require the penalty card to be played. Any other card exposed by defender at that juncture becomes a penalty card.

Auction: A player who exposes a ten or higher during the auction must leave it face up on the table. His partner must pass at his next turn. If the other side plays the hand, the card becomes a penalty card. No penalty is imposed for exposing a card of lower rank.

A player who offers an insufficient bid suffers no penalty if he substitutes the lowest sufficient bid of the same denomination. But if he substitutes any other bid, his partner must pass throughout the remainder of the auction. And if he substitutes a pass, a double or a redouble, not only must his partner pass for the rest of the auction but declarer may either name the suit to be led to the first trick or may forbid a specific suit.

A player may change his call without penalty if he does so immediately and if the second call is legal. Delayed changes are punished. In some cases, the original bid—if legal—remains in effect, but offender's partner must pass his next turn to bid. But if offender prefers to make another legal call, his partner must pass for the remainder of the auction.

If a player gives unauthorized information in process of changing his call, and if his side becomes the defense, declarer may require that the suit illegally named be avoided when offender's partner gets the lead, and for as long as that player retains the lead. Or if no-trump was named illegally and if offender's partner has the opening lead, declarer may specify the suit to be led.

If a player bids out of turn, but before any other player has bid, his partner is barred from the bidding throughout. If the player bids at his partner's turn, the partner not only is barred from the rest of the auction but must use or avoid whatever opening lead suit the declarer prescribes (provided that he has the opening lead). If player bids when it is his right-hand opponent's turn, he suffers no penalty if opponent passes. But if opponent bids, offender may bid but his partner must miss a turn.

If a player passes out of turn before anyone else has bid or if it was his right-hand opponent's turn, he must pass when his proper turn comes. If he passes out of turn after the bidding has started and when it actually is his partner's turn, the offender is barred from the remainder of the auction. Moreover, offender's partner may not double or redouble at that turn. If he passes, and the other side plays the hand, declarer may select or forbid a specific suit for the opening lead.

If a player doubles or redoubles when it is his partner's turn, he may not repeat the call when his proper turn comes. Also, his partner is barred throughout the auction and may be forbidden by declarer to lead the illegally doubled suit at the opening trick (if he happens to have the opening lead).

If a player doubles or redoubles when it is the turn of his right-hand opponent, he must repeat the double or redouble if that opponent passes. If the opponent bids, offender may make any legal call and his partner must miss a turn in the auction.

Review of the Bidding: Either member of the defending team may ask for a review of the auction before the opening lead. Declarer may ask for a review before any part of the dummy has been displayed.

Dummy's Deportment: Dummy may call attention to irregularities in play, and may recite the laws, but not if he has looked at another player's hand. If he has forfeited his rights in that way and is the first to call attention to an infraction by the other side, declarer may impose no penalties. Or if he warns declarer about leading from the wrong hand, either defender may choose the hand from which defender leads to the next trick.

Exposed Cards: Declarer can expose a card without penalty. But if a defender exposes a card so that his partner can see it before entitled to see it, the card must remain on the table face up and becomes a penalty card (*see page 42*).

Play out of Turn: If declarer leads from the wrong hand, and is required to play the trick properly, he must lead the same suit from the correct hand if he has a card of that suit in that hand. If he plays when it is a defender's turn, there is no penalty. If a defender leads out of turn, declarer can treat the led card as a penalty card, or can specify or forbid a suit when offender's partner gets the lead.

If a defender plays out of turn before his partner has played, declarer may direct the partner to play his highest or lowest card of the led suit, or a card of another suit. If the defender cannot comply, he is allowed to play any card. However, if declarer has played to the trick from both his own hand and the dummy, he cannot penalize a defender for playing before his partner.

Revoke: A revoke is the failure to follow suit when able to do so. A player who revokes must correct the misplay before it becomes established—that is, before he or his partner play to the next trick. A revoke card withdrawn by offender becomes a penalty card. But when a revoke becomes established, it stands as played, unless it is the twelfth trick, which must be corrected, but bears no penalty. Otherwise, the penalty for an established revoke is two tricks, if available. The penalty can be paid only from tricks won by the offending side after the revoke. If only one such trick is available, it becomes the total penalty. And if no trick is available, no penalty is imposed. Neither is there a penalty for a second established revoke by the same player in the same suit.

Customs and Proprieties: The laws of Contract Bridge are intended to provide remedies when accident or carelessness delivers an undeserved advantage to one or the other side. But the laws cannot prevent dishonorable practices. As the official document itself observes, "Ostracism is the ultimate remedy for intentional offenses."

Breaches of propriety often occur not so much because the offender wishes to gain maximum advantage but because he is insufficiently aware of the game's traditional etiquette. Basic to this code is the concept that the only permissible communication between partners is through bidding and card signaling. Gestures, display of cards, vocal inflections and verbal instructions violate the rule and spirit of the game. Among the significant differences between Bridge and Poker is the freedom of the Poker player to profit from any weakness of his opponent. In Bridge, for example, it is unethical to attempt to read another person's hand by learning how he arranges his cards and watching to see the part of the hand from which he draws each card.

Among breaches of ethics itemized in the rules are these:

A remark, question, gesture or mannerism that might convey information to partner or might mislead an opponent.

A call or play made with special emphasis, inflection, haste or hesitation.

An indication of approval or disapproval of partner's call, or of satisfaction with an opponent's.

Indication of expectation of winning or losing a trick before all four cards have been played.

Using any convention of bidding or play that is not understood by the opponents.

Recommended Reading

Whoever wants to delve more deeply into the theory and playing techniques of Contract Bridge will be rewarded by any of the following books:

Charles H. Goren, *Goren's New Contract Bridge Complete* (Doubleday).
———, *Point Count Bidding* (Simon and Schuster).
———, *The Precision System* (Doubleday).
Terence Reese and Albert Dormer, *The Complete Book of Bridge* (Saturday Review Press).
Alfred Sheinwold, *Five Weeks to Winning Bridge* (Pocket Books).
Louis H. Watson, *Play of the Hand at Bridge* (Sterling).

American Contract Bridge League publications, available from the ACBL headquarters, 125 Greenwich Ave., Greenwich, Conn. 06830, are extremely useful to the serious student. For example, the *1969 World Team Championship Book* summarizes the Italian systems and the Precision systems, and reconstructs the bidding and play of 300 selected hands from the championships of that year. And *The Official Encyclopedia of Bridge,* prepared by ACBL staff, contains more than 600 pages, discusses every worthwhile bidding system and convention, offers biographies of more than 2,000 celebrated players, itemizes the histories of all leading Bridge competitions, etc.

2 DUPLICATE BRIDGE

The best player does not necessarily log the highest score in an evening of straight rubbers of Contract Bridge. Luck is a crucial factor in the deal of the cards. Although a superior player almost invariably loses a minimum on the poor hands and exploits the good hands to their outer limits, the luck of the deal sometimes defeats him.

To ensure fairer tests of skill, Duplicate Bridge is played in virtually all tournaments. This form of the game requires players to compete against one another in the play of identical hands. When the scores are totaled at the end of a Duplicate Bridge session, the partners with the highest score may not be the very best Bridge players in the place, but the fact is indisputable that they have played the most effective Bridge of the night.

Central to this merciless game is the Duplicate Bridge board, a small tray that contains the four hands of a deal. Each hand is segregated in its own pocket, readily identifiable as North, East, South and West because an arrow points to the North hand. Vulnerability and the location of the dealer are also clearly indicated on the tray.

The trays come in numbered sets of sixteen, which rotate the deal and vulnerability in the following sequences:

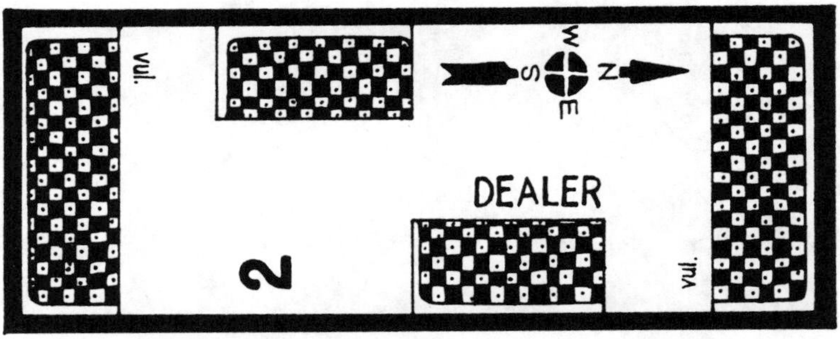

Dealer

North 1, 5, 9, 13
East 2, 6, 10, 14
West 3, 7, 11, 15
South 4, 8, 12, 16

Vulnerability

Neither 1, 8, 11, 14
North–South 2, 5, 12, 15
East–West 3, 6, 9, 16
Both 4, 7, 10, 13

Boards 17 through 32 and 33 through 48, if used, are marked in exactly the same sequences as above. For a typical evening of neighborhood Duplicate Bridge, in which one team of four competes against another, sixteen boards suffice. In tournaments, twenty-four boards per session are more likely, although as many as thirty-six or forty may sometimes be played.

The Play

Having been assigned seats at a table (either by a tournament director or by the traditions of a weekly game), the players proceed thereto and find three to eight boards, usually with cards already in the pockets. Unless the cards have been predealt, the shuffle and deal are the first order of business. Each board's cards remain *as dealt* throughout the evening. After the hand is played, the cards are returned to their respective pockets and are conveyed in the tray to the other tables, as scheduled.

To keep the hands separate, tricks are not melded in the center of the table. Each player exposes his cards one at a time during play, but keeps them directly in front of him. At the conclusion of a trick, each card is turned face down—still in front of the player—with its long sides pointing to the pair that won the trick. After the score of the hand is totaled and recorded (*see below*), each hand is returned to its pocket and the board is ready to proceed to its next table.

Scoring

Because actual rubbers are not played, the scoring differs slightly from that of ordinary Contract Bridge. For making a game contract when not vulnerable, a team earns 300 bonus points. If vulnerable, the bonus is 500. For making a contract of less than 100 trick-points, the bonus is 50. Where scoring is on a match-point basis, no bonus is recorded for holding aces or trump honors. Otherwise each deal is scored exactly as in rubbers of Contract Bridge.

Rotating Players and Boards

Whether duplicate competition is among individuals, pairs or teams of four, it is necessary to follow an equitable traffic pattern in deploying the players and the trays. The logistics are sometimes complicated.

Individual Play: The objective is to have each contestant play one hand in partnership with every other and to face the other twice as an opponent. For home competition, the most manageable game involves eight players. Each is given a number and is assigned a seat in accordance with this design:

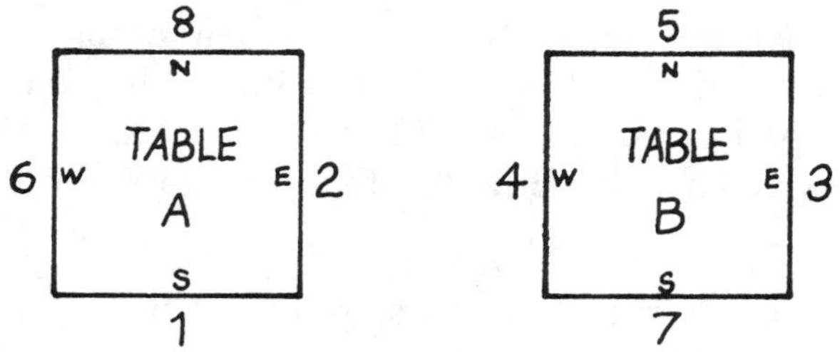

Three or four boards are played at each round. During the round, the boards are passed from one table to another, so that both tables play the same hands. Each board is accompanied by a scoring slip that shows how each player fared (*see below*). At the end of the round, player Number 8 remains seated. Everyone else moves to the position just vacated by the player with the next-lower number (Player 1 takes the seat of Player 7). If four hands are played per round, twenty-eight hands are necessary—a long session.

For individual competition among twelve, the tables are organized this way:

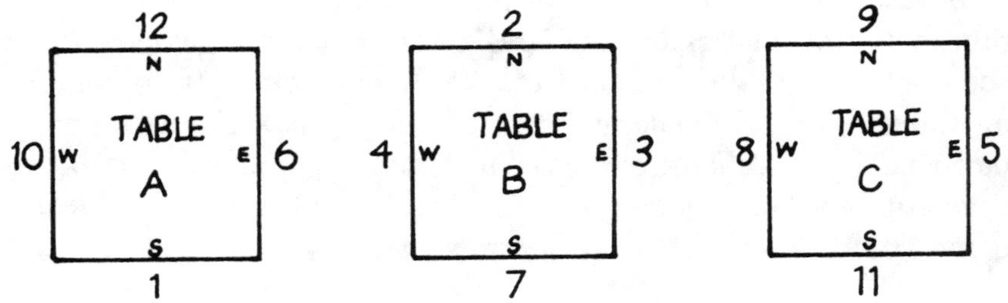

Once again, the player assigned the highest number is regarded as anchor man and remains in the same seat for the entire session. Each of the other players moves to the seat being vacated by the person with the next-lower number, except that Player 1 replaces Player 11. A full session involves play of thirty-three hands—a marathon.

Pair Competition: Partnerships remain constant throughout the session. Those assigned the North-South positions remain in their seats after each round. The East-West teams move to the table with the next higher number, while the three, four or five completed hands are conveyed in the duplicate boards to the table with the next lower number. When each East-West pair has played at each table, the session is over. In this, the Mitchell system, two teams become winners—the North-South team with the highest score and the team that performed best in the East-West seats. Another, much more complex system, the Howell, produces one winning pair per session.

Teams of Four: Half the team sits as North-South and the other half plays the same hands at another table in the East-West positions. If North-South wins by 100 points at Table "A" and their teammates lose by only 50 when playing as East-West at the other table, it is clear that the team has scored a 50-point victory. Tournaments for teams of four are conducted either on a so-called knockout schedule (the familiar athletic-tournament pattern that culminates in semifinals and finals) or on a round-robin basis, with each team confronting each of the others. Teams of four may actually include five or six players. By agreement or by directive of their captain, four of the players and their seating positions are designated before each round.

Team-of-four competition is a fine diversion for any group of eight or ten players able to convene for weekly or semimonthly play at two tables. Most participants find this form of Duplicate Bridge preferable to the usual two tables of ordinary Contract Bridge.

Recommended Reading

The strategy and tactics of Duplicate Bridge differ substantially from those of regular Contract Bridge, due mainly to the systems of scoring. One of the most useful treatises on this subject is Alfred Sheinwold's *Complete Book of Duplicate Bridge*, Putnam (hardcover), Harper (paperback).

3 BRIDGE PARTIES

Because the procedures of rubbers of Contract Bridge are more familiar than those of Duplicate Bridge, social evenings that include Bridge are likely to feature Progressive Bridge—especially if at least a dozen players are available. Fewer players make for a lively game of Pivot Bridge.

PROGRESSIVE BRIDGE

The host or hostess gives each player a tally card that designates a table number and a seating position. Every effort is made to emphasize the social character of the pastime by dividing the sexes as equally as possible among the tables.

A round of play ends after four deals—one by each player. Each deal is separate. No points are carried from one to the next. The first deal is played with neither pair vulnerable. The second and third are played as if dealer's side were vulnerable. The fourth deal finds both pairs vulnerable. Scoring of each hand is the same as in Duplicate Bridge. Each player's team score is recorded on his own tally card, along with the points made by the opponents.

At the conclusion of the round, the losing pair remains and the winners move to the table with the next lower number—except that the winners remain at Table 1 and the losers move to the table with the highest number. Depending on local preferences, partnerships for each round are determined on the basis of sex or by cutting the cards. It is best that all players change partners for each new round.

At the end of the evening, the winner is the player with the highest net score (comparing his own tally with those recorded for his opponents on his own tally card).

A variation, Progressive Rubber Bridge, is played on the basis of six or eight deals per round and is scored as regular Contract Bridge. At the end of each round (which may be limited by time as well as the number of hands), the player enters his *net* score on his tally card.

PIVOT BRIDGE

This game is for four or five players per table, and permits each to play as partner with each other. Play may involve four deals per round, as in Progressive Bridge, or may carry a time limit and be scored exactly as in ordinary Contract Bridge. With four players, the person who cuts highest becomes first pivot. He remains in his seat for the first three rounds. Second-highest cut becomes his partner in the first round, his right-hand opponent in the second and his left-hand opponent in the third. Third-highest cut begins as pivot's left-hand opponent and moves clockwise around the table for the subsequent rounds. The lowest player begins as pivot's right-hand opponent, moves to the opposite position for the second round and finishes as pivot's partner.

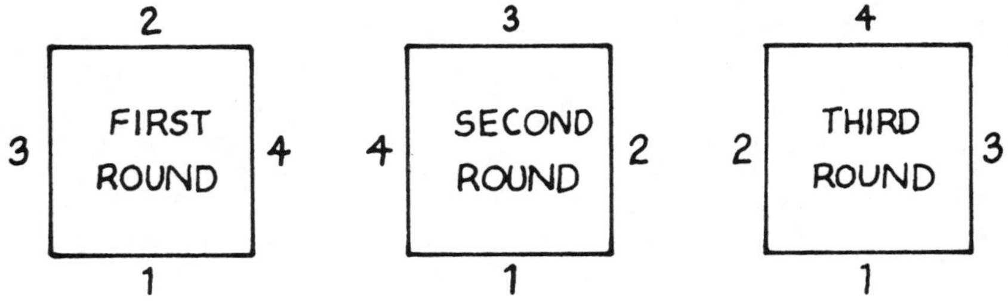

With five players per table, the logistics are more complicated. Note from the illustration that five rounds are necessary, that pivot remains seated until the final round, when he sits out and is replaced by the second-highest cut.

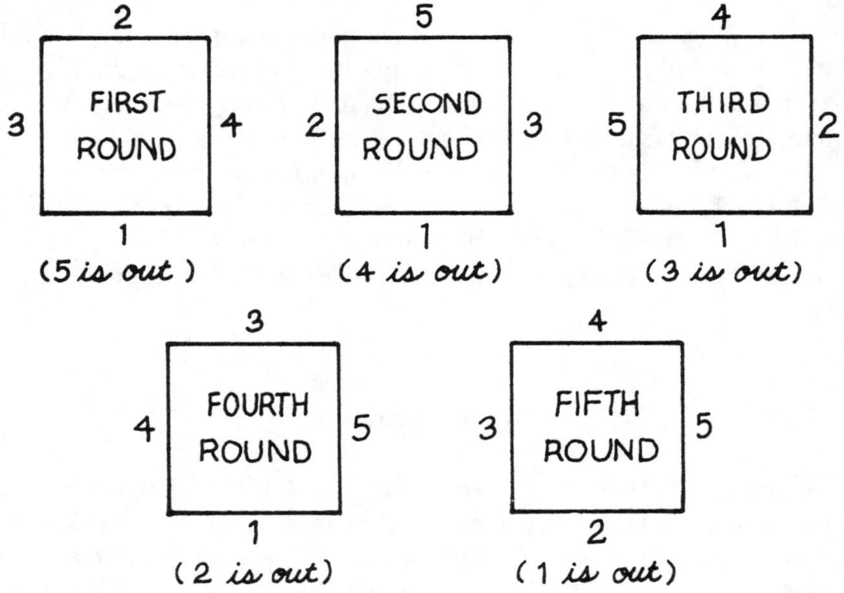

Whether four or five players are involved, a new cut is made at the completion of the third (or fifth) round, and a new cycle begins. At the end of the session, the winner is the player with the highest net score (comparing his own tally with that recorded on his tally card for his opponents).

Pivot Bridge often is played with large numbers of people at numerous tables. Its virtue is that it spares the players the trouble of moving from table to table.

4 BRIDGE VARIATIONS

AUCTION BRIDGE

The predecessor of Contract Bridge differs from the modern game only in its scoring.

If declarer makes his contract, his side scores for all odd tricks, including any won in excess of the contract.

Odd-Trick Values:	In No-Trump	10
	In Spades	9
	In Hearts	8
	In Diamonds	7
	In Clubs	6

Thus, to bid two no-trump and make three odd tricks is to earn 30 points—as many as would be earned had the partnership bid three no-trump in the first place.

Undertricks: If defenders set the contract, they get 50 points above the line for each undertrick and 100 if doubled, 200 if redoubled.

Declarer Bonuses: When declarer makes a doubled contract, his side scores the doubled value of the odd tricks below the line. For making the doubled contract, 50 goes above the line. Overtricks earn an additional 50 above the line on doubled contracts. When contract has been redoubled, each bonus is 100 points and odd tricks count four times their normal value in the trick score.

Game: Thirty points below the line.

Slams: These earn 100 for grand slam, 50 for small slam. If contract is for grand slam but declarer takes only twelve tricks, he gets 50 for small slam, even though the contract was set.

Honors: In trump, three honors in either hand or the combined hands earn 30 above the line; four honors in the combined hands are worth 40; five in the combined hands get 50. Four in one hand earn 80; one in one hand and four in the other count 90; all five in one hand get 100.

At no-trump, all four aces in one hand are worth 100; four divided count 40; three get 30 whether in one hand or divided.

Rubber: For winning two games, a pair gets 250 points above the line. Side with the most total points at the juncture wins the rubber.

CHICAGO

Known also as Club Bridge or Four-Deal Bridge, this variation limits each round to four deals, after which the players cut again for partners or, as in Pivot Bridge, simply change places in conformity to pattern.

Vulnerability: On the first deal, neither side is vulnerable. On second and third, dealer's side is vulnerable. On the fourth, both sides are vulnerable.

Scoring: Part scores are carried from one deal to the next, until one side makes game, after which existing part scores cannot be carried into the next game.

For making game not vulnerable: 300.
For making game vulnerable: 500.

The net score of the four-game set is converted into even hundreds by crediting as 100 points any fraction of 50 or more. Thus, 650 counts as 700, but 640 counts as 600.

To avoid confusion as to how many deals have been played, and where vulnerability lies, the official rules of the American Contract Bridge League recommend that a large "X" be drawn near the top of the score sheet:

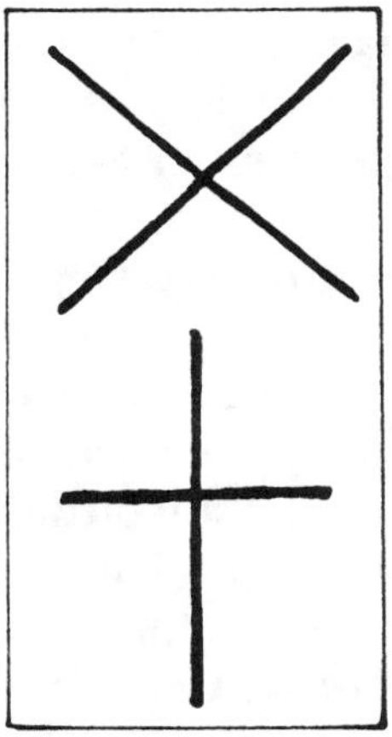

Before the first deal, the figure "1" should be written in the angle that faces the first dealer. After the hand, a "2" goes into the next angle, in the usual clockwise rotation. This helps stave off the disputes that otherwise mar a fast-moving game like this one.

GOULASH

This favorite pastime of commuters and other high-spirited types is known also as Mayonnaise, Hollandaise and Ghoulie. Originally, a Mayonnaise was a hand played during a normal game of Bridge immediately after a deal in which nobody had opened the bidding. The Mayonnaise took the game to the other extreme. Dealer placed his sorted hand face down on the table, after which each player (in clockwise sequence) put his own sorted hand face down on top of the pile. Then, with or without a cut, the dealer distributed the cards five at a time and, on the last distribution, three at a time. Unusual hands resulted and were played and scored by the regular rules.

Many Bridge groups continue to play the occasional Mayonnaise hand. Others play nothing else. Of the various versions, the most popular is the following.

Passing Goulash

A hand is dealt. The players arrange their cards but do not bid. Instead, they place them in a pile on the table, as in Mayonnaise. The dealer then distributes them in 5-5-3 fashion, after which the passing begins.

Each player passes four cards face down to the player on his left, hoping to build length and strength in one suit. After sorting the proceeds of this, the players again pass four cards to the left. On the third pass, each player passes four cards to his partner. The tactic usually is to weaken a weak hand still further by passing one's highest cards to partner's presumably strong hand.

Slam bidding is unexceptional in this game.

In another version of Passing Goulash, cards are passed only to one's partner. On the first exchange, each passes one card. On the second, each passes two. On the third and last, three are passed.

HONEYMOON BRIDGE

No two-hand Bridge game is more than a pallid imitation of the real thing. Nevertheless, Honeymoon Bridge and its various permutations have been played for decades by countless addicts, demonstrating that a two-hand game is better than no Bridge at all.

In one popular version, four hands are dealt, including a face-down dummy for each player. The players bid their hands without looking at the dummies. When the contract is established, each player arranges his dummy in a rack that displays the cards to him but not to the opponent. Play and scoring then proceed as in Contract Bridge.

In another version, both dummies are exposed after the bidding concludes, and each player, having surveyed his own cards and those in the dummies, is able to tell what his opponent holds. If the players are not evenly matched, a game like this can shorten the honeymoon.

One fairly popular variant requires that only twelve cards be dealt to each hand. A so-called *widow* of the four remaining cards is distributed after the bidding and often affects the play considerably. To inhibit reckless overbidding, some players favor a game in which undertricks not only earn the defender the usual penalty points but entitle him to a below-the-line bonus equivalent to the normal value of each such trick—as if he had been the declarer and had made a contract of that many odd tricks.

A version of Honeymoon Bridge that resembles Rummy is known variously as Draw or Strip Honeymoon. No dummies are dealt. Instead the hand is played in two phases. First, the undealt cards (twenty-six of them) are played like the *stock* in a Rummy game. Dealer's opponent leads to the first trick and play proceeds as if in no-trump. Winner of each trick draws from the stock, after which loser also draws. After the stock is exhausted, the first thirteen tricks are set aside and the bidding begins. Because the adversaries have each built the best possible hand, bidding is sometimes quite spectacular. Scoring is based on the contract and on the play that follows.

OH HELL

This is one of the many first-rate card games that can be played with exquisite skill by good players yet is good fun for others. It should never be played with strangers over the age of six. There is more to Oh Hell than meets the uninformed eye.

Essentially a game for four, it can be played with as few as two or three (not much fun) to as many as six or seven (very tricky). Play resembles that of the parent, Bridge, except that each player is on his own, without a partner.

The first hand consists of only one card per player. The second hand is played with two, the third with three, and so forth. With seven players, seven deals make a game. With four players, thirteen deals occur. As the reader can see, each game ends with the play of the deal on which all the cards are distributed, or when no more cards can be distributed without making the hands uneven in length.

Bidding is done on each hand—including the first, the one-card hand. Each player announces the exact number of tricks he proposes to win. Thus "pass" signifies an intention to win no tricks.

The last hand of each game is played at no-trump. For all other hands, trump is designated immediately after the deal by turning up the next undealt card in the pack. After which the bidding starts.

A player who takes exactly the number of tricks for which he contracted (including a bid of "pass" or "zero") scores 5 points plus the number of cards dealt to him for the particular hand. A player who wins *fewer or more* tricks than he bid scores nothing.

A somewhat less satisfactory scoring system awards the successful player 10 points plus the number of tricks for which he contracted. Unsuccessful players get nothing. At the end of the game, the player with the most points wins.

PLAFOND

In this French approach to Contract Bridge, the trick score is identical with that of Auction Bridge, but no odd tricks may be scored below the line unless they have been bid. Overtricks are worth 50 points. For fulfilling a contract, the bonus is 50, unless the contract was doubled or redoubled, which increases the bonus to 100 and 200, respectively.

Each undertrick earns 100 points undoubled, 200 doubled, and so on. Four honors in one hand are worth 100. If partner has the fifth honor, the side gets 150. If one player has all five honors, or all four aces at no-trump, they are worth 200.

A small slam counts 100 and a grand slam 200. These bonuses are awarded even if the slam was not bid.

There is no vulnerability. A partnership gets 100 points when it wins its first game. First side to win a second game and rubber earns another 400. If the session ends with a rubber incomplete, a partnership that has won the only game of the rubber gets 150.

THREE-HAND BRIDGE

Cutthroat

The dummy remains face down until the opening lead from player at left of the highest bidder, who then plays his own hand and the exposed dummy, just as in a regular game of Contract Bridge. Scoring is on an individual basis. If declarer makes his contract he gets full points—with a 500-point bonus for rubber if either opponent is vulnerable and 700 if neither has won a game. When a contract is set, each defender is awarded the full penalty points.

Exchange

After the auction, declarer exposes his own hand as dummy and plays the concealed hand.

Towie

After looking at his own cards but before bidding, dealer turns up six of the dummy's cards. If the contract (including doubles, if any) is insufficient for game, the hand is not played but is redealt as in Goulash. In the Goulash phase, dealer must shuffle dummy before exposing the six cards.

Many players score Towie according to the obsolete 1927 rules of Contract Bridge. No good reason exists to perpetuate this. Newcomers to the game will enjoy it more with normal scoring procedures.

5 THE BEST GAMES OF WHIST

When it was known as Whisk, this sturdy ancestor of Bridge was played with a 48-card deck in which the lowest card was a trey. Trump was determined by turning up the forty-eighth card and playing the game in that suit.

In 1734, one Richard Seymour, Esq. (as he identified himself), published *The Compleat Gamester, for the Use of Young Princesses,* in which he described an extension of Whisk that had become highly popular in Britain under the name Ruff and Honours. The full 52-card deck was used. Each of the four players was dealt twelve cards. Trump was designated by turning up the top card of the remaining four. Whoever held the ace of trump was entitled to take the four cards, discarding the four least desirable ones from his original hand. Seymour wasted little time on the details of the rules. His main concern was teaching the young princesses how to win by fair means or foul, including hand signals and peeking at an opponent's cards. The game had come to be known as Whist, explained Seymour, because "the very name implies, Hold your tongue."

And then along came Hoyle, whose best-selling advice was more technical than that of his predecessors, and considerably more high-minded than that of Squire Seymour. For example, his method of remembering the fall of the cards would stand a modern Bridge player in fairly good stead.

General Procedures

The deck, preliminary cuts, partnerships and deal are the same as in Bridge.

Dealer turns up the last card, which becomes a trump card along with every other card of the same suit. Dealer then takes the card into his hand and play begins with the dealer's left-hand opponent, known in this and most older games as the *eldest hand.*

Opening lead may be any card, and play proceeds *from all four closed hands* without a dummy. Each player must follow suit if he can, but may trump if he cannot follow suit. One player on each side gathers the tricks won by his partnership.

Scoring: Each odd trick counts 1 point. First side to score 7 wins the game. An odd trick, as in Bridge, is any trick won in excess of six during the play of a single hand.

BID WHIST

In this popular variation, the trump suit is designated by the highest bidder. All fifty-two cards are dealt face down. Player at dealer's left starts the bidding and may pass or bid a number of odd tricks from one to seven. Each player has one turn to bid, but each bid must be higher than the preceding one. After highest bidder names trump, play proceeds as in ordinary Whist.

In what some call Auction Whist, bidding continues until three successive passes have been offered in response to the highest bid—just as in Bridge. In another version, highest bidder's side plays in whatever trump he names but is required to make only the number of odd tricks called by the highest *previous* bidder.

In some games, highest bidder can order the game played in no-trump, which doubles the score.

Scoring: If bidder's side fulfills its contract, it gets 1 point for each trick it makes. If the contract goes down, opponents get the amount of the bid plus 1 point for each trick *more than one* that the contract has gone down.

In many games, each of the top four trump honors counts 1 point, as does each trick. The lowest bid is seven (equivalent to a bid of one in a regular game of Whist or Bridge), and the highest is seventeen (a bid to win all the tricks by someone who holds all four honors).

Because each hand is relatively fast, games of Bid Whist can be contested for whatever number of total points the players prefer, or settlement can be made after each hand.

CAYENNE

In this lovely but almost extinct game, the dealer chooses the trump suit after looking at his hand. Rather than name a trump, he can announce that he will play *grand* (no-trump) or *nullo* (in which his object is to lose every possible trick in no-trump, with aces as the lowest-ranking card). If unable to choose among these possibilities, he defers to his partner, who then must decide the terms of the contract.

The *cayenne* itself is a complicating factor. Before the denomination of the hand is named, player to dealer's left cuts a second deck and exposes the top card of the bottom pile. The card's suit is known as the cayenne, and has a delightful effect on strategy and scoring.

If trump is the same as the cayenne, all trick scores are multiplied by four. If trump is the next-highest suit, the multiplier is three. The third-highest makes the multiplier two. And the lowest means no multiplication at all. The hierarchy of suits:

Cayenne	Spades	Hearts	Diamonds	Clubs
Second	Clubs	Diamonds	Hearts	Spades
Third	Hearts	Clubs	Clubs	Hearts
Fourth	Diamonds	Spades	Spades	Diamonds

If the hand is played in nullo or grand, the multiplier is eight.
All odd tricks count 1 point.

Each of the top five cards in a trump suit counts as an honor. If the partners have all five, they score 6 points. If they have four, they score 4. And if they have three, they get 2.

A score of 10 wins the game. Points above 10 are carried over to the next game.

If a game ends before the losing side has 4 points, the winners get a bonus of 4. If losers have 4 but less than 7, the bonus is 2. And if losers have 8 or more, the bonus is 1.

The first side to win four games gets 8 points for the rubber, but the final accounting for the rubber requires that losing side's points be deducted from winners' total.

No side can win a game by scoring a hand for honors alone. Lacking a trick score on the particular hand, the side cannot bring its point total above 9, regardless of honors.

CONTRACT WHIST

The bidding and scoring are identical with those of Contract Bridge. The only difference is that dummy is not exposed. All four players participate in each hand.

DUMMY WHIST

A three-hand game in which lowest cut plays opposite an exposed dummy for the first rubber, second-lowest cut gets the dummy for second rubber, and so forth. Dummy is not exposed until after the opening lead.

ENGLISH WHIST

Differs from the American version only in the scoring. Game is for 5 points. Honors score along with tricks—4 points if one side has all four, and 3 for three. Established *revokes* cost three tricks, which can be deducted from the offending side's haul and added to the other side's. Or 3 points can be deducted from or added to the appropriate game score, depending on the nonoffending side's preference.

Rubber points are scored at the end of each game. If losers have made no score, the game is called a *treble,* earning the winners 3 rubber points. If losers have only 1 or 2 game points, the game becomes a *double,* adding 2 points to the winners' score. If losers have more than 2 points, game is a *single,* adding 1 point to the winning score.

Winning the rubber (two games) adds 2 extra rubber points. A *bumper* is a rubber of two triples and a rubber score of 2, against no points for the opponents.

As in other forms of Whist, tricks must be scored before honors. If a side has 4 points at the beginning of a deal, they must win the odd trick to take game—a game cannot be won on honors alone. If one side goes out on tricks and the other on honors, the tricks win and the honors count zero. On the other hand, if one side goes out on honors, the losers' tricks take precedence and may reduce the score from a triple or a double to a single.

NORWEGIAN WHIST

Eldest hand (player to dealer's left) speaks first and may either pass or bid *grand* or *nullo.* All hands are played in no-trump. Grand is a contract to win at least seven tricks. Nullo is a contract to *lose* at least seven.

If the bid is grand, the player to the bidder's right leads the first card. If nullo, lead comes from the bidder's left. Each trick goes to the highest card of whatever suit is led.

In grand, bidder's team scores 4 for each odd trick made. If contract is set, the defenders score 8 for each odd trick they make.

In nullo, the procedure is reversed. Bidder's side gets 4 points for each odd trick *lost.* But if his side loses the contract by *winning* seven or more tricks, the other team gets 8 points for each odd trick won by bidder's side! Game is usually 50 points.

SOLO WHIST

This is four-hand Whist without partnerships. Trump is determined by dealer's display of the deal's final card, which becomes part of his hand when play starts. Player to dealer's left is first to speak. (He also leads to the first trick, unless a *slam* is being played.) Bidding continues until a bid is followed by three passes. A player who passes must continue to pass, but player to dealer's left may accept a *proposal* (*see below*), even if he has already passed. Each bid must overcall the previous bid. Here are the bids, listed from the lowest to the highest.

I Propose: Player contracts to win eight tricks, provided another player will be his partner. Next bidder may pass, overcall or say "I accept," which means that he agrees to be the other's partner in that particular contract (which involves whatever trump suit has been designated).

Solo: Bidder contracts to win five tricks in a trump contract, playing alone against the other three.

Misere: Bidder contracts to win no tricks, playing a no-trump contract against the others.

Abundance: Bidder must win nine tricks while playing alone, but can name whatever trump suit he pleases.

Abundance in Trump: Nine tricks playing alone, but in the designated trump suit.

Spread Misere: Bidder contracts to expose all his cards at the start of play, and win no tricks playing alone in a no-trump hand.

Slam: Bidder says he will win every trick, playing alone in whatever trump suit he names, and leading to the first trick.

Scoring: Players begin with equal numbers of red and white chips (each red worth five white). If bidder is successful, he (and his partner, if any) is paid by each of the opponents. If unsuccessful, he (or he and partner) pays opponents. The payment schedule:

Solo	2 red chips
Misere	3 red chips
Abundance	4 red chips
Abundance in Trump	4 red chips
Spread Misere	6 red chips
Slam	8 red chips

For each overtrick or undertrick, payment is one white chip.

In Proposal, successful bidder and partner win one chip each from each opponent. If they lose, they pay at the same rate.

6 EUCHRE

Before Poker emerged, Euchre was beyond challenge as the most popular card game in the United States. Its cousins among trump games played with five-card hands included Ecarte, Napoleon and Spoil Five—respectively the national games of nineteenth-century France, England and Ireland. All seem to have descended from Triomphe, which was well liked in the fifteenth and sixteenth centuries and may have been of Spanish origin.

Euchre deserves the loyal following that it continues to command in the northeastern United States. It and a multitude of close relatives offer a wide range of challenging diversion to any card lover seeking a change of pace from, for example, Bridge.

Players and Deck

Four players in two pairs. A 32-card deck with the usual suits, and cards ranking downward from A through 7.

Trump and Bowers

After trump is established, it becomes a nine-card suit in which the highest card is the jack (known as *right bower*) and the second-highest card, *left bower,* is the other jack of the same color. That is, if spades are trump, then the J ♠ becomes right bower and the J ♣ left bower. The A ♠ becomes the third-highest trump and the rest rank downward as follows: K, Q, 10, 9, 8, 7.

Thus the suit of the same color as trump (called *next suit*) becomes a seven-card suit, and the two suits of the other color (*cross suits*) remain eight-card suits.

The word "bower" is the Americanized spelling of *Bauer*—German for "farmer," a name by which the jack has been known in various times and places, especially Pennsylvania Dutch country.

Cut, Shuffle and Deal

If partnerships have not been prearranged, as they are in most neighborhood rivalries, the players draw cards. The two lowest become partners. The very lowest is the first dealer. Two decks are used, with dealer's partner shuffling and then placing one deck at his right for the next dealer. Player to dealer's right always cuts the deck. Deal and play rotate clockwise.

To distribute the five-card hands, dealer passes three cards at a time to each player and then two at a time. Or he may reverse that order. After finishing the deal, he turns up the next card of the deck. Its suit will be trump for the hand, unless the players indicate otherwise in their bidding—known in this game as *making.*

Making

Player at dealer's left (still called *eldest hand* in many places) may pass or may say "I order it up." This means that he accepts the proposed trump suit and is willing to play the hand. Dealer then discards a card from his hand, face down, and slips it crosswise beneath the deck. He takes the turned-up trump card into his hand.

If eldest hand passes, dealer's partner may pass or may order up by saying "I assist," whereupon dealer discards, takes up the trump card and play begins. If dealer's partner declines, dealer's right-hand opponent can "order it up" or not. If all three pass, dealer can take up the trump card and play the hand, or he can show that the proposed trump has been *turned down.* He does this by taking the turned-up card and placing it crosswise under the pack. In some games it remains face up as a reminder that its suit can no longer serve as trump in the particular hand. Elsewhere, it is turned face down.

Eldest hand now has the right to designate a trump suit (*make it*). If he names a suit of the same color as the one already turned down, he *makes it next.* If he names a suit of the other color, he *crosses it.* Should all four players pass again without *making trump,* the hand is abandoned and deal passes to the next player.

The Play

The *maker*—the player who has ordered up, taken up or otherwise designated trump—has the right to play the hand without assistance from his partner. He must announce this intention as soon as he becomes maker. And it is considered a heinous breach of etiquette for his partner to protest the decision. All partner should do is immediately discard his own hand, face down, and await the next deal. In some games, the dealer has the right to play alone even if he has passed, provided that his partner has ordered up the trump by saying "I assist."

If the maker plays alone, the first lead comes from the player to his left. Otherwise, first lead is from *dealer's* left-hand opponent—the eldest hand. This rule holds regardless of where the maker sits.

All hands must follow suit if able. If not, any card may be played, including trump. Highest trump wins the trick. If no trump is played to the trick, it goes to the player of the highest card in the led suit. The winner of each trick leads to the next.

If maker's side wins all five tricks, it scores *march.* To take fewer than three tricks is to be *euchred.*

Scoring

If maker and partner both play the hand, they score 2 points for march and 1 for taking three or four tricks. A lone player also scores 1 for taking three or four tricks, but gets 4 for march. Whenever maker's side is euchred, the opponents score 2.

By local custom or special agreement, a game may consist of 5, 7 or 10 points. In some games, the scoring is enlivened by rubber play, in which rubber (with a bonus of 2 points) goes to the first pair to win two games. Other bonuses and penalties may be agreed upon, and settlement usually involves subtracting the smaller total from the larger.

In case of *revoke* during the play of the hand (that is, failure to follow suit plus failure to correct the error before play of the next trick), the nonoffending side may prefer to let the hand be scored as if no revoke had occurred. Otherwise, the penalty for revoke is 2 points, which some subtract from the offending side's score and others add to the other score. If opponents of a lone maker are caught in a revoke, the penalty is 4.

Errors and Penalties

Euchre resembles other civilized card games in exacting no penalties for inadvertent errors that impose little disadvantage on opponents.

Misdeals: In most cases, the same player simply redeals. However, if a player deals out of turn and the mistake is noticed before he exposes a card, the deal reverts to the proper player. But after a card has been turned up, the deal stands and the other player misses his turn.

If a player has the wrong number of cards in his hand and nobody notices this until after the first trick is completed (*quitted* is the technical term), play continues and the side of the player with the misdealt hand may not score on the deal. If the mistake is noticed in time, a new deal is made.

If dealer is also maker and plays to the first trick before discarding, he is required to play the entire hand without discarding. The turned-up trump therefore is not used in that particular deal.

Errors in Making: No penalty for mistaken terminology such as saying "I assist" when the proper term is "order it up." But declaring out of turn deprives the offending side of the right to make trump on the deal unless the player who spoke out of turn simply passed and did not attempt to make trump. Also, a player who tries to make a trump suit that has already been turned down is not allowed to change his call and his side may not make trump on the deal.

Mistaken Leads: If a player leads out of turn and the mistake goes unnoticed until the trick has been gathered, there is no penalty and play proceeds as if the lead had been proper. But if the trick is still incomplete, the erroneous lead becomes an exposed card and other cards played to the trick may be restored to the hands without penalty. When it next becomes the offending pair's right to lead, the right-hand opponent of the leader is entitled to name the suit in which the trick is to be played.

Exposed Cards: Cards accidentally exposed or deemed exposed because of out-of-turn plays must remain face up on the table and must be played at the first opportunity.

Strategy

Because things happen so quickly in a low-scoring game based on five-trick deals, good Euchre players strike while the iron is hot, expecting few rewards for the patience that is so serviceable in other pastimes.

When ordering up, assisting, taking up or otherwise making trump, it is essential to keep the score in mind, as tactics must be altered accordingly.

With three sure tricks in hand (such as both bowers and ace), the player hopes to make it alone. But most holdings are uncertain. In doubt, most players incline to order it up even with only two likely tricks in hand, hoping that partner will produce the other.

One of the most crucial situations is when eldest hand and partner are *at the bridge*—within 1 point of game and 2 or 3 points ahead. When this happens, eldest hand often orders it up with any ordinary holding, preferring to suffer a euchre rather than risk the consequences of having dealer or dealer's partner making it alone. Therefore, should eldest hand pass, his own partner knows that possibilities are good in the turned-up trump suit. With a couple of trump cards of his own, he can order it up and expect to win the game.

Dealer's partner relates his own bidding not only to the cards in his hand, and to the score, but to the fact that the turned-up trump becomes part of dealer's holdings. At the bridge, he may order it up to block his left-hand opponent. Or, if the turned-up card is a high one (such as a bower), he may pass in hope that his partner can play alone.

When dealer turns down trump, all hands deduce that he holds no bower. This encourages eldest hand to make it next if he can.

In play, as in bidding, it is reasonable to assume that an average deal will involve six trump cards. If trump is ordered up, dealer probably holds at least two, maker three and the others one each.

Play tends to be aggressive. Players grab tricks as soon as possible, lest their aces be trumped toward the end of the hand. Only with a strong trump holding are side aces reserved.

Keeping the Tally

In rubber games it is best to use pencil and paper and follow procedures akin to those of Bridge. In more traditional games, it is convenient and amusing for each side to keep its own tally with the three and four of any suit:

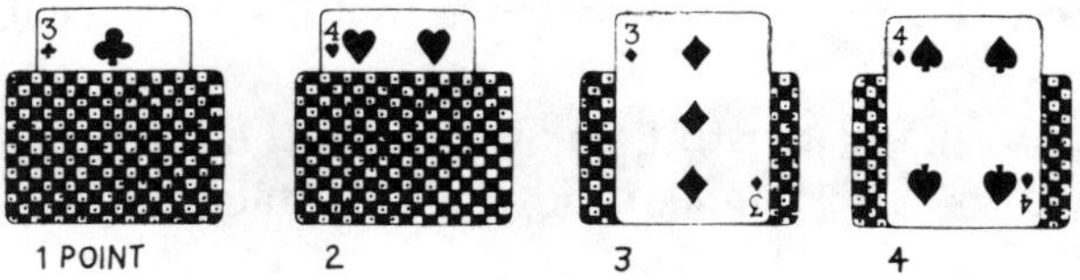

AUCTION EUCHRE

For five to seven players, with rules that vary broadly from place to place. Five use the customary Euchre deck of 32. Six play with that deck plus the sixes. And seven use a conventional 52-card deck, with seven-card hands.

The routines of dealing to five or six players are the same as in four-handed, except that dealer sets aside two cards, face down, as a widow, after serving the first round of cards and before completing the deal. In the seven-hand game, the widow contains three cards. Local dealing ritual may require that a seven-card hand be served in a round of four followed by a round of three, or vice versa. And the five-card hand may be out of order unless dealt in a round of three before a round of two, or contrariwise.

Maker gets the widow and discards an equal number of cards from it and/or his hand before play begins. Where custom allows, maker has option of making it alone without the widow, which doubles the point score.

Trump is named either by a bidding system akin to that of Bridge (except that there is only one round of bidding) or—in some circles—by maker after inspecting the widow.

Partnerships are determined by numerous methods, varying with local custom. In Call-Ace Euchre, maker may designate as partner whatever player holds a particular card that he thinks he needs for successful play. As a fillip, the rules may conceal the identity of that partner until the card drops onto a trick. If maker holds the card himself, its fall shows that he is playing alone. Obviously, this procedure is suitable only where the entire deck is used in each hand—as is the custom in some places.

In other games, a bid of three entitles the maker in a five-hand game to name one partner. But a higher bid gets him two partners. In the seven-hand game, bids of four or five earn one partner, and six or seven get two. In the six-hand game, partners may be designated by cutting the cards before the deal, or by prearrangement. They then sit in this pattern:

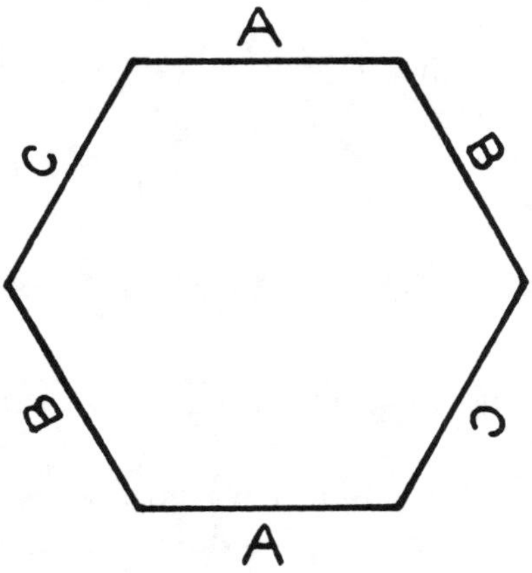

Play: In many games, the maker leads to the first trick. Some games require him to lead a trump.

Scoring: Game is usually 21 or 25 points. To score, maker and his partner (if any) must take no fewer tricks than the bid. Tricks are worth 1 point each. If maker fails, his side is penalized the total amount of the bid.

In the five- or six-hand game, lone hand scores 8 for *march* with widow and 15 without. In seven-hand game, 10 for march with and 20 without. Where rules permit bidding in terms of these points rather than of tricks, failure by maker means a bonus score of 5 to each opponent on a bid of eight or ten, and 10 on bids of fifteen or twenty.

CUTTHROAT EUCHRE

For three players, using the 32-card deck. *Maker* always plays alone and other two are always partners. Maker scores 3 points for *march*, and 1 for three or four tricks. If opponents *euchre* him, each scores 2. Each player's score accumulates separately.

TWO-HAND EUCHRE

Played exactly like the regular game but with a 24-card deck (all cards from eight down are eliminated).

HASENPFEFFER

A partnership game for four, using a 24-card deck, plus joker, dealt in six-card hands.

After the deal, the remaining card goes face down as a *widow*. One round of bidding is allowed. Bidders call the number of tricks. High bidder names trump and takes widow, discarding it or any other card. But if all players pass, holder of joker must bid three.

High bidder leads to first trick. If he and partner make their contract, they score 1 point for each trick. Otherwise, the amount of the bid is deducted from their score. Minus scores are permitted. Defense always gets 1 point per trick.

DOUBLE HASENPFEFFER

For two partnerships of four or six players, using a 48-card Pinochle deck, no joker. The entire pack is used in each deal, without a *widow*. Most dealers distribute four cards at a time.

Lowest bid is six. If bidder thinks he can take every trick, he has the privilege (after naming trump) of discarding two cards and getting his partner's two best—or in a six-hand game, the best from each partner. He then plays the hand solo.

Game is 62 points, scored at rate of 1 point per trick. Successful lone player scores double for his side. If defeated, he loses as many points as there are tricks per deal. But if dealer is forced to bid and play the hand, he loses only half the ordinary number of points.

JAMBON AND LAPS

Among variations that lend themselves to regular Euchre, Jambon (or Hambone) and Laps are quite popular. In Jambon, lone hand may elect to play from a completely exposed hand (or may be required to by local custom). Some games allow *maker's* left-hand opponent to call the first card played from the exposed hand. In this variation, *march* is worth 8 points.

Laps is a scoring variation that carries the winners' unnecessary extra points into the succeeding game.

RAILROAD EUCHRE

A hyped-up version of the good old game, using the regular Euchre pack plus a joker that ranks above *right bower.* Also utilizes features of Double Hasenpfeffer, plus Jambon, Laps and an option entitling either of *maker's* opponents to play alone—in which case *that* opponent's partner gives him a card or two, just as a lone maker gets a card or two from his own partner in Double Hasenpfeffer. But in case of Jambon, a lone opponent is not permitted.

Lone maker who can win with his own hand is awarded extra

points for doing so without taking partner's best card or cards. Similarly, if dealer wants to play *pat,* not taking up trump, he also gets extra points. Usual scoring awards 5 for lone, pat *march.* But if maker is *euchred* in these circumstances, opponents score 3. Neither opponent may play alone against a lone, pat maker.

In some games, maker gets a 16-point bonus for holding the five highest trump. Known as *jamboree,* this also rewards dealer even if one of the pieces in his five-trump holding is the taken-up card.

7 FIVE HUNDRED

The U.S. Playing Card Co. copyrighted this ingenious extension of Euchre in 1904, and it eventually replaced the older game at many urban tables.

Players and Deck

The popular three-hand version uses a regular 32-card Euchre deck plus a joker, which outranks the jack of trump (*right bower*), which in turn outranks the *left bower* (the other jack of the same color as the trump suit). Below these in descending order of value, trump rank A, K, Q, 10, 9, 8, 7. In suits other than trump, the jack ranks in its normal position between queen and ten.

The suits rank downward—hearts, diamonds, clubs and spades.

Cut, Shuffle and Deal

In draw for deal, low card wins but joker is regarded as lowest, ace next and then the seven on up. After cut by player to his right, dealer serves three cards at a time to each player, then four, and then another three for a total of ten per hand. A *widow* of three cards goes face down in center of table, usually after first round of the deal.

Bidding

Each player has one opportunity to bid, beginning with *eldest hand* (player to dealer's left). Bidder announces the number of tricks he will contract to win (from six to ten) and the trump suit in which he proposes to play the hand. Each bid must exceed the previous, either in the number of tricks or by naming a higher-ranking trump suit. A bid of no-trump is higher than a bid in any suit.

A bid of *nullo* is an offer to play in no-trump and lose every trick. It is regarded as a bid higher than eight spades but lower than eight clubs.

The Play

Highest bidder plays alone against a partnership of the other two. He takes the widow and can then discard any three cards, including cards from the widow. He makes the opening lead and others must follow suit if they can. If void in the suit, they can play any card. Each trick is won by the highest card of the led suit, or if one or more trump are played, by the highest trump.

In no-trump contracts, joker may be led to any trick, but player who leads it must announce the suit in which the trick is to be played. Also, the leader must be void in that suit. Similarly if a player in one of the other two seats plays the joker to a trick, he must be void in the led suit.

Scoring

Tricks	*Spades*	*Clubs*	*Diamonds*	*Hearts*	*No-Trump*
6	40	60	80	100	120
7	140	160	180	200	220
8	240	260	280	300	320
9	340	360	380	400	420
10	440	460	480	500	520

A successful contract in nullo scores 250.

The bidder who fulfills his contract gets no points for winning extra tricks unless he bid less than 250 but won all ten tricks, whereupon his score becomes 250. If he is defeated (*set back*), he loses the entire value of his contract and may even have a minus total, which usually is indicated by circling the figure on the score sheet.

Whether bidder fulfills the contract or not, each opponent scores 10 points per trick. Note that opponents only *play* as partners, but score individually, according to the number of tricks captured by each.

Game is 500 points. If two reach that total (*go out*) on the same deal and one of them is the bidder, the bidder wins. If neither is the bidder, victory goes to the first to reach 500 by means of winning defensive tricks. As soon as player with the decisive trick *counts out*, the rest of the deal is discarded.

Errors and Penalties

In case of misdeal, no penalty and same player deals again. However, if bidding starts before the error is discovered, and if one hand and the widow have an incorrect number of cards, the player loses his right to bid but the hand continues after the error has been corrected. If two players are found with an incorrect number of cards at this stage, a redeal is mandatory.

Should the dealing error go undiscovered until the bidding has finished, bidder loses immediately if he and widow have an incorrect number of cards. But the hand is played to see how many tricks opponents can score. If a player is short of cards and cannot play to a trick in these circumstances, he is held to lose the trick. If bidder and widow have correct cards but the opponents have not, bidder wins immediately and may choose to continue play in an effort to win all the tricks.

If bidder and an opponent have the incorrect hands, the cards are tossed in for redeal by the same dealer.

Exposed Card: No penalty if bidder exposes a card. If opponent does, the card must remain face up. Bidder may order it played whenever the player's turn comes, except that the card may be played only to a trick on which it could have been played legally if unexposed. Should player toss a card onto a trick before bidder has had an opportunity to order the exposed card played, the second card is now treated as an exposed card.

Revoke: If illegal failure to follow suit is corrected before the trick is gathered and stacked (*quitted*), the mistakenly played card becomes an exposed card but a card of the proper suit may be substituted without other penalty.

After a trick containing a revoke has been quitted, if someone calls attention to the revoke, play of the hand terminates immediately. If the bidder revoked, he loses the value of his bid and opponents score whatever tricks they have already taken. If opponent revoked, bidder makes his contract and opponents get no points.

Strategy

Bidding: Experts base their bids entirely on what they hold in their original hands. They expect nothing from the widow. Thus, they prefer to bid five-card trump suits, and will name a four-card suit only if it is top-heavy with bowers and an ace or king.

To evaluate the hand, credit it with ability to win one trick for each bower and ace of trump, each trump card in excess of three, each ace or protected king in other suits, and, of course, the joker.

Play: With a normally powerful trump holding, bidder attacks in that suit at once. His secondary objective is to develop his extra cards in other long suits.

Opponents strive to sandwich the bidder by keeping the lead in the hand of his right-hand opponent. Otherwise, he has the advantage of playing last.

FOUR-HAND

Twos, threes and black fours are stripped from deck, leaving 42 cards, to which joker is often added. Played and scored in partnerships.

FIVE- OR SIX-HAND

Full 52-card deck, sometimes with joker, is played by five hands. Each player bids for himself, but top bidder plays with one partner if he bids six or seven and two partners if he bids more.

If entitled to two partners, he names them. In some circles, when entitled to one partner, he simply names the highest card of a suit. Whoever holds that card becomes identified as the partner during subsequent play when dropping the named card onto a trick.

In the six-hand game, a 62-card deck is formed by adding special cards—four each in denominations of eleven and twelve and two thirteens. These are ranked above the ten but below the jack (or in trump, below the queen).

ONE THOUSAND

Winning total becomes 1,000 or 1,500. Some players enjoy counting trick-bonus points: Opponents or the successful bidder (but *not* a *set-back* bidder or his partnership) riffle through their captured tricks and score 1 for each ace, 10 for each king, queen, jack or ten, and the face value of each other card.

8 LOO

This good gambling game was a British national pastime at the beginning of the last century and is still played in Britain, as well as in most of the former colonies, including the North American. Known at various times as Division Loo or Lanterloo, it is a fast game, full of punishing surprises.

Players and Deck

Usually for five to eight players, although as few as three or as many as seventeen can be accommodated. The full 52-card deck is used, and cards rank normally from A down through 2.

Cut, Shuffle and Deal

Anybody hands out cards in clockwise rotation, faces up. First to get a jack becomes first dealer and antes three chips into the *pool,* which increases and diminishes according to the results of each hand. After cut by right-hand opponent, dealer distributes, face down, one card at a time, clockwise, until each player has three.

Simple Pools

On the first deal of the game, and on any subsequent deal that finds only the dealer's three chips in the pool, the circumstances are called *single pool* or *simple pool,* and the deal is a *bold stand* or *force,* in that everyone must play. Cards as played are not gathered but remain face up in front of each player.

Eldest hand (player to dealer's left) leads whatever he chooses. Others must follow suit if they can and, if possible, must try to *head* the trick by playing a card higher than any previous card. Trump is identified by a procedure that begins the first time a player is unable to follow suit. He simply plays what he can and after trick is won by the highest card in the led suit, dealer turns up top card of the undealt portion of the deck (*stock*). Its suit designates trump. If one or more trump were played to previous trick or tricks, the highest trump played wins each trick. The winner of the latest trick becomes leader to the next and must lead a trump if he can.

After the three tricks have been played, the winner of each takes a chip from the pool. All other players are *looed.* Each looed player contributes three chips to the pool for the next deal.

Double Pools

A *double pool* is any that begins with more than three chips. Deal proceeds as before, except for a *widow* hand (sometimes called the *miss*) to the right of dealer's. When deal is complete, dealer turns up next card. Its suit becomes trump.

Before play of the first card, each player, beginning at dealer's left, declares whether he intends to *pass, stand pat with his hand* or *take the miss.* If a player passes, he is out of the hand and his cards go face down beneath the stock. If a player takes up the miss, his original cards also go face down under the stock. Whoever stands or takes the miss is looed unless he wins at least one trick.

If all players pass except the player to the dealer's immediate right, that player must either take the miss or stand. Otherwise, dealer collects the pool.

If only one player ahead of him stands, dealer must *defend the pool* by playing, with or without the miss. But dealer can neither win nor lose chips in such a situation. If looed, he does not pay. And if he wins tricks, he collects nothing.

After all declarations, remaining player nearest dealer's left leads to first trick. He must lead ace of trump if he has it, and lead king to next trick if he has that. In any case, lead to each trick must always be a trump, if possible. Lacking a trump, leader to each trick must use the higher card of a two-card or the highest card of a three-card suit, if he has one.

Again, winner of each trick collects one-third of the pool. Whoever is looed pays three chips into the next pool.

Errors and Penalties

A player must pay three chips to the current pool if he exposes a card, deals the wrong number of cards, turns up the top card of the stock for trump before the proper time in a simple pool or declares out of turn in a double pool. Three chips also are levied for playing out of turn or neglecting to pay for loo before trump is turned on the next deal. The penalty for failing to follow suit when able is six chips (paid to the next pool), unless the error is corrected before the next player plays his card. As soon as the penalty is imposed, the hand ends and the existing pool is evenly divided among all but the offending player.

FIVE-CARD

With two additional cards in each player's hand, the ante and penalties become five chips.

FLUSHES

In either three- or five-card games, player with all cards in one suit (*blaze* or *flush*) is permitted to pass until all others have been heard from. He then exposes his hand and all who have bid are looed. Trump flush beats any other. If two players hold trump flushes, the one closest to dealer's left wins, but other is not looed.

IRISH LOO

All deals are double pools. Players who stand may discard any or all of their cards for others taken from the top of the stock. Trump is always turned up before this exchange.

UNLIMITED

A looed player pays the next pool twice the number of chips in the present pool.

PAM

The J ♣, called *pam,* serves as highest trump, or as a wild card to fill a *blaze* in any suit.

9 SPOIL FIVE

A grand old Irish game guaranteed to drive any moderately high-strung beginner straight up the wall.

Players and Deck

Full 52-card deck, for two to ten players, but better with five or six.

The five is always the highest trump, followed by the jack and then, regardless of the trump suit, the A ♡. After that, *in the red trump suits,* the remaining cards decrease in the usual order from A through 2.

But *in the black trump suits,* the order of the numbered cards is reversed. Thus, if spades are trump, the trump suit ranks as follows: 5, J, A ♡, A, K, Q, 2, 3, 4, 5, 6, 7, 8, 9, 10.

If a red suit is *not trump,* its highest card is the king and the others rank downward in normal order, except that the A ♢ becomes the lowest, after the 2 ♡ or 2 ♢.

If a side suit is *black,* its four highest cards rank downward as follows: K, Q, J, A. The next highest is the 2, followed downward by 3, 4, etc., as in black trump suits.

Cut, Shuffle and Deal

Any player deals cards one at a time, face up. First player dealt a jack becomes first dealer. Each player contributes one chip to the first *pool.* If nobody wins the pool, next dealer or dealers each ante up an extra chip. After pool is won, all ante one chip again.

Each hand consists of five cards, dealt in two servings—three and two or two and three. After all hands are dealt, top card of remaining deck is turned up for trump.

Robbing Trump

If anyone holds the trump ace, he can get the turned-up card in exchange for any other in his holding. To do this, he simply hands his discard face down to the dealer when it is his turn to play to the first trick. After getting the turned-up card, he then plays to the first trick, and may play any card he pleases. If the dealer holds the ace of trump he can have the turned-up card by discarding before the opening lead.

The Play

Player at dealer's left leads to first trick. Others must follow suit if they can. If unable, they may trump or discard from a side suit. Highest card of the led suit wins, unless it is trumped or the trick is played in trump, whereupon the highest trump wins. Winner of trick leads to the next.

Player who holds one of the three highest trump (five, jack or A ♡) is allowed to *renege.* That is, if a lower trump is led to the trick, the player need not follow suit with one of the three highest. However, if he holds a lower trump he must follow suit. Furthermore, if a trump higher than one of his is led, he must follow suit. Thus, if spades are trump, and a player leads the J ♠, holder of the lone A ♡ must play it, but holder of the singleton 5 ♠ would be permitted to renege.

Whoever takes three tricks first wins the pot at once unless he chooses to *jink it.* This obliges him to win all five tricks. If successful, he gets an extra chip from every player.

Players unable to win three tricks devote themselves to *spoiling* the deal. In effect, they play as partners, doing everything possible to prevent the presumably stronger hands from taking enough tricks.

If a player tries to jink it but wins only four tricks, the deal is spoiled, and next dealer must ante up a chip before proceeding.

Strategy

Although it is a quick game, Spoil Five is a carefully defensive one, in which players hoard their high trump in hope of spoiling the deal. Hence, good players are unlikely to become aggressive unless they hold extremely good hands, including long trump suits.

AUCTION 45

A partnership game for four (two against two) or six (three against three). No spoiling. Each trick is worth 5 points. Bidding begins with player to dealer's left and proceeds clockwise, with each player either passing or bidding in multiples of five to a maximum of thirty (which can be made by the team that takes all five tricks and holds the highest trump in the deal). A successful bid of thirty is scored as 60.

High bidder names trump. Before play, each may discard any or all of his cards and take new ones from the pack.

Game usually goes to the first team that scores 120. In an older version, 45 points won—hence the name.

10 ECARTE

A splendid two-hand game for gamblers and kibitzers. Like most games of chance, this one rewards knowledge of the percentages. Custom permits each player to have his backers, who make side bets with one another or with the active opponent and are free to give advice.

Players and Deck

A 32-card deck, in which the ace of each suit ranks between the jack and ten, but the rest of the suit is ranked normally enough, from K (high) down through 7.

Cut, Shuffle and Deal

Higher card deals first. Other cuts. Dealer hands out three cards and then two, or vice versa, and should continue to deal in that sequence for the remainder of the session. He cannot change without announcing his intention to do so just before the cut on a subsequent game.

Having dealt the ten cards, dealer turns up top card of deck, establishing trump. If the turned-up card is a king, dealer gets 1 point.

Maneuvering

Each player tries to delay actual play until confident that his hand can win. Meanwhile, repeated discards are made, and hands are replenished from the deck.

After the original deal, the opponent examines his hand and decides whether to play immediately or exchange some cards. To play, he says "I play" or "I stand." If he wants to improve his holding, he says "I propose." If dealer also wants to get some new cards, he replies "I accept" or, to save time, "How many?" He then gives the opponent from one to five cards and either *stands pat* or draws from one to five himself. When dealer prefers to play, he says "I refuse" or "Play," and play commences.

If dealer discards and draws, opponent again has his choice of proposing or playing, and dealer can again accept or refuse. This continues until someone elects to play or deck is exhausted, at which time the hand must be played. When insufficient cards remain for a complete new draw, dealer's opponent has first drawing privilege as usual, and dealer may take any of the remaining cards or stand pat.

The Play

Dealer's opponent leads to first trick, after saying "I play," which gives dealer a chance to claim 1 point for holding the trump king. If opponent holds that card, he claims the point before leading.

Whoever leads to a trick calls its suit. Other player must follow suit, with a higher card if possible. If unable to follow suit, a player must trump if he can. If not, he may discard. Higher trump always wins. If no trump is played to the trick, it goes to higher card of the led suit.

Winner of each trick leads to next.

Scoring

If a player stands with his original cards and wins three or four tricks, he scores 1. When he makes *vole*—winning all the tricks—he scores 2. If he does not win three tricks, his opponent gets 2.

If the hand is played after discards and draws, whoever wins three or four tricks gets 1 point, with an extra point for vole.

Game is 5 points. If someone has 4 points and gets the trump king, he ends the game immediately by exposing it.

Strategy

To survive in this game it is necessary to know *les jeux de règle*—the "regulation" hands likely to win the necessary three tricks in most circumstances. Whoever learns these need exercise little judgment to defeat the uninformed. Looking at his hand and recognizing it as a *jeu de règle,* he simply stands. And wins much more often than not.

A hand without a single trump may be a *jeu de règle* if each side suit is headed by queen–jack or king.

With only one trump, the hand qualifies if it contains three jacks and a queen, or a side suit topped by king–queen, or two side suits headed by queen–jack or king.

With two trump, one side king, two side queens or three side jacks are usually enough.

And any hand with three or more trump is a likely winner.

General practice is to discard all cards except trump and kings. If player cannot discard more than two cards, he probably has a *jeu de règle*. By this reasoning, when a player draws fewer than three cards, his opponent usually stands, unless he has reason to think that he can win in any event and wants to try another draw in hope of making vole.

The opening lead is usually the highest card of the strongest side suit.

11 NAPOLEON

Nap succeeded Loo in the affections of the post-Victorian British.

Players and Deck

Full 52-card deck, ranking from A down through 2. Four players are best, although two to six can play.

Cut, Shuffle and Deal

Low card deals, and ace is regarded as lowest for that purpose. Deck is cut by dealer's right-hand opponent. Each player gets five cards, one at a time.

Bidding

Eldest hand (player to dealer's left) opens either with a pass or with a bid of two (promising to win that many tricks). Some games permit an opening bid of one. Each successive player must make a higher bid or pass. If all hands pass, dealer must bid one and play the hand. A bid of five is known as *Nap*.

The Play

Highest bidder leads to first trick. The suit he leads becomes trump. All must follow suit if possible. Highest trump wins each trick. If no trump is included in a trick, trick is won by the highest card of the led suit. The winner of each trick leads to the next.

All players join forces against the high bidder, willingly sacrificing tricks in the effort to defeat him.

Scoring

If he fulfills his contract, the bidder collects from each opponent as many chips as equal the number he bid. If he loses, he pays that many. Nap is worth ten chips if accomplished, but costs the bidder only five if he fails to make the required five tricks.

Strategy

The probabilities have been worked out fairly well, so that experienced players know the worth of their hands with reasonable certainty. Four trump are likely to win three tricks. Three trump headed by a jack or better are worth two tricks. Headed by a lower card, they should be equivalent to one and a half tricks. Two trump including an ace or a king are worth one trick. Any other two trump are valued at half a trick. In the side suits, an ace or a king is rated as a trick, and a queen with one or two smaller cards is thought to be worth half a trick.

After the bidding reaches the level of three, expert Nap players usually evaluate their hands entirely in terms of the trump holdings plus the side aces and kings.

BLÜCHER AND WELLINGTON

Carrying out the Napoleonic theme, many localities permit a bid of *Nap* to be exceeded by *Wellington,* the bidder of which contracts to win all the tricks at double the usual stakes. And *Blücher* means all the tricks at triple stakes.

MISERY

This bid (from *misere* in Solo Whist and identical with *nullo* in other forms of Whist) offers to win none of the tricks, playing without a trump suit. It is higher than a three bid but lower than four and wins or loses three chips.

PEEP

After hands are distributed, a one-card *widow* is dealt face down. At each player's turn to bid, he may elect to peep at the widow, but it costs him a chip to do so. High bidder gets the widow and discards one card before play starts.

POOL

Pool goes to first player to bid and make *Nap*. On first deal everybody antes two chips, and on subsequent deals the dealer antes two. Unsuccessful Nap bidder must double the pool. The *peep* feature (*above*) increases the stakes still more.

PURCHASE

Before bidding, each player is permitted to discard as many cards as he chooses, drawing new ones from the *stock* in return for a payment of one or more chips per card. This variation is also known as Ecarte Nap.

WIDOW

On the table, between his right-hand opponent and himself, and before dealing his own hand, dealer places a five-card *widow*, face down. Any player who wants to can pick up the widow at his turn to bid. This indicates a bid of *Nap*. Playing with the best five of the ten cards, the bidder subjects himself to extra penalties that vary from place to place. In the game called Sir Garnet, the player who uses the widow must pay ten chips to each opponent if he fails to make Nap.

12 SKAT

An American Skat League was established by a solemn congress of enthusiasts at St. Louis in 1898. Such an organization had been flourishing in Germany for more than a decade. The game itself seems to have been developed in a card club at Altenburg, near Leipzig, about 50 years earlier. Its ingredients were borrowed from Tarok, Schafkopf and Kalabrias, the first two of which remain popular in the Western world without having been formalized as ceremoniously as Skat. We shall get to them presently. Skat is described first because it is perhaps more widely played in the Western Hemisphere than other games of its type. Also, whoever familiarizes himself with its exotic terminology will find the going easier when the other games are discussed.

Players and Deck

A game for three, using a stripped 32-card deck, with no card lower than a seven. The suits rank downward: clubs, spades, hearts and diamonds. The jacks of those suits are the four highest trump, ranking in the same order. Thus, the ace of trump is the fifth-highest card in its suit. Side cards rank in the usual order, from A down through 7 and the J, of course, omitted.

Like other games of what may be regarded as the Euchre family, this one involves trump, the taking of tricks, the use of a *widow* (called the *skat*), and—unlike most of the games reviewed previously—requires the player to capture certain cards for their point values.

If four players are involved, the dealer gets no cards. With five, the dealer and the third player to his left remain out of the hand.

Cut, Shuffle and Deal

Low card deals. If cards are of the same rank, suit rank decides. Dealer's right-hand opponent cuts. Each player gets ten cards in batches of three, four and three. After the first helping of cards is dealt, two cards go face down as the skat, then dealing proceeds.

First hand to dealer's left is called *leader* (*Vorhand*), next comes *middlehand* (*Mittelhand*) and then *endhand* (*Hinterhand*). Whichever of these becomes highest bidder is known as the *player*, and the other two team up as the *opponents*.

Bidding

Middlehand is first to speak. If he chooses not to pass, he must name a number of points ranging upward in even intervals from ten. The evaluation of the hand and the size of the bid depend on the points that can be won in various types of play and by holding or capturing certain cards. These values are given below.

If middlehand bids, the response comes from leader, who says "Yes" or "Stay" if he feels that he can equal or exceed middlehand's bid. When this happens, middlehand must increase the bid. This continues until one of them passes, whereupon endhand enters the bidding against the survivor. If both middlehand and endhand pass, leader is required to *name the game* (*see below*) and play the hand, even though he may prefer to pass.

Naming the Game

The player can choose to play with or without a trump suit, with or without using the skat, or by using only the four jacks as trump. He can contract to win all the tricks in process of achieving the score he has bid. Or he can contract to win no tricks at all. And he can attempt various combinations of the foregoing propositions. Whatever plan he chooses has a specific name and is worth a specific number of points. The final value of his hand (should he succeed) is based on that established value multiplied by other values that derive from the kinds of cards held and captured and the number of tricks taken. We shall itemize the multipliers below, when we discuss scoring.

Here are the basic games:

Tournée: The player looks at the top card of the skat, concealing it from his opponents. If its suit pleases him, he displays it to identify trump. He then puts it into his hand with the other skat card (which he keeps concealed). If he dislikes the suit of the first card, he puts it in his hand without exposing it. He then must turn up the second skat card, which establishes trump. This *passt mir nicht* tournée—as traditionalists of the game call it in their Franco-German patois—costs the player double penalties if he fails to make his bid. In the United States, this play is known as *second turn.*

Having picked up the skat cards, the player discards any two cards from his hand. These later are used in calculating his score.

If the exposed skat card is a jack, the player has the right to play *grand tournée.* In this and all the other Skat games called *grand,* the four jacks are the only trump. Player picks up both skat cards and discards two other cards.

Solo: Without looking at the skat, player names a trump suit. He then plays the hand in that suit, without using the skat. However, the values of the skat cards are later included in his score. Player also may elect to play *grand solo*—playing with only the jacks as trump, and without looking at or using the skat cards.

Guckser: Known in most games as *gucki grand,* this begins when the player picks up both skat cards at once. After he discards, play proceeds as in all grand games, with jacks as trump.

Nullo: When he declares *nullo* or *null,* player contracts to lose every trick without looking at the skat. The hand is played without a trump suit.

Ouvert: Player exposes his entire hand before the opening lead, contracting either to win all the tricks with jacks as trump (*grand ouvert*) or to lose all the tricks (*null ouvert*).

Ramsch: When middlehand and endhand pass without bidding, leader must play the hand. He has the option of declaring this game, which plays like a grand, with jacks as the only trump. Player's object is to win no tricks. Skat cards are not used in play but go to whoever wins the last trick of the hand.

The Play

Leader makes the opening lead. Others must follow suit. If unable, they may play any card, including trump. Highest card of led suit, or highest trump, wins. Winner of trick leads to the next.

The Values

Apart from the artificial valuations attributed to different suits, the reader will note in the tabulation below that the basic rewards and penalties of each Skat hand reflect its difficulty.

	Trump			
	Clubs	Spades	Hearts	Diamonds
Tournée	8	7	6	5
Solo	12	11	10	9

	Using the Jacks as Trump
Ramsch	10
Grand Tournée	12
Guckser	16
Grand Solo	20
Grand Ouvert	24

	No-Trump
Gucki Nullo*	15
Nullo	20
Gucki Nullo Ouvert*	30
Null Ouvert	40

* Not played in all localities.

The Multipliers

The allure of Skat lies in its complexities. Of these, the most interesting are devices whereby the player may multiply the basic value of whatever game he elects to play.

Card Values: Except for the seven, eight and nine, each card captured in a trick has a specific value:

Ace	11
Ten	10
King	4
Queen	3
Jack	2

Thus, there are 120 points in the deck—30 points per suit.

Except at nullo, player contracts to win enough tricks to amass high-card points ranging from 61 up. In some games, as we shall see, failure to fulfill the contract means doubled penalties.

Schneider: If player takes cards worth 91 points or more, he *schneiders* the others (or, in some settings, scores a *little slam*). This achievement multiplies his score, as shown below. To win fewer than 31 points is to be *schneidered.*

Schwarz: To win every trick in the hand is to score *schwarz,* or *grand slam.* Except at nullo, failure to win a trick incurs the penalties of *schwarz.*

Announcing: Before the opening lead in solo games, player may multiply his potential winnings (or penalties) by announcing that he expects to score schneider or schwarz.

Matadors: Here is one of Skat's ultimate complications. The player who holds the J ♣ is "with" as many *matadors* as he holds in sequence from that card down. For example, to hold the J ♣, J ♠, J ♡ and the ace of trump is to be "with" three matadors—the J ◇ being missing.

On the other hand, a player who does *not* hold the J ♣ is "without" matadors. Specifically, he is "without" as many matadors as the number of trump *higher* than his highest trump. If he holds the J ♡, he is "without two."

Using the Multipliers

The multipliers are valued as follows:

Making game (61 to 90 points in high cards)	1
Schneider without prediction	2
Schneider announced and made	3
Schwarz without prediction	3
Schneider announced, schwarz made	4
Schwarz announced and made	5
Each matador, "with" or "without"	1

Except when playing nullo or ramsch, the score for a fulfilled contract is arrived at by adding the applicable multipliers (which always total at least two, because of the inevitable matador and game credits), and then multiplying the basic game value (*see page 101*) by the total multiplier.

At nullo, no multipliers are used. For that reason, a player who bids more than 20 is forbidden to declare null. If he has bid more than 40, he is not permitted to declare null ouvert.

At ramsch, the player taking the fewest points is considered winner of the game and gets 10 points. If he has taken no tricks, he gets 20. In case of a tie among all three players, the leader gets 10. If two tie for low points, game and 10 points go to the one who did not take the most recent trick taken by either. If a player takes all tricks at ramsch, he loses 30.

Other Scoring

A player who fulfills his declaration and the full value of his game equals or exceeds his bid scores that full value.

If player falls short of the necessary points for game, he loses the basic value of the game. The penalty is doubled at guckser or second turn (*passt mir nicht* tournée).

If player fulfills his declaration yet amasses fewer points than his bid, he loses whatever multiple of his declared game's basic value exceeds his bid. For instance, if he declares and plays a heart solo tournée, takes 72 points in high cards (enough for game), and is "with one" matador, his game is worth 20. If he bid 22, he is in trouble. His penalty is computed by multiplying the basic value of his declared game (10 for heart solo tournée) by whatever number it takes to exceed his bid. This means multiplying 10 by 3—30 being the first multiple of 10 that exceeds the overbid of 22. The penalty, therefore, is 30. At guckser or second turn it would be doubled—60.

Settling

Cumulative scores are kept for each player. At the end of the session, one or more may have minus scores. To avoid confusion, it is customary to calculate the number of points by which each player's score differs from average. Those below average pay the indicated number of chips (or dollars or dimes) into the pot, and those above average pocket their swag by the same method. To illustrate:

Joe	*Jack*	*Tom*	*Bill*
52	31	−40	117

Adding the plus scores 52 + 31 + 117 = 200
Subtracting the minus 200 − 40 = 160
Dividing by the number of players 160 ÷ 4 = 40
The average score is 40.
Joe wins 12 chips.
Jack loses 9.
Tom loses 80.
Bill wins 77.

Bidding Strategy

It is not good business to count on help from the skat.

To be considered biddable, with a declaration of tournée in mind, a hand should contain at least one jack—in which case the other nine cards should be divided evenly among three suits. With two jacks, two-card suits in all four denominations are acceptable, as is one three-card suit, two two-card suits and a singelton.

For solo, a five-card trump suit is considered essential. Side cards should include two aces, or the ace–king of one suit and the ten of another. With hands as strong as this, experienced players usually count the potential losing tricks. Having long since memorized the point value of each card, it is easy for them to calculate the maximum number of points they are likely to lose, assuming that luck abandons them completely. Having done this, they can tell the minimum number of points they are likely to win. This simplifies bidding and, of course, the subsequent declaration of game.

With two jacks and two aces, or any combination thereof totaling four, leader considers a declaration of grand. In other positions, it is best to have a total of five such cards.

Discarding

One does not always throw junk into the discard. It often is sensible to discard high-point cards, especially tens, which are unlikely to win tricks but which count heavily when time comes to add up the score.

Playing Strategy

With a solid trump holding, it is essential to exhaust the opponents' trump by leading one's own. With a less impressive trump suit, it usually pays to force out the opponents' trump winners early by leading one's own low ones. Games have been lost by allowing one opponent to *ruff* (trump) a late trick on which the other opponent discards (*smears*) a high-point card of another suit.

Errors and Penalties

In a game as complex as this, the slightest deviation from the rules of procedure can cause havoc. Therefore, punishment is harsh.

At *passt mir nicht* tournée (second turn), failure to show the second skat card before putting it in the hand costs the player a 100-point loss of game.

Anyone who accidentally looks at the skat before qualifying to do so is fined 10 points. And if the player of a solo hand looks at the skat, he loses immediately, unless opponents require him to continue play so that they can pile up points.

Player's failure to follow suit costs him the game. But no player can win because of an opponent's misplay. Revokes and other errors by opponents must be corrected, even if portions of the hand have to be replayed. In tournaments, problems of this kind are resolved by the tournament director—known as the *Skatmeister.*

STANDARD SKAT

Some North Americans play a less complex version of the game, in which tournée play is scored at solo value, and solo play—known as *handplay*—adds one multiplier to the score. Base value of grand play is 20, and guckser, grand solo and grand ouvert are eliminated. Nullo scores 23, open nullo (null ouvert) 46, and handplay open nullo 59.

RÄUBER SKAT

In this variant, the player looks at the skat before choosing his game. Tournée is scored as if it were solo, and solo (or *handplay*) is worth one multiplier. Basic value of grand is 20. Nullo is worth 23, open nullo 46, ramsch 10 and open handplay 59. Multipliers are for matadors (1 to 11), game (1), handplay (1), little slam (1), big slam (2), little slam announced (3) and big slam announced (4).

Failure to make game or to amass points equal to his bid costs player the value of the game at handplay, double if he plays with the skat. A player who realizes after seeing the skat that he will lose can surrender to avoid losing a slam. But he must name a game so that points can be levied against him.

SCHAFKOPF (SHEEPSHEAD)

This immediate ancestor of Skat has never been organized and promoted like the newer game. Rules differ widely from place to place. Often played by three, but just as often by four. Trump may be exactly as in Skat, or may find the four queens outranking the four jacks. In some games, the permanent trump is diamonds, headed by the four queens and then the jacks. In others, permanent trump cards are, in descending order, Q ♣, Q ♠ and the four jacks.

In the four-hand game, partners may be predetermined, or high bidder can name a card, holder of which becomes his partner. In these versions, bidding is in terms of number of points beyond 60 that bidder contracts to win. In others, no partnerships are formed and each player tries to win at least two tricks. He loses one chip for each trick less than two and gains one for every trick more than two.

Most groups continue to count high cards, using values identical with those of Skat.

SIX-BID SOLO

This offshoot of Skat is believed to have originated in Utah. It uses a 36-card deck (the Skat deck plus the sixes) and is for three players, who hold eleven cards each. The *widow* is called "widow" rather than "*skat*," consists of three cards, and is used only for counting points, not for actual play of the hand. High-card points are the same as in Skat. So are the bidding procedures.

Trump is simplified in that each jack remains in its own suit. Cards rank downward: A, 10, K, Q, J, 9, 8, 7, 6.

High bidder names one of six games.

Simple Solo: Bidder names any suit but hearts and plays without looking at widow. He wins or loses two chips for every point above or below 60.

Heart Solo: With hearts as trump, bidder wins or loses three chips per point above or below 60.

Misery: Without using trump, bidder tries to lose every trick. Widow cards are neither used nor counted. As soon as bidder wins a trick, hand is over and he drops thirty chips. If he makes contract, he wins thirty from each of the others.

Guarantee Solo: With hearts as trump, bidder tries to win at least 74 points. In any other suit, he must win 80. Game is worth forty chips, win or lose.

Spread Misery: Bidder plays *misere,* turning his whole hand face up before playing to the first trick. His left-hand opponent makes opening lead. Bidder wins or loses sixty chips depending on whether he is successful in losing every trick. Widow cards are not counted.

Call Solo: Bidder must win all 120 points. As soon as opponents take in a point-valued card, bidder loses 100, unless game is in hearts, which loses him 150. To help him, he is allowed to call for a card not in his hand before he names trump. Whoever holds the card must exchange with him for any discard he pleases. But if card is in the widow, he is out of luck and no exchange is allowed.

FROG

In Middle-European Skat, the *Vorhand* (*leader*) opens the bidding by saying "*Ich frage,*" that is, "I ask." Hence, the Anglicized Frog, which is known in its various guises by numerous other names, some of which—like Solo, Heart Solo, Tarok and Sluff—are also used for other games.

Frog resembles Six-Bid Solo, except that the scoring is simpler, bidding can be more adventurous, and only three games are played.

Frog: Hearts are trump. Widow is taken into hand and three cards are discarded. Bidder wins or loses 1 point (or a chip) for each high-card point above or below 60.

Chico: Any suit but hearts may be trump. Widow remains closed during play, but its cards count toward high-card points. Bidder wins or loses two chips for each point above or below 60.

Grand: Same as chico but with hearts as trump and 4-point reward or penalty for each point above or below 60.

In some games, when four or five are at the table, the dealer and the other player inactive on the particular hand may be entitled to receive points or chips when the bidder loses. Elsewhere, they may also be required to pay when he wins. Sometimes they are involved in the settlement only when frog is played, or only on chico and/or grand.

DENVER PROGRESSIVE SOLO

Five different games are played. The lowest is *frog,* which wins or costs one chip per point above or below 60. Then, in order, come *spade solo* (two chips), *club solo* (three), *diamond solo* (four) and *heart solo* (five). Each player also chips into a *frog pot* and a *solo pot.* When bidder makes his contract he takes the designated pot. If he is defeated, he must double the pot. Meanwhile, regular payments are made for high-card points.

13 GERMAN SOLO

In some places, this game is known simply as Solo. Among card scholars, this causes a certain amount of confusion in that the name is also used for other games that this one resembles superficially but to which it relates only distantly. Aside from its merits as a pleasant pastime, German Solo deserves interest because it traces to Quadrille, one of the few games explored in the writings of Edmond Hoyle. It also is kin to Ombre, a Spanish game developed more than 500 years ago.

Players and Deck

For four, scoring individually, with a 32-card deck in which the Q ♣ is always the highest-ranking trump, followed by the 7 of the trump suit and the Q ♠. These top three trump, classified as *matadors,* are known individually as *spadilla* (Q ♣), *manilla* (7 of trump) and *basta* (Q ♠). In side suits the cards rank downward from A through 7, with the 10 in its familiar place below the J. Note that red trump suits contain ten cards, whereas black ones have only nine.

Cut, Shuffle and Deal

Seating positions are no issue. First player to draw a club from the deck becomes first dealer. After cut by his right-hand opponent, dealer dispenses eight cards to each in packs of three, two and three.

The Games

Three basic games are played, either *in suit* or *in color.* In color usually means a game played with clubs as trump, and in suit is a game in which one of the other three suits is trump. Some groups play in suit until somebody fulfills a contract. Thereafter, the trump used in the successful contract becomes *the color.*

The types of games:

Frog: A contract to win five tricks. High bidder announces color or suit and then asks for a strategic ace that he lacks in his hand. Player holding that card becomes bidder's partner for the remainder of the hand, but does not identify himself except by playing the particular ace to a trick. If the high bidder holds all the aces, he asks for a king. Frog in suit is worth 2 points and in color 4. Both bidder and partner collect the full amount from each opponent if contract is made and pay the full amount to each if contract is defeated.

Solo: High bidder calls color or suit and plays for five tricks alone against the others. Game is worth 4 in suit, 8 in color. Bidder either collects full amount from each opponent or pays each the full amount.

Tout: Bidder contracts to win every trick, solo. Payment or collection involves full amount, all opponents—16 in suit, 32 in color.

Bidding

Player at dealer's left either passes or announces "I ask." This means readiness to play the hand, and indicates curiosity about the readiness of others. Next player (in the usual clockwise order) may now pass or enter the bidding by questioning the first bidder. This process begins with the assumption that the bidder has already declared willingness to play a frog in suit. So the first question is always "Is it in color?" If the answer is affirmative, the questioner either passes or continues, "Will you play solo?"

In short, each "Yes" by the bidder is equivalent to a bid one step higher than his previous bid. And each question by the other is itself a commitment to undertake a contract as high as the one mentioned in the question. If the previous bidder finally answers "No," the questioner must now respond to queries—if any—from players as yet unheard from. Or, if the questioner passes, the previous bidder must then answer questions from the others, should any wish to capture the contract or push the bidder into an excessively high contract. Each player has one chance to bid or pass.

If all four pass without bidding, whoever holds spadilla—Q ♣—must show it and play a frog. If anyone holds both black queens (spadilla and basta), he must either bid a solo or push the previous bidder into accepting a solo contract.

After high bidder hears the final pass, he names his contract, which may be higher than any mentioned during the bidding, but cannot be lower. He also calls color or suit.

The Play

Player at dealer's left leads. All must follow suit when able. If not, any card may be played, including a trump. Trick goes to highest trump or, lacking any trump, highest card of led suit. Winner of each trick leads to the next.

Bidder of frog or solo has the privilege of attempting to achieve a tout. If he continues play after taking his fifth trick, he is obligated to take all the tricks or must pay the penalties of a losing tout.

Strategy

As may be imagined from the description of its bidding procedure, this game offers prime opportunities to shrewd psychologists. To avoid falling afoul of such sharks, it is best to bear in mind that legitimate tout hands seldom appear. To play solo, it is best to have five sure tricks in the hand and not rely on luck. At frog, no fewer than three sure tricks are the minimum, inasmuch as partner should be able to supply an extra trick along with his ace.

14 SCOTCH WHIST

Remote from Whist but with overtones of Skat, this is an entertaining partnership game for four, although it is played solo in some circles and may involve as few as two or as many as seven or eight players.

Players and Deck

A regular pack, stripped to 36 cards, which rank in normal order from A down through 6. In the trump suit, the jack ranks above the ace.

Cut, Shuffle and Deal

In draw for deal, highest deals first. Player at dealer's right cuts. Deal is clockwise, one at a time, until each has nine cards and pack is gone. Dealer shows his own last card, which designates the trump suit.

The Play

Object is to capture the points represented by the higher trump cards. In process, points may also be gained by capturing tricks.

Trump cards score 11 for jack, 4 for ace, 3 for king, 2 for queen and 10 for the ten. This explains the name by which this game is known in some places—Catch the Ten.

Play begins with opening lead by dealer's left-hand opponent. Others must follow suit. If unable, they may play anything, including trump. Highest trump wins trick, or if no trump is played, highest card of led suit. Winner of trick leads to next.

Scoring

Each captured card in excess of eighteen is worth a point. These credits plus the ones for top trump honors constitute the scoring on each hand. Both sides can earn points on any hand. First to get 41 points wins the game.

Strategy

As any player of Bridge or Whist will understand without even thinking of it, the player holding the ten of trump likes to be void in one or more side suits so that he can ruff with the ten on an early trick. If unable to do this, he often is well advised to lead the card as soon as possible. If partner has the ace, the card is safe. If not, it may smoke out the other side's ace. With ace and king of trump, it pays to lead them pronto. The ten probably will fall.

FRENCH WHIST

Same as Catch the Ten, but the 10 ◇ also counts 10 points, making the game somewhat livelier.

15 CASINO

This splendid game is sometimes spelled Cassino, possibly in celebration of the Italian city of that name, or possibly because some early authors did not know how to spell Casino. The modern consensus (for whatever it may be worth) is that the game *does* hail from Italy but is properly spelled with only one *s* because it is a gambling pastime. Among games in which players strive to capture specific point-scoring cards, Casino is unsurpassed as a test of card memory and card sense. Although it often is among the first adult card games taught to children—and therefore is widely known as a child's game—this should mislead nobody. For example, it is foolish to play a fourth game of Casino for cash stakes with anyone who has already won the first three. Some people are just too good at this kind of recreation and do not hesitate to exploit the advantage.

Players and Deck

For two, using the regular 52-card deck. In play of hand, ace counts as 1 and other numbered cards rank at face value.

Cut, Shuffle and Deal

Dealer is designated by draw for high card. Dealer shuffles, opponent cuts. Dealer serves two cards to opponent, two cards face up in center, two cards to himself and then repeats the procedure, leaving four face up in center and four in each hand. After each hand is played, dealer serves new four-card hands, but adds no new cards to center of table.

The Play

Beginning with dealer's opponent, each plays in turn, taking one of the following alternatives.

Trailing: Player puts one of his cards face up on the table, along with the other exposed cards, and the turn passes to his opponent.

Taking: Player may take (or *take in*) any exposed face or number card by displaying a hand card of the identical denomination. Or he may add the face values of two or more of the exposed number cards and take them with a hand card whose denomination equals the sum of their face values. It sometimes is possible to accomplish both these kinds of take in one turn, using a card from the hand to take not only an arithmetical combination of exposed cards but another exposed card of the same rank as the taking card.

If a player takes every exposed card on the board in one turn, it is a sweep and, in some versions, entitles the player to extra credit in the scoring. Taken cards are stacked face down in front of the player.

Building: The player places a card from his hand on one or more of the exposed cards, so that the sum of the combined face values equals the face value of another, higher card held in his hand. In doing this, he declares his intentions: "Building eights" (if that is what he is building), and may supplement the build with any eight that happens to be exposed in the center of the table, or with any additional combination of exposed cards whose sum equals eight. At his next turn, he may display the eight from his hand and take in the build. Or he may expand the build with a new card or a new combination of the same value, provided that he fulfills the minimum requirement of any Casino turn by playing a card from his hand. In this case that card would either be an eight or would combine with one or more from the table to form a new combination totaling eight. Or he may increase the numerical value of the build with a card from his hand plus one or more from the table, provided that the cards from the table are of the new denomination or if their face values total that sum. Note that the value of a build can be increased *only* by a card from the hand and that additional cards may be added from the table *only* if they are of the right denomination or form a proper build of that denomination. Moreover, a build may *not* be increased in value if it already contains a card of the denomination being built. Thus, a player who holds a seven in his hand may build sevens by taking the 3 ♡ from his hand and placing it on the 4 ♠ in the center. At his next turn, if he also holds a ten in his hand, he may increase the build by taking the 3 ♣ *from his hand,* placing it on the build and saying "Building tens."

A player may not build face cards, but when three of the same denomination are on the table he may capture them with the fourth.

Taking an Opponent's Build: A player may capture an opponent's build with a card of the proper value, and may also increase the value of an opponent's build in hope of capturing it at a subsequent turn. Thus, if a player has placed the 3 ♡ on the 4 ♠ and announced sevens, as in the example above, his opponent may drop a three on it and call "Building tens," whereupon the original player may capture the whole pile with a ten of his own. Remember that a player may not increase the value of any build if it already contains a card of the rank being built.

Last Hand: Before dealing for the sixth time and exhausting the deck, dealer is required to announce "Last." Whoever is the last to take a trick during the final hand takes in whatever cards remain exposed.

Scoring

After completion of the last hand, the players count their cards and announce their own scores, based on the following point schedule:

Cards (having taken at least 27)	3 points
Spades (having taken at least 7)	1
Big Casino (having taken the 10 ◇)	2
Little Casino (having taken the 2 ♠)	1
Aces (each counts 1)	4
Total per game	11

In some games, each sweep counts 1 point. A player who sweeps usually places one of the swept cards face up in his pile of taken cards as a reminder.

Occasionally, each player captures twenty-six cards, in which case no score is credited for *cards*.

In most places, the game is won by whoever is first to score 21 points. At any stage, a player who believes that he has accumulated that many points is allowed to make the claim and *count out* the total points in his present pile of captured cards, plus the total credited to him on the score sheet. If he proves wrong, he loses. But he may count out and become the victor over an opponent who actually had reached 21 sooner but had not realized it and had failed to count out.

Winner deals the next game.

Errors and Penalties

The most heinous crime in Casino is to build a combination without holding a card of the rank needed to capture the build. When the error is discovered, the opponent has the right to add 1 point to his own score. And, of course, the build becomes invalid and the cards are spread face up on the table for the opponent to deal with as best he can.

If a player trails instead of taking or increasing his build, his opponent may require him to take the build. The trailed card remains on the table and the offender misses his next turn.

It is a gross breach of Casino etiquette to peek at cards that one took prior to one's most recent turn. In some games, a 1-point penalty is imposed for the violation.

Strategy

As observed at the beginning of this chapter, Casino offers good card players ludicrously easy opportunities to exploit the ineptness of poor card players. In the days of his innocence as a young soldier, the author of this book lost eight or ten successive games of Casino to an otherwise harmless comrade who knew the game and was eager to profit from the knowledge. Having played at Casino all my life, I assumed that I was a victim of bad luck. But an older and wiser man took me aside and advised me that I was being fleeced. Until that day I had not realized that it pays to keep track of every card. If you can. It was the beginning of my education in matters of this kind.

At an absolute minimum, remember the whereabouts of the point-scoring cards. And play to capture as many cards as possible, preferring spades to cards of other suits. Obviously, it is unwise to trail with counting cards if a face card can be dropped. And nondealer has the advantage of being able to trail a counting card on his final turn of each deal, getting first crack at it on the first play of the next deal.

In the rare games that continue to permit the building of face cards, it is necessary to remember which have been played, so that when an uncapturable one appears on the table during the last hand, you will not assume that your opponent has a good chance to take the final trick.

DRAW CASINO

After first hand is dealt, remainder of deck goes face down as a *stock.* After each play, top card of stock is taken, Rummy-fashion, to restore the hand to its proper four cards. When stock is finished, play continues as in straight Casino.

FOUR-HAND CASINO

A partnership game in which, for scoring purposes, cards captured by each partner are merged with those taken by the other. Good players manage to help each other a great deal but nobody can begin a build for his partner unless he, too, holds a card of the denomination being built.

ROYAL CASINO

A challenging version in which the picture cards are treated like other cards, and can be built. Jack counts as an eleven, queen as twelve and king as thirteen. An ace is either one or fourteen, depending on the player's option at the time.

SPADE CASINO

The A ♠, J ♠ and 2 ♠ count 2 points each, and every other spade is worth 1. The game is otherwise unchanged, except that it usually is scored on a Cribbage board, which makes a winning total of 61 convenient and logical.

16 CALABRASELLA

This Italian antecedent of Skat contains some elements of Casino and may be one of the most subtle three-hand games ever developed.

Players and Deck

If four play, the dealer gets no cards. Deck is stripped to 40 cards by discarding eights, nines and tens. Cards rank, downward: 3, 2, A, K, Q, J, 7, 6, 5, 4. No trump suit is involved.

Cut, Shuffle and Deal

Draw for deal. Low card deals after cut by right-hand opponent. Each player gets twelve cards, two at a time. The remaining four cards become a *widow,* face down.

Bidding

Player at dealer's left either passes or announces "I play." If he passes, bidding proceeds clockwise. If all pass, cards are tossed in for the next dealer. First to say "I play" becomes the *player* and tries to take tricks worth at least 18 of the 35 points represented by (a) the high cards (32 points in all) and (b) the last trick of the hand (3 points). The other two join forces to prevent this.

The Play

Player begins by naming denomination and suit of the highest card missing from his hand (it usually will be a three, occasionally a two). If either opponent holds the card, he passes it to player in exchange for a card from player's hand. This card must not be exposed to the other opponent.

Player's second move is to discard from one to four cards. These are reserved face down for the winner of the final trick of the hand. Player now turns the widow face up and chooses the card or cards with which to replace his discards. If any cards remain in the widow, they also go to the winner of the last trick.

Player's left-hand opponent leads to first trick. No trump are used. Highest card of led suit wins each trick, and winner leads to the next.

Scoring

Each ace is worth 3 points. The three, two, king, queen and jack are each worth 1. After the last trick, each counts his high-card points. Player must have at least 18 points to the combined opponents' 17 or he loses the hand and pays each opponent the full difference in points. Thus if he has 14, when one opponent has 10 and another 11, the opposing total is 21 and he pays each opponent 7. If he wins, each opponent pays him the total difference. If player takes all 35 points, he gets 70 points from each opponent. If player gets no points, he pays 70 to each opponent.

Errors and Penalties

If either opponent leads out of turn, player immediately gets their remaining cards plus the widow and scores 3 for the last trick, along with the high-card value of all his previous tricks plus those of the cards collected as penalties. Opponents tally only whatever they earned before the mistake.

A *revoke* (failure to follow suit when able to do so) costs the offender 9 points. If he is one of the opponents at the time, the other opponent must also pay 9.

STRATEGY

Beginners are advised to emulate experienced players, who seldom take chances. For success as player, it is necessary to have protected high-card strength in each suit. It is a mistake to count on help from the widow. During actual play, victory goes to persons able to remember the fall of cards and to "read" the hands of other players.

17 ALL FOURS

This good old game and such of its relatives as Cinch and Pitch have been favored by many generations of plain folks. All Fours itself was mentioned in Charles Cotton's *Compleat Gamester,* published in 1673. It apparently was second in popularity only to Whist as a pastime of the unfashionable. With the upheaval of social attitudes that occurred in the eighteenth century, All Fours moved from the scullery to the parlor. And with the immigration of Englishmen to all parts of North America, All Fours established itself here.

Readers who have played Seven Up or Old Sledge were actually playing All Fours.

Players and Deck

Two or three players, or four (two against two), using the full 52-card deck, with cards ranking in normal order from A through 2.

Cut, Shuffle and Deal

High card deals. Right-hand opponent cuts. Hands of six cards each are dealt clockwise, three cards at a time to each player. Top card of the remaining pack is turned up to establish the trump suit. If that card is a jack, dealer gets 1 point.

Bidding

Player at dealer's left may *stand* (which means he accepts the trump) or *beg* (asking that another hand be dealt and another trump designated). If dealer prefers that the hand be played in the exposed trump, he says "Take it." The opponent then gets a point for *gift* and play begins. But if dealer does not mind taking his chances on a new trump, he *refuses gift*. He must do this if the opponent is within 1 point of winning the game (which goes to the first player to get 7).

After refusing gift, dealer discards the trump card face down and *runs them,* dealing another round of three to each player and turning up the top card of the remaining pack as a new trump. If this card turns out to be in the rejected suit, another round of three is dealt and another trump card is exposed. As soon as a new trump suit appears, play begins.

Whenever cards are run, each player discards any three to bring his hand to the required six.

If cards are being run and dealer turns up the jack of the rejected trump suit, dealer gets no points. But he gets a point if the card is a jack of another suit.

The Play

Player at dealer's left leads to first trick. Others may follow suit, if they can, or trump if they wish (even if able to follow suit). If unable to follow suit, others may play any card, including a trump. Highest trump wins each trick. If no trump has been played, trick goes to highest card in led suit. Winner of the trick leads to the next.

Scoring

Play yields a total of 3 or 4 points—one each for *high, low, jack* and *game*.

High: Holder of the highest trump played during the hand gets 1.

Low: Holder of the lowest trump gets 1.

Jack: Winner of the trick (if any) that contains the jack of trump gets 1.

Game: Whoever captures tricks containing the most high-card points gets 1 point. High-card points are calculated as follows:

Ace	4
King	3
Queen	2
Jack	1
Ten	10

Counting Out: Points are always counted in high–low–jack–game sequence, with each type of credit taking precedence over the ones named after it. For example, if a player reaches 7 (*counts out*) during the play of a hand and if no other player has a chance to top that total with points of higher priority, the game ends at once. But if some other player has a chance to score points of higher precedence, play continues and he gets the opportunity. Note that this issue arises more frequently in some of the game's variants, which award points to the capturers of certain cards, rather than to the original holders.

Errors and Penalties

If a player able to follow suit or play a trump fails to do so, and does not correct the *revoke* before a card is led to the next trick, he is allowed to accumulate no score beyond 6 on that deal. Also, if jack of trump was held by the offender or an opponent, revoker loses 2 points to each opponent and cannot score a point for jack if he happens to capture it. If jack is not in play, revoker pays 1 point to each opponent.

CALIFORNIA JACK

For two. After the deal of six cards each, dealer places remainder of pack face up in center. Exposed card designates trump. Dealer's opponent leads to first trick without any bidding. Dealer must follow suit if able. If not, he may play any card. High trump wins or, if none is played, trick goes to high card of led suit. Winner of trick takes the top card of the stock, loser the next. When stock is exhausted, final six tricks are played. Scoring as in All Fours. Strategy demands memory of opponent's draws and plays. This helps a good player decide whether to try to win the next trick or, by playing low, lose it so that opponent will be forced to take an undesirable card.

ALL FIVES

California Jack scored on a Cribbage board, with 61 points (once around the board) the winning total. Scoring as in All Fours, except that each five is worth 5 points.

SHASTA SAM

California Jack or All Fives, but played with the stock face down. Trump is established by cutting before the deal.

AUCTION PITCH

A very popular game, at its best when played by four players, but suitable for from two to seven. One clockwise round of bidding is permitted, beginning at dealer's left. Bids range from one to four. To bid four, player simply *pitches* opening lead onto the table. Its suit becomes trump. Scoring as in All Fours, except that failure to make bid means that defeated player is *set back* the number of points he bid. If this leaves a minus score, player is said to be *in the hole.*

BUNCH

In some two-hand games, dealer is allowed to offer *bunch.* Opponent then rules whether the dealer shall play a bid of two or redeal.

SET BACK

Another name for Auction Pitch but applied also to a three-hand southern version in which bids may go as high as five because the deck includes a joker worth 1 point. Joker usually is lowest trump for playing purposes, but the actual trump card continues to earn the *low* point. In *counting out* (*see page 126*), the joker point usually ranks between *jack* and *game.* Ten points usually wins.

SMUDGE

Whoever bids and makes four wins the game, unless in the hole, whereupon his score becomes four and the game proceeds. To make four without bidding it does not end the game, unless it brings player's total above the winning total of 7 or 10. In some 10-point games, *smudge* is worth 8.

PEDRO

A good 50- or 100-point game for four to seven in which the five of trump (*Pedro*) scores 5 and the nine of trump (*Sancho*) scores 9. The ten of trump is known as *game* and gets the point awarded in other versions to the player with the most high-card points. As in other Pitch variants, *high, low* and *jack* score 1 each, making the total count per deal 18. Count-offs in this order: *high, low, jack, game, Pedro, Sancho.*

DOM PEDRO

Sometimes called Snoozer, the name given to the joker, which always plays as a trump ranked below the two, scores 15 points and counts off last, after *Sancho.* Total count per deal is raised to 36 with the trump three, which is worth 3 and counts off after *game* but before *Pedro.*

18 CINCH

This offspring of Pitch has also been called Double Pedro and High Five. It emerged in the western United States at the turn of the century and became so popular that several instructional books were published about it. Until the twenties, when Bridge settled the issue, it was possible to argue in many localities that Cinch, rather than Whist, was America's favorite among card games requiring skill.

Players and Deck

A partnership game, two against two, using the conventional 52-card deck. Cards rank downward from A through 2. The trump five (*right Pedro*) and the five of the same color as trump (*left Pedro*) rank in that order in the trump suit.

Cut, Shuffle and Deal

If partnerships are not prearranged, cards are drawn and two highest oppose the others. Highest chooses his seat and deals first. Right-hand opponent cuts. Deal moves clockwise, three cards at a time until each has a nine-card hand.

Bidding

Beginning at dealer's left, players either pass or bid a number of points not higher than 14, which is the total number of points scored on each deal. Player unwilling to top the previous bid must pass. Only one round of bidding is allowed. Highest bidder names trump, without discussing the question with his partner. If all three pass, dealer must name trump but is not liable to the same penalties as a high bidder who has contracted to make a certain number of points.

Robbing the Deck

After trump is announced, the players (except dealer) discard all nontrump from their hands. Then player at dealer's left declares the number of cards he needs to hold a six-card hand. Dealer gives him the cards from the top of the deck, and does the same for the other two in clockwise order. Dealer then states how many cards he needs for a six-card hand after discarding his own nontrump holdings. Instead of dealing himself these cards from the top, he *robs the deck*. That is, he fans through the pack and draws all the remaining trump. If there are not enough to give him a six-card holding, he adds whatever other card or cards he chooses. But if his own hand and the deck contain more than six trump, he is required to display the extra trump face up on the table.

The Play

High bidder leads to first trick. If others can follow suit they may do so or may trump. If unable to follow suit, they may play any card, including a trump. Highest trump wins. If no trump is played to the trick, highest card of led suit wins. Winner of trick leads to the next.

Scoring

Unless dealer dredges up more than six trump while robbing the deck, each deal produces a total of 14 points, as follows:

High (trump A) 1
Low (trump 2) 1

Jack (trump J)	1
Game (trump 10)	1
Right Pedro	5
Left Pedro	5

These values are scored by capturing the counting cards in play.

If bidder's partnership fulfills its contract by scoring not less than the bid number of points, the other side's score is deducted from that of the successful bidder's side and the difference is awarded to the bidder's side.

In some circles, however, each side scores whatever number of points it captures during the play of a successful contract.

If bidder's side makes fewer than the bid number of points, the opponents score that number plus the points they actually captured during play.

Most experts favor a 51-point game, but higher cutoff totals are customary in some places.

Errors and Penalties

During the discard-and-draw phase, if bidder or his partner discards a counting trump, no penalty is imposed, except that neither side can then score that particular card. But if an opponent of bidder discards such a trump card, and does not retrieve it before dealer gives him a replacement card, the value of the wrongly discarded trump is credited to the bidder's side.

If a player fails to trump or follow suit when able to follow suit, and if he does not correct the *revoke* before a card is led to the next trick, his side scores no points on the deal.

If a player bids out of turn, his side is out of the bidding thereafter, unless offender's partner had already offered a legal bid that turns out to be the high bid.

Strategy

Opponent at dealer's left and dealer's partner usually try to communicate information about their hands to their partners, who can then appraise their combined strength for purposes of bidding at an ideal level. This information must be conveyed by the nature of the bid rather than through actual discussion of the holdings.

For example, an opening bid of 5 indicates possession of a Pedro. A bid of 6 means an ace plus three or four lesser cards in the same suit. Ace and king of the same suit are announced by an opening or second-position bid of 7.

With extremely strong holdings, such as ace–king–queen and one or more lesser tickets in a suit, it is practical to bid 11.

Bridge players should remember that Cinch players able to follow suit may decide to trump a trick. Not at all surprisingly, this puts a premium on high trump cards while making a long trump suit less reliable than in Bridge.

RAZZLE DAZZLE

For five or six, each playing alone. After high bidder names trump and the discards and draws are finished, he calls a high trump card that is missing from his hand. Whoever holds it becomes his partner against the others. No seats are moved. The temporary partners sometimes occupy adjoining seats, which complicates their tactics. If contract is made, each of the partners scores the full amount. If the partners lose, each opponent scores the number of points bid plus the number of points he captured in play. The game also is known as Auction Cinch.

SIXTY-THREE

A 162-point game in which the highest bid is 63. The usual high-card points are increased by 25 for the trump king, 15 for the trump three and 9 for the trump nine.

19 PINOCHLE

This staple of urban America is now the most popular of a group of highly intricate games that seem to date from the fifteenth century, if not earlier. The group includes Bezique, Klob, Piquet and Sixty-Six, all of which add the interest of melding to the subtleties of bidding, trick-taking and high-point counting. They are extremely demanding pastimes in which card sense and a good memory are paramount. Years of experience do no harm, either.

AUCTION PINOCHLE

Players and Deck

A three-hand game using a 48-card deck of four twelve-card suits—two each of nine through ace in each suit. Cards rank downward: A, 10, K, Q, J, 9. Often is played by four, with dealer getting no cards. May also be played by more, provided that no more than three participate actively in any hand. With five, dealer and second player from dealer's left usually get no cards. With six, dealer's right-hand opponent also sits it out.

Cut, Shuffle and Deal

Players cut for deal, low winning. Second low customarily sits to dealer's immediate left and others sit clockwise according to ascending rank of the cut cards. Dealer shuffles. Right-hand opponent cuts. Each player gets fifteen cards—three at a time or in three rounds of four and a final serving of three. After dealing first batch of three or four, dealer places a three-card *widow* in center of table. Orthodoxy requires that the widow lie face down, but a more exciting game results when dealer exposes one of the cards, leaving only two face down.

Bidding

Bidding starts at dealer's left and proceeds clockwise. In many places, first bidder is forbidden to pass and must bid 200 or—depending on local custom—250 or 300. The other two players must then pass or offer bids at least 10 points higher than the previous. A player who passes remains out of the bidding thereafter. After passes by two successive players, latest bidder plays the hand.

In some circles, player at dealer's left may decline to bid. If the others also pass, the cards are tossed in and deal moves to next player. Elsewhere, bidding may be limited to one opportunity per player.

The basis of bidding (without as yet exploring matters of strategy) is the player's estimate of the number of points he may earn through *melds* and by capturing high-card points in tricks. He knows that the high bidder names trump, imparting considerable value to certain patterned holdings.

Melds: Before the actual play of the hand, *bidder* (as high bidder is known) displays his melds—the point values of which count toward fulfillment of his contract. The melds are:

Pinochle (Q ♠ and J ♢)	40
Deece (9 of trump, originally called *dix*, which is French for ten)	10
100 Aces (one A in each suit)	100
80 Kings (one K in each suit)	80
60 Queens (one Q in each suit)	60

40 Jacks (one J in each suit)	40
Marriage (K-Q in a side suit)	20
Royal Marriage (K-Q of trump)	40
Royal Flush (A-K-Q-J-10 of trump)	150

A king or queen melded in a *royal marriage* may not also be melded in a *royal flush* (or vice versa).

In some games, bidder who holds *80 kings* and *60 queens* is said to have a *round trip* (or a *roundhouse*), worth an extra 100 points. If that bidder also holds a royal flush, the combined value is 350 rather than 390.

Trick-Points: The last trick of the hand scores 10 points. Cards captured in that and previous tricks are valued at 11 for each ace, 10 for each ten, 4 for each king, 3 for each queen, 2 for each jack. The deck contains 240 points in high cards (plus the 10 for last trick).

The Widow, Melding and Burying

Immediately after the bidding, bidder turns up the widow. After the other players have seen the three cards, he adds them to his hand. He now displays his melds (which identify trump). While the melds are exposed on the table, he discards (*buries*) any other three cards from his hand face down. After play of the hand, their values are scored for him. Bidder may change his melds, his buried discards or the trump suit before leading to the first trick.

Concessions

Bidder may concede defeat before or after looking at the widow. So may his opponents (if they both agree to). And if his melds total no fewer points than he has bid, the game ends without play, the contract already having been fulfilled.

A bidder who concedes without exposing the widow saves money (or chips or points) because he pays only the value of his bid to the *kitty*—a pool of chips that pays and collects after resolution of each hand, just as if it were a fourth player. When kitty has a deficit, players replenish it equally.

A bidder who concedes after exposing the widow but before leading to the first trick is said to have suffered *single bete* (pronounced "bait") and must pay each player and the kitty.

The Play

Having completed the process of burying, and having returned his melds to his hand, bidder leads to the first trick. Each player must follow suit if possible. If unable to follow suit, the player must trump if he can. If second player has trumped instead of following suit, the third player need not play a higher trump. But if the lead card of the trick is a trump, each player must attempt to win the trick if possible. When a trick includes two cards of the same rank and suit, the first played is higher.

Opponents play in partnership, one of them gathering all tricks won by either. Bidder piles his own captured tricks atop the cards he buried.

Scoring

If bidder's score for melds and trick-points falls short of his bid, he is *double bete* and must pay to each other player (and in some games the kitty) a double penalty, calculated in accordance with one of the preferred formulas offered below. If bidder makes or exceeds his contract, he collects from each other player and the kitty whatever amount his contract entitles him to under the chosen formula.

No extra payment is made for extra points.

The value of a contract is doubled if the contract is played with spades as trump. This means that double bete costs four times the normal value. In some localities, the basic values are tripled for a successful contract in hearts. Elsewhere, each suit is scored equally.

Here are five standard scoring formulas, each of which has adherents in one part of the country or another.

Bid	*Base Values*				
Below 350	3	3	1	1	1
350–390	5	5	2	2	3
400–440	10	10	4	4	7
450–490	15	20	7	6	10
500–540	20	40	10	8	13
550–590	25	80	13	10	16

Note that unsuccessful bidder must pay kitty and *all* players, including those who held no cards in the particular hand. Bidder who makes contract collects from kitty and *all* players, including those who held no cards. If kitty comes up empty at any point, it is replenished by equal contributions from all players. Whenever a player leaves before the end of the session, he draws his fractional share from the kitty. At end of a session, kitty is divided equally.

In some circles, a running score is kept, with game (and settlement thereof) going to first player who reaches 1,000 points.

Strategy

Good players expect nothing much from the widow (it usually contributes about 20 points to the hand). They bid on what they already have, and never overbid unless confident that it will provoke an opponent to hang himself with an even rasher overbid of his own.

In estimating the value of the hand, it helps to bear in mind that the deck contains 240 high-card points to be won or lost in actual play. For a conservative estimate of one's own playing strength, it is best to assume that each losing card in the hand will fall on a trick in which the suit's highest cards will also be played. Thus, with two losing hearts and no winners in that suit, the player assumes with good reason that one or both of his opponents will accumulate the six highest hearts in the two tricks on which his losers fall. These high cards—the two aces, two tens, two kings and two queens—are worth 56 points. A player in such a position bids accordingly.

In the play of the cards, it is essential to remember that a high percentage of hands goes to the player who manages to win the final trick. If your hand is only moderate, it will pay to concentrate on capturing that last trick.

Bidder tries as best he can to use his discard privilege to produce a hand in which the long, powerful trump suit is accompanied by one other long suit. Where this is not entirely possible, he settles for a holding in which he is void of one suit. This enables him to capture all the highest cards in the void suit by playing trump of his own. In most situations, he exploits his trump advantage by leading trump, exhausting the opponents and setting up the high cards in his side suits.

The defense looks for opportunities to weaken bidder's trump holding (if it is of dubious strength to begin with). If his melds left him more than 100 points short of his contract, defense usually tries to complicate his problem by forcing him to trump sooner than he wants to. This is done by leading cards in his shortest (or void) suit. If he requires fewer than 100 points, opponents sometimes find it effective to lead trump—especially when bidder has not been doing so.

A standard defensive tactic is the *schmier* (smear)—throwing high-point cards onto a trick that one's defensive partner is in process of winning.

Errors and Penalties

If a player bids out of turn, others may decide to treat the bid as if it were proper and may pass or bid over it. Otherwise the bid is void and there is no penalty.

If a player bids insufficiently to exceed the previous bid, the error is usually treated as if the player had passed. But the others may decide to accept the misbid as legitimate by bidding over it.

If bidder buries a card he has melded, or leads to the first trick before burying, or buries an incorrect number of cards, he is double bete.

If bidder looks at his buried cards after he has played to the second trick, he is double bete.

If bidder fails to follow suit when able, or fails to play over on a trump lead, or fails to play a trump if he has one but does not have a card of the led suit, and if he fails to correct the error before playing to the next trick, he is double bete. If he corrects the error in time, opponents may withdraw any cards played to the next trick, and there is no other penalty. If an opponent *revokes* and does not correct the error in time, the contract is held to have been made and play ends. If the offending opponent or his temporary partner corrects the error in time, play continues but the bidder need not pay if he fails to make his contract.

Variations

Exposed Widow: One of the widow cards is exposed after the first round of bidding, or before bidding begins. If 400 or more is bid, two cards of the widow are usually exposed before bidding on the next deal, and only one round of bidding is allowed.

No Widow: In the original three-hand Pinochle, a 64-card deck was used (the 48-card deck plus two eights and two sevens in each suit), and there was no widow. Game was 1,000 points. Auction Pinochle has replaced this version almost everywhere in the United States.

In the Mitt: For melding *100 aces* without using the widow, bidder collects an extra chip from each other player if he goes on to fulfill his contract. In some games, the value of *in the mitt* increases by one chip for each 50 points bid above 300.

TWO-HAND PINOCHLE

The deck and card values are the same as in Auction. Dealer gives twelve cards to opponent and himself, three at a time. He turns up the next card to designate the trump suit and places one of its edges under the remaining deck, known as the *stock* because the players draw cards from it.

Dealer's opponent leads to the first trick. Dealer need not follow suit. During these first twelve tricks, which are the drawing phase of the game, high trump takes any trick, or if no trump card is played, high card of led suit wins. After each trick, each player takes a card from the stock and adds it to his hand. Dealer's opponent always draws first, but winner of each trick always leads first to the next.

The winner of the first trick may meld once before drawing and leading to the next trick. He may also take up the exposed trump card, replacing it with the *deece* and earning the customary 10 points. If dealer turns up the deece as the original trump card, he gets 10 points.

On last trick of the drawing phase, winner shows the card he draws and loser takes up the trump card (which may now be a deece).

During play of the next twelve tricks, a player able to follow suit must do so, and must try to win each trump trick, and must trump if he can when unable to follow suit.

For convenience, scores are kept and settlements are made in multiples of 10. A score that ends in a 7 or higher is accepted as the next higher multiple of 10. In some games, settlement is made after each hand. In others, 1,000 points wins.

Pinochle strategists use the drawing phase for purposes of developing melds. During the early play, they do not chase high-card tricks if that would jeopardize later melds. When it becomes apparent that certain aces and tens are no longer usable in melds, they are expended in capturing other high cards.

The winner of this game is invariably the player with the best recollection of cards already played and unavailable.

64-CARD PINOCHLE

The most severe test of a two-hand Pinochle addict occurs with a 64-card deck (sevens and eights add the extra sixteen cards). The trump seven becomes the *deece*. Each player gets a sixteen-card hand, dealt four at a time.

PARTNERSHIP PINOCHLE

For four—two against two—using the 48-card deck. Everyone gets twelve cards, three at a time, except dealer, who gives himself eleven and exposes the last card to designate the trump suit. If the card is a nine, dealer's side gets 10 points. If not, other players each get a turn (in clockwise rotation) to replace the trump card with the *deece*. That process completed, dealer takes up the exposed trump card or its replacement and *melding* begins.

Melds are scored as in Auction, except that a *double royal flush,* or *eight kings,* or *double pinochle,* or any other double meld counts ten times the value of the single meld. In some games, this is varied by awarding double pinochle only 300. Another variation permits partners to score the bonuses for double melds when each has the needed single meld. In other places, each partner's melds are added separately and no tenfold bonuses are claimed unless one player can make the extra meld himself.

In the best partnership games, the usual Pinochle rules apply. A player unable to follow suit need not attempt to win the trick with a high trump if his tactics suggest that he should hold off. He must play a trump, but it can be a low one. Only after a trump lead is it mandatory to try to win. In some games, tactics are simplified by obliging each player to try to win every trick he can.

Some players use traditional Pinochle values when scoring high cards. Others count 10 for each captured ace or ten and 5 for each king or queen. Other cards do not count. Last trick always counts 10. Game is 1,000 or any higher amount agreed upon. No melds are entered in the score unless the team has taken at least one trick, which renders the melds "official."

A pleasing variation on the usual scoring becomes possible when both sides reach or surpass the winning total on the same hand. Instead of awarding the victory to the first side that reaches the total, or the one with the higher total, the number of points necessary for victory is automatically increased by 250 or 500 points. This adds excitement.

PARTNERSHIP AUCTION PINOCHLE

A variation of Partnership Pinochle in which one round of bidding establishes trump, eliminating the turned-up card. High bidder names trump and leads to first trick. Opponents always score what they make in *melds* and high-card points. If bidder's side fails to make contract, it loses the full amount of the bid. Game goes to first side to reach 1,000, and bidder's side always counts first, which means that it can win even when other side has more total points. In some places, bidding is not restricted to one round, but goes on until everybody but high bidder has passed. A player who passes is barred from the subsequent bidding. The game also can be played with a *widow*. Each players gets an eleven-card hand. Before the melding, high bidder picks up the four-card widow, chooses the one he wants and gives one of the other cards, face down, to each of the other players.

CHECK PINOCHLE

A variation of Partnership Auction Pinochle in which lowest bid is 200, and bidder must have a *marriage* unless he is the dealer, who is required to bid 200 if the others have passed. He may bid more with a *marriage*. Bidding is continuous until all but high bidder have passed. High bidder leads to first trick. If high bidder and partner make their contract, they score all the points they make. If they fall short, they lose the full value of the bid. Game usually is 1,000 points, with interest heightened by payment in chips (often called *checks*) for various achievements. The most usual payment schedule:

Meld	*Value in Chips*
Roundhouse	4
Flush	2
100 Aces	2
Kings, Queens or Jacks	1
Double Pinochle	1
Fulfilled Contract	
Below 250	2
250–290	4
300–340	7
350–390	10
400–440	13
450–490	16

Higher contracts earn three chips for each 50 points. When a contract is defeated, losers pay double the number of chips.

When game is won, victors get seven chips (double in some circles when losers have a minus score) plus one chip for each 100 points by which their total score exceeds that of the losers.

When one side wins every trick in a hand (*slam*), it collects four chips.

FIREHOUSE PINOCHLE

Partnership Auction Pinochle in which the smallest permissible bid is 200 but nobody may bid without a *marriage*.

DOUBLE-PACK PINOCHLE

A partnership game, two against two, using an 80-card deck (two regular Pinochle decks from which the nines have been removed). Each player gets a 20-card hand (four or five at a time). Minimum bid is 500. Partners communicate during bidding by using the privilege of announcing (but not yet showing) *melds* and other strengths. When bidding, a player may add that he has a lengthy suit or a trump sequence (without naming the suit). Or he may declare the point-value of a meld he holds. Before bidding begins, a player who declares a long suit or a sequence has, in effect, bid 500. At that stage, announcement of the number of points in a meld does not commit the player to a bid, but simply imparts information. After the first actual bid—or the first declaration of a long suit or sequence—each declaration of the point-value of a meld is an *overcall,* at the rate of 10 points per 100, or fraction. For example, if the highest previous regular bid has been 600, a player who declares possession of a meld worth 300 automatically boosts the bidding to 630.

High bidder announces trump by exposing the first card of his first meld. Or he simply places the entire meld on the table, and the bottom card in the display is trump.

Melds are scored as in Auction Pinochle, except that large bonuses are awarded for doubled, tripled or quadrupled melds *other than marriages and flushes.* Thus, three marriages are worth only 60 points. But *80 kings* held three times in the same hand are worth 1,200.

The formula provides that *double melds* (other than flushes and marriages) are worth ten times as much as a *single meld* of the same type. And *triple melds* are counted as half again as valuable as a double. And a *quadruple meld*—should it occur—yields twice as much as a double. Therefore, 80 kings double is worth 800. Triple earns 1,200. Quadruple is 1,600.

Partners meld separately and score the bonuses separately. If each has *100 aces,* the team's score is only 200 for those melds. But if one has the 100 aces twice, the team gets 1,000 points.

Melds are not scored for a team unless it captures a trick that contains a high-point card.

Scoring of high-card points is as in Partnership Pinochle, although some groups prefer to count 10 for each ace, ten and king and nothing for any other captured card. Bidding side's opponents always score what they earn in melds and tricks. If bidding side fulfills contract, it gets all the points it melds or captures. If not, it loses the total amount of the bid. Game goes to the first side to reach 3,550. Bidding side counts first in such circumstances.

Revokes: If uncorrected before the offending side plays to the next trick, *revoke* costs the offenders as many points as their melds are worth.

WIPE-OFF

In this variation of Double-Pack Pinochle, a team must score at least 200 in high-card points or its melds and high-card points do not count.

20 BEZIQUE

This forerunner of Pinochle remains popular enough in Britain, Western Europe and North America to deserve inclusion here.

Players and Deck

Two hands with a 64-card deck—the ordinary Pinochle pack plus sevens and eights. Card rankings follow the usual German sequence of A, 10, K, Q, J, 9, 8, 7.

Cut, Shuffle and Deal

Players cut for first deal. Low card deals, after shuffling and allowing opponent to cut. If opponent chooses, he may also shuffle, but dealer shuffles last. Each player gets an eight-card hand, dealt in batches of three, two and three. Dealer turns up next card to establish the trump suit. The card then is placed face up but partly underneath the face-down pack, which serves as a *stock* from which the players draw during the early phase of play.

The Play

After opponent makes the opening lead, dealer may play any card on it. That trick and all subsequent ones go to the higher card of the led suit or to the higher trump. If each plays the same card, the leader wins the trick. Winner of the trick leads to the next.

Object is to score points by (a) capturing aces and tens (each of which is known as a *brisque* and counts 10) and (b) *declaring* (*melding*) various combinations of cards. The values of the *declarations* are:

Marriage (K-Q of same suit)	20
Royal Marriage (K-Q of trump)	40
Sequence (A-10-K-Q-J of trump)	250
Bezique (Q ♠ and J ◇)	40
Double Bezique (two beziques)	500
100 Aces (one A in each suit)	100
80 Kings (one K in each suit)	80
60 Queens (one Q in each suit)	60
40 Jacks (one J in each suit)	40

After winning a trick, player may make a declaration by putting down a value-bearing combination of cards face up. Only one declaration is permitted at one turn. The displayed cards remain on the table but may be used as if they were part of the hand—that is, any of them can be played on tricks. After declaring and before leading to the next trick, the declarer must replenish his hand by drawing as many cards from the stock as he has declared.

Cards used in declaration of a *royal marriage* may be used in enlarging the declaration to a *sequence.* But after declaring a sequence, the player may not declare a royal marriage with cards used in the sequence.

Once a declaration has been made and one or more of its cards have been played to tricks, the player may not claim credit for the same declaration again unless able to display an entirely new combination of cards.

Within those limits, a single card may be used in several different declarations. A J ◇ may be used in a *bezique,* a *sequence* and *40 jacks.* But if it then is played to a trick, the player cannot claim a new bezique without producing a new Q ♠ with his new J ◇. Nor can he claim a new 40 jacks without displaying four new jacks.

If bezique is declared and 40 points are scored, *double bezique* and an additional 500 points may be claimed on a subsequent turn. But if both are declared on the same turn, the score is only 500.

When only one card remains face down in the stock, the winner of the next trick takes it and the loser takes the face-up trump card. Players then pick up the declared cards that remain on the table and play the final eight tricks of the deal. In this phase, it is compulsory to follow suit if able, and to try to win each trick.

Last trick is worth 10 points.

Scoring

Game usually is 1,000 or 1,500 points. If both reach or exceed the winning figure on the same deal, player with the higher total wins. In the rare event of a tie, the game is prolonged to 1,500 or 2,000 points.

Strategy

Play is largely maneuvering for declarations, which are more valuable in the long run than brisques. The greatest effort is expanded in attempting to retain cards usable in high-count declarations. To enlarge the possibility that such declarations can be made, good players strive to keep other cards with which to win tricks—remembering that only the winner of a trick is permitted to declare.

RUBICON BEZIQUE

Two 64-card Bezique decks are shuffled to make a 128-card deck. Each player gets a nine-card hand. Establishment of trump is delayed until declaration of the first *marriage. Declaration* procedures resemble those of traditional Bezique but are more lenient and, therefore, more exciting. After a card has been played from a declaration, the full value of the declaration may be claimed again if the player is able to replace the card. The range of declarations is also increased. A nontrump *sequence* (*back door*) earns 150. *Triple bezique* is worth 1,500 and *quadruple bezique* scores 4,500. The trump seven is without value but a player without a face card in his original hand may show it and score 50 for *carte blanche*. He gets another 50 for each ace, seven, eight or nine he draws from the *stock* before drawing a face card.

Tricks are not taken until a *brisque* is played. Winner of that trick collects all the cards that have accumulated. Winner of final tricks scores 50. At end of deal, a player with fewer than 1,000 points is *rubiconed*. His opponent scores all points made by both, plus 320 for the brisques and a 1,000-point bonus. This holds true even if winner has less than 1,000—just so his total is higher than opponent's. Bonus for winning a game without rubicon is 500. In settlements, fractions of less than 100 are disregarded. Brisques usually are counted only when they might affect the outcome of the deal or might prevent rubicon. Winner of hand deals next one.

CHINESE BEZIQUE

A 192-card deck is formed by shuffling three 64-card Bezique decks. Twelve-card hands and procedures resembling Rubicon Bezique, except that brisques are never counted and tricks are never gathered but remain in mid-table. Besides *rubicon*, this version permits 1,000 for four aces of trump, 900 for four tens of trump, 800 for four kings of trump, 600 for four queens of trump and 400 for four jacks of trump. *Carte blanche* scores 250, as does the final trick.

Before dealing, dealer tries to lift exactly twenty-four cards off the top of the pack in one attempt. Without touching the removed cards, opponent guesses at their exact number. If count reveals exactly twenty-four, dealer scores 250. If opponent's guess is correct, he earns 150.

Winning bonus is 1,000. If loser has fewer than 3,000 points, he is rubiconed.

EIGHT-PACK BEZIQUE

Chinese Bezique is sometimes enlarged by use of a 256-card deck (eight regular decks stripped of twos through sixes) and 15-card hands. *Quintuple bezique* is worth 9,000. Five aces of trump score 2,000, five tens of trump 1,800, five kings of trump 1,600, five queens of trump 1,200, and five jacks of trump 800. Loser must score at least 5,000 or he is rubiconed.

NO-TRUMP BEZIQUE

Conventional Bezique in which trump is established by declaration of the first *marriage*.

THREE-HAND BEZIQUE

A 96-card deck (three regular decks stripped of twos through sixes), with *triple bezique* worth 1,500. Game is usually 2,000.

FOUR-HAND BEZIQUE

With two 64-card Bezique decks shuffled to make a 128-card pack, each player operates individually. The fourth *bezique* is worth 1,500, as is the third. In partnership play, winner of trick may declare or may defer to partner. Partners are permitted to add to each other's combinations. In some localities, a player may make all his possible declarations at the first opportunity.

CINQ-CENTS

An earlier form of Bezique (possibly the earliest), using a regular deck and scoring high-card points exactly as in Skat (*see page 98*). In this version, *bezique* is called *binage* (which sounds enough like *pinochle* to justify speculation about the origins of that newer pastime's name). Aside from the usual *declarations* of conventional Bezique, players may declare a *nontrump sequence* worth 120. High-card points are not counted until end of hand. A player who believes that his declarations plus captured points total 500 is allowed to knock on the table. If his count is accurate (or if he has more than

500), he wins even though his opponent's total may be higher. If neither player knocks before the end of the hand, and only one has reached 500, he wins. If both have reached 500, game continues with 600 as winning score. If player miscounts his total and knocks with fewer than 500 points, he loses.

21 SIXTY-SIX

This simple variant of Bezique commands a chapter of its own for no reason other than the difficulty of explaining all the differences in a smaller space.

Players and Deck

A two-hand game using a 24-card deck, with cards ranking downward: A, 10, K, Q, J, 9. Players score by *melding* and by capturing high-point cards, which are valued exactly as in Skat—ace earns 11, ten 10, king 4, queen 3 and jack 2.

Cut, Shuffle and Deal

Player who draws high card becomes dealer. After cut, he gives opponent and himself three cards at a time for six-card hands, then turns up top card of deck to establish the trump suit. Trump card is placed face up alongside or partly beneath the remaining pack, which now is used as a *stock* (or *talon*) for drawing purposes.

The Play

Dealer's opponent leads to first trick. Each trick is won by the higher card of the led suit, or by the higher trump. It is not compulsory to follow suit. Winner of each trick draws first from the stock and leads to the next trick.

If a player holds a king and queen of the same suit, he scores 20 (40 if the suit is trump) by displaying the cards and leading one of them to the next trick.

For tactical reasons, at any point during the play the winner of the latest trick may declare the stock closed by turning the trump card face down. No further draws are made, but in the remaining six tricks it is compulsory to follow suit if possible. If unable to follow suit, a player may play any other card he chooses, including trump. Melding of *marriages* (king and queen of same suit) is permitted during this phase. Should neither player close the stock, play of the final six tricks occurs after the stock is exhausted.

A player who has won at least one trick may exchange the trump nine for the face-up trump card. But if the last card of the stock is the trump nine, the player who draws it is required to keep it and the other player gets the other trump card.

Scoring

If stock was not closed by either player, final trick is worth 10 points. Otherwise it earns no bonus. After the final trick, players add up their points for marriages and captured high-point cards. First player to reach 66 gets 1 game point. If loser gets fewer than 33, he is *schneidered* and winner scores 2 game points. To win no trick is *schwarz,* which earns the winner 3 game points.

If a player closes the stock and goes on to score fewer than 66, his opponent gets 2 game points. Also, if opponent had not won a trick when the stock was closed but now restricts the closer to fewer than 66, he scores 3 game points.

Game goes to first to earn 7 game points.

At any stage, a player who thinks that he has 66 is allowed to knock. If his count is correct, he wins. If not, opponent gets 2 game points.

22 KLABERJASS

The name and spelling vary greatly but the far-flung adherents of this complicated Middle-European game proclaim it more enjoyable than any other member of the Bezique family. Whoever has played Clabber, Clobber, Klob, Clob, Clab, Klab, Evansville Clabber, Kalaber, Cloberyash, Yoss or the French version called Belote (or Belotte) has played Klaberjass.

Players and Deck

For two, with a 32-card deck. In the side suits, cards rank downward: A, 10, K, Q, J, 9, 8, 7. In trump the high card is the J, followed by 9, A, 10, K, Q, 8, 7. The trump jack is called *jass* (yoss) and the trump nine is *menel.*

Cut, Shuffle and Deal

Player who draws the lower card becomes dealer. After cut he deals six-card hands in two rounds of three each. Then he turns up the next card, which is known as the trump but does not necessarily establish the trump suit in which the deal will be played.

Bidding

Dealer's opponent opens the bidding. He has three choices.

Take: If he says "Take," he accepts the suit of the exposed card as trump. He thus becomes the trump *maker.*

Schmeiss: Bidder asks that the entire deal be tossed in. If dealer refuses by saying "Take it," the exposed card establishes trump and *schmeisser* is trump maker.

Pass: Opponent abstains, making dealer the bidder. Dealer has same choices as his opponent had. If dealer passes, opponent may now schmeiss, pass again or name a trump suit other than the one exposed on the table. Moreover, if he schmeisses and dealer refuses, opponent must name trump and become maker. If opponent passes, dealer has choice of naming trump or abandoning the deal.

After trump is named, dealer distributes three more cards from top of pack to opponent and himself. He then exposes the bottom card of the remaining *stock* and places it on top (face down in some circles, up elsewhere).

Declarations

Before action begins, one player is entitled to score points for holding the highest *sequence* of three or more cards. For this competition, cards rank downward from A, K, Q, J, 10, 9, 8, 7. A sequence of three scores 20. A longer sequence scores 50. A trump sequence outranks one in a side suit. In case of a tie (sequences of identical length headed by cards of identical rank in side suits), dealer's opponent gets the points.

To settle the issue, dealer's opponent speaks first, declaring the point value of his best sequence. If this beats the dealer's best, dealer says "Good." If dealer holds a sequence of higher value, he says "No good," and makes a declaration of his own. If the matter is in doubt, dealer responds with "How high?" Opponent then reveals the rank of his sequence's highest card, and if another question is asked, he discloses whether the sequence is in trump.

Player who scores for high sequence may also score for the other sequences (of three cards or longer) that he holds. To earn the score, he must display the sequences after the first trick has been played.

If the exposed card has been accepted as trump, a player who has the trump seven (known as the *deece* or *dix*) may exchange it for the higher exposed card. This must be done before playing to the first trick.

The Play

Players try to capture high-card points according to this schedule of values:

Jass	20
Menel	14
Each Ace	11
Each Ten	10
Each King	4
Each Queen	3
Each Side Jack	2

The last trick is worth 10 points. Players must follow suit, if able. If unable to follow suit, they must play trump, if able.

A holding of both the trump king and queen is called *bella* and scores 20, provided the player announces "Bella" when he plays the second card of the combination.

Scoring

After the final trick, each scores his own points for sequences, bella, last trick and captured high-point cards. If maker of trump has the higher score, the total credited to each is recorded on a score sheet. If scores are tied, maker gets nothing but opponent gets credit for his own total. When nonmaker gets the higher score, he gets both his own total and maker's—a calamitous situation in which maker is said to have *gone bete* (pronounced "bait").

First to earn 500 points wins. A player who reaches that goal during the play of a hand may claim victory and count out his total.

Strategy

Without jass and menel, maker probably goes bete. Experienced players prefer to duck the issue unless they hold a potential jass and can count 35 or 40 points in the first six cards. High trump cards and all side aces and tens can be counted at their face amounts in evaluating the hand for bidding. Some experts count the ten as worth only 5 points unless protected by its ace.

Although the three cards dealt after the bidding usually add around 20 points to the value of a hand, good players never count on finding a needed card among the three. They bid on their original holdings.

Nondealer rarely uses the schmeiss on the first round of bidding, lest dealer refuse, force nondealer to be maker, and clobber him for all the points. Some authorities recommend that nondealer never deviate from this principle, but use the schmeiss on the second round, to stop dealer from naming his own trump. Unfortunately Klab is a crueler and more subtle game than that. Precisely because good players rarely schmeiss on the first round, the nondealer who does so may succeed in bluffing his opponent into a costly refusal.

In play, nondealer usually leads from a four-card suit, if he has one, and avoids early trump leads unless he holds jass (which should usually be led as soon as possible) or has a four-card trump suit. Lacking jass or a four-card suit, nondealer prefers to lead from solid sequences, hoping to promote a relatively low card to win a later trick.

THREE-HAND

Turns start at dealer's left. Whoever becomes *maker* must tally more points than both opponents combined. When maker loses, opponents divide his points between them and each also scores whatever he made on his own *sequences* and play.

FOUR-HAND

A good partnership game. Team with high *sequence* scores for the sequences in both hands. Can also be played solo, with dealer getting seven-card hand and the others eight. Holder of *dix* gives it to dealer and takes the trump card.

23 PIQUET

Legend insists that this is among the oldest surviving games of cards. It may have originated in Spain but its vocabulary is now French. More than 400 years ago, Rabelais mentioned it as one of Gargantua's pastimes. Known also as Le Cent (One Hundred), it was taken up by the sixteenth-century British, some of whom pronounced "Cent" as if it were "Saint"—a name that persists in many localities, as does the name Picket or Pick It. More than a historical curiosity, Piquet remains a pleasant game in its own right. Readers who try it will notice strong resemblances to Rummy, Casino and Whist.

Players and Deck

Two hands, with a 32-card deck in which cards rank downward in normal fashion from A through 7. Suits are of equal rank, and no trump suit is used. The game is divided into three phases—discarding, declaring (or *calling*) and play.

Cut, Shuffle and Deal

Each draws a card. Low card designates dealer (known as *minor* or *mineur*). He shuffles and his opponent (*major* or *majeur*) cuts.

Minor then deals two cards at a time until each has a twelve-card hand. The other eight cards go face down as the *stock*.

Discarding

Nondealer discards at least one but not more than five cards, replacing them from the stock. The twin objectives are to form point-scoring combinations for the game's declaration phase, while improving the hand's trick-taking powers for actual play. If nondealer takes fewer than his maximum of five cards from the stock, he may look at the ones that he did not take, and need not reveal them to dealer.

Dealer is not required to discard but may do so, taking as many of the remaining stock cards as he pleases. Like his opponent, he must discard before drawing. If any cards remain in the stock after dealer has exercised his discard option, he may set them aside face down or may turn them up. Each player's discards are segregated, so that he may look at them and refresh his memory during play.

Declaring

If nondealer holds no kings, queens or jacks before the draw, he calls *carte blanche,* which earns him 10 points at once. Dealer who holds such a hand does not declare it until after his opponent has discarded and drawn.

After completion of the draw, players declare their holdings in three categories of point-scoring combinations. Nondealer speaks first, and the categories are declared in the following sequence.

Point: Player who holds the longest suit scores 1 point for each card in that winning combination. Nondealer begins by declaring the length of his longest and strongest suit. Chances are that he says "Five." If dealer has no suit that long, he responds "Good," and nondealer scores 5 points. If dealer has a longer suit, he says "No good" or "Not good" and scores the length of his own suit. If dealer's suit is the same length as nondealer's, dealer asks "How many?" or "How much?" and each player then evaluates his long suit by counting 11 for an ace, 10 for a picture card and pip value for cards of lower denomination. Higher value wins. In case of a tie, nobody scores in this category. If nondealer has no long suit, he may concede the issue by saying "No point," whereupon dealer makes his own declaration and gets the score.

Sequence: Nondealer now calls the number of cards in his longest one-suit sequence of three or more cards. If he lacks such a sequence, he declares "No sequence," and dealer makes his own announcement. The calls may be given as "Three," "Four" or "Five," although many players prefer "Tierce" for three, "Quart" for four and "Quinte" for five. If nondealer makes a positive declaration, dealer's answer is "Good," "Not good" or "How high?" If each player's best sequence is the same length, the one with the higher top card wins. If both are topped by a card of equal rank, nobody scores. Winning sequences score 3 for a three-card combination, 4 for four, and for a sequence of five or more, 10 plus an extra point for each card in the sequence. If holder of the best sequence has other sequences in his hand, he may also score for them.

Sets: The highest-ranking holding of four of a kind scores 14, but no *set* counts unless the denomination is ten or higher. If nobody holds four of a kind, three of a kind wins—again provided that the card is a ten or better. No ties are possible. Scorer of top quart (four of a kind) or tierce (three) is entitled to score extra for all other triplets and fours in his hand (tens or better).

Repic and Start

If one player scores 30 before the other has scored at all, he gets 60 more for *repic.* After declaration of the sets, nondealer and dealer (in the usual sequence) announce the score with which they start actual play of the hand: "I start with nine." Thereafter, each player announces his new total after every trick.

The Play

Nondealer leads to the first trick. Dealer must follow suit if he can. Otherwise he can play any card he pleases. Higher card of the led suit wins each trick. The winner of each trick leads to the next.

Player gets 1 point for each lead and 1 point for capturing a trick to which his opponent has led.

After actual play begins, if a player reaches 30 points while his opponent remains scoreless, the successful one gets a bonus of 30 for *pic.* Note that points scored during the declaration phase are carried over into play (which is why the players announce beforehand the number of points with which they start play).

Other points scored in play:

Winning all the tricks (called *capot*)	40
Winning seven to eleven tricks	10
Winning final trick (except when *capot*)	1

Scoring

The first to reach 100 wins the game. In the version most popular nowadays, known as Rubicon Piquet, each game lasts for six deals. If both players score 100 or higher, the player with the higher score gets the difference between his score and the other's, and also gets a bonus of 100 for game. If either or both players score below 100, the loser is *rubiconed,* which awards the winner the total of both scores plus 100 for game.

In some circles, a four-deal game is played, with scores doubled during the first and last deals.

Some games do not award a point for leading to a trick unless the led card is a ten or higher. Similarly, no point is given for capturing an opponent's lead if the led card was a nine or lower. These rules tend to slow the game, and are less widely accepted than in the past.

One particularly vicious (and intensely interesting) feature of Rubicon permits a player to score for point, sequence or set without declaring his best holding in the particular category. An obvious example would be to declare three kings when also holding three aces. After play ends, the player is permitted to score for the better, undeclared holding. Meanwhile, having analyzed his own hand and recognized his opponent's weakness, he has concealed his aces, making them more powerful during play.

Strategy

Nondealer usually discards and draws with aggressive intent, hoping to button up point, sequence and set. Experienced players are able to estimate the opponent's potential after studying their own hands. After all, only twenty cards are out, and the number is reduced to fifteen after nondealer examines the top five cards of the stock. A good card player can draw important inferences in a situation of that kind.

To fortify his hand and—he hopes—spoil opponent's chances, nondealer generally draws his maximum of five cards. To retain aces, kings and the longest suit is fundamental, of course.

Dealer is usually on the defensive and takes care to do whatever promises to protect him from repic, pic or capot. During the declaration phase he may *sink* (not mention) a weak holding, such as three jacks, simply to keep his opponent in the dark about the full weakness of his hand. Nondealer also finds sinking a useful tactic on occasion.

By the time play of the cards begins, good players can read each other's hands with considerable certainty. If they are closely matched, the struggle may revolve around an attempt to win a majority of the tricks or the final trick. Nondealer usually leads his longest suit, watching for the weaknesses created by opponent's forced play of cards from other suits. Card-counting and other exercises of memory are essential here.

PIQUET À ECRIRE

A good game for three to five. Each deals twice in succession, first to the player on his left and then to the player on his right. After the play of the second hand, each pays the difference between his total and that of the other two.

THREE-HAND PIQUET

Known also as Piquet Normand. Each player gets ten cards, leaving a stock of two. Dealer may take it after discarding two. Left-hand opponent declares first, and calls proceed clockwise. Only one player may score in any category of declarations. Repic is worth 90, but player need score only 20 to earn it. Pic counts 60, also on a score of 20. Capot is worth 40, as in other forms of the game, and player with most tricks gets 10. If two tie for most tricks, they each get 5, unless the third player has won no tricks, in which case the other two get 20 each.

FOUR-HAND PIQUET

Also called Piquet Voleur. A partnership game with eight-card hands. Player to dealer's left (eldest hand) begins by declaring his holdings in all categories. Dealer's partner then *overcalls* in whatever category he can. After all calls have been made and points scored, eldest hand leads to first trick. Scoring is identical with that of the three-hand game. Play follows rules of two-hand game, with highest card of led suit winning the trick for the player and his partner.

24 HEARTS

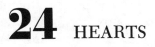

This unfailingly interesting game rewards the player able to avoid winning certain tricks. It is the ultimate application of the *nullo* idea encountered earlier in forms of Euchre, Whist and Skat.

Players and Deck

For three to six, each playing solo. The 52-card deck is used, with cards ranked in the customary order from A down through 2. If three play, a black two is stripped from the deck. With five, both black twos are removed. With six, the 2 ♡ is retained but the other twos are eliminated along with a black three.

Cut, Shuffle and Deal

Cards are drawn, with low card designating first dealer. Dealer shuffles, right-hand opponent cuts. Dealer distributes entire deck, one at a time.

The Play

No bidding takes place, nor is a trump suit used. The object is to play cleverly enough to avoid winning any tricks that contain one or more hearts. Failing that, the player attempts to win all the hearts. Player at dealer's left leads to first trick. Others must follow suit if able. Otherwise, they may play any card. Highest card of led suit wins trick. Winner of each trick leads to the next.

Scoring

In the simple form described above, a traditional scoring method requires each player to ante one chip into a kitty. Whoever finishes a hand without having been *painted* (without having won a heart) is said to be *in the clear* (or *clear*) and wins the pot. If more than one is clear, they divide the pot. If all have been painted, or if one has taken all the hearts, the pot is called a *jack* (jackpot), remains on the table, and is enlarged by another ante for the next hand.

Another approach, known as the Howell method, requires each player to multiply the number of hearts he won by the number of other players in the game and contribute that many chips to the pot. Thus, in a five-person game, someone who had taken three hearts is required to hand over twelve chips. After these contributions, each player takes from the pot as many chips as represent the difference between the number of hearts he won and thirteen—the total number of hearts in the deck.

Errors and Penalties

A player who fails to follow suit when able is charged with a *revoke* unless he corrects the error before play of the next trick begins. Because a revoke is as serious a breach in this game as in any other that depends on the taking of tricks in specific suits, the penalty is severe: the offender is charged with all points at stake in the hand.

AUCTION

In one round of bidding which starts at dealer's immediate left, players either pass or overcall previous bid. Each bid offers to sweeten the pot with a number of chips in exchange for the right to name "trump" (a misnomer, inasmuch as no trump plays exist in Hearts). Known also as the *minus suit*, the suit named by the top bidder serves throughout the particular hand as if it were the heart suit in a conventional game. As usual, the objective is to win no tricks containing a "trump." In case of a jackpot (all players are painted or one captures all the trump), no bidding precedes the next hand. After the deal, previous top bidder again names trump and play begins.

BLACK LADY

This is the most popular version of the game. The Q ♠ (known variously as *Black Lady, Black Maria* or *Calamity Jane*) plays a role identical with that of the Q ♠ in Old Maid, the childhood pastime. After inspecting his hand, each player passes three cards face down to his left (or in some localities, the right). Since the unfortunate who captures the Black Lady in a trick is charged with 13 points, a Q ♠ unprotected by at least two smaller cards of that suit is usually disposed of by being passed to a neighbor before play begins. In some games, a player unable to follow suit to a trick must play the Black Lady, and is charged with a revoke for neglecting to do so. Scoring is as usual, except that each hand counts for 26 points. In some circles, the player who captures all 26 points (all thirteen hearts plus the Q ♠) is counted a winner. Elsewhere, points are recorded on paper for settlement at the end of the session, and whoever takes all 26 in a hand has that many deducted from the total charged against him on the score sheet.

DOMINO HEARTS

Play begins with six-card hands. The remainder of the pack serves as a *stock,* face down in the center. A player unable to follow suit to a trick draws from the stock until he gets a card of required suit. After stock is gone, hands unable to follow suit may play from any suit. When a player has no more cards, he becomes a spectator for the remainder of the hand. If he happened to win a trick with his last card, his left-hand opponent leads to the next trick. Scoring methods vary, but the most familiar brings the game to an end after someone is charged with 31 points, at which point the player with the fewest points is the winner. The Black Lady variation is seldom embodied in this game.

HEARTSETTE

A black two is eliminated from the deck when three or four play. Otherwise, the full deck is used. For three players, sixteen-card hands are used; for four, twelve cards; for five, ten; and for six, eight. The remaining cards become a *widow,* face down. Winner of first trick is required to take the widow, as if it were a trick. All hearts in the widow count against him but only he is allowed to see what cards the widow contains.

HOOLIGAN HEARTS

Like Black Lady, except that the 7 ♣ costs 7 points to whoever captures it. But a 10 ♢ is an asset, permitting its capturer to deduct 10 from his debits. If a player takes all hearts, plus Black Lady and 7 ♣, each opponent loses 33, except the player with the 10 ♢. And if a player wins all hearts, plus Q ♠, 7 ♣ and 10 ♢, opponents pay him 43 each. Or, in games where a running tally is recorded, the victor's score is reduced by 43, while his opponents are penalized 33 apiece.

JOKER HEARTS

The joker is substituted for the 2 ♡. If players prefer a *widow,* as in Heartsette, the joker may be added after elimination of a black two and the 2 ♡ for three- or four-hand games and after elimination of the 2 ♡ in games for five or six. Joker is ranked just below the J ♡ and is treated as a kind of trump card. It wins any trick except one on which the J ♡ or a higher heart is played.

OMNIBUS HEARTS

Resembles Hooligan, except that the 7 ♣ is not used as a penalty card, and the 8 ◊ or J ◊ may be used instead of the 10 ◊ as a plus card. Game usually ends after the score sheet discloses that one or more players have been charged with 100 points.

PINK LADY

Hooligan, complicated by charging the captor of the Q ♡ with 13 points. In most localities, the 7 ♣ penalty is not included. Properly played, this may be the most demanding of all Heart games. As suggested under Strategy (*below*), the play of both the heart and spade suits becomes enormously subtle.

POLIGNAC

Known also as Four Jacks (*Quatre Valets*), this game implements the Hearts principle, but with other penalty cards and less elaboration. A 32-card deck (aces through sevens) is used for four players. Two black sevens are eliminated when five or six play. The objective is to avoid capturing jacks. The J ♠ is called *polignac* and costs its captor 2 points. The other three jacks cost 1 each. If a player thinks he can take all the jacks, he declares *capot* before play starts. If he succeeds, he gets five or ten chips from each opponent. If he fails, he pays the same penalty. In some places, settlement is on the basis of a running score. When a player is charged with 10 (or 20 or 30) points, he pays each opponent the difference between 10 and the opponent's score.

RED JACK HEARTS

Straight Hearts, except that the J ◊ is desirable, being worth 10 points to its captor. This feature may be incorporated in almost any version of the game and, in one fashion or another, is found in Hooligan, Omnibus and other popular variations.

SLOBBERHANNES

Resembles Polignac but involves only three losing plays per deal. Whoever wins the first trick loses 1 point. So does taker of the last trick. And it costs 1 point to win the Q ♣. If a player is stuck with all three losers during a single hand, it costs him 4 points instead of 3.

SPOT HEARTS

The A ♡ costs 14 points, K ♡ costs 13, Q ♡ 12, J ♡ 11, and the other hearts their face value down to the 2. This makes the game more intricate and, depending on taste, more costly—especially when combined with features of Black Lady or Hooligan.

TWO-HAND HEARTS

Using a full deck, with thirteen-card hands and the remainder face down as a *stock*. Nondealer leads. After each trick, winner draws top card from the stock and loser takes the next. After stock is gone, final thirteen tricks are played. In most versions, only the hearts count, but other penalty cards can be added by the adventurous.

Strategy

In Black Lady and other variations that involve the passing of cards to an opponent, it is important to unload high spades and high hearts, which are sure to win undesired tricks. Low spades are prime cards to have. The player who leads them will inevitably force out the Q ♠.

When a plus card of medium rank, such as the 10 ◇, is used, the player to whom it is dealt should pass it on in hope of capturing it with a higher card. As often as not, the plus card drops as a discard because its holder cannot win a trick with it.

In play of the hand, skill consists mainly of card memory and common sense. In games with the jackpot feature, it pays to take chances in hope of not being painted. But once having taken a heart, cooperation with other painted players is essential—so that every effort can be made to paint the opponents.

In versions that reward the player able to take all tricks, the attempt should not be made without a hand free of potential losing cards. The passing feature makes this unlikely but not impossible. After passing his only three losers to an opponent, the player may discover that three high cards have been deposited in his hand by the opponent on his other side. If so, he has a good chance at *take-all*. Otherwise, he should abandon the idea at once.

PART TWO

Rummy and Its Relatives

Dozens of enjoyable card games are races in which each player tries to get rid of his cards before anyone else beats him to it. Rummy is the chief of these. Some of its variants, such as Gin, require great skill in accumulating specific combinations of cards that permit the player to meld his hand and win the deal. Others, such as Canasta, place more emphasis on accumulation than on riddance. Closely related to Rummy in spirit, if not ancestry, are games of the Stops group, in which the player not only tries to divest himself of his hand, but uses certain cards as weapons to prevent competitors from unloading their own hands.

Rummy may be a rather new game. Its best-known antecedent is Conquian, of Spanish derivation and extremely popular in Mexico. Brought to the United States, the game was known as Coon-Can and then, with elaborations, as Rum or Rummy. In South America, it evolved into Canasta, Samba and such. And, despite myths about the antiquity of the Chinese pastime Mah-jongg, the tile game probably is nothing more exotic than a spin-off from Conquian.

Before World War II, surveys indicated that Rummy was known by more Americans than any other card game. Recent interest in Gin and Canasta signifies that the Rummy group probably retains a following comparable to those of Bridge and Poker.

1 STRAIGHT RUMMY

Players and Deck

For two to six, with a regular 52-card deck in which the cards rank downward from K through A.

Cut, Shuffle and Deal

Player who draws the lowest card becomes first dealer. After he shuffles and deck is cut by his right-hand opponent, dealer delivers seven-card hands (in a game for three or four players), or six-card hands (for five or six players), or ten-card hands (in a game for two). Remainder of deck is placed face down in center as a *stock.* Play begins after dealer turns up top card (the *upcard*) of stock and places it alongside to begin a discard pile.

The Play

The object is to get rid of cards by *melding* (placing face up on the table) *groups* of three or four cards of the same rank or *sequences* of three or more cards of the same suit, such as the J ♠, 10 ♠ and

9 ♠. Being low, an ace can be used only at the bottom of a sequence that contains the two and three of its suit.

Play begins at dealer's left. A turn starts with the player taking either the exposed upcard from the discard pile or the face-down top card from the stock. If able to meld a group or sequence (either of which may be called a *set*), he may do so or not, according to his preferred tactics. He may also add to melds previously exposed by other players or himself. This is called *laying off* and simply involves adding the fourth card of a denominational group or an additional card at the top or bottom of a sequence.

Each turn ends when the player discards a card face up on the discard pile.

Whoever first empties his hand (*goes out*) by melding is the winner. Or a hand can be won by melding all but one card and using that as a discard. If the stock is used up before anyone has gone out, dealer reshuffles the discard pile, exposes a new upcard and play continues until someone wins.

In some games, winner deals next hand. In others, deal rotates to left.

Scoring

Winner gets 10 points for each picture card in the losing hands. Each ace costs 1 point and the other cards are charged their face values. If a written tally is maintained, the game may end at 100 or 200 points, depending on mood or custom. In some games, of course, settlement is made after each hand.

Errors and Penalties

When a player makes an improper meld (meaning that he actually does not have the group or sequence), he must put the cards back into his hand. If the error is not discovered until another player has laid off the faulty meld, the laid-off card remains on the table and any player may later add a *full* group or sequence (but not one or two cards).

A player who draws out of turn or draws more than one card and, for either reason, sees a card that he should not have seen, must place that card face up on the stock. If the next player does not want the card, it is turned face down and inserted in the middle of the stock.

Strategy

The best Rummy players remember every card in the discard pile, and who dropped it there. They also remember every card that has been taken from the discard pile, and who took it. Before the hand ends, they usually have a clear understanding of what everybody else is trying to accomplish.

Not everyone is gifted with this ability, or is motivated to enlarge whatever ability he has. This means that not everyone should play Rummy for cash. Indeed, hardly anybody should play *any* card game for money unless sure that persons of approximately equal ability are involved—an assurance of reasonably fair sport.

Whether playing for fun, blood or coin, it is wise to watch the discards and note their effects on the potential of your own hand. For example, a holding that includes the J ♡ and J ♠ suffers if both other jacks get buried in the discard pile. From observations of this kind it is but a short step to selecting discards in terms of (a) the kinds of cards that have been taken from the discard pile and (b) the variable likelihoods of using one's remaining cards in melds.

For example, given a choice between holding a pair or playing for a sequence, it usually is better to play for the sequence (although previous discards may alter the situation). A three-card sequence can, after all, be improved in two ways—by adding a card at the bottom or one at the top. But a three-card group can only be improved in one way—by coming up with the fourth card of the particular rank.

Obviously, if no other factors intrude, it is better to discard a face card than a card of low rank, especially if the holding is bad and chances of being stuck are increasing.

Variations

Among elaborations that add to the interest of the game without masking its identity as plain old Straight Rummy, the following are the most popular.

Ace High: In some places, the ace may be used at the top of a suit sequence with the king and queen as well as at the bottom with the two and three. Sophisticates sometimes allow a K-A-2 sequence, known as *melding around the corner.*

Borrowing: If a meld contains more than three cards, the player may choose to remove one of the cards from the set (provided that he was the one who melded the particular card) and use it to complete a new meld.

Calling: When a player discards a card that could have been added to a meld already displayed on the table, any other player may say "Rummy" without awaiting his proper turn, and may then take the card, add it to the meld and discard a card of his own.

Going Rummy: In some games, no partial melding is allowed. As soon as a player can meld his entire hand (in any permissible arrangement of groups and/or sequences), he declares "Rummy" and exhibits his winning hand.

Showdown: Winner collects double points if he goes rum with his entire hand, without partial melds, in a game where partial melds are allowed.

2 GIN RUMMY

This cutthroat game got enormous publicity when its possibilities as a high-stake pastime were discovered in Hollywood. As a result, it quickly became the most fashionable two-hand card game in show business and in other action-loving sectors of urban North America. Its resemblance to Straight Rummy is unmistakable but its intricacies are pronounced and—for the unwary—can become painfully expensive. The game is said to have been devised in 1909 by Elwood T. Baker of New York's Knickerbocker Whist Club. It was known for a while as Gin Poker, a misnomer, but had become Gin or Gin Rummy by the mid-thirties, when its vogue accelerated. After World War II, it really came into its own.

Players and Deck

For two, with the regular 52-card deck. K is high, A low. Two decks often are used. While one is being dealt, the other is shuffled for the next hand.

Cut, Shuffle and Deal

In draw for deal, high card has choice of whether to be first dealer. In case of tie, card of higher suit prevails (for this purpose, suits rank as in Bridge, from spades down—hearts, diamonds, clubs). Because nondealer has the slight advantage of playing first, it has become customary in many games for drawer of low card to deal first. Dealer shuffles, opponent cuts. Each hand gets ten cards. Remainder of pack goes face down as a *stock.* Dealer exposes its top card and places it next to stock. This *upcard* serves as first card of discard pile. Winner of each hand deals next. In some circles, stock card is not exposed and dealer's opponent gets eleven cards.

The Play

If nondealer does not want the first upcard, dealer may either take it or draw the top card from the stock. Each turn consists of taking either the upcard or the top card from the stock, making decisions about combinations and/or declarations and, finally, adding a new exposed upcard to the discard pile.

In games that begin with the nondealer holding eleven cards, he takes no card at his first turn, but ends it by placing an exposed upcard next to the stock, reducing his hand to the normal holding of ten and beginning the discard pile.

Unlike many other forms of Rummy, this one permits no piecemeal melding of cards. To *go gin,* a player must be able to display his full ten-card holding in *sets* (*denominational groups* or *suit sequences*) like those of Straight Rummy. With a lesser hand, he may choose to *knock*—forcing the opponent to compare hands. To knock, a player must hold *deadwood* (unmatched cards that fit into none of his groups or sequences) worth not more than 10 points. Each picture card counts 10, each ace counts 1 and each numbered card counts its pip value.

Before knocking, the player must take his regular turn, adding an eleventh card from the discard pile or the stock. When knocking he discards an eleventh card face down and displays the other ten in their sets, with deadwood separate.

If only two cards remain in stock and neither player is able or willing to knock, the game is a draw and the dealer starts anew with the next deck. However, a draw may not be declared until the fiftieth card has been drawn and the discard offered to the other player.

Scoring

When a player knocks and displays his hand, his opponent is permitted to *lay off* as many of his unmatched cards as are compatible with the *knocker's* groups and sequences. If this process leaves the opponent with a deadwood count equal to or lower than that of the knocker, he has *underknocked* or *undercut* the knocker. For this he gets a bonus of 25 points plus the number of points, if any, by which the knocker's deadwood count exceeds his own. Note that the knocker is not allowed to lay off any of his own deadwood on sets that have been enlarged by the opponent's layoffs.

If a player goes gin, the opponent is not allowed to undercut him. Going gin is worth 25 points plus opponent's deadwood count.

First player to reach 100 (150 or 200 in some places) wins game, which entitles him to a game bonus of 100. Each also gets a *line bonus* or *box bonus* of 25 for each hand won. Final settlement is based on the difference between the two total scores.

If one player reaches 100 (or whatever winning total local rules require) before opponent scores a point, the loser is *skunked* and the game is a *schneider* (more familiarly known as *schneid, blitz* or *shutout*), for which the winner is credited with double his total score.

For convenience, each entry on the Gin Rummy score sheet is a cumulative total, except at the end of each game when a certain amount of subtraction is necessary. Example:

	YOU	ME	
①	42	13	②
⑤	72	24	③
⑥	83	77	④
⑦	120 100 100 320 152 178		

① You go gin. I have 17. You score 42.
② I knock with 8. You have 21. I score 13.
③ I knock with 5. You have 16. I add 11.
④ I go gin when you hold 28. I add 53 for a total of 77.
⑤ You knock with 6. I hold 36. Your total grows to 72.
⑥ You knock with 8. I have 19. You add 11.
⑦ You go gin when I hold 12. The 37 gives you a winning total of 120. To that you add 100 for game bonus and 100 for your four box bonuses (the four hands you won). From your total of 320, we subtract the 152 I earned with 77 points plus three box bonuses. I now owe you 168 jellybeans.

Hollywood Scoring

Certain sharpshooters in the Film Capital are said to have devised the scoring method now in widest use among Gin addicts. It contributes mightily to the high-flying action of the game. In essence, it consists of playing three games at a time. The scorekeeper sets up three adjoining double columns—each pair of them like the one above. A player's first score is credited to him in the tally column reserved for the first of the three games. His next score becomes his first entry in the second game's tally, and also is added to his first-game score. And his third score becomes his first entry in the third game, his second in the second game and, of course, his third in the first game. In case of a schneid in the first game, the player who has been skunked registers his first score in the second game—unless he is skunked again. Needless to say, persons of stamina often continue these epics far beyond the third game.

Errors and Penalties

As in other good games, the emphasis is on common-sense correction of inadvertent errors. If one or both players are dealt the wrong number of cards and play has already begun, civilized rules suggest a simple redeal. In some circles if dealer holds an improper number of cards and opponent does not, opponent has the right to demand a new deal or to penalize the dealer. This is accomplished by requiring the dealer to play as many turns with discards but no draws, or draws but no discards, as may be necessary to leave him with the proper number of cards.

When a player draws out of turn, he must place the drawn card face up on the table and miss the remainder of his turn. If opponent does not choose to pick up the card, it is buried in the discard pile.

In the unlikely event that a player is found with too few cards or too many after opponent knocks, it is customary to deprive the incorrect hand of the undercut bonus or, in some places, the entire undercut privilege.

When a player knocks with a hand that contains too few or too many cards, opponent is entitled to a new deal, but may choose to force the mistaken knocker to continue play with a fully exposed hand and to correct its size by draws without discards or discards without draws.

If a player knocks with deadwood in excess of 10 points, opponent is permitted to decide whether to accept the knock as valid (and undercut it) or require the knocker to continue play with an exposed hand.

It is considered a breach of etiquette to look into the discard pile unless custom or specific agreement permits that practice. In some settings, violation of this rule is penalized by loss of a turn.

Strategy

This is a cruel game in which the best players supplement card memory with a talent for bluffing and other forms of psychological warfare. Beginners may be relieved to know that experts are not nearly as reckless as they may seem to the innocent bystander. Instead, they play close to the vest—going with the percentages as best they can and varying their tactics only enough to keep the opponent off balance.

Most hands end within nine turns. Thus, the longer a hand lasts, the greater the dangers become. It is a rule of thumb to knock with 10 points or less before the sixth turn (being wary on the fifth if opponent has discarded a low card or two and/or has taken a couple of upcards). As this implies, a good player makes important deductions from cards taken and other cards tossed away by the opponent. By the ninth or tenth turn, it is seldom advisable to knock with 6 or more points, and play becomes defensive, each hoping to undercut the other.

It rarely pays to delay knocking in the hope that gin will become possible on a later turn. Again, opponent's activities contribute to the decision.

Bluffing arises through the tactic known as *advertising,* in which the player discards a relatively useful card, hoping to mislead opponent into the supposition that it is safe to discard other cards of the same rank or suit. Experts do not usually unload useful cards except early in the game, when gin seems to be only two or three turns away and chances can be taken. Because this is so, a good player might try to improve his prospects with an *ad,* discarding something as useful as the 9 ◇, hoping to lull opponent into unloading the 9 ♣—which he then snatches to form a sequence.

Early discards are all-important in this fast-paced game, because they tell so much of the player's intentions (or whatever he wants to convey about those intentions). In general, of course, it is best to unload high cards, retaining low cards for inexpensive deadwood.

After noting, interpreting and, above all, remembering not only opponent's discards but the kinds of cards he has not been discarding, an expert develops a rapid picture of the other's hand. In choosing his own discards, he tends to prefer cards of adjacent ranks but of different suits than the opponent has been dropping. The logic behind this and other refinements is complicated. For readers who want to pursue Gin Rummy strategy that far, the following books are highly recommended:

Charles H. Goren, *Go with the Odds* (Macmillan).
John Scarne, *Scarne on Cards* (New American Library).
Irwin Steig, *Play Gin to Win* (Cornerstone Library).

OKLAHOMA GIN

The upcard's rank determines the maximum points with which a knock may be offered during the particular deal. For this purpose, as in scoring deadwood, picture cards count 10, aces 1 and others their face values. When upcard is a spade, all scores are doubled. Usually, 150 or 200 wins.

ROUND THE CORNER

As in one variant of Straight Rummy, an ace may be used either as a top or bottom card in sequences, and may also be used as the corner card in a K-A-2 sequence. Players of this game usually score the ace at 15 when it turns out to be deadwood.

DOUBLING

At any turn, a player may *double,* offering to play the hand for twice the customary number of points. This enhances the bluffing aspect of the game. A player with an enormous deadwood count may double after picking two upcards and frighten his opponent into *resigning*. At that juncture, game is scored as if the doubler had knocked. But the doubler gets a bonus (10 or 20, depending on locality), even if undercut. The player who resigns must pay the bonus plus the difference, if any, should he fail to undercut. And he collects nothing for undercutting. On the other hand, if double is accepted, play continues until one or the other knocks. In some games, a redouble is permitted.

THREE-HAND GIN

An amusing game when each plays the other two in turn, with the partnership consulting in management of a single hand. Or whoever draws low card sits out first hand, but plays its winner on the second hand. Each player's score is kept separately.

FOUR-HAND GIN

This is simply two tables of regular Gin, except that each player is the partner of a player at the other table. After each hand, each team's score is combined. An entertaining feature permits a player to advise his partner if his own hand is completed but partner is still struggling.

3 CANASTA

This Uruguayan development was elaborated in Argentina and became a North American fad of phenomenal dimensions about 1950. Its sudden vogue was the most spectacular in the history of cards. The tide has ebbed in recent years. Hard-bitten card players prefer Gin. Canasta being more neighborly and considerably less demanding than Gin, it now occupies a place comparable to that of Mahjongg, another former fad, which employs tiles much as Canasta uses cards. Both games command the interest of persons for whom sporting challenges are less attractive than opportunities to have friendly fun. More power to them. By any objective measure, Canasta is a good game. And it is not nearly as complicated as it seems on first acquaintance.

Players and Deck

Ideally, a four-hand game of partnerships, using two regular decks plus four jokers—108 cards in all. With five players, two play against the other three, who take turns sitting out hands. With six, it is three against three, with one member of each team sitting out by turns.

Cut, Shuffle and Deal

If partnerships are not a matter of established neighborhood rivalry, cards may be drawn, with the two higher joining against the two lower. High card plays first, which means that player at his right deals first. In circumstances where it is necessary to keep everything tidy, seats may also be assigned on the basis of the original draw. In case two draw cards of the same rank, suits rank downward: spades, hearts, diamonds, clubs.

After shuffles by any players who want to shuffle, dealer shuffles last and right-hand opponent cuts. Everyone then gets eleven cards, one at a time, in the usual clockwise rotation. Remaining cards go face down as a *stock*. Dealer exposes top card of stock and places it next to stock as an *upcard*, on which discard pile (the *pot* or *pack*) will be built. If this upcard is a red trey, a deuce or a joker, it is covered by another exposed card from atop the stock and play proceeds.

The Play

Among the distinguishing characteristics of this game and its kin is the emphasis on accumulating cards that can be fit into point-scoring groups. Getting rid of cards as quickly as possible is not a primary objective.

Furthermore, suit sequences are not used. Each player in turn strives to form groups containing at least three cards of the same rank. Other features include the following.

Wild Cards: The deuces and jokers take on the rank of whatever natural cards with which the player chooses to combine them in *melds*. They also are *stoppers* in play (*see below*).

Freezing: The discard pile is frozen for both sides at start of play. Players must therefore take cards from stock. The pile remains frozen for each side until one of its members has made the team's first meld of the hand. The compulsory minimum point value of this meld increases as the partnership's total score increases (*see below*). The discard pile also is frozen for both sides at *any* stage of the game when it contains a wild card. And, if the first upcard exposed is a red trey, the pile remains frozen even for a partnership able to make its first meld. When the pile is frozen, no player may take the top discard unless able to use it at once in a meld that includes two cards of the same natural rank. After this happens, the pack no longer is frozen for either team (unless one of them has not yet made its first meld). When the pack is not frozen, a player may take its top card for immediate use in a meld containing not less than one natural card of the same rank and including a wild card. In most places at least two natural cards are required, whether the pack is frozen or not.

Red Treys: Whenever a player has one of these in his hand, he is required at his first opportunity to display the card (which is worth points) as if it were a meld, replacing it with a card from stock. If he has more than one red trey, he must do the same. However, if he gets the red trey when he picks up the discard pile, he need only place it on the table face up and does not replace it with a card from the stock.

Stoppers: When a black trey or a wild card (joker or deuce) is discarded, the next player is not permitted to take it. And, as noted above, the pack becomes frozen as soon as a wild card is discarded. Stoppers are also called *stop cards* or *blockers.*

Canastas: A *pure* (or *natural*) *canasta* is a melded group of seven cards of the same natural rank. A *mixed canasta* contains at least one wild card but not more than three. During play, additional cards may be *laid off* on a canasta, but one wild card converts an existing pure canasta into a mixed one. And no mixed canasta, even if it includes more than seven cards, may contain more than three wild ones.

Other Melds: A meld must include at least three cards of the same rank, at least two of them natural, and no matter how many cards in the meld, not more than three wild cards. A partnership is not allowed to meld more than one group of the same rank—all additions must be laid off on the original meld. During his turn, a player may lay off as many cards as able on his own side's melds, but may not lay off on melds made by the other side.

Initial Requirement: For melding—and later, for scorekeeping purposes—each card has a point value. Each joker is worth 50; each ace and two is worth 20. Kings down through eights are worth 10, and sevens down through black treys are worth 5. If a team's total score is below 1,500, a first meld of cards worth 50 points is permitted and unfreezes the discard pile. Indeed, if the team has a *minus* score (which happens), its first meld need contain no more than 15 points. If the team's score is 1,500 or higher—but not more than 3,000—its first meld may contain not less than 90 points. And if it has already registered 3,000 or more on the tally sheet, it cannot unfreeze the pack for itself with a meld worth less than 120 points.

Taking the Discards: A player able to take the top discard is required to do several other things. First he displays the cards with which he plans to meld the top card of the pile. He then takes the card, completes the meld on the table, and *adds the entire discard pile to his hand.* Here, of course, is the heart and soul of the game. The player who grabs the whole, fat pot is immediately allowed to make as many melds as the new cards permit. He ends his turn with a discard, beginning a new pack.

Going Out: Play ends when a player disposes of the last card in his hand, either by melding or discarding it. No player may go out unless his side has already melded at least one canasta. To warn his partner that he is about to go out, a player who has not yet melded during his current turn may ask, "May I go out?" He is required to abide by his partner's Yes or No, but if the answer is No, he need not ask the question at his next turn. Neither need the question be asked in the first place, except as a tactic. A player is said to have gone out *concealed* (with a concealed hand) when he does so in one fell swoop, without having melded during the earlier play of the particular hand. Whether concealed or not, a player who goes out may meld at that time groups of three or more black treys (without wild cards). Previous to that, the black treys are used only as stoppers.

Forcing: Play continues even after the last card of the stock is gone. *Forcing* occurs at this stage and consists of making a discard that the next player *must* take if he is able to add it to one of his side's existing melds. If the player declines the card although able to add it to a meld, the hand ends at once and the score is computed. Play also ends if last card of stock is a red trey. The player who draws it may not meld or discard.

Scoring

When a player goes out, each side counts the points contained in its melds. The side that went out adds 200 if it went out concealed, or 100 for having gone out unconcealed. Each side also adds 500 for each natural and 300 for each mixed canasta, and 100 for each red trey (800 for all four of them).

If a side has made no melds, each red trey counts as a minus 100—minus 800 for all four.

After adding these factors, each team subtracts from its score the number of points represented by its unplayed cards. Thus, cards that remain in the hand of the player whose partner went out are now counted against that side's total. And the cards with which the opposing team was stuck are counted against that side's total.

Each team's net figure is entered on a tally sheet. The cumulative totals show how many points must be contained in the first meld made by each side during play of the next hand. First team to reach a total of 5,000 wins. If both reach 5,000 during play of the same hand, the hand is completed and side with the higher final total wins. Settlement is always based on the difference between the winning and losing scores.

Strategy

Although Canasta does not rank among the most demanding of games, the better card players in the crowd always seem to have the best luck, which means that Canasta is less a game of luck than of skill.

The heart of Canasta skill is to grab the first big pack (the pot or discard pile) before the other side does. The advantage gained in that maneuver can seldom be overcome during the play of the particular hand. A standard tactic is to discard one's useless—and potentially dangerous—cards early, when the pack is small. The opponents may need those cards for their own melds but can usually be counted on to pass them up, waiting for the pack to enlarge. As the pack grows, the good player begins dropping cards less likely to fit into the opponent's scheme of things—for example, small ones already matched in one's own hand, or black treys.

If the other side manages to get the first large pack, good players often abandon hope for that particular hand and try to go out as quickly as possible so as to reduce the other team's total and spoil its advantage.

Thus, the emphasis is on accumulating cards when the issue is still in doubt, or when things are going well on a particular hand. The emphasis reverses itself when the other side gains the advantage.

One mark of the good Canasta player is the care with which he resists the burden of a higher-than-necessary score. To keep the minimum size of his initial meld at a manageable level in the next hand, he sometimes sacrifices a few points during the present hand. His slightly lower total gives him a tremendous advantage when jockeying for the first sizable pack in the ensuing deal.

Errors and Penalties

If a player neglects to declare a red trey at his first opportunity (his first turn after getting the card), and if the hand ends before he corrects that error, his side is penalized 500 points.

If a player displays an initial meld containing insufficient points under the rules governing such melds, he restores the cards to his hand and the minimum count for his side's first meld increases by 10.

In extremely serious games, a side is penalized 100 points for returning a card to the hand after trying to meld it improperly. Such a card can be added to another meld (if it belongs there) or can be discarded without penalty.

TWO-HAND CANASTA

Fifteen-card hands. To go out, the player must have melded two canastas. In taking from stock, each player gets two cards per turn but discards only one.

THREE-HAND CANASTA

Thirteen-card hands. First player to take discard pile plays alone against the other two. In drawing from stock, player takes two cards per turn, discarding only one. Lone player records his full score. Opponents each get their full partnership score, as if playing a four-hand game. Usual practice raises minimum winning total to 7,500.

SAMBA

The great Philadelphia card player John R. Crawford is credited with this elaboration, which employs a 162-card deck composed of three regular ones plus six jokers. Whether played by two or three or as a partnership game for four, the hands contain fifteen cards. The two-card draw from stock and the one-card discard are standard. Melds may be made in suit sequences (with ace high) as well as in denominational groups. A seven-card sequence without wild cards is a *samba,* which earns a bonus of 1,500 and is interchangeable with a canasta as a qualification for going out. Wild cards are not permitted in suit sequences. No wild cards may be added to canastas already melded, and no canasta may contain more than two wild cards. Sequences may be melded only from the hand, not by immediate use of the top card of the discard pile. Either side may build as many sets as it pleases of the same denomination, and they may be combined to form canastas. When pack is not frozen, it can be taken by adding its top card to a group already melded. Otherwise, it can be taken only when top card is added to a natural pair from the hand to form a new meld or to increase an existing meld by three cards. Game is 10,000 points. Side with 7,000 or more points must assemble a first meld of not less than 150 points. Otherwise, rules on first melds remain the same. No bonus is given for going out with a concealed hand, but going out is worth an extra 200. A side with all six red treys gets 1,000.

BOLIVIA

Same as Samba but with a canasta formed of seven wild cards known as a *Bolivia* and worth 2,500. And the samba is called an *Escalera.* At least one Escalera and one canasta are required before going out. Red treys count against a side that has not melded two canastas of some kind. Player stuck with a black trey loses 100. Black treys melded when going out count only 5 points each. Game is 15,000. First meld requirements are exactly as in Samba.

BRAZILIAN CANASTA

A hairsplitting variant of Bolivia. With 5,000 but fewer than 7,000 points, first meld must contain 150. With 7,000 but fewer than 8,000, first meld must be a canasta of some kind. With 8,000 but fewer than 9,000, the first meld must contain 200 points. Above that, the first meld must be a natural canasta. Game is 10,000. Wild-card canasta counts 2,000. Five red treys earn 1,000. Six are worth 1,200. When one side goes out, both sides lose 1,000 for every melded sequence of fewer than five cards. Black treys are not melded.

CUBAN CANASTA

Like regular Canasta, with the one-card draw from stock and no melded sequences. But the pile is always frozen and no canasta may be built beyond seven cards. Game is 7,500. With a score of 5,000 or more, first meld must contain 150 points. Wild-card canastas are permitted. One composed of seven deuces is worth 4,000. Four jokers and three deuces count 3,000. Any other wild-card canasta scores 2,000. Two canastas are needed to go out. One red trey scores 100; two earn 300; three count 500; and all four are worth 1,000, except that they become minus values if the side has not melded a canasta. Black treys are not melded, but are set aside when taken. If a side gets all four, it earns 100.

CHILE

The chief version of this game is identical with Samba, except that a four-deck pack of 208 (including eight jokers) is used and wild-card melds are permitted. A wild canasta counts 2,000.

ITALIAN CANASTA

Played like Samba, except that red treys are displayed and replaced before upcard is turned. Denomination of upcard determines the number of cards to be taken face down from the top of the stock and placed face down beneath the upcard to form the beginning of the discard pack. For this purpose, aces and jokers count 20, kings 13, queens 12, jacks 11, and others are taken at face value. Discard pile is always frozen. Deuces may be melded, with or without jokers, but the side that does it may meld no other wild cards until completing a canasta of deuces. Game is 12,000. First melds must be naturals. Requirements for first melds are as in Canasta, except that 160 is needed with 5,000 but fewer than 7,500; requirement is 180 with 7,500 but fewer than 10,000. Above 10,000 the first meld must be a natural 200. Bonus for going out is 300, but side cannot go without two canastas. A wild-card canasta does not count for that purpose. On the other hand, only the side that goes out can score the 3,000 awarded for melding seven deuces or the 2,000 scored by a mixed canasta of deuces. If side does not go out, it scores only the regular point value of those melded cards. If a side melds five pure canastas it earns an extra 2,000. Four pure plus one mixed count 1,000, and ten canastas of any variety score a bonus of 2,000.

URUGUAY

Regular Canasta, except that wild cards may be melded independently. A wild-card canasta scores 2,000.

4 CONQUIAN

In its native Spanish, the oldest surviving ancestor of modern Rummy games was known as Con Quien, meaning "With whom." Perhaps the game involved unpredictably shifting partnerships, as in Three-Hand Canasta. Otherwise the name makes no sense. Neither do the New World corruptions, Conquian and Coon-Can. In the process of adapting to these mispronunciations, the original game (whatever it was) must have changed a great deal. Some believe that another old game, Panguingue, described later, is more like the original Con Quien than Conquian is. In any case, Conquian is sheer Rummy, with emphasis on melding and going out. In some places it used to be called Rum Poker.

Players and Deck

For two, with a 40-card deck. Traditionally, the eights, nines and tens are eliminated from a regular deck of fifty-two, which then ranks downward from K through A, with the J one notch higher than the 7. A more comfortable arrangement for gringos is the elimination of picture cards, leaving a deck in which the high card is 10, the low A and nothing is missing between them.

Cut, Shuffle and Deal

Cards are cut, low card shuffles and deals. Ten-card hands are served, two cards at a time. Remainder of deck goes face down as a *stock*. Loser of game deals next.

The Play

Dealer's opponent turns up top card of the stock. If he wants it, he adds it to his hand. Otherwise, he says "Pass" and dealer has the right to take the card. Should dealer not want it, he puts it face down and turns up the next top card of the stock. If dealer does not want this one, he passes and opponent either takes it or turns it face down. This process continues until somebody takes a card, which obliges him to discard one from his hand. Such discards go face up on the stock. Other player may then take the discard or turn it face down and cast it aside before turning up the stock's top card. Note that each player knows what the other is adding to his hand because each card is exposed before being taken.

The object is to form sequences of three or more in the same suit or groups of three or more of a kind and to *meld* these sets when ready.

Melding is done immediately before passing the *upcard* or immediately before making one's discard. It is permissible to add to one's existing melds, and also to borrow from one meld of four cards or more to form an additional meld of three cards or more.

One of the maddening features of the game is *forcing*, which has found its way into other forms of Rummy. If the turned-up card fits into one of the exposed melds of the player whose turn it is, he is forced to take the card, which obliges him to discard another. This can bring ruination, because the only way to go out in this game is by melding eleven cards, without a discard after going out. Good players use the forcing feature as a winning tactic. For example, if a player has melded all his cards but two tens, his opponent carefully holds on to the ten that would enable the player to go out. At the first opportunity, the opponent discards something that fits onto one of the unfortunate player's melds. The victim is forced to take it, discarding one of his tens and leaving himself with poor prospects.

If the fourth ten has already been seen and buried, the player's outlook is really dim.

The hand ends as soon as a player goes out. If neither can manage this before the last card is gone from the stock, the hand is a tie. Where the game is played for money (which is virtually wherever it is played at all), both players ante a chip before each hand, and the pot from a tied hand is added to the pot for the following hand.

5 KNOCK RUMMY

This is Gin Rummy's father.

Players and Deck

For two to five, with an ordinary 52-card deck, ranking downward from K to A. Two-hand game is played with ten-card hands. Otherwise, seven-card hands.

The Play and Scoring

Stock cards and *upcards* are taken one at a time, as in Straight Rummy, but, as in Gin, there is no intermediate melding. Object is to form a hand in which the unmatched cards (*deadwood*) carry a minimum penalty. Unmatched picture cards count 10 and all other deadwood counts at face value. As soon as a player believes that his hand has a lower count than others, he may choose to *knock,* whereupon each player counts deadwood. If *knocker* proves to have lowest count, he collects difference from each opponent. If another player has a lower count than the knocker, he becomes the winner, getting the difference from all, plus a penalty payment (usually double) from the knocker.

If an opponent ties the knocker, that opponent becomes the winner, collecting from all but the knocker, who need pay nobody in this case. And if two tie in process of beating the knocker, they divide the spoils.

A player *goes rum* by knocking with a hand that contains no deadwood. This feat earns 25 points from each opponent, plus the usual difference between each loser's deadwood count and the winner's. If another player's hand also is formed into sets without any unmatched cards, the knocker who goes rum collects the 25-point bonus regardless.

Strategy

Apart from the usual strategy of Rummy games and the necessity of remembering previously exposed cards and their whereabouts, success at Knock Rummy depends to some extent on a knowledge of probabilities. It is taken for granted among veteran players that the average hand in a three-hand game contains about 45 points immediately after the deal and before the player's first draw and discard. The figure derives from the fact that an average card counts 6.5 points. Accordingly, most players believe it reasonably safe to knock with a hand of 35 at the very first turn in a three-hand game, reducing that figure to 30 in a game for four or five. At each succeeding turn, the deadwood count should be at least 5 points lower for safe knocking. After three turns, nothing above 10 is safe. In the two-hand game, the average hand being about 65 points, a knock with 55 or 60 on the first turn is considered sound, as is one with 35 or 40 on the next, and so on in steps of 10 or more points per turn. Obviously, no hope lies in slavish adherence to this mechanical formula. It merely provides guidelines. Hawklike observation of the discards remains essential.

6 500 RUMMY

Those who resisted the Canasta craze pointed out with some justice that 500 Rummy, which had been around for years, was quite similar but more sensible. Not many resisted for long, and 500 Rummy (or Pinochle Rummy) began to fade from the scene. But the game has a lot to recommend it. For that reason it continues to be played widely enough to justify prominence in these pages.

Players and Deck

For three or four with a regular 52-card deck, ranking in the usual Rummy order from K down through A. Also for six to eight or, more enjoyably, for five, with a double deck of 104 cards. Can also be played by two, but is not nearly as good for that purpose as Knock or Gin.

Cut, Shuffle and Deal

After the usual dealer shuffle and the cut by right-hand opponent, seven-card hands are distributed (thirteen cards in the two-hand game). Remainder go face down as a *stock*, with top card exposed by dealer as *upcard*, on which discards are placed.

The Play

As in other Rummy games, players try to form meldable sets—either three or four cards of the same rank or suit sequences of no fewer than three cards. The cards in the discard pile are spread, rather than stacked, so that each card is visible to all the players at all times. Whoever can use any card in the discard pile for an immediate meld is permitted to take it when his turn comes but must take all the cards above it in the spread pile.

Players may *meld* not only from their hands and on their own previously melded sets, but on melds made by opponents. This last is done simply by placing the melded card face up at one's place and declaring the particular opposition meld with which it fits. The card remains with the player who melded it, face up.

A player who takes a card from the discard pile, along with cards that have been placed above it, is required to declare and show the specific meld on which the desired card is to be played. He then does not add the other cards from the discard pile to his hand, but leaves them on display until his next turn. This permits opponents to use their memories in relative leisure.

Hand ends when any player goes out, having melded all his cards. It also ends when no cards remain in stock and the player whose turn it is to meld is unable to do so. But play continues as long as players can draw and meld in turn.

Scoring

After one player goes out or stock is emptied and a player passes, all count the value of their melded cards. Note that credit cannot be taken for meldable sets that exist in the hand but have not been exhibited and declared prior to the end of play. Aces count 15, unless melded in a sequence, whereupon they count 1. Picture cards count 10 and others count at face value. After computing melded points, each player other than the one who went out subtracts from the meld total whatever number of points remains in his hand. Occasionally a player is stuck with more points than he melded, which means that he scores a minus. A cumulative score is kept on paper. Whoever reaches 500 first wins the game, collecting points or pennies from defeated opponents, depending on the difference between the winning score and that of each loser.

Strategy

Because discards remain exposed, card memory is burdened less than usual. However, it is important to remember who has taken which cards. And common card sense prevails in all other respects as well. Completed groups of four of a kind are usually melded as soon as possible to avoid being stuck with them. On the other hand, good players tend to retain open-ended sequences rather longer than that to prevent other players from melding on them and, perhaps, going out in the bargain. As in Canasta, the wish is to take as fat a pack as possible as early as possible because the advantage thereby gained is often a guarantee of victory. On the other hand, a player far behind in the scoring is likely to concentrate on going out, hoping to stick his opponents with large hands and overtake them on the score sheet.

BOZENKILL RUM

A variation of 500 Rummy. Using a single deck, six-card hands are dealt when five or more play. Otherwise, seven-card hands.

MICHIGAN RUM

A scoring variation in which each player scores his melds as he makes them, and the player who goes out adds to his own score the values represented by the cards remaining in the opponents' hands.

OKLAHOMA RUMMY

Thirteen-card hands, using two regular decks (104 cards), with deuces wild (which means that any of the eight twos in the double deck may be substituted for any other card in a meld). In some versions, jokers also are used as wild cards. The player who has melded a wild card may replace it with the natural card for which it has been substituting, and may then use it as a wild card in another meld. If a player wants the top card on the discard pile, he must take the entire pile and must use the top card immediately in a meld before completing his turn. At any turn, a player may add to his existing melds with cards from his hand, or with the top card of the discard pile, or with any other card he may have taken up when taking the discard pile. But players may not add to group melds that already contain four of a kind, and also may not lay off cards on an opponent's melds. Aces are used either at the top of picture-card sequences or in low sequences with twos and threes.

In the Canasta spirit, this game includes an Old Maid feature. No player may discard the Q ♠ if able to unload another card. The sole exception occurs when discarding the Q ♠ enables the player to go out. The process of going out must always involve melding one's next-to-last card and discarding the last card. After a player goes out, which earns him 100 points (250 for going out without having melded previously), everyone adds the value of his own melds and subtracts the value of cards that remain in hand. This is also done when hand is *blocked* by a situation in which the stock is exhausted and a player completes his turn without going out. For scoring purposes, melded jokers count 100 each, a melded Q ♠ counts 50, a melded ace is 20, sevens down through threes count 5 and all others count 10—except that each melded deuce scores the value of the card for which it substitutes, unless it replaces a Q ♠, which earns it 10. Cards that remain in hand are usually counted as minus scores of the same number of points as they would earn when melded, although some groups prefer to charge double these values, and in other circles stuck deuces are penalized 20 points, the jokers and Q ♠ cost double, and all other cards are charged at the normal rate. Winner is the first player to reach 1,000, for which he gets an extra 200. If more than one reaches 1,000 on the same deal, the higher score wins. In some games, the 250 bonus for going out without having melded previously is not credited toward the 1,000 total. In games where it is, the winner may be required to score 1,500 or 2,000 points.

PERSIAN RUMMY

A partnership game of 500 Rummy for four, using a regular deck enlarged with four jokers, which count 20 and are treated not as wild cards but as a separate rank that is meldable only in groups of its own kind—three or four jokers to the meld. Aces are melded only at the top of picture-card sequences or in groups of aces, but not in low-card sequences. If a group of four of a kind is melded all at once, it counts double. But adding a fourth card to a three-card group does not earn the double value. When a player goes out, his side gets an extra 25. After last card is drawn from stock, play continues as long as the player whose turn it is can draw from the discard pile. Most games end after two deals. Higher score wins, which gets it an extra 50, after which settlement is made by subtracting the losing total from the higher.

7 JAVA RUMMY

This game differs enough from other Rums to be treated separately here. Its chief virtues are speed and an elimination feature that enables losers to stretch their legs while potential winners continue play.

Players and Deck

For four or five, with a regular 52-card deck plus two jokers. If more play, two such decks are used.

Cut, Shuffle and Deal

To choose dealer, cards are drawn and low card deals, unless local practice favors the high card. In some places, first dealer is designated by passing out cards face up, one at a time. First player to get a jack becomes the dealer.

After usual cut by right-hand opponent, dealer serves seven-card hands. Remainder of deck goes face down as a *stock*. Dealer exposes top card, to serve as beginning of discard pile.

The Play

Player at dealer's immediate left begins by taking either the exposed card or the top card of the stock. Turn ends with a discard. Any player at his turn to play may meld, but must do so *before* drawing a card.

In general, the object is to meld all seven cards at once. Aces can be used in groups of their own kind, or at the top of suit sequences involving the appropriate kings and queens. The jokers and all deuces are wild. A player may go out by melding only six cards, provided that his seventh is a five or less (for this purpose an ace is regarded as a one). In doing this, the player announces, "Taking a *sting* of two"—or whatever face value the card may have. If stock is exhausted before anyone goes out, discards are shuffled and placed face down as a new stock.

Scoring

Scoring is negative. Players add the value of unmeldable cards remaining in their hand and are penalized by having the total added to their running scores. An unmelded or unmeldable joker counts 25. Picture cards count 10. Others count at face value, with the ace scoring 1. No laying off on opponents' melds. A player who takes a sting is penalized by having the value of the sting added to his total. When a player reaches 100, he is eliminated from the game, and survivors continue until only one remains.

A player who holds or melds a seven-card suit sequence is entitled to a deduction of 25 from his running score. If he reaches a minus total of 100, he wins the game.

Final settlement is based on the differences between the winner's score and those of his defeated opponents.

Strategy

At first, everyone tries to play for a minus score. But after a player earns as much as minus 50, the opposition attempts to go out as soon as possible, hoping to chip away at the leader's advantage.

CHICAGO RUMMY

A variation that uses a 108-card deck (two regular decks plus four jokers) and ten-card hands. No going out with a sting of more than three. Ace counts 10. A sequence of ten cards in more than one suit is worth minus 25. So is a hand consisting entirely of cards of the same suit. And a *straight flush*—a ten-card sequence in a single suit—scores minus 50. Obviously, the jokers and wild deuces facilitate this kind of scoring.

8 LIVERPOOL RUMMY

Also known as Contract Rummy, Progressive Rummy or Joker Rummy, this is among the best of the Rum group when played by five or more players. Its main feature is a fixed number of deals in each of which the melds must conform to a different, predetermined pattern.

Players and Deck

For five to eight, using three regular decks plus two jokers—158 cards. With three or four players, two decks plus one joker. In addition to jokers, deuces may also be used as wild cards but need not be.

Cut, Shuffle and Deal

First dealer is selected by whatever means the local sports prefer—usually a draw of cards with high man getting the deal. Each game consists of seven deals. On the first four, each player gets a ten-card hand. On the final three, twelve-card hands are used.

The Play

The name Contract Rummy arises from the rule that each player's first meld during play of a hand must conform to "contract" requirements specified for the particular hand. First-meld requirements follow and, except for the seventh deal, are stated in terms of three-card groups (three of a kind) or three-card sequences (three cards of adjacent rank in a single suit).

First Deal—Two groups.
Second Deal—One group and one sequence.
Third Deal—Two sequences.
Fourth Deal—Three groups.
Fifth Deal—Two groups and one sequence.
Sixth Deal—One group and two sequences.
Seventh Deal—Three sequences of four cards each.

If the contract requires a first meld including two or more sequences, the sequences may not be in the same suit unless actually unmeldable as one longer sequence. That is, a six-card sequence may not be divided in half and melded as two sequences. But it would be perfectly all right to meld the Q ♡, J ♡ and 10 ♡ with the 8 ♡, 7 ♡ and 6 ♡.

Wild cards may be used in any group or sequence.

Aces may be used as high or low cards in suit sequences.

If a player does not want to take the latest discard, each other player in turn is given an opportunity to take it, but must also take the top card of the stock along with it. Furthermore, he may not discard. After that, the original player resumes his turn, taking the top card of the stock, but not the newly exposed top discard.

Having complied with the contract requirements for an initial meld, a player may *lay off* cards on any meld already showing—including melds made by other players. But no player may meld additional complete sets after his first meld.

In laying off a natural card, a player may make room for it by shifting a wild card to either end of a sequence. But no sequence may become longer than fourteen cards—A (high)-K-Q-J-10-9-8-7-6-5-4-3-2-A (low).

All other aspects of play are identical with Straight Rummy.

Scoring

Aces and wild cards count 15; picture cards are 10; and others are counted at face value. When a player goes out, each opponent is charged the value represented by the cards remaining in hand. At conclusion of seventh hand, winner is player with lowest total and settlement is based on difference between his score and that of each opponent.

KING RUMMY

A splendid four-hand game, using two regular decks and four jokers, which are the only wild cards. Ten-card hands. Each game consists of four deals, each carrying a contract requirement for first meld. These are:

First Deal—One group and one suit sequence of four or more cards.
Second Deal—Three groups of three or more each.
Third Deal—Two sequences of four or more each.
Fourth Deal—Two groups of three or more each plus one sequence of four or more.

On the fourth hand, to make an initial meld is to go out altogether. On earlier hands, player may go out in one large meld or may meld first and go out subsequently by laying off on his own melds or those of opponents.

Jokers count 25, aces 15, picture cards 10 and others their face value.

In most places, the ace may be played above the king or below the two, but fourteen-card sequences are not permitted.

When a joker is melded, the melding player's turn is suspended long enough for every other player in turn to have an opportunity to replace the joker with the natural card for which it substitutes in the meld. The player able to do this takes the joker into his own hand and play resumes.

9 PANGUINGUE

Known more familiarly as Pan, and played with great gusto in the Far West and Southwest, this intricate game is a linear descendant of Conquian. Evidence suggests that it is more faithful to the original Spanish pastime than is our present Coon-Can.

Players and Deck

For no fewer than six, and better with as many as fifteen players, using eight (occasionally five) 40-card decks. These Spanish decks are obtained by removing the eights, nines and tens from ordinary 52-card decks. The same result is achieved by removing picture cards but violates tradition. The 320 cards rank downward in normal Conquian order, from K through A, with the J immediately above the 7.

Cut, Shuffle and Deal

Draw determines who shall be eldest hand, the first player to receive cards in the deal (low card usually captures that privilege) and dealer (second-lowest card). In the Pan clubs of the West, action proceeds in counterclockwise rotation, to the dealer's right. Dealer's left-hand opponent presides over the shuffle, a chore that usually involves several players. After the huge deck is regrouped, cards are dealt five at a time in two rounds, forming ten-card hands. Remainder of deck is divided in two. The top half (*head*) goes face down as a *stock*. The bottom half (*foot*) is set aside in reserve. Dealer turns over the top card (*deck head*) of the head and places it nearby to begin the discard pile.

The Play

The object is to go out by melding a total of eleven cards from a hand that begins with ten and becomes smaller as the game progresses. Interest is added by rules governing the picking of cards from the stock and discard pile. An especially lively feature requires immediate payment by each opponent when a player displays certain crucial melds.

Going on Top: Before actual play begins, each player (beginning at dealer's right) announces whether he intends to play the hand (*stay*) or drop out (*go on top*). A player who drops out pays a forfeit in cash or chips (usually twice the minimum unit), which is placed atop the foot for later collection by whoever wins the hand. The dropped cards are discarded, usually by being slipped crosswise under the foot.

Spreads: The game's melds, known as *spreads,* are formed in denominational groups of not less than three cards each and in suit sequences (*stringers*) of three or more cards. A denominational spread may contain cards of the same rank and a single suit or of three or four suits. But unless aces or kings (known here as *non-comoquers*) are grouped, it is not permissible to have two cards of one suit in a spread with one card of a second suit.

Permissible	*Not Permissible*
4 ♠ 4 ♡ 4 ♣	5 ◇ 5 ◇ 5 ♣
4 ◇ 4 ◇ 4 ◇	
K ◇ K ◇ K ♣	

Conditions: Spreads that entitle the player to collect at once from his opponents are called *conditions.* For this purpose, the threes, fives and sevens are known as *valle* (value) cards.

Any group of valle cards in one suit earns two chips from each opponent—double if in spades.

Any group of non-valle cards in one suit extracts one chip from each opponent—double in spades.

Either a low suit stringer (A-2-3) or a high (K-Q-J) means one chip from each opponent, double in spades.

Draw and Discard: At his turn, the player exposes the top card of the stock and either uses it in a spread or discards it. In some localities, no player may draw from the discard pile. In others, the player to the immediate right of the one who discarded the card may take it in turn, but nobody else may. Regardless of local rules, whoever takes a discard must use it in an immediate spread. As this game is played in most places, no card is *ever* taken into the hand, but is either used for melding or is discarded. After a meld, the player ends his turn by discarding.

Laying Off: As usable cards present themselves to him, a player who has already melded may *lay off* these cards (use them to expand) on his existing melds or, of course, use them for new melds. Whenever a player lays off on a condition, he collects the full penalty payment from each opponent, just as if he were spreading the condition for the first time. Moreover, spreads of more than three cards may be split to join other cards in new spreads—and if the process (called *borrowing*) results in a new condition, payment must be made. The only restriction is that the borrowing process must leave a full spread of three or more cards. Melds may not be destroyed to form others.

Forcing: In most places, any opponent may order the player whose turn it is to take the card atop the discard pile and lay it off. This forces the player to make a discard that may be the ruination of his chances. On the other hand, no player is permitted to discard a card that fits into the next player's spreads—unless he has no alternate discard to avoid that problem.

Going Out: The first player to meld eleven cards is the winner. From those of his opponents who did not go on top he collects one chip for winning, plus the full value of his conditions—his second bonus for the conditions. He also collects the forfeits paid earlier by those who went on top. And he becomes eldest hand in the next deal, which makes his left-hand opponent the dealer.

Errors and Penalties

A player who makes an impermissible meld is allowed to correct it without penalty. But if unable to correct it, he returns any chips he may have collected for it and then resumes play. If the error is not discovered until his turn has been completed by a discard, he pays back all chips collected during the play of the hand. He then turns down his cards and abstains from the remainder of the hand, except to pay for conditions spread by others and, of course, to pay the ultimate winner. The same penalties are imposed on a player found, after his first draw, to hold an improper number of cards. But a player who discovers the improper length of his hand before making his first draw is permitted to toss in his cards and get new ones from the top of the stock.

10 OTHER GOOD RUMMY GAMES

BOAT-HOUSE RUMMY

This is essentially Straight Rummy except that a player who draws from the discard pile is required to take a second card—either the next card on the pile or the top card of the *stock*. No intermediate *melds* are made. Winner is the first player able to *go rum* (go out) with conventional melds involving his entire hand. Settlement methods vary, but usually are on the basis of 1 point (or chip) for each unmatched card in each loser's hand.

CONTINENTAL RUM

For at least six players, using three full decks plus three jokers. For nine players or more, four decks—212 cards in all. Fifteen-card hands, with no intermediate *melding*, and no melding of denominational groups. To go out, player must meld his entire hand in *sequences,* using aces either at the top or bottom. Before the Canasta era, this was a popular afternoon diversion. It has several variations. Chief of these is the requirement that a player can go out only with five three-card sequences, or three four-card and one three-card sequences, or one sequence of five, one of four and two of three. Many games use deuces as wild cards, along with the jokers. Settlement usually is on the basis of payment by each loser at the end of each hand—one chip on general principles, plus one for each wild card melded, or ten if no wild cards were melded, plus seven for going out on the first turn. Elsewhere, the winner gets one chip from each opponent, plus two for each melded wild card. And in some adventurous circles, the dealer collects an immediate chip from each if he begins by picking up the exact number of cards needed to distribute the fifteen-card hands.

DOUBLE RUMMY

This is very much like Conquian except that two 52-card decks are used, plus two jokers. Melded jokers may be shifted about and the natural cards substituted for them. In scoring, jokers count 15, aces 11, picture cards 10 and the others are counted at face value.

11 EIGHTS

Here is the best of all games classified as members of the Stops family. Like most of the Rum group, these games emphasize a race to get rid of cards. But they permit the player to drop obstacles in an opponent's path. Of older Stops games that survive, the oldest is Comet, said to have been popular during the eighteenth century, when Europe was obsessed by the approach of Halley's Comet. Eights (sometimes misnamed Swedish Rummy) is a more recent development. Deservedly, it is the most popular of the lot.

Players and Deck

For two, using the full 52-card deck, with cards ranking downward from A through 2. Sometimes played by three, or as a partnership game for four.

Cut, Shuffle and Deal

Cards are drawn for deal. Low deals. After he shuffles, his right-hand opponent cuts. When two play, seven-card hands are dealt. Otherwise, five-card hands. After the deal, the rest of the deck goes face down in the center for use as a *stock*. Dealer turns over the top card of the stock and places it nearby as the *starter*.

The Play

Beginning at dealer's left and proceeding clockwise, players add to the pile that begins with the starter. Each player must put down a card of the same suit or denomination as the card atop the pile. Or, if the occasion warrants and he has an eight, he may play it. All eights are wild. When player places one on the stack, he is allowed to choose the suit (but *not* the rank) of the card to be played by the next hand. A player unable to match the rank or suit of the top card, or unable to provide the suit designated by someone who has played an eight, or unable or unwilling to play an eight of his own, must take cards from the stock until able to play. *But he may also choose to take cards from the stock even when able to play.*

The hand ends when a player puts his last card on the pile, or in four-hand play, when both members of a team are void. If no cards are left in the stock and nobody is able to play, the hand ends in a *block*.

Scoring

After the winner has dropped his final card on the pile, he scores for the remaining cards held by his opponents. Each eight counts 50, all face cards are worth 10, aces count 1 each and the numbered cards fetch their own face values. If the deal ends in a block, the hand with the lowest point count collects the difference from the others. In most games a running score is kept, with 100 winning and the victor getting an extra 100 for the accomplishment. Deal rotates clockwise.

Strategy

An outstanding feature of this game is the right to draw from the stock even when able to play from the hand. This rule confers an extra advantage on a competent player whose opponent is unable to keep track of cards already played. For example, a superior player can *corner* a suit by taking up the entire stock, using the eights in his hand to paralyze his opponent while disposing of his own large number of cards.

It is unwise to use eights too early in the game. Unless the opponent seems close to going out, it is better to go to the stock than to waste an eight.

12 COMET

This is not as good a game as Eights. It merely is more complicated. The same may be said for most other members of the Stops group. Those now to be described remain popular in the Western world.

Players and Deck

For two to five, with two 48-card decks. Form the decks by removing the aces from two regular 52-card packs and separate the red and black cards in two groups of 48. Finally, place the 9 ♣ in the red deck and the 9 ♢ in the black. Cards rank downward from K through 2. Suits are not used. The odd nines are known as *comets* and are wild.

Cut, Shuffle and Deal

Cards are drawn. Low card shuffles and, after cut by right-hand opponent, deals. Opponent also shuffles the other deck for use on next deal. In two-hand game, each gets eighteen cards. For three, the hands contain twelve cards. For four, ten-card hands are used; and for five, nine cards are the rule. After hands are dealt, the remaining cards are placed face down as a *dead hand.*

The Play

Object is to get rid of all cards in the hand. Player at dealer's left starts by placing any card face up in the center and, if able, adding others in an unbroken upward sequence. He calls the denomination of each card as he plays it, and when unable to continue the sequence, he says "Without." Thus, if he begins with a two and supplies a three, four and five but lacks a six, his call of "Without" permits his left-hand opponent to continue the sequence, if able. A player unable to enter play (lacking a card of the proper rank) calls "Pass." A player able to play is required to do so, and to prolong the sequence as far as able, unless his only playable card is the comet, which he prefers to save.

After playing a king, ending a sequence, a player may begin a new sequence with any card that suits him. If a player has called "Without" and none of the others is able to continue the sequence, the player is permitted to begin a new sequence with any card.

The comet may be played during any of its holder's turns to play, and may be played at any stage of a sequence, substituting for a card of any rank. As soon as it is played, the player is entitled to begin a new sequence with any card.

A player who holds three nines, or all four cards of any other rank, may play them all at once.

Scoring

When the comet is played, its holder gets two chips from each opponent. For each successive deal in which the comet is dealt to the dead hand, its playing value increases by two. Thus, after being found in the dead hand twice in succession, it is worth six chips. But after being played, and paid for, it is worth only two if exposed on the succeeding deal.

The player who wins by playing the last card in his hand gets ten chips for each picture card held by his opponents, plus the face value of each other card they hold.

A player stuck with the comet when an opponent goes out must pay double the value of each card in his hand, including the comet.

A player who goes out by playing the comet as his last card collects double penalties from each opponent—quadruple if he uses the comet as a nine. These are in addition to the usual rewards for playing the comet, which are *also* doubled or quadrupled to reward such timing.

In some games, an ancient feature called *opera* awards a double bonus to *eldest hand* (player to dealer's left) if he is able to go out on his first turn.

Some of the following variations may have diverse ancestry. Nevertheless, they resemble each other sufficiently to be grouped here.

BOODLE

Known sometimes as Newmarket, but differs from the fairly popular game of Michigan, which also is called Boodle and Newmarket. Uses full 52-card deck ranking downward from K through A. An A, K, Q and J, each of a different suit, are taken from another deck and are placed face up on the table. These are the *boodle* cards. Dealer announces how many chips each player must bet as an ante before the deal. The usual amount is four, but it may range to ten or twelve, depending on the value of the chips. Each player may bet this ante on any one of the boodle cards or may distribute them as he pleases on any combination of cards. In a three- or five-hand game, a dead hand of seven cards is dealt and the remaining cards are distributed equally. In four-, six- and eight-hand games, the dead hand contains four cards. In a seven-hand game, the dead hand holds three.

Eldest hand leads his lowest card in any suit he chooses. Whoever holds the card of next higher rank in that suit then plays. Play continues in that fashion until a sequence is stopped by play of the king or by the fact that the required card is in the dead hand. Last hand to play a card before the sequence stops is entitled to begin a new sequence, playing his lowest card of any suit.

Whoever plays a card that matches one of the boodle cards collects the chips that were bet on that card.

Player who goes out gets a chip for each card remaining in opponents' hands.

In some versions, the 9 ◊ is a *comet,* and earns one chip when played or costs two if it remains in a loser's hand after an opponent goes out.

COMMIT

An antique British version of Comet, using a regular 52-card deck minus the 8 ♢, and regarding the 9 ♢ as a *comet*. Comet is played as an alternative to saying "Without." Whoever plays it gets two chips from each opponent. Player of a king collects one chip from each other player. Player who goes out gets one chip for each king that remains in other hands, plus two from the unfortunate stuck with the comet, plus a kitty into which all players ante before each deal.

ENFLÉ

Known also as Schwellen. Low cards are eliminated from regular deck until just enough cards remain for eight-card hands. Cards rank downward from A. Eldest hand leads any suit. Others must follow suit if able. Highest card wins trick, which is then set aside. Player unable to follow suit must take up all cards already played to the trick and must then lead to the next trick. First to go out wins. Stake is usually a pool formed by a predeal ante.

FAN TAN

Presumably named after a Chinese gambling game that uses beans rather than cards, this provides a lot of action for four or five players and is almost as interesting when played by as few as three or as many as eight. After an ante, all cards of a regular 52-card deck are dealt. Eldest hand must place a seven face up in center of table or pass and contribute a chip to the pool. If he passes, next player goes through same procedure. As soon as a seven is played, next player may either place another seven below it or may play the six or eight of the first seven's suit. Thus, after each seven appears, it becomes permissible to play the sixes and eights of the appropriate suits. Ultimately the sixes, sevens and eights form a twelve-card tableau. Before the tableau is complete, however, players are permitted to

build downward sequences (in each suit) on the sixes and upward sequences (in each suit) on the eights. Aces are regarded as low and are played after the twos. Whoever is unable to play in turn must contribute a chip to the pool. First player to go out wins. Losers augment the winner's pool with a chip for each card remaining in their hands.

FIVE OR NINE

First player can put down a five or nine, either of which corresponds to the seven in Fan Tan. Game then proceeds with fours and sixes or eights and tens.

GO BOOM

One or two regular decks, depending on the number of players. Seven-card hands, with remainder of deck face down as a *stock*. Aces are low. Eldest hand leads and others must either follow suit or play a card of identical rank. If unable to do so, player must draw from stock until able to play. If stock is gone and player cannot play, he knocks on table and next player tries. Highest card of led suit wins trick. Winner of trick leads to next. First to get rid of all cards wins, an achievement that he announces by calling "Boom." Losers are penalized face value of numbered cards, 10 for picture cards and 1 for each ace.

I DOUBT IT

A bluffing game is which aces are low, suits are ignored. Entire 52-card deck is dealt. Eldest hand places one to four cards face down on table and announces the denomination ("One ace" or "Three sixes" or whatever), after which next player may either place one to four cards face down and represent them as being of the next higher denomination or may say "I doubt it." If previous player's cards turn out to be other than those he declared, he must pick up all the cards on the table. If doubter's doubts prove unfounded, *he* must take up all the cards on the table. Sequences continue up to king and ace and thence to two and upward again. First to dispose of all his cards wins. This is child's play for a good bluffer with card sense.

LIFT SMOKE

For four, five or six, using regular 52-card deck with aces high. Hands contain as many cards as there are players. Remainder of pack goes face down as *stock*. Top card is exposed and set aside to designate *trump*. Or dealer may show his own last card for the same purpose. Eldest hand leads any card. Others must follow suit if able. If not, they may play any card. Highest trump wins trick or, if no trump is played, highest card of led suit. Winner of trick takes top card from stock and leads to next trick. Last player with cards in hand wins the kitty, into which antes are deposited before deal. Thus, this game is a kind of reverse *nullo*. Winner deals next.

MICHIGAN

Known by several other names, including Chicago, Stops, Newmarket, Boodle, Saratoga. For five to eight, using a regular 52-card deck with aces high. *Boodle* cards are used as in the game of that name described above. Dealer antes two chips on each boodle card, other players ante one on each. Entire deck is dealt. A *widow* hand, between dealer and eldest hand, gets a full helping of cards. If dealer dislikes his own hand, he can exchange it for the widow. If not, he must sell the widow for chips to the highest bidder, who then discards his own original hand without exposing it to anyone. Play then proceeds as in Boodle, except that after each *stop,* the next sequence must be in a different suit than the sequence that was stopped.

PLAY OR PAY

An antecedent of Fan Tan, described above. Eldest hand leads any card and play continues in an upward sequence that continues from king to ace to two to three, etc. Player of thirteenth card in a suit begins the next sequence with another card. Chips are paid for inability to continue play, as in Fan Tan.

SNIP SNAP SNOREM

For four to eight, with a regular 52-card deck, all cards of which are dealt. Eldest hand leads any card, and each player in succession must either play a card of identical rank or pass. After two hands play in succession, the first of the two is penalized, depending on whether he played the deal's first, second or third card of the particular rank. If it was the first card of the rank to appear, he is *snipped* and pays one chip to the pool. If his was the second card of the rank, he is *snapped* and pays two. If his was the third card of the rank, he is *snored* and pays three. Note that these penalties are exacted only after two successive plays. An intervening pass gets the first player off the hook. Whoever plays the fourth and last card of a particular denomination is permitted to play again, leading any card he pleases. When a player gets rid of his last card, the others add one chip to the pool for each card in their hands, and winner takes all.

SPIN

Also called Spinado. A variant of Boodle, permitting holder of the A ◇ to use it as a *stop*, after which he is permitted to begin a new sequence. To use it as a stop, he plays it *with* the card called for in the original, normal sequence.

13 CRIBBAGE

This unique game was devised early in the seventeenth century, allegedly by the romantic young English poet Sir John Suckling. The invention owed much to an old game called Noddy, which featured scoring on a pegboard, just as Cribbage does.

Originally for two—and much the best that way—Cribbage adapts to play by three or four.

Players and Deck

For two, with a regulation 52-card deck. A is low, K is high. Each card counts at its face value and picture cards are worth 10.

Cut, Shuffle and Deal

Low draw deals six-card hands, one card at a time. The remainder of the pack goes face down as a *stock*, which is placed next to the scoring board.

The Play

Each player *lays away* two cards in the *crib*. These four cards remain face down until after the hand is played and the game's counting phase begins. Once the crib has been formed by the lay-aways, nondealer picks up the top half (or thereabouts) of the stock without exposing any cards and dealer takes the top card from the remaining half. This card, the *starter*, goes face up on the stock after dealer's opponent has put the top half back. If the starter is a jack—known in these circumstances as *His Heels*—dealer scores 2 points immediately, moving one of his pegs along the board in accordance with procedures described below.

Actual play begins with dealer's opponent choosing one of the four cards in his hand, placing it face up on the table directly in front of him and calling its value. Dealer then plays a card in the same fashion, announcing the sum of the values of the two cards that have now been played. If the combined values at this point—or subsequently—add to exactly fifteen, the player whose card produced that sum pegs 2 points on the board.

The same number of points rewards the player whose card brings the total count to exactly thirty-one.

The count is not allowed to exceed thirty-one. If a player is unable to put down a card without pushing the total count beyond thirty-one, he says "Go." For this, his opponent pegs 1 point and is permitted to play as many more cards as he can without enlarging the count beyond thirty-one. When this player either scores thirty-one or runs out of plays, the count resumes at zero and the player who said "Go" begins play again.

Whoever plays the last card of the two four-card hands pegs 1 point, after which *showing* points are tallied by means now to be described.

Scoring

The Cribbage board contains four columns (*streets*) of holes and comes with two pairs of pegs (each pair of a different color) that

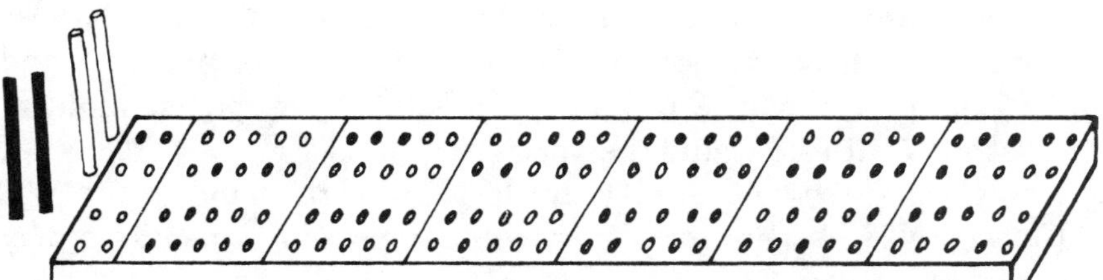

are moved down the streets in the scoring. At the start, each player's pegs are in his *game holes.* At his first score, the player moves a peg forward, away from the game holes, along the outside column (sometimes called *first street*). He moves the peg one hole for each point he has scored. At his second score, he moves his second, or rearward, peg the appropriate number of holes beyond the first peg. In conventional games, the winner is the first player to peg *twice around* and return to the game hole after having traveled each street twice. This means that the first player to score 121 points wins. In some places the game is played only *once around* for 61 points.

Because the game ends when the winner reaches the game hole, scores must be recorded as soon as they are earned, both during play and during the *showing* phase, which we shall discuss shortly.

Before Cribbage can be played seriously or enjoyably, the following credits must be committed to memory. As might be assumed, these credits not only determine the score but are the basis of all strategy and tactics.

Scoring Before Play:

His Heels—2 for dealer.

Scoring During Play:

Fifteen—2 for player whose card brings total to fifteen.

Thirty-one—2 for player whose card brings total to thirty-one.

Pair—2 for player whose card matches rank of opponent's latest card.

Pair Royal—6 for player whose card matches rank of pair just played.

Double Pair Royal—12 for player who puts down fourth consecutive card of same rank.

Sequence—3 or more points for player whose card makes a *sequence* of three or more cards (such as 5-6-7, 5-7-6, or 5-6-4). Each card in a sequence is worth 1 point to the player whose card creates or extends the sequence. Thus, after play of 8 and 9, the player who exposes a 7 pegs 3. The opponent able to respond with a 6 would then peg 4.

Last Card—1 to whoever plays the last card of the hand.

Closest to 31—1 point for player whose opponent is unable to play and says "Go."

Scoring in Showing: After the hand has been played, dealer's opponent pegs whatever number of points may be earned by the combinations formed of his four-card hand plus the starter card. Dealer then does the same with his own hand and the starter, and finally with the crib and the starter. The values:

His Nobs—1 point if hand or crib contains jack of same suit as starter. Also called *Right Jack.*
Fifteen—2 for each combination totaling fifteen.
Pairs—2 for each.
Sequences—1 point for each card in a sequence of three or more.
Double Run—8 for hand or crib that contributes two runs of three made possible by a pair, such as 2-3-4-4.
Double Run of Four—10 for a sequence of four with a pair, such as A-2-2-3-4.
Triple Run—15 when three of a kind make possible three sequences of three, as in 9-9-9-10-J.
Quadruple Run—16 when two adjacent or nearby pairs make four three-card sequences, such as 9-9-10-J-J. Sometimes called *Double Double Run.*
Four Cards of Same Suit—4 to player whose hand meets this standard. Does not apply to cards in crib.
Five Cards of Same Suit—5 when starter and all four cards in hand *or* crib are of the same suit.

Each combination is scored separately and immediately. The highest possible count while showing is 29—when the hand contains J-5-5-5, and the starter is a five of the same suit as the jack. After taking 1 point for Right Jack (His Nobs), player would then score 8 points for the four fifteens formed by his jack with the fives, after which he would score 8 more for the four combinations of fifteen made by the fives. Finally, the double pair royal would add 12, for the total of 29.

In pegging all those points, or any others to which he may be entitled, the player calls them aloud. If opposed by a newcomer to the game, he may spread the four fives before him and point to each combination as he calls and pegs, "Fifteen-two, fifteen-four, fifteen-six, fifteen-eight." With more experienced opposition, he would simply call "Fifteen-eight" and peg the points.

After the dealer has done whatever pegging he can with his hand and the crib, nondealer shuffles and becomes dealer for the next hand. In some circles, if a player notices that his opponent has failed to take full credit for points held in the hand or crib, he may peg the points on his own side after calling "Muggins."

In the conventional game of 121 points, or four streets, a player who has proceeded less than halfway to the finish by the time his opponent has won is said to be *lurched* or *skunked*. If money is riding on the game, the lurched loser usually pays for a double loss.

Errors and Penalties

Before layaways have formed the crib, a misdeal of any kind simply requires a new deal and no penalties are exacted. In the unlikely event that either hand turns up with an incorrect number of cards after the layaways, dealer's opponent may call for a new deal or may peg 2 points and require either that excess cards be buried at the bottom of the stock or that shortages be supplied from the top of the stock.

If a player calls "Go" when actually able to play, he may not withdraw that call after opponent has played.

A failure to peg the full number of points scored during play may not be corrected unless no new card has been played since the mistake. Similar mistakes during showing cannot be corrected after the cut for the next deal. Where the Muggins feature is used, such errors of underscoring can be turned to the opponent's advantage. Where a player pegs more points than are actually earned during play or showing, his opponent is entitled to correct the error and take 2 bonus points.

Strategy

Dealer tries to maximize the prospects of the crib by laying away cards that might help form valuable sequences with the starter or with the cards laid away by opponent. Nevertheless, he rarely breaks up sequences already in his hand, a bird in hand being more dependable than a pig in a poke.

By the same logic, the dealer's opponent tries to spoil the crib with cards of widely separated denominations, hoping to avoid sequences.

To begin play, the safest card for dealer's opponent is a two, three or four, since dealer cannot possibly make fifteen with his own first play.

FIVE-CARD CRIBBAGE

This predecessor of the standard game uses five-card hands instead of six. Game is 61 points. On first deal of every game, dealer's opponent scores 3 at once, to compensate for a statistical advantage enjoyed by dealer. Since the four-card crib is of greater importance than the three-card playing and counting hand, dealer's opponent must be extremely careful about the two cards he lays away.

THREE-HAND CRIBBAGE

Players get five-card hands and one card is dealt to the crib. Each then lays away one card in the crib, producing hands and crib of conventional size. Game proceeds as in two-hand play. Showing begins with player at dealer's left. Special Cribbage boards with three sets of peg holes are used in this version. If none is available, the score may be kept with pencil and paper.

FOUR-HAND CRIBBAGE

A partnership game, with teams chosen by whatever means may be preferred, including the time-honored cut in which drawers of the two lower cards join forces against those with the two higher. Five-card hands are dealt, and the crib is formed when each player lays away one card. The rules of Three-Hand Cribbage apply, with each team's points being combined. First pair to score 121 wins.

PART THREE

Poker, the Money Game

Games mimic life. Great games do more than that. The great game of Poker, which we shall now examine at length, not only imitates but magnifies and exalts some elemental features of contemporary life.

Poker demands an enormous range of skills—far more diverse than those of Contract Bridge or Chess. In a better world, some of these skills would be against the law. For example, cruelty and deceit are among the chief weapons of the good player, whose sole purpose is to victimize others.

Friendliness, generosity, compassion, sportsmanship and other humane weaknesses are out of place at the Poker table. They adulterate the game. In fact, there probably is no such thing as a sociable game of real Poker. When played by amiable types who don't care whether they win or lose, the game is not Poker but a corruption.

Poker stakes may be the dimes of the poor or the hundred-dollar chips of the mighty, but the game is authentic only if the biggest losers suffer genuine pain. Depending on the economics of the particular group, the stakes must be high enough to permit full exercise of Poker's major tactic, bluffing. That tactic is empty unless bluffer and opponents have reason to fear the price of error.

Accordingly, Poker causes more anguish than all other card games combined. And the discomfort occurs in direct ratio to the harmlessness of the individual personality. The less predatory you are, the more you suffer. And if *that* does not imitate certain patterns of life, what does?

Our national sense of solo competitiveness—the old frontier spirit—undoubtedly accounted for the swift spread of Poker at the beginning of the nineteenth century. Its first vogue was as a gambling pastime on Mississippi riverboats, where it had been compounded from bits and snatches of Bouillotte, Poque and Ambigu (French games) and an English game called Brag.

Poker's endless modern variations come in two main types. Draw Poker is played with closed (*concealed*) hands, while Stud, or Open, Poker features hands in which some or even all of the cards are exposed. Local customs and the preferences of the individual group dictate so many procedural differences that universal rules are out of the question. Yet certain widely accepted traditions are honored at more tables than not, and should be cultivated.

Standard Procedures

The typical game has from five to eight players, although versions are played with great skill and enthusiasm by as few as two and as many as fifteen. In most games, the regular 52-card deck is used. Some groups add a joker as a wild card. Many high-powered gatherings of three, four or five players strip the deck of its twos, threes and fours. Some prefer a 32-card deck for a four-hand game, playing with nothing lower than a six.

At Draw Poker, it is highly unusual to permit play by more than seven players at a time. In Stud, the upper limit often is nine. To accommodate more players, various systems of rotation are used, with some playing and others waiting. Most often, supernumerary players must wait until one of the earlier comers vacates a seat and goes home.

Regardless of its myriad variations, the essence of Poker is always the bet—the confrontation between an individual and his opponents, with money as the prize. Bets being so crucial, it follows that the size and circumstances of each bet are elaborately regulated at most tables. Here are the main approaches, which are combined to suit the preferences of individual Poker groups.

Variable Limit: The size of the maximum bet changes at a mutually agreeable rate at various stages of play. In Stud, the limit may also be governed by the strength of the cards exposed in the individual hand. Thus, the limit might be two chips until a pair is exposed, whereupon the limit might become four.

Pot Limit: No bet may exceed the value of cash or chips already in the pot.

Bet the Raise: A bettor who wants to raise may double the bet made by the opponent who made the latest bet. In this kind of game the number of raises is limited, usually to three in any round of betting.

Table Stakes: A player may bet as many chips or as much money as he has. But he may not buy new chips or go to his wallet after a hand begins.

Freeze-out: If a player loses the money or chips with which he entered the game, he must drop out. Play continues until one player has everybody's money.

Side Pots: A player with insufficient chips to call a bet at table stakes or freeze-out may bet what he has in a side pot. All other players at the table are permitted to match this supplementary wager if they choose.

Chips

Cash is perfectly acceptable in most Poker pots, but chips are tidier. One player is elected banker (possibly after having drawn low card) and sells chips to the others. When a player leaves or the game ends, the banker redeems chips for money. White chips are usually valued at 1 unit, red 5, blue 10 and yellow 25.

Cut, Shuffle and Deal

Dealer is chosen by a draw for high card or, in some places, by getting the first jack in a deal of exposed cards. After dealer shuffles, player to his right cuts. Deal proceeds clockwise, one card at a time.

Most groups play *dealer's choice,* which implies that the dealer chooses whatever variety of Poker he will deal. In actuality, however, true dealer's choice is extremely rare and quite impracticable. Poker players have pronounced feelings about the range of variations they will tolerate. The dealer who announces Seven-Card Stud with deuces and one-eyed jacks wild will not be invited back to a game where wild cards are abhorred.

Whatever variety is played, chances are great that each player will be required to *ante* (bet) a nominal amount before getting his cards for each hand. These antes are the only Poker bets that force the expert to take outright gambles, risking money before looking at and appraising some cards.

For convenience, some groups dispose of the ante problem by having each dealer contribute an ante for himself and everyone else at the table. And in other games, the pot begins with a *dealer's edge,* a minimum contribution likely to equal whatever minimum bet is permitted on the first round of betting. This may or may not be accompanied by antes from the other players.

The Betting Phase

In Draw Poker, competitive betting begins with the player at the dealer's left, after all hands have been dealt and the player has seen his cards and is ready to declare himself. In most versions of Stud, betting starts as soon as one or more cards have been exposed. The first to be heard from in Stud is the player showing the highest cards. In case two or more are tied in that respect, the first voice is that of the high hand closest to the dealer's left.

On any round of betting, a player may take one of the following courses.

Drop Out: Turn his cards face down without betting, thus withdrawing from contention for the particular pot. Among ways of announcing this, "*I pass*" is the most common.

Check: If nobody has yet offered to bet on a particular round of betting, "*I check*" signifies a wish to remain in the game without opening the betting. In these circumstances, a player may also say "I pass" without dropping out.

Bet: To make a wager within whatever limits the particular game prescribes.

Raise: To make a bet larger than one already made by an opponent during the round.

Sandbag: In any Poker game, a player who has checked is given another chance to get into the pot in case one of his opponents has bet since he checked. In many games, the player who checks is permitted only to match (*call* or *see*) the latest bet when his next turn arises during the particular round of betting. In other games, he is allowed to raise. This form of treachery—raising the stakes after having behaved like someone on the verge of surrender—is known as *bumping* or *sandbagging*. It makes for lively evenings.

Blind Betting: Many forms of Poker lend themselves to a practice that permits the opening bettor on certain rounds to bet *blind*—that is, without having looked at his cards. Later, after looking, he may raise during the same or a later round. Blind betting is an interesting alternative to sandbagging since it involves less deceit and spreads the risk, so to speak. In forms of Draw Poker (*see below*) that require no minimum hand for whoever begins the first round of betting, blind betting is permissible for the first player on the first round and after the draw. In Stud Poker (*see below*), first bettor may be permitted to bet in the blind for as many rounds as he remains the first bettor—provided that no opponent spoils his fun by raising in the blind. In most places, such a raise must double the opening blind bet. Late in the play of Seven-Card Stud hands, whoever is entitled to be heard from first after the final round of cards is dealt may also bet blind.

After any bet—raise or not—the opportunity to match the bet or, if rules permit, to raise it is given to every player who has not already dropped out. After this, the game moves to its next phase. In Stud, that may simply be the deal of another card all around, followed by another spell of betting. In Draw, it may be the process of discarding unwanted cards and the drawing of new ones in efforts to improve hands, followed by more betting. Ultimately, however, the deal reaches its climax in the final round of betting and—as often as not—in the famous *showdown*.

The Showdown

After the final round of betting, all players who have not dropped out expose their cards for the comparison that determines who takes the pot. If only one player remains, the others having been driven out by his latest bet, no showdown is required. Here, of course, is one of the rewards of the successful bluff: the victor's hand is never seen. Without a showdown, nobody can be absolutely sure that the winner had the best hand.

In games played with five-card hands and no wild cards, the showdown goes to the bettor with the highest-ranking hand. He need only show the cards, which "speak for themselves" without any declaration from him. But in seven-card games or if wild cards are used, the player must announce the value of his holding and must stick with that value even if he has underassessed his hand. On the contrary, if he has overrated his cards, claiming a higher rank than that to which he is entitled, any of his opponents may correct him. In some places, this error is penalized by automatic loss of the pot.

In seven-card games, each hand's value is determined by whichever five cards produce the best pattern.

Poker hands rank as follows.

Five of a Kind: Four cards of the same denomination plus a wild card or a joker (A-A-A-A-joker ranks as five aces and outranks five kings).

Straight Flush: Five cards of the same suit in uninterrupted sequence—2 ♠, 3 ♠, 4 ♠, 5 ♠, 6 ♠. The highest straight flush is topped by the ace, descends to the ten of the same suit and is called a *royal flush*. In some games the ace may be used in a small straight flush, with the two, three, four and five, as well as at the top.

Four of a Kind: Four cards of the same denomination, or including wild cards if such are in play.

Full House: Three cards of one rank and two of another—J-J-J-9-9 being a *jack full.*

Flush: Any five cards of one suit. In European Poker, which usually finds the deck stripped by removal of several low denominations, the flush outranks the full house. This occurs for the best of reasons—it being more difficult to get a flush from a stripped deck.

Straight: Any uninterrupted sequence of five cards in more than one suit. For example, Q ♡, J ♠, 10 ♣, 9 ♣, 8 ◇ is a *queen-high straight.*

Three of a Kind: Three cards of like denomination (including a wild card or two if they are being used). The other two cards in the hand match neither each other nor the three of a kind.

Two Pairs: Two cards of the same rank and two of another with a fifth that matches neither of the sets (9-9-6-6-K—*nines up*).

One Pair: Two cards of the same rank with three others that help form none of the better hands described above.

No Pair: Five cards without any of the foregoing patterns (K-J-10-8-4—*king high*).

Wild Cards and Bugs

The great schism among Poker players is not really about whether to play Draw or Stud. Whether or not to use wild cards is a much graver question. On the extreme right wing are those who brook no wild cards of any kind and often refuse to play anything but five-card Draw or five-card Stud. On the far left are those whose juices do not really begin to flow unless the game is a way-out version of seven-card Stud with at least one denomination wild.

Where wild cards are permitted, it is customary to allow the holder to assign to them any rank he chooses. Thus, if deuces are wild, A ♠, A ♡, A ◇, A ♣, 2 ♡ become five aces. In another hand at the same table, a deuce might be called the 3 ♠, to fill a straight or a straight flush.

In some circles, the joker is used as a *bug*—accepted only as an ace or to complete a straight or a flush.

The ranks most usually used as wild cards are, besides the joker, the deuces, one-eyed jacks and one-eyed kings. In some forms of Stud, the lowest concealed card held by the player becomes his wild one.

Although purists argue with some vehemence that wild cards adulterate Poker, the truth is that they only elaborate Poker. They modify the game's percentages. More guile and knowledge are needed in a high-stakes game with wild cards than in one without them.

Bonuses

Many groups award the holder of a royal flush a penalty payment from everybody else at the table, regardless of whether any stayed until the showdown. Straight flushes of lower denomination also get the bonus in some quarters, as may five of a kind and four of a kind.

Exotic Hands

As if Poker did not contain enough suspense to begin with, numerous exotic hands are given high rank at some tables. The principal effect of these variations is to keep losers in each pot longer than might otherwise be the case. The main exotic holdings are the following.

Big Tiger: No pair, but king high and eight low. Beats a straight but loses to a flush. Known also as *big cat*.

Little Tiger: No pair, but eight high and three low. Beats a straight but loses to big tiger. Also called *little cat*.

Big Dog: No pair, but ace high and nine low. Beats a straight but loses to *little tiger*.

Little Dog: No pair, but seven high and two low. Beats a straight but loses to big dog.

Groups that do not use the tigers and dogs sometimes favor these.

Skeet or *Pelter:* No pair, but nine high, two low and a five in the middle. The fourth card must be either a three or a four and the fifth either a six, seven or eight. Beats a straight but loses to a flush unless all cards are of the same suit, whereupon the skeet beats anything but five of a kind.

Skip Straight: A numerical sequence counted off by twos—such as 2-4-6-8-10 or 5-7-9-J-K. Beats three of a kind but loses to a straight. Known also as *Dutch straight* or *kilter*.

Round the Corner: The denominations are viewed as an unbroken, circular sequence. Therefore, someone holding Q-K-A-2-3 is allowed to claim a straight. Such a straight beats three of a kind but not a skip straight.

Blaze: Five picture cards, which, if they include two pairs, are better than an ordinary two pairs but not as good as three of a kind. And if the holding includes three jacks, queens or kings, it beats three of a kind but nothing higher.

Four Flush: In some games, a holding of four cards of the same suit is accepted as superior to a pair. Loses to two pairs.

Ties

When the showdown reveals that the two or more best hands are of the same class, the tie is broken by conceding that the holding with the highest cards is the winner. Thus a pair of aces beats any other one-pair holding. But if more than one player holds a pair of aces—or three aces or four (utilizing wild cards)—the pot goes to the hand with the highest side card.

When evaluating straights or flushes or no-pair hands, the highest card in each hand is compared to the highest card in the competing hand. And with full houses, the rank of the triplet prevails—A-A-A-2-2 (*ace full*) defeats K-K-K-Q-Q (*king full*).

And, between hands showing two pairs, the hand with the highest-ranking pair wins. If there is a tie in that respect, then the lower pairs are compared, after which comparison is made—if necessary—between the fifth, unmatched cards.

In games played with six- or seven-card hands, ties are settled as above, with reference to the five-card hands chosen for the showdown by each player. If the tie remains unbroken, the player with the highest sixth or, if necessary, seventh card takes the pot in some quarters. Elsewhere, the tie is looked on as binding and the pot is divided.

If the game accepts the exotic, optional hands previously described, the same principle governs ties. In round-the-corner straights, it is convenient to rank aces and kings as lower than the twos, threes or fours with which they combine in the sequence. Thus, ties of that kind are resolved by the highest low card.

When wild cards are used and ties occur, the wild card retains whatever rank it simulates in the particular holding. A joker used as a ten cannot be called an ace for tie-breaking purposes. But if a winning hand at Seven-Card Stud can be patched together so that the joker becomes a side card, it may then pass for a tie-breaking ace.

Errors and Penalties

The roughhewn etiquette of Poker permits the widest latitude barring outright cheating. For example, it is permissible to look at an opponent's cards if he is unwary enough to expose them. Also permitted are all manner of psychological diversions such as banter, groans, grunts and misleading facial expressions.

In the resultant skirmishes, the only effective rules are those imposed by the group itself. A good beginning is to agree that each dealer will settle whatever disputes arise during his deal—and that the group can always vote him down if his verdict is obnoxious.

Poker procedures are really so simple that it takes a conspicuously humorless bunch to impose penalties for the kinds of errors that occur. However, some groups feel more secure when governed by "rules" promulgated in Hoyles. For example, if the dealer in a game of Stud is in such a fog that he dispenses the first two or three cards face up, he can always spare himself trouble simply by dealing the next one face down. However, the ancient rules thunder that if he deals the first *four* cards face up, whoever receives them may take back all his money from the pot and abstain from the rest of the hand. And the errant dealer is supposed to pay a fine of twenty white chips. No mention is made of flogging.

A more intelligent rule requires anyone who drops out of a Stud hand to turn over his *faced* cards at once and never expose his *hole card.* Various penalties have been prescribed for failure to perform this simple, obvious sporting courtesy. The most sensible would be to stop inviting such a slob to the game.

Sometimes disagreements arise about the need for a new deck. Where stakes are high, any player is usually permitted to demand a new deck, even if nothing is wrong with the one currently in use. The only limitation is that everyone at the table must have had a deal with a deck before it is discarded. Naturally, an imperfect deck is tossed out at once. And some rule books state that the first player to deal with a new deck must examine it closely to make sure that it is complete and unflawed. To deal from an imperfect deck is to incur a fine of five white chips. If the error is not noticed until after completion of a hand, the winner retains his spoils.

If dealer forgets to shuffle or cut or both, or deals out of turn, or exposes a card while dealing or cutting, anyone may demand a new shuffle and cut provided that matters have not proceeded as far as the deal of the second round of cards.

When a card is accidentally exposed during the draw, it must be kept. When a player receives a second exposed card during the draw, the card is removed from the game. The player then waits to complete his draw until all others have finished.

Whoever gets too few cards on the draw may demand the correct number provided that he hasn't seen any of the drawn cards and the next player has not yet drawn. If he has seen his cards, he simply plays with a short hand. Or, if a player gets too many cards in the draw, he may discard the excess card or cards provided that he has not looked at any of the drawn cards. If he has already looked, his hand is dead and he must drop out, losing whatever he may already have contributed to the pot.

When insufficient cards remain in stock to complete a draw, or if discards accidentally become mixed with undealt cards, all discards and undealt cards are shuffled, cut and dealt to finish the hand.

In many circles, the bottom card of a deck is never dealt, the assumption being that anyone in his right mind would have been trying to peek at it.

To prevent out-of-turn betting and the costly confusion to which it leads, most groups penalize the impetuosity by forbidding the guilty party to raise. When his proper turn comes, he may call or drop out. At some tables, he also is required to leave his out-of-turn bet in the pot and either bet again (without raising) or drop out when his turn comes.

In Jackpots and other Draw games requiring the opening bettor to hold a hand of some value, the opener may later be required to prove that he held a hand of the prescribed worth. In most games, proof is demanded only of an opener who later wins the pot. In others, the opener must show his qualifying combination (for example, a pair of jacks or better in Jackpots) whether he wins or not. Where this rule is regarded as necessary, penalties for violation have ranged as far as a bullet in the head. In any event, when opening bettors discard part of the required opening combination during the draw (such as discarding one of the jacks in an effort to buy a straight), they take pains to keep the discarded proof close at hand for later display.

In this vein, all undealt cards and discards are untouchably dead. No player is allowed to look at them except when trying to check a claim that something is wrong with the deck. In some games, however, peeking at dead cards is so troublesome that it makes sense to fine the violator a few white chips—assuming that it is necessary to have him around at all.

As much of the above material implies, the best approach to errors and other behavioral problems is whatever suits the individual group. Let the game's senior members develop their own congenial rules and, in time, their own traditions. Whoever finds that the resulting code conflicts with his own sense of logic or sportsmanship will do himself and everybody else a favor by playing elsewhere.

1 DRAW POKER

The most popular form of Draw Poker is Jackpots, in which the player who opens the betting is required to hold *jacks or better*—a hand containing at least a pair of jacks. Before this feature came into vogue (supposedly about 1870 in Ohio), anybody could start the betting with any holding at all and bluffing required less wit than it now does. In many modern Poker sessions, the dealer's choice of a minimum opening hand may vary from Jackpots to Queens or Better, or even kings or aces, and, for laughs, the old-fashioned Anything Opens.

Players and Deck

When using the regulation 52-card deck, six or seven players are ideal, although as few as two and as many as eight are traditional. For fewer than six, interest is added by stripping the deck to forty cards, removing its twos, threes and fours. With eight players, dealer may sit out the hand to avoid running out of cards during *the draw.*

Cut, Shuffle and Deal

Mixing and cutting follow usual procedures. Before the deal, each player *antes* or, for convenience, the dealer may ante for all. One face-down card then goes to each player in clockwise rotation until five-card hands are held. Remaining cards are kept by dealer for subsequent draw. Deal rotates clockwise.

The Play

Betting begins at dealer's left. First player may *check* with any holding but cannot open the betting unless he holds a pair of jacks or better. If he checks, his left-hand opponent then exercises the same options. If all players check, the hand is *passed out.* Another ante then goes into the pot, and the first checker now becomes dealer. However, in games of dealer's choice, where a wide range of Draw and Stud games may be accepted, the deal does not move until a hand has been bet and the pot won.

After someone opens the betting, each player in turn must *call* (agree to match the previous bet), *raise* or *drop out.* When everyone has had the chance to match or surpass the previous call or raise, the round of betting ends and the draw begins.

Beginning at dealer's left, players who have not dropped out may now discard as many as four of their original cards, although in most games for six players or more only the dealer may draw four and others are limited to three.

Dealer replaces each opponent's discards by dealing one card at a time from the stock. Player at dealer's left completes his draw first, followed by others clockwise, with dealer last. When dealer takes his own cards, he is required to announce how many he is discarding. When players other than dealer are permitted to draw four, it is customary to deal the first three but to withhold the fourth until everyone else has drawn.

The second round of betting begins with the player who opened the betting on the previous round. If he has dropped out, the player to his left begins, although in some circles, this priority goes to the player who offered the latest raise (if any). Once again, the opening bettor may either check or bet. If he bets and nobody calls, he wins the pot. If he checks and nobody bets, a showdown follows. If he or anyone else bets, each player is given an opportunity to call or raise the highest previous bet.

Strategy and Bluffing

As in all Poker, sound play rests on knowledge of the statistical probabilities. The tables on pages 273 through 280 provide that foundation.

Except when facing weak players or launching a bluff, experts tend to open the betting only when the holding conforms with well-established percentages. These depend not only on the cards in the hand but on the number of opponents yet to be heard from. The more players yet to speak, the greater the possibility that someone holds a superior hand. Table A lists the minimum hands considered good enough for a sound opening in each situation.

TABLE A

Opponents Not Yet Heard From	*Minimum Pair for Safe Opening*
7	Aces
6	Kings
5	Kings
4	Queens
3	Jacks

It is customary to lower these standards by one notch when holding a side card of higher rank. With a pair of jacks and a side ace, one might open the betting against four opponents. For example, in a game against six when two others have already checked.

After an opponent opens, the decision to call or drop depends on another set of probabilities. Where more than one opponent has already called, a relatively strong hand is needed to remain safely in the game. Table B summarizes the conventional wisdom.

TABLE B

Players Staying	*Minimum Hand to Stay*
6	Three of a Kind
5	Two Pairs (Aces up)
4	Two Pairs (Kings)
3	Two Pairs (Queens)
2	Any Two Pairs
1	Pair of Kings

Of course, these guidelines and all others are ignored when the pot is large enough to justify a long chance. If only a few chips need be risked on the possibility of winning five or ten times their worth, it is sensible to adjust tactics accordingly. Once again, knowledge of the probabilities is all-important, and pages 273 to 280 will help immensely.

As implied earlier, no good Poker player remains inflexibly with the percentages, hallowed though they may be. The unimaginative tactician is a patsy. His opponents know beyond doubt when he holds a strong hand and when he does not. Good players cut their tactics against the grain now and then, attempting to keep everyone else off balance.

Which is where the bluff arises. It is exactly what its name suggests—a misrepresentation. The hand is weak but the bluffer bets as if it were powerful.

He holds a pair of aces and behaves as if it were three of a kind. During the draw, he airily requests only two cards. He then bets his head off. Sometimes he scares out opponents who hold two pairs. Indeed, he sometimes intimidates opponents who hold three of a kind.

So he steals an occasional pot. But the benefits of the bluff range even farther than that. The bluffer makes most headway when his deception is unmasked. Someone calls his bets and the showdown reveals the bluff. Havoc!

How often had he bluffed and not been caught? The next time he bets heavily, will he be bluffing? How does one go about divining the actual strength of such an opponent's hands?

He has made his point. For the rest of the session—unless his opponents are strong players—he can count on profits from the confusion he has caused. Indeed, when party to a weekly game against weaker players, a good bluffer can feather his nest for an entire season by getting himself caught in a showdown once or twice a month. Doing so, he lays the groundwork for the occasions when he can bet his full house as if he were bluffing with a pair of threes.

In a game against competent players, the bluffer is less likely to make money on his bluffs than on his strong hands. As suggested, he prefers to lose a bluff—*advertising*, as the Poker lexicon has it. Furthermore, he does not bluff frequently. To do so is as unproductive as never bluffing at all. And much more expensive, because opponents learn to ignore the bombast.

Not surprisingly, the bluffer is at a disadvantage against the kinds of weak players who see every bet "just to keep you honest." How can you bluff someone who refuses to be bluffed? Persons of that kind can be fleeced by a good player's simple adherence to the percentages of the game. Another circumstance in which it seldom pays to bluff arises when a big winner becomes expansive and decides to call every bet in an apparently guilt-ridden desire to refund his opponents' losses. Winners of that kind are only accidental. They are not good players. But they can harm a bluffer who does not lie low in their presence.

By all means the least promising environment for the bluffer is the game in which the stakes are too low. If one or more opponents are unimpressed by the amounts of money involved in calls and raises, it may be impossible to bluff them.

Finally, to every bluffer comes the evening when his opponents call his first, second and third bluff, and drop when he finally bets a legitimate hand. He has met his masters. They are reading him as if he were graffiti. He is in the wrong game. No real Poker player makes such a mistake twice. Instead, he moves on to greener pastures.

PROGRESSIVE JACKPOTS

This begins like Jackpots, but when nobody opens the betting and the hand is passed out, the minimum opening for the next try becomes queens or better. Then kings and aces and, if necessary, back one step at a time to jacks. An extra fillip is provided by increasing the ante one unit after each passed hand. Thus, if the ante is one chip for the first hand and three are passed, every player will have contributed ten chips before seeing the aces-or-better hand.

STRAIGHT DRAW

The daddy of Draw Poker, permitting an opening bet regardless of the strength of the holding. The option of checking is usually omitted, which means that everyone either bets or drops on every round.

BET OR DROP

Betting begins after a single card is dealt to each player, and another round of betting follows after each subsequent card. Betting always begins at dealer's left and ends with dealer. Because this puts the dealer at a disadvantage, Bet or Drop is not suitable for groups that play dealer's choice.

COLD HANDS

A simple game of showdown Poker. After the ante, all cards are dealt face up until everybody has five. Highest hand wins. If a draw is permitted, a round of betting precedes it.

BLIND TIGER

Still popular in Europe, this is Straight Draw with rigid betting procedures. Before serving the cards, dealer antes a chip and player at his left (known to oldsters as the *age* or *eldest hand*) does the same. Age's bet is called the *blind.* The player at his immediate left is required to ante two chips—the *blind raise* or *straddle.* After these formalities, cards are dealt. Competitive betting begins with the player at the left of the blind raiser. He and those who follow must either call or raise the blind raise, unless they prefer to drop out. In some circles, the first bet after the deal must raise the blind raise—even double it. And versions of the game make all first-round betting absolutely blind. Nobody is permitted to look at his hand until the blind round is over, whereupon another round of betting takes place and then the draw is held.

After the draw, the surviving player nearest to dealer's left begins the final betting. In some games, he is allowed to check if he wants.

In groups that require the first bettor (on the first round of betting) to raise the blind raise, it often happens that nobody cares to take the risk. At that stage, eldest hand (the last to be heard from) has option of calling the blind raise, or raising it, or offering to split the pot with the blind raiser. Or the local rule may require him to offer to share only the dealer's ante, the blind raiser's ante being returned whole.

LOWBALL

Poker backwards. At the showdown, low hand wins. Aces rank below twos. Since straights and flushes have no value, the best possible holding is A-2-3-4-5 (a *wheel* or *bicycle*).

Many prefer to play with all standard card and hand rankings intact. In that version, the lowest and best hand is 2-3-4-5-7—and A-2-3-4-5 is a losing straight, just as it might be a winning one in conventional Poker.

Another kind of Lowball is played in Stud Poker.

HIGH-LOW

Poker both ways. At the showdown, highest and lowest hands share the pot, with odd chips going to high hand. In some games, each player who has stayed to the end declares his intentions (competing for high, low or both) before the final round of betting. To prevent dealer (the last to speak) from gaining unfair advantage by (for example) declaring "Low" simply because everyone else has said "High," it is customary to require simultaneous declarations. This can be done by each holding a chip (blue for high, white for low) and revealing them at dealer's command.

Whether played with wild cards or not, this is a tremendously demanding game, worthy of the most sophisticated Poker talent. Most experts agree that the original holding had better be nice and low in its own right—or good and high—before the player should risk important money on a draw.

SHOTGUN

Betting begins after three cards have been dealt to each. Additional rounds follow the fourth and fifth cards. Next comes the draw and the final betting. Anything opens. Known also as Pig.

DOUBLE-BARRELED SHOTGUN

Shotgun with a vengeance. High and low hands share the pot. Moreover, after the draw, each player exposes (*rolls*) one card on the table before him. This is done at dealer's signal and must take place simultaneously. If anyone is too slow about it, the opponents may change their own choices of exposed cards. A round of betting begins with holder of the highest exposed card, and then comes another roll. Declarations and showdown come after four such rounds of betting, each of which starts, as in Stud, with the highest holding displayed. If two are tied in that respect, the privilege goes to player nearest dealer's left hand.

PASS THE GARBAGE

If fewer than eight play, dealer serves closed hands of seven cards (six cards for eight). After a round of betting, each player passes three of his cards to his left-hand opponent. Discards then reduce each hand to the conventional five. Next comes a series of rolls, as in Double-Barreled Shotgun. As if all this were not enough activity, the game is usually embellished with the high-low feature plus a wild card and a joker.

TWO-CARD POKER

Lovers of congested tables will appreciate this, which can be played by as many as fifteen. After an ante, each player gets two down cards. A round of betting precedes a showdown with no draw. Best hand is a pair of aces. Flushes and straights are not recognized. Can be played high-low and/or with deuces or some other wild card. Declarations are made after the final bets. Whether played high-low or not, betting restrictions apply as in Bet or Drop.

ENGLISH DRAW

Player at dealer's left is allowed to draw four cards. Everyone else is limited to three.

CANADIAN DRAW

Exactly like Jackpots except that it is permissible to open betting with a four-card flush or a four-card straight. At the showdown, the four-flush beats the four-straight and both beat any pair but lose to two pairs.

LOW DRAW

If nobody holds jacks or better, the hand is not tossed in but continues as a game of Lowball. Known also as Double-Barreled Draw.

BRAG

This ancestor of modern Poker features three-card hands, permitting large groups to play. After dealer serves and antes, others must either call or raise. At the showdown, only pairs and threes of a kind are recognized. An added attraction are three wild cards (*braggers*) ranking downward from the A ♢ to J ♣ to 9 ♢. A pair formed with any of these wild cards stands below a natural pair of the corresponding rank.

AMERICAN BRAG

Here all jacks and nines are wild and rank equally. Pairs or threes formed with wild cards outrank naturals.

RED AND BLACK

Not really Poker, although it begins like Straight Draw. At the showdown, hands rank according to point values assigned to the cards: ace is worth 1 point, jack, queen and king get 10 and the others rate at pip value. All red cards are tallied as plus points, all black as minus. The hand that nets the highest plus count wins the pot. If high-low is favored, half the pot goes to the hand with the largest net minus total or the lowest plus.

WHISKEY POKER

Ante and deal as in Draw, except that an extra hand (*widow*) is dealt just before dealer's own. After the deal, eldest hand has option of taking the widow, passing or *knocking*. If he passes, the option devolves on his left-hand opponent. When someone takes the widow, his original hand goes face up on the table as a new widow and each succeeding player may then exchange one or all of his own cards for any or all of those exposed. The game proceeds in this fashion until somebody knocks, which is the signal for a showdown. However, all but the knocker get one more turn to exchange with the widow.

To settle, high hand may win the antes or—where the game is played without an ante—low hand pays high a predetermined penalty. This often is one chip for every player at the table. In other places, low hand matches the original ante and high hand takes all.

KNOCK POKER

A good game that combines elements of Poker and Rummy. For two to six but best for three or four. After everyone antes, closed hands of five cards are dealt. The remainder of the pack forms a stock, top card of which is faced to begin a discard pile.

Beginning at dealer's left, each player takes either the top card of the stock or the top card of the discards. He then discards a card face up on the pile. A player may knock immediately after taking a card and before discarding. This signifies readiness for showdown and means that each opponent has only one more turn. The final turns completed, the showdown takes place and high Poker hand wins. Some groups make the mistake of having the showdown immediately after the knock, which gives the knocker an unfair advantage.

When knocker proves to have the best hand, he collects the ante plus two chips from whoever lingered to the finish. Players not caring to risk that may escape after their final turns and before the showdown by paying knocker one chip—whether he turns out to be the actual winner or not.

When knocker loses the showdown, he pays high hand two chips. In a variation, the losing knocker pays all parties to the showdown. Added rewards (*royalties* or *premiums*) go to victorious knocker in special circumstances:

Royal Flush—four chips from each loser.
Straight Flush—two chips from each loser.
Without Drawing (Standing Pat)—two chips from each loser.
Four of a Kind—one chip from each loser.

2 FIVE-CARD STUD

Because it lacks the variety possible in games that use seven cards, Five-Card Stud is no longer as popular as it was half a century ago. It used to be a favorite of big bettors, but they have moved on to the newer and more challenging seven-card games. Indeed, with its four open and one concealed card, the average Five-Card Stud now shapes up as scarcely more entertaining than a game of straight showdown. Time marches on.

Players and Deck

The conventional game is for seven to nine, with the full 52-card deck. However, it is more fun to strip the twos and threes and whatever other low denominations must be removed to leave the deck with fewer than seven cards per player.

Cut, Shuffle and Deal

All ante before dealer serves a face-down *hole card* to each. Then comes a second card (*up card*), face up, followed by the first round of betting. An additional round of betting comes after players get each of the three other up cards. At each turn, the player displaying the highest exposed card or cards is the first to bet. In this sense, a pair of deuces is taken as higher than ace–king. In case of a tie, the tied player closest to the dealer's immediate left is first to bet.

Limit and Showdown

In most circles, a relatively severe limit may be imposed on the sizes of bets and raises during the first two rounds, with a higher limit on the last two rounds. Another widespread practice is to allow an increased limit as soon as anyone's exposed cards include a pair. After the final round, if more than one player survives, they expose their hole cards and the best Poker hand wins. In this game, the cards "speak for themselves," and the rare player who underestimates the strength of his hand is not penalized for the mistake.

Strategy

Except when played for punitively high stakes, whereupon the bluff becomes the primary separator of sheep from goats, this is a dull game. Four-fifths of everyone's hand being exposed to view, the proceedings are only one step removed from straight Showdown Poker, in which all five cards are dealt straight up.

Regardless of the stakes or the talents of various bluffers, good players rarely gamble that a holding will improve with the next dealt card. They drop as soon as they see that their present combination is beaten by someone else's. They depart from this practice only when trying to bluff, or to be caught bluffing.

A player adept at creating confusion becomes most dangerous when his hole card contains the basic strength of his hand. If it turns the other four into a straight or a flush or even a pair of kings, the shark exploits whatever anxieties he has managed to cultivate in the minds of his inferiors. Clever though he may be, his powers rest on firm knowledge of well-established percentages and probabilities. In Five-Card or any other brand of Poker, the newcomer is helpless until he begins to grasp the realities set forth on pages 273 to 280.

Five-Card Stud can be played with a wild card or a joker, which tends to make it even more of an exercise in showdown. The game's best variations are more entertaining than that.

MEXICAN ROLLOVER

Known also as Flip, this has the virtue of allowing the player to expose his hole card and keep a newly dealt card face down. In most versions, all cards are dealt down. Betting begins after two cards have been dealt and each player has faced one. The round of betting concluded, each player gets a new down card and then exposes his hole or the new down card, depending on which he prefers to keep in the hole. As in all other Stud games, each new card means a new round of betting.

Some groups streamline the game by dealing the first card down and the second up, with the player asking for the subsequent card up or down as he chooses (down if he faces his hole card, up if he does not). Thus the choice of hole card is made blindly, heightening the element of luck.

CHICAGO

At a Chicago showdown in any Stud game, the player with the highest spade in the hole wins half the pot. Thus, whoever has a concealed A ♠ is a sure winner and is said (as with any other cinch holding in any other form of Poker) to hold an *immortal.* The K ♠ becomes an immortal when held face down during a deal in which the A ♠ appears face up.

NO PEEKIE

Everyone gets five cards down and is forbidden to look at any of them. Player at dealer's left begins by exposing a card (without looking at it beforehand). He then bets or checks. After the betting—totally blind except for the one exposed card—the next hand turns up a card of his own and continues to turn cards until (a) exposing a card higher than the first player's or (b) developing a partial or whole Poker hand better than the first player's—such as a pair of deuces, beating the first player's single ace. As soon as the first player's showing has been surpassed, another round of betting takes place, and then the third player begins rolling cards.

A player who turns up all his cards without becoming highest at the table is automatically out. The hand ends when only one player remains, or when the last two have faced all their cards and have acknowledged the outcome. This game is also known as Sweat, an apt description, although its resemblance to Poker lies mainly in its suspense and its ranking of the hands. No bluffing is possible.

LAST CARD DOWN

This hard-boiled game involves two hole cards and only three up cards. In one version, the second hole card is dealt last. In another the first two cards dealt are down and are followed by the first round of betting.

LOWBALL STUD

Exactly what the name implies, with first bet in each round by whoever holds the poorest exposed cards.

SUBSTITUTION

This Five-Card Stud offers the high-low feature that is more fun in Draw Poker or Seven-Card Stud, where the possibilities are larger. To heighten the gambling possibilities, the final betting round of a regular high-low game is followed by from one to three substitutions, or draws, depending on dealer's prescription or group preference. In most versions, the player who wants to discard something from his hand must pay for the privilege—usually the game's minimum bet for the first draw, double for the second and triple for the third. After each round of substitutions comes a new round of betting. Exposed cards are substituted for exposed cards and down cards replace hole cards.

PIG STUD

A testing game in which each player gets three hole cards and two up cards and the fourth round of betting is followed by conversion of each holding into a closed hand and draw, as in regular Draw Poker. Naturally, the draw produces a final betting round.

ENGLISH STUD

Another good game combining Stud and Draw. After deal of two down and one up, betting begins. Fourth and fifth cards are face up, and each is followed by a round of betting. After the third round, each player may discard and replace as many of his cards as he pleases, getting down cards for down cards and exposed cards for the others.

This and all games like it are out of place in a game of dealer's choice. Indeed, someone who tries to get away with dealing it in such a game should be viewed with deep suspicion. The dealer's position as last bettor is a large advantage. He sees everybody else's discarded up cards before committing himself.

MURDER

Well named. A game of Two-Card Stud in which any player can draw as many as three cards. Betting begins after deal of one down card all around. Second card goes face up, followed by more betting. Then comes the draw, with fees as in three-card Substitution.

This game is best when played high-low. Straights and flushes don't count. Aces always are high, above kings. But a pair of sevens automatically wins both high and low. And the next-best low hand, obviously, is 2-3. Expert Poker players dislike this kind of game except for the opportunities it provides to exploit pigeons. A poor player with a seven is all too likely to overlook the fact that the odds against drawing another are around 16–1. To warrant the expense of the draw and continued betting, the pot should contain seventeen times the cost of the draws and bets.

Study of the tables on pages 273 through 280 will help develop the kind of probabilistic thinking helpful in this and other forms of Poker. Meanwhile, the 16–1 odds against drawing a second seven are computed by noting the ratio between the remaining sevens (three of them) and the forty-eight other cards in the deck. To be sure, the probability also depends on the number of sevens already dealt, the number of opportunities to try for another seven and the number of undealt cards remaining in the deck.

ACEY-DEUCEY

A variation of Murder. Players can draw up to three cards on the two-card hand, but only one at a time. Turns continue until everybody is ready to stand pat. Fees are paid for cards as in Murder. Betting begins when everyone has either dropped or has declared himself ready to bet.

THREE-CARD STUD

Some call this Three-Card Monte, although it does not resemble that carnival hustler's version of the old shell game. After antes, a down card goes to each and bets are made. Another round of betting follows a second card (up) and a third (also up). High wins, with hands ranking as follows:

1. Straight flush
2. Three of a kind
3. Flush
4. Straight
5. Pairs
6. High card

PUSH

Deal as in Five-Card Stud. When player at dealer's immediate left gets his first up card he may keep it or pass it (*push*) to the player at his left. He then gets a new up card from dealer and must keep it. The push privilege now devolves on the player to first player's left. He may fob off the unwanted up card on his own left-hand opponent (whether he got the card from the dealer or from the player to his right). And he then must keep the next card dealt him. Matters proceed thusly until dealer's turn. If he decides to push, the unwanted card becomes dead and goes to the bottom of the pack.

As soon as everyone has five cards, players are permitted to discard and draw one card. The usual price for this draw is three times the game's minimum bet. In some quarters, the price is set at three times the usual betting limit.

Can be played high-low. Should not be allowed at tables where dealer's choice is the rule because the dealer has the advantage of not having to make his own move on the draw until he sees what everyone else is up to.

The decision to push or not should be based on estimates of the probabilities of improving one's own hand. Pushing defensively, to spoil somebody else's hand, is not as productive.

BIG SQUEEZE

Six-Card Stud, with the sixth dealt down as a second hole card. Betting as in Five-Card Stud. After round of betting that follows deal of sixth card, a one-card draw is permitted and then come final betting and showdown. Usually played high-low.

3 SEVEN-CARD STUD

For at least a quarter of a century, experienced Poker players have recognized that Seven-Card Stud games are the most challenging of all. Traditionalists and other purists held out as long as they could for five-card varieties, but the tide has been too powerful. Anybody who continues to maintain that Seven-Card Stud isn't "real" Poker is probably not a Poker player.

DOWN THE RIVER

After two hole cards are dealt, a third card arrives face up and betting begins. Each subsequent round of betting comes after each survivor has received another card. The fourth, fifth and sixth all come face up and the seventh is down as a third hole card. The complex percentages (*see pages 280 to 283*) become even more challenging and exciting when wild cards are judiciously introduced.

EIGHT-CARD STUD

Seven-Card Stud plus a fourth hole card, dealt last.

HIGH-LOW

To many, this is the quintessence. When played well, it embodies the entire bag of Poker techniques and is death for anyone whose own play is weak. As in the Draw varieties of High-Low, this awards half the pot to high hand and the rest to low hand. Being able to select any five-card combination available in a seven-card holding, a player sometimes qualifies for both high and low, or thinks he does. Declarations of intent are made either before or immediately after the final round of betting, depending on local preference. First to speak is highest exposed hand, with others following in usual clockwise sequence. Or simultaneous declarations may be made by exposing chips—red for high, white for low and both colors for the whole pot.

A pretty feature penalizes a player who declares for both high and low and fails to win both at the showdown. Having offered to win both, he must do so or lose the half of the pot that he might otherwise have won.

Low hands rank as in Lowball (*see page 251*).

LOW HOLE CARD WILD

In any seven-card game, each player's lowest hole card may be regarded as wild, along with any other card of the same rank in his own hand. In older versions, the last card is always dealt down, which places too great a premium on luck: if the seventh card turns out to be too low, a perfectly nice hand can be ruined. In a better version, each player gets the last card up or down, depending on his best guess about the probabilities. If he wants the card down, he turns up one of the two down cards already held. If he wants the card up, he retains the original two hole cards.

FOUR-FOUR-FOUR

Stud with four cards up, four down and the fours wild. First three cards are dealt down, and so is the eighth. Betting starts after deal of the first up card. Anything less than a full house is probably a loser.

THREE-THREE-THREE

Three up, three down and threes wild. Betting starts after deal of two down and one up. Last card arrives down.

FOLLOW THE QUEEN

In any Stud game, it can be decided that a queen dealt face up converts the player's next card into a wild one, along with any others he holds of like rank. But if he gets another queen, it cancels the effect of the earlier one, and if followed by a new up card, makes it wild.

When dealer's fourth up card is a queen, everyone's wild cards revert to their face value. In this circumstance, the deal of the final down card is followed by a card face up in the center of the table (a *spit* card). Whoever holds one or more of the deck's three other cards of the same rank may use them as wild ones.

FIVE AND TEN

Fives and tens are wild provided that the player holds both ranks. Holding only one or more fives or one or more tens does not entitle the player to use them as wild cards. Hands lower than four of a kind are seldom productive.

BASEBALL

This far-out variation is mainly luck, yet a player aware of probabilities has an advantage, as in any other even remotely legitimate form of Poker. Here are Baseball's features:

1. All nines are wild.
2. A three in the hole is wild.

3. A face-up three may eliminate the player.
4. A face-up four entitles the player to an extra card.

In some games, a three dealt face up requires the player to drop at once. In others he can remain by betting an amount equal to the entire pot. When he does this, all threes become wild.

Warning: When dealt an up three, do not match the pot unless your hand is an absolute immortal.

CHICAGO PIANO

Here's another for persons who prefer games of chance. It combines features of Mexican Rollover, Low Hole Card Wild and High-Low. And it departs the realm of real Poker by making every player's low hole card wild not only for him but for everyone else. Thus, in a seven-player game, it is possible to have a showdown involving twenty-eight wild cards.

The fracas begins with a deal of three down cards, followed by simultaneous exposure of one of them. Then a round of betting. Then another deal, another rollover and more betting. The final card always remains face down and, since it can be lower than the other down cards, can ruin the hand.

SEVEN-CARD NO PEEKIE

The two extra cards compound the anxieties of regular No Peekie (*page 258*).

ANACONDA

This resembles Pass the Garbage (*page 252*) and falls somewhere among Draw, Stud and insanity. Closed seven-card hands are dealt. After a round of betting, each player passes three unwanted cards to player at his left. Another round of betting is followed by a pass of two cards. Then more betting and a pass of one card. Each player now discards two cards, after which all roll one card at a time, betting after each roll. This is best played high-low, with wild cards.

TNT

Or Big Sol. Like Anaconda but without the passing of unwanted cards. Betting begins after deal of first three cards of the closed hand. More betting after each additional card. After the seventh card and fifth round of betting, play is identical with that of Anaconda.

PICK UP AND ROLL

Like Seven-Card Stud until the final down card is dealt. At that point each holding is taken up as a closed hand, as in Pig Stud (*page 260*). Each player is allowed to discard and draw up to two cards. After this come two rolls and other proceedings identical with Pass the Garbage (*page 252*). Better when played high-low.

4 CENTER-CARD POKER

In recent years Poker fashion has embraced a group of games that feature small closed hands, a draw and one or more cards exposed at center table and shared by all. After years of cutthroat Stud, the Poker now favored among players of high-stakes "championship" freeze-out is Hold 'Em, a game of enormous subtlety. In Hold 'Em and other members of this family, cards displayed on the table must be counted as part of each contending hand at the showdown. This complicates the percentages of ordinary Draw or Stud. The individual must now reckon with the fact that everyone else has been drawing in hope of matching the same exposed card or cards. The daddy of this good trend is Spit in the Ocean, long popular in its own right.

SPIT IN THE OCEAN

After ante, each player gets four cards down. A single card then goes face up on the table. It is wild, along with the others of its denomination. After a round of bets (often with a minimum opening requirement as in Jackpots), a draw is held. Each player is allowed to draw up to three cards. After another spell of betting comes the showdown. Each player's hand includes the four cards he holds plus the wild card exposed on the table. A popular variation eliminates the draw but features betting after the deal of each round of down cards. And some groups follow this with a draw.

HOLD 'EM

Known in the West by this name or Hold Me, Hole Me, High Hold 'Em or Hold Me Darling, this one challenges the best efforts of the foremost Poker operatives in the land. Betting begins after two down cards are dealt. Then come three up cards on the table and another round of bets. Two more rounds follow exposure of a fourth and then a fifth card at the center of the table. For the showdown, each survivor must use both his closed cards with any three from the center. Wild cards are rarely used in this game and are not necessary. Strategy and tactics are held to be almost occult, but need not be. In this as in all other Poker, it is elementary to refrain from betting important money in *hope* of improving a bad holding. If the two closed cards are ill matched and of low rank, it pays to drop. If they are somewhat more prepossessing but produce nothing in combination with the first three exposed cards, it is suicidal to stay. In the variation called Omaha, center cards are exposed one at a time, with betting after each is turned up.

WILD WIDOW

Like Spit in the Ocean, except that the center card only establishes the denomination of the wild cards. After center card is exposed, players get a fifth closed card and play proceeds as in Draw. The chief difference, of course, is that a round of betting follows exposure of the wild widow, and another one occurs before the draw.

CRISSCROSS

Several dozen games feature a tableau of down cards at center table. The most familiar looks like this:

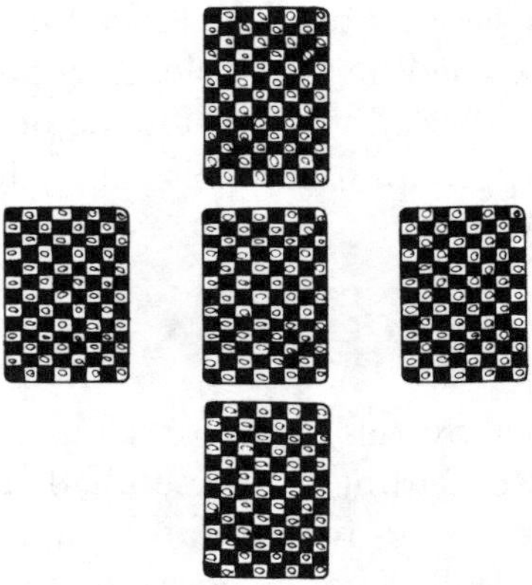

The individual holding is usually two closed cards, although as many as five are dealt in some places. A round of betting comes after each of the tableau cards is exposed by dealer. In most places, the center card of the crisscross is wild, and so are others of its rank. If the individual closed hand contains more than two cards, discards are made before the showdown, in which the player's own two cards are combined with either the vertical or horizontal three of the tableau.

Innumerable variations are possible. In one, allegedly imported from Colombia and known as The Elbow, only three cards appear at center table:

The card at the point of the elbow is wild, along with the other three of its rank. After the wild one has been exposed and the third round of betting takes place, each player is permitted to discard and draw one card if he chooses.

Yet another variation, a European monster called Tablatura, calls for two-card closed hands and a closed tableau like this:

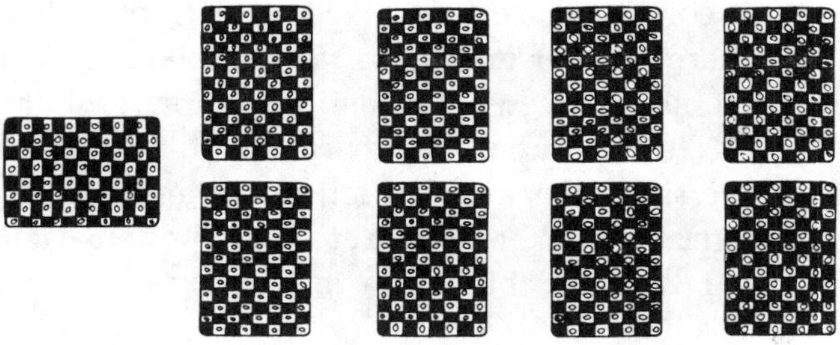

The vertical pairs of cards are exposed one at a time, followed by a round of betting. The card at the end is faced last and is wild, along with the deck's other three of that rank. After another round of bets, showdown requires the player to use his own two cards, plus the wild card, plus two from any *horizontal* row. If by some chance he does not want the wild card, he has the option of using three from one of the horizontal rows.

In a game called Cincinnati, the tableau of five closed cards includes no wild ones, but at showdown—after the usual series of exposures and betting rounds—any or all of the tableau cards may be used for improving the individual hand. Another kind of Cincinnati permits the dealer to designate one of the down cards as wild before betting begins. And in Dizzy Liz, each player gets a closed hand of five, opening bet can be made only with jacks or better, and facing of a four-card tableau does not begin until after the opening round of bets.

In all these tableau games it is highly unusual to win with less than a full house.

TWIN BEDS AND THE LIKE

This carries the new trend to excess. Five-card closed hands plus a tableau of ten cards—five to a column. Betting begins as in Tablatura, after exposure of the first pair of center cards, one from each column. First to be heard from is player at left of dealer. The next round of bets begins with the first player's left-hand opponent, after exposure of the next pair. And so on. After all ten of the center cards have been faced, a period of rolling occurs, as in Pass the Garbage (*page 252*). At showdown, high-low is customary. In some games the player can use only two of the tableau cards (selected from only one column in certain places and from either or both columns elsewhere). Other groups permit the player as many of his own cards in combination with as few or as many of the tableau cards as he needs to come up with the best possible high or low hand. One popular version allows construction of seven-card hands to compete for high, for low, or both. Yet others permit each to build two five-card hands, one for high, the other for low.

5 POKER PROBABILITIES

As indicated earlier, Poker success is less a matter of shrewd psychology than hard knowledge. Whoever combines a grasp of the game's percentages with a sufficiently cool temperament and adequate powers of concentration can play as well as he or she might care to. But without the percentages, the cool, the concentration and the desire will be of little avail.

The casual Poker player (that confirmed loser) need not memorize the following tables. For that matter, neither need anyone else. But a reading of them provides a feeling of the principles in which effective play is rooted.

Table One sets forth the statistical basis for the ranking of conventional Poker hands.

TABLE ONE

Odds Against Drawing Any Hand in a Five-Card Deal

Hand	*Possibilities*	*Odds*
Royal Flush	4 (one per suit)	649,739–1
Straight Flush	36	72,192–1
Four of a Kind	624	4,164–1
Full House	3,744	693–1

TABLE ONE (*Cont.*)

ODDS AGAINST DRAWING ANY HAND IN A FIVE-CARD DEAL

Hand	*Possibilities*	*Odds*
Flush	5,108	508–1
Straight	10,200	254–1
Three of a Kind	54,912	46–1
Two Pairs	123,552	20–1
One Pair	1,098,240	1.4–1
No Pair	1,302,540	1–1
Total	2,598,960	

NOTE: The existence of only four royal flushes is obvious enough, since only one such five-card hand occurs in each of the four suits. The odds are calculated by subtracting 4 from the total number of possible five-card hands in a deck and making a ratio of the remainder and the 4. Thus the odds against a royal flush are 2,598,956–4, or 649,739–1. Less apparent is the table's justification for asserting the possibility of 624 hands containing four of a kind. After all, only thirteen denominations exist, and only thirteen fours of a kind can be hoped for. Right? Wrong. The table's statistics are quite properly based on all possible five-card deals. Each four-of-a-kind combination can be dealt in forty-eight different hands, each of them including a different fifth card. And 13 × 48 is 624.

An indispensably valuable set of statistics enables the player to learn how the number of players at the table affects the probabilities on a given hand.

TABLE TWO

Depending on the number of players, here are the percentages of hands in which a given holding is likely to be the strongest hand after the deal but before a draw.

	Players					
Hand	7	6	5	4	3	2
Three of a Kind	84%	87%	89%	92%	94%	97%
Two Pairs	63%	68%	74%	80%	86%	93%
Pair of Aces	49%	55%	62%	70%	79%	89%

TABLE TWO (*Cont.*)

Hand	*Players* 7	6	5	4	3	2
Pair of Kings	48%	54%	61%	69%	78%	88%
Pair of Queens	32%	38%	46%	56%	68%	83%
Pair of Jacks	25%	32%	40%	50%	63%	79%

NOTE: As a rule of thumb, a Poker expert is unlikely to call any bets unless his chances immediately after the deal rate at least 50% on the chart. Exceptions arise when he is bluffing.

In deciding whether to remain around for the draw, it is essential to compare the odds against improving the hand with the odds likely to be paid by the pot. A good player does not accept 5–1 odds if the chances against winning are that high. He looks for much more favorable payoffs than that. Playing only when percentages are favorable, or when opponents can be hornswoggled into making them favorable with ill-considered bets, the expert assures himself of the margin he needs. He loses minimum amounts on his losing hands and insists on being overpaid for his winning hands.

TABLE THREE

ODDS AGAINST IMPROVING FIVE-CARD HANDS

Holding After Discards	*Cards Drawn*	*New Holding*	*Odds*
Ace	4	Any Pair	4–1
Ace	4	Three Aces	63–1
Ace and King	3	Pair of Aces or Kings	3–1
One Pair	3	Anything Higher	2½–1
	3	Two Pairs	5¼–1
	3	Three of a Kind	8–1
	3	Full House	97–1
	3	Four of a Kind	359–1
One Pair and a Third Card	2	Anything Higher	3–1
	2	Two Pairs	5–1
	2	Three of a Kind	12–1
	2	Full House	119–1
	2	Four of a Kind	1,080–1
One Pair and an Ace	2	Two Pairs (Aces Up)	8–1

TABLE THREE (*Cont.*)

Odds Against Improving Five-Card Hands

Holding After Discards	*Cards Drawn*	*New Holding*	*Odds*
	2	Three of a Kind	12–1
Two Pairs	1	Full House	11–1
Three of a Kind	2	Anything Higher	8½–1
	2	Full House	15½–1
	2	Four of a Kind	22½–1
Three of a Kind and Any Other Card	1	Anything Higher	11–1
	1	Full House	15–1
	1	Four of a Kind	46–1
Possible Straight (open at both ends)	1	Straight	5–1
(open at one end or inside)	1	Straight	11–1
Two Cards, Same Suit	3	Flush	96–1
Three Cards, Same Suit	2	Flush	23–1
Four Cards, Same Suit	1	Flush	4½–1
Possible Straight Flush			
(open at both ends)	1	Straight Flush	22–1
(open at one end or inside)	1	Straight Flush	46–1

NOTE: Among interesting wrinkles in this table is the revelation that chances of catching two pairs when drawing to a holding of one pair are slightly better when only two cards are discarded. And chances of drawing four of a kind with the same hand are markedly larger (although absolutely remote) when discarding three rather than two cards. Note how readily this material adapts to Five-Card Stud.

In the same statistical vein, the following table gives an important hint of what can happen to a good player's strategy when the deck is stripped of some of its lower cards. Stripping the deck is an excellent idea. It makes a livelier game for four or five players. But it changes some of the probabilities.

TABLE FOUR

Odds Against Hands on Deal with 40-Card Deck

Hand	*Odds*
Straight Flush	23,499–1
Four of a Kind	1,827–1
Flush	670–1

TABLE FOUR (*Cont.*)

ODDS AGAINST HANDS ON DEAL WITH 40-CARD DECK

Hand	*Odds*
Full House	304–1
Straight	91–1
Three of a Kind	28–1
Two Pairs	12–1
No Pair	1.6–1
One Pair	1.04–1

NOTE: The plot thickens. When playing with a stripped deck, it helps to know that a flush is more than twice as difficult to obtain as a full house. If, as usually happens in North America, the players continue to consider the full house higher than the flush, it becomes foolish to chase flushes. And it is interesting to observe that a blank hand is harder to find than one with a pair!

When a joker is added to a regular deck, strange things happen to the probabilities, as the next table shows.

TABLE FIVE

ODDS AGAINST PAT HANDS BEING DEALT WITH JOKER IN 52-CARD DECK

Hand	*Odds*
Five of a Kind	220,744–1
Royal Flush	119,569–1
Straight Flush	13,285–1
Four of a Kind	919–1
Full House	437–1
Flush	367–1
Straight	139–1
Two Pairs	22–1
Three of a Kind	20–1

TABLE FIVE (*Cont.*)

Odds Against Pat Hands Being Dealt with Joker in 52-Card Deck

Hand	*Odds*
One Pair	1.3–1
No Pair	1.2–1

Note: The joker makes two pairs slightly harder to obtain than three of a kind.

This effect is maintained and others are added when the game is played with deuces or any other denomination wild. Nobody in the United States or Canada will budge from the traditional ranking of hands, but with a denomination wild, the ranking should be like this:

TABLE SIX

Odds Against Pat Hands with a Denomination Wild

Royal Flush	5,369–1
Five of a Kind	3,867–1
Straight Flush	637–1
Full House	204–1
Flush	196–1
Four of a Kind	83–1
Straight	38–1
Two Pairs	26–1
Three of a Kind	6–1
No Pair	2–1
Two Pairs	1–1

And with a stripped deck, other interesting things occur:

TABLE SEVEN

Chances of Dealing Pat Hands with 40- and 32-Card Decks

	40-Card Deck	*32-Card Deck*
Straight Flush	23,499–1	10,068–1
Four of a Kind	1,827–1	986–1
Flush	669–1	888–1

TABLE SEVEN (*Cont.*)

CHANCES OF DEALING PAT HANDS WITH 40- AND 32-CARD DECKS

	40-Card Deck	*32-Card Deck*
Full House	304–1	150–1
Straight	91–1	39–1
Three of a Kind	28–1	18–1
Two Pairs	12–1	7–1
No Pair	1.5–1	3–1
One Pair	1.3–1	1–1

At Stud Poker, a key problem is that of catching a card to form a pair with the hole card. The next table gives an indication of the chances.

TABLE EIGHT

MATCHING THE HOLE CARD IN FIVE-CARD STUD

		Odds If:	
Up Cards Already Dealt	*Number of Players*	*Hole Card Already Matched in Another Hand*	*Card Not Visibly Matched*
1	6	6.7–1	4.31–1
1	8	6.4–1	4–1
2	6	9–1	5.7–1
2	8	7.8–1	5.1–1

NOTE: This table shows that chances of pairing the hole card decrease by about 50 percent when a card of the desired rank has already been dealt elsewhere. Chances also worsen as the game proceeds, verifying the ancient belief that it is a mistake to throw good money after bad. If the holding does not beat everything in sight and a bluff is not appropriate, the expert drops out rather than gamble on a steadily diminishing likelihood.

Several times a night, the Stud player finds himself with a pair in the first two cards and a third card that does not match. What are his chances of improving the pair with the final two cards of the hand?

TABLE NINE

Improving a Pair on Final Two Cards

Players	*No Card of Desired Rank Showing in Another Hand*	*One Card of Desired Rank Showing in Another Hand*
6	2.4–1	3–1
8	2.2–1	2.8–1

Note: This is strong testimony to the advantages of catching an early pair. In a six-hand game, the odds against improving are only 5–2, and even with an opponent showing a card of the desired rank, the odds are only 3–1.

Seven-Card Stud offers percentages more generous than those of the five-card games. The trouble is that its percentages apply to everyone at the table, putting the individual back where he started —with nobody but himself to blame for his losses. We have already noted the odds against filling a straight in five-card games. The following table shows how much easier it is to get such a hand at Seven-Card Stud. Which means, among other things, that a straight is less often a winner at Seven-Card.

TABLE TEN

Odds Against Filling a Straight (Seven-Card Stud)

Hand	*Odds*
5-6-7-8	1.3–1
5-6-7-8-x	2.2–1
5-6-7-9	2.7–1
5-6-7	4.3–1
5-6-7-9-x	4.6–1
5-6-7-8-x-x	4.7–1
5-7-8-9-J-x	4.7–1

TABLE TEN (*Cont.*)

ODDS AGAINST FILLING A STRAIGHT (SEVEN-CARD STUD)

Hand	*Odds*
2-3-4 or J-Q-K	6.6–1
5-6-7-9-x-x	10.5–1
2-3-4-x	12.2–1
A-2-3 or Q-K-A	12.9–1
5-6-7-x-x	21.7–1
A-2-3-x or Q-K-A-x	24–1

NOTE: Apparent slight differences in hands may cause wide fluctuation of the odds against filling. For example, 5-6-7-8 has more than twice as good a chance of panning out as does 5-6-7-9. On reflection, we realize that the first holding needs only one card at either end (a 4 or 9), whereas the other must have either two cards at one end (3-4) or a single card in the middle (8).

Filling a straight open at only one end (A-2-3) is three times as difficult as making one with a sequence open at both ends (5-6-7).

And now a table showing how easy it is to fill a flush at Seven-Card Stud provided you begin with four successive cards in the same suit.

TABLE ELEVEN

ODDS AGAINST FILLING A FLUSH (SEVEN-CARD STUD)

Hand	*Odds*
S-S-S-S	1.1–1
S-S-S-S-x	1.9–1
S-S-S-S-x-x	4.2–1

TABLE ELEVEN (*Cont.*)

Odds Against Filling a Flush (Seven-Card Stud)

Hand	*Odds*
S-S-S	4.6–1
S-S-S-x	8.4–1
S-S-S-x-x	22.8–1

NOTE: In a typical game of Seven-Card Stud, with no wild cards, a flush is good enough to win most hands. This table is well worth committing to mind. For example, note how the odds rise when the fourth card is of a suit different than the first three.

To beat a flush, somebody must hold a full house or better. The next table shows the odds against achieving this in Seven-Card Stud.

TABLE TWELVE

Odds Against Full House or Better (Seven-Card Stud)

Hand	*Odds*
7-7-7	1.5–1
7-7-7-K	1.6–1
7-7-7-x-x	2–1
7-7-7-x-x-x	3.6–1
7-7-6-6	4.2–1
7-7-6-6-x	7.1–1
7-7-6-6-x-x	10.5–1
7-7-x	12.7–1
7-7-x-x	18.6–1
7-7-x-x-x	37.5–1

NOTE: Here again is dramatic evidence that the first three cards of the deal are critically important in Stud. If they match, the odds against filling a high hand remain comfortable until the very end of the deal. But if the third card does not match the first two, the odds soar with each successive unmatching card. Again, it simply is not good Poker to defy these odds—except when bluffing in hope of fattening the opponents for a later kill.

Recommended Reading

In the vast literature of Poker, the authorities and their books tend to repeat themselves and one another. Serious students of the game will find that the following works avoid that dreary pitfall, each containing material of extreme interest:

Irwin Steig, *Poker for Fun and Profit* (Cornerstone Library).
Herbert O. Yardley, *Education of a Poker Player* (Simon and Schuster).

6 BLACKJACK

In addition to being the most popular card game played in American gambling casinos, Blackjack turns up in many a living room. Known in those circumstances as Twenty-One, Van John or Vingt-et-Un (as well as Blackjack), it offers rules more equitable than those of the casino version and is a first-rate game for sociable gamblers. Its ancestry has been traced to a simpler pastime, The Farm, which originated in France and with which we deal later.

The difference between private and casino Blackjack is that the casino pits the player against the house under rules that give the dealer (a house employee) an advantage. This will be discussed in our section on casino gambling. At home, each player also competes against the dealer (rather than against the other players), but the advantage lies with whoever can remember exposed cards and appraise the interesting likelihoods of the game.

Players and Deck

Five to nine make the best game, but two or three can also pass the time enjoyably, and more than twelve can be accommodated at a large table with a double or triple deck. The regular 52-card deck is used, with ace counting 1 or 11, picture cards 10 and others their pip value.

Cut, Shuffle and Deal

First player to draw a jack becomes dealer and banker, remaining so until someone captures that privilege by getting *blackjack* (a *natural*), a combination of an ace and a picture card as the first two cards of a hand.

In dealing, care is taken to prevent exposure of the deck's bottom card. To avoid this, the best procedure, after cutting, is to place a joker at the bottom of the deck. Another way is to *burn* the top card of the deck—showing it to all before putting it on the bottom.

Dealer gives one card face down to all. Beginning with player at dealer's left, each looks at his card and announces how much he will bet on the hand (limits may be set according to group preference). Having seen his own card, dealer may double the bets. And, in response, any player who continues to think he will beat the dealer may then redouble his own bet. Whether or not dealer chooses to launch the doubling-redoubling process, he then deals a second down card, except to himself. His own second card is dealt up.

The Play

Player at dealer's left starts. If he holds blackjack, he turns up his ace and 10-count card at once and dealer pays him twice his wager (eight times the original wager if he redoubled). But if dealer also has blackjack, the player loses his bet. And if dealer is the only one to catch blackjack on the hand, all pay him double their bets.

If player at dealer's left holds cards with a count of considerably less than 21, he usually asks for another card by saying "Hit." Or he may choose to *stand* (*stick*) by saying either of those words or "I'm good." He may continue to hit, one up card at a time, until he reaches 21, comes as close as he dares, or *busts* (accumulates cards counting to 22 or more).

If he busts, he must expose his cards at once, losing his bet to the dealer. After he has busted or stood or collected on a natural, dealer moves to the next player.

When a player's first two cards are of the same rank, he may turn both up and *split the pair*, getting a new down card on each and playing two hands at twice his previous bet. If one of the new down cards matches the earlier pair, that part of the hand may again be split, giving the player three hands in all. When one part of a split hand turns up with blackjack, it is not treated as a natural. If it wins, it earns only the payment that would be made if it were a winning hand of a different count, and its holder does not win the deal.

Another option arises when a player's first two cards count to 11. On revealing them, he may then get a single down card. This is called *doubling down.* The player's original bet is doubled, and he may collect no additional cards.

After all deals to other players are complete, the dealer turns his down card up (assuming that he had not already done so because he held blackjack and needed to show it to defeat an opponent's blackjack).

Dealer may hit or stand as he sees fit. He may not split or double down. When satisfied with his hand, he announces "I'm good." Surviving players now expose their hands. Dealer wins from all those whose counts are not higher than his. If he holds a lower count, he pays. And, of course, if he hits and busts, he pays everyone except those who busted during the earlier phase of the deal.

When deal changes hands because someone caught blackjack, a new shuffle is in order. If two had blackjack, deal passes to the one who got his cards first.

In some places, deal rotates, which is not as much fun. One variation requires each new dealer to post a *bank,* passing the deal clockwise after he has lost or doubled whatever sum he chose to risk as his bank. In yet another variation, the deal is auctioned off to highest bidder, who then posts his winning bid as the bank. He retains the deal until he loses the money in the bank, or doubles it, after which another auction is held.

Most groups award bonuses to players who hit three times without busting (Five-Card Charlie). A player with such a hand is paid double and cannot lose, even if dealer draws 21. A Six-Card Charlie is sometimes paid four times his bet. Dealer cannot collect such bonuses, but only pays them.

Strategy

Because the rules of parlor Blackjack are fair to the player vis-à-vis the dealer, the game is not quite as popular as it used to be. This paradox is traceable to the best-selling *Beat the Dealer* by Edward O. Thorp and other published computer studies that enable any good card player to keep track of exposed cards, recognize when the remainder of the pack is balanced in his own favor and tailor his bets accordingly. Indeed, these techniques put the innocent living-room dealer at a dreadful disadvantage.

A simple basic strategy for noncounters of the cards is to stand with as little as 13 when dealer's up card is an eight or less. When dealer shows a nine or higher, the player stands on no less than 15.

Dealer generally hits with 16 or less. His usual assumption is that surviving opponents hold 17 or more, especially if his own face card is a ten or eleven. To be sure, if dealer exercises his own card memory, and combines it with awareness of his opponents' pet tactics, he varies his play to suit the immediate situation.

As to splitting and doubling down, the casual player is best advised to split no pair but aces and avoid the other kind of extra play entirely.

THE FARM

This oldest surviving ancestor of Blackjack uses a regular deck stripped to forty-five cards by removal of the eights and all sixes but the 6 ♡. Players try to hit exactly 16.

Dealer, called *farmer,* wins that honor in an auction after all ante. His winning high bid goes into the pot. Cards are dealt from the bottom of the deck, the first down and the rest up. When a player goes over 16, he does not reveal his *hole card* until after the farmer completes his own turn. Losing players pay farmer one chip for each point over 16. Players who stop below 16 but lose to the farmer pay only one chip for the loss.

Any player who hits exactly 16 becomes farmer. In case of a tie at 16 (which can include the farmer), winner is whoever holds the 6♡. If none has it, the one with fewest cards wins. If tie still prevails, winner is player closest to farmer's left.

If nobody hits 16, the player closest to 16 without busting gets a chip from everybody else, including farmer, and ties are broken as above. The game is best played defensively, standing on 9 or better, which limits losses to one chip but pays off when the first two cards total 16 and the pot can be collected.

SEVEN AND A HALF

Like Blackjack, except that deck is stripped of eights, nines and tens. Players try for a count of 7½, with aces counting 1, pictures ½ and others pip value. Dealer may double the stakes, but no redouble is allowed. Dealer wins ties.

MACAO

Here the 10-count cards of Blackjack count zero and the goal is a count of 9. Before getting first down card, player bets. He wins triple if dealt a nine. For an eight, he wins double. For a seven, he wins whatever he bet. Dealer wins if his own first card counts higher than the player's. From then on, the routines resemble those of Blackjack.

QUINZE

A game for two, with deal alternating. After each gets a down card, play proceeds as in Blackjack, with stake going to whoever hits 15 or closest to it (without busting). If nondealer busts, he does not reveal it until dealer has finished own play. When both bust, or if they tie, the bet doubles on the next hand.

7 OTHER SHOWDOWN GAMES

PUT AND TAKE

Sheer luck, but fun for as many as eight players. Each gets five cards, dealt face up from a regular 52-card deck. Dealer then places the first of five *put* cards face up at center table. Any player who holds one or more cards of the same rank as a put card must pay the kitty for each such coincidence. In some games the penalty is one chip on the first put card, two on the second, through five on the fifth. In stiffer games, payment equals the face value of the matched put card—thirteen for king down to one for ace. Or the price may double on each round, starting with one chip on the first round and reaching sixteen on the fifth.

After the five puts, dealer turns up the first of five *take* cards. Players able to match it now withdraw money from the kitty at whatever rate governed earlier payments. If the kitty runs short during this phase, dealer pays the difference. And if any money is left over at the end of each hand, the dealer gets it. The deal rotates clockwise. First dealer is designated by cut for high card.

BANKER AND BROKER

Although it is possible to generate elaborate procedures for this game, it is a simple cutting of the cards, with high card winning and the banker collecting on ties. Ace ranks high, two low. Almost any number can play. Having won the deal by cutting high card, banker cuts deck into as many piles as there are players, including himself. Each player places a bet on whichever face-down pile appeals to him —except the one already selected by the dealer. In most versions, a player may place separate bets on as many piles as he pleases (except dealer's), but the amount of any bet is limited by prior agreement. After all bets are down, dealer flips over his own pile, exposing the bottom card. If it is an ace he collects all bets without further ado. Otherwise, he turns over the other piles, paying those whose cards are higher than his own, but winning all ties. Deal passes to first player who wins with an ace. The deal is highly desired because of the advantage of collecting on ties.

RED DOG

A game of skill for as few as two or as many as eight, using a regular 52-card deck.

Ante and deal as in Draw Poker, with dealer selected by cut for high card. Player at dealer's left decides whether the percentages give him a bettable chance of holding and displaying a card of like suit and higher rank than that of the card presently face down atop the remainder of the deck. If he believes his chances are good, he places his bet in front of him in an amount ranging as high as the entire pot. Dealer then faces the top card of the stock. If the player guessed right, he collects from the pot, and places his entire hand, along with the stock card, face down on a discard pile. If he loses, he must reveal his full hand to the other players before discarding it. His losing bet becomes part of the pot. And now it is the next player's turn, in the usual clockwise rotation. Whenever the pot is exhausted, all players ante again. And when the pot gets too large, it is divided equally among the players. Deal rotates clockwise.

In a good variation, players are allowed to bet that they *cannot* beat the next exposed card. This two-way option places an even greater premium on card memory and knowledge of percentages, making for a livelier game.

Beyond his memory of cards already exposed, the successful player must know how to compute percentages. The simplest example would be the situation of the first player, before he has seen any cards but his own. To estimate his chances, he calculates the number of cards that can beat his own in each suit. If he holds no spade, for example, thirteen cards can beat him in that one suit. If he holds the A ♡, no heart can beat him. If the total of all cards likely to beat him is below twenty-five, the odds are distinctly in his favor. More precise odds may be computed by remembering all cards previously exposed. A good player sitting in the catbird seat, after all others have played and the stock is low, can tell to within a few percentage points what the odds are. With a holding full of picture cards, and all aces previously exposed, the odds are overwhelmingly in his favor.

IN BETWEEN

This is a tough gambling game for as few as two or as many as can sit at the table. Dealer is selected by cut for high card. After an ante, everybody gets two down cards from a regular 52-card deck. In the usual order beginning at dealer's left, players bet whether the top card of the remaining portion of the deck will rank between the two cards of his hand. Suits and colors do not matter. Cards rank from ace down to two. In most versions, a player can bet an agreed-on minimum or may increase the stake as he pleases, limited by the total amount contained in the pot. If he wins, he collects from the pot. When he loses, he pays the pot. Whenever the pot empties, a new ante takes place. Deal passes clockwise after each complete round, and each new deal is preceded by a new ante. A player who holds an ace and a two has the best possible hand, but loses if the top card of the stock is an ace or a two. For drama and convenience, dealer tosses top card of deck to the bettor, face up, immediately after the bet is made. After everyone has bet, including dealer, the deal moves clockwise, cards are shuffled and a new ante is made.

PART FOUR

The Best Games of Solitaire

Solitaire sounds lonely. The melancholy is not relieved by the alternate name—Patience. Yet the best games of Solitaire are among the most interesting pastimes ever devised for card play. Solitaire need not be played in dark parlors. It need not even be played alone. When gambling casinos were more numerous and less industrialized than they now are, Solitaire could be played against the house, for big money. Solitaire was fun in those days, and still is.

During Hoyle's era, this group of games was deemed unfit for male attention. The direct descendant of ancient attempts to tell fortunes, Patience was strictly a lady's amusement. And it was a woman who finally popularized the games. In 1870, Lady Cadogan's *Illustrated Games of Patience* converted Solitaire from a sitting-room time killer into an international fad. By the end of the century, a good deal of money was changing hands on the outcome of the casino versions.

The varieties of Solitaire are beyond number. One modern student of games, Norman Monath, has managed to search out and appraise hundreds of the more popular. We are indebted to him for introducing order into the subject with his observation that all Solitaires fall into one of three main categories. The more prominent games, such as Klondike and Canfield, are games in which the object—as

Monath points out—is to *build* numerical sequences. In other Solitaires, the object is to *match* cards or *add* cards.

The building games, which form the largest group, usually involve a *tableau,* a center-table arrangement on which the player attempts to develop patterns from which individual cards may be conveyed to the *foundation,* where the final test of luck and skill occurs. In process, the player may be allowed to draw cards from a *talon,* which gets its own cards from a *stock* or a *hand* or both.

1 KLONDIKE AND BUILDING GAMES

For countless North Americans, Solitaire begins and ends with Klondike or one of its many variations.

The Tableau

After shuffling, the player places a horizontal row of seven cards face down. Then, beginning with the second card from the left, he places another face-down card on each, and returns to the third card from the left to continue building piles of cards. The pile at the extreme right finally contains seven cards, the adjoining pile has six, and so on to the extreme left, which has only one.

The top card of each pile is face up. The remaining cards go face down in front of the player as his hand.

The Play

Top card from the hand goes face upward alongside it to begin the talon. It may be used on the tableau or on the foundation, which begins to develop at the instant an ace appears. This ace and (the player hopes) each other ace go above the tableau to form the beginnings of piles in which the cards of each suit will be stacked sequentially, from ace (at bottom) to king (at top).

Building takes place not only on the foundation but on the tableau, where crafty management of the cards—plus a little luck—makes them available for use on the foundation.

In building on the tableau, the player is challenged by the need to get at the twenty-one cards that are concealed face down on six of the piles. To reach them, he must move the top exposed cards from each pile, making a face-down card accessible. Klondike's rules permit tableau building when the player finds that he can place on one exposed tableau card another card that is of the opposite color (red or black) and of next lower rank. Thus:

Cards for tableau building may be taken from the top of the talon or from the tableau itself, but not from the foundation. Cards placed on the foundation are frozen for the remainder of the game.

Note that tableau building produces vertical rows in which all exposed cards are left visible by partial overlapping. If the card at the low end of a tableau column turns out when exposed to be the Q ♡ and an exposed card in another column is the J ♠, the player can get to the card concealed beneath the J ♠ simply by moving the jack *and the cards that rest on it* to a position partly overlapping and extending downward from the queen. Or if the jack were not toward the head of its column but the player wanted the card on which it rested, he would move the jack and the cards (if any) below it to the Q ♡.

When vacant spaces develop in the tableau, which occurs when building exhausts the individual piles, new piles may be started, but only with face-up kings. Such kings are taken from the tableau or the talon as they become available.

When the top talon card is not usable either on the tableau or the foundation, the next card from the hand is turned up and becomes the top talon card. If it can be used, the previous top talon card is again exposed and is again a candidate for use.

The game ends after every card in the hand has been exposed and no further moves are possible.

Scoring

Most Solitaire fiends believe that the game is not won unless all fifty-two cards are on the foundation. Those inclined to gamble will have a fair chance if they charge themselves 52 points at the outset and credit themselves with 5 points for each card that ends on a foundation pile. This is fair because the proper odds against complete victory are about 4–1.

FIVE-DEAL KLONDIKE

If Klondike is not won on the first hand, and no more moves are possible, the foundation is left on the table, but the tableau and the talon are reshuffled and a new deal begins with six, rather than seven, tableau piles. If necessary, this continues into a third deal (with five piles), a fourth (with four) and a final fifth (with three). For gamblers, 5 points are credited for each foundation card placed during the first deal, 4 for each that reaches the foundation during the second, and so on down to 1 per foundation card placed during the final deal.

CANFIELD

Among American casino operators at the turn of the century, none was more glamorous than Richard A. Canfield. This Solitaire was among the attractions at his establishments in New York and Saratoga Springs.

After shuffle, player deals a pile of thirteen cards face down. He turns it over and places it at his left as a stock of which only top card is visible. Next card goes face up just above and to right of stock to begin the foundation. As other cards of the same rank turn up during play they go alongside the first. Cards are played to the foundation cards in ascending sequence and must follow suit: Q ♠, K ♠, A ♠, 2 ♠, etc.

Four more face-up cards in a row at the right of the stock form the tableau. And the remainder of the deck is the hand, which is kept face down in a squared-up pile.

Player counts off three cards from the hand and turns the three up so that only the third is visible. This becomes the first talon card. Play now proceeds as in Klondike, with cards taken as player chooses, either singly from stock, singly from talon or in threes from hand. When a space occurs in the tableau, top card of the stock must be used to fill it. If stock is exhausted, then top card of talon is used. Failing that, the player fills the space from the hand.

After hand has been run through, player picks up talon, turns it face down (without shuffling) and uses it as a new hand. Process continues until game is completed or player is stalled without a possible move.

In casino play, high rollers paid $50 for the deck and won back

$5 for each foundation card. Those who managed to place all fifty-two on the foundation won $500, which suggests that the proper odds against beating this game must be much more than 10–1.

THE RAINBOW

Canfield, except that it uses a stock of twelve rather than thirteen cards, and player runs through the hand one card at a time, rather than three. Finally, the game ends after the hand has been used three times.

WHITEHEAD

A Klondike tableau, but all cards are exposed. Another card is dealt face up to start the foundation, as in Canfield. Hand is used one card at a time. Top talon card is playable as in Klondike or Canfield. Tableau building follows a descending sequence without regard to color or suit. However, it is useful to build in the same suit because a suit sequence (10 ♠, 9 ♠, 8 ♠) may be moved as a unit to another column for placement on the proper card (J ♠). Tableau spaces are filled by any uncovered card the player chooses.

CORNER CARD

This is good for play in limited space. Deal begins with the tableau—a five-card cross, all face up. A sixth card goes face up in the upper-left quadrant and establishes the foundation rank. As other cards of that rank appear, they go into the other three corners of the layout. Play to foundation cards follows the continuous sequence of Canfield—by suit and in ascending order. Play to tableau is in descending sequence and alternating color, as in Klondike, except that the cards are piled in squared stacks and only the last card of each stack is visible or usable. Hand is used one at a time, with unused cards going into a face-up talon. As space develops on the tableau, it is filled either by the top card of the talon or the top card at one of the other tableau positions. Such space must be filled before a new card can be turned up from the hand.

ACES IN THE CORNER

Corner Card except that foundation begins with aces, which are placed in the corners as they emerge during play.

THREES IN THE CORNER

In this one, the corners are occupied by threes as they appear during play. In building on tableau, three ranks below two (for some reason or other) and both color and suit are ignored. Foundation cards are built as in Canfield.

THE MASKED TWELVE

A lenient Klondike with a fancy layout. Deal begins with a horizontal row of eight face-up cards. A second row of six cards goes face down upon and partly overlapping the middle six cards of the eight already placed. A third row of six faced-up cards overlaps the previous six. On the third, fourth, fifth and sixth of the columns now come two more rows of four cards each—continuing the alternating pattern of closed and exposed cards. The layout is completed with placement of four more cards in the same pattern on the fourth and fifth columns. The finished tableau contains twelve cards face down and twenty exposed. Play proceeds as in Klondike, but is easier because of (a) all the exposed cards and (b) a rule permitting movement of partial tableau columns.

LUCKY THIRTEEN

The entire deck is dealt in a row of thirteen piles, each containing four cards, of which the top is face up and the rest are down. From there, the lenient rules of The Masked Twelve apply. A more challenging version permits tableau movement of only one card at a time, but disregards suit and color.

GOOD MEASURE

This is a difficult game to win because play begins with forty cards concealed. After removing two aces and setting them aside, player deals a row of ten piles of five cards each. Only the top card of each pile is face up. The two aces go above this tableau to start the foundation. Tableau building goes in the customary descending sequence but without regard to suit or color. Only one tableau card at a time may be moved. As kings turn up, each may be used to form an additional tableau pile. Tableau spaces are not filled. In some versions, when player forms a new tableau pile with a king, the building rules for that new pile revert to the stricter ones of Klondike, requiring alternating colors.

IDIOT'S DELIGHT

This is a Klondike played with all cards exposed. Tableau begins with a row of nine cards, each of which heads a column. As deal of tableau continues, the pattern emerges with only the one original card in the first column, two in the second, three in the third and so forth to nine in the ninth. The tableau uses forty-five cards. The remaining seven are spread in a display below the tableau and are used as the hand. Foundation play is exactly like that of Klondike. In tableau building, only one card at a time may be moved. Any hand card may be used when player chooses. As spaces appear they may be filled from the hand or with the card at the bottom of a column. The game becomes more difficult if the tableau consists of piles rather than columns so that player is unable to anticipate future moves by scanning the entire tableau.

FLOWER GARDEN

Six vertical columns of six overlapping cards each form the tableau (called *flower beds*). The undealt sixteen cards form the hand, which may be spread out below the tableau or may be held. Foundation is formed as in Klondike, but the tableau is built differently, ignoring suit and color. Only the bottom card of each column may be moved. When spaces occur they cannot be filled except with a king.

THE BELEAGUERED CASTLE

Known also as Sham Battle, this is played in much the same fashion as Flower Garden except that the layout begins with placement of the exposed foundation aces in a vertical column. Remainder of deck is the tableau, dealt in rows of six partially overlapping exposed cards—one such row to the left and another to the right of each ace. Any uncovered card may fill a tableau space.

STREETS AND ALLEYS

This is The Beleaguered Castle except that the aces are not exposed in advance. Instead, they are left in the deck and are dealt into the tableau. But spaces are left for them. Thus, each row consists of seven overlapping cards, a space for the ace (if it ever becomes available) and six more overlapping cards.

FORTRESS

A changed tableau and stricter rules of building distinguish this good game from its relatives. All fifty-two cards are dealt face up in five rows. The top row holds twelve cards divided into two groups of six separated by a space. The six cards of each group overlap, remaining visible. The four lower rows hold ten cards each, divided into overlapping displays of five each, separated by a space. Foundation begins with aces as they become available. Tableau building permits movement of only one card at a time (the exposed end card on any half row). The card must be placed only on a card of identical suit and neighboring rank. Thus, the 9 ♡ can be placed only on the 8 ♡ or 10 ♡. But a tableau space may be filled with any uncovered card the player chooses.

CHESSBOARD

This is Fortress with an option that requires skill. Foundation need not start with aces. After reviewing the problems presented by the tableau, the player can decide which rank of card is most suitable as a foundation base. All four cards of the chosen rank are then used for that purpose, with the foundation developing in the Canfield manner.

LA BELLE LUCIE

This is one of the many Solitaires in which the hand is also the tableau. Known also as Alexander the Great, Midnight Oil and Clover Leaf, it begins with a display of seventeen three-card columns (all fifty-one cards visible), with the last card also exposed. Foundation play follows the Klondike pattern. Tableau building takes place as in Flower Garden, but the descending sequences must each be in a single suit. When unable to make any more moves (a frequent problem), player leaves foundation cards intact but takes up, shuffles and redeals the tableau for a fresh attempt. After three such failures, some players grant themselves a feature called *merci,* which permits transfer of any tableau card to the foundation or, for that matter, to any convenient position on the tableau. With this lenience, the question is not whether the player will win but how many deals he requires before winning.

GOLF

Here we combine talon and foundation, playing from the tableau to the talon, instead of vice versa.

The tableau consists of seven five-card columns with all thirty-five cards visible. The seventeen undealt cards are the hand. The first card of the hand is turned over to begin the talon. Any card fully exposed at the very bottom of a tableau column may be placed on the talon if it forms a sequence with the top talon card. Suits are ignored. Example: If the top talon card is a ten, any nine or jack that happens to be available at the bottom of one of the tableau columns may be placed atop the talon pile. If all thirty-five tableau cards fit onto the talon, the player has won.

However—and here's the rub—no card may be put on a talon king, and only a two may be placed on an ace.

When play is blocked, the next card in the hand is faced and an attempt is made to find a place for it on the talon. If it does not fit, it is dead. After hand is exhausted, game ends. The name "Golf" derives from a scoring feature whereby at game's end the number of remaining tableau cards are counted and are scored as "strokes above par." Nine "holes," or deals, constitute a full game, with a net score of +36 regarded as a victory.

AULD LANG SYNE

The simple version of this good game permits the player to begin his foundation with the four aces before shuffling and beginning play. The entire shuffled pack (minus the aces) is face down. No tableau is used. Instead, the player turns over the top card of the pack and if it is not a two, which belongs on a foundation, it is used to start the first of four talon piles. Some players rule that the talons must get unusable hand cards in strict order. Others put the hand cards on whichever talon offers the best possibilities. The top card of each talon is always available for foundation play, of course. To make an even more interesting game, some do not deploy the foundation aces before the deal, but leave them in the pack and segregate them only when they turn up in the hand. Game ends when hand is exhausted or foundations are full.

CALCULATION

No tableau, but four foundation cards, one beginning with an ace, the next with a two, the third with a three and the last with a four. Suits do not matter. These basic foundation cards are removed from the deck and are placed in position before the deal. After shuffle, the pack is placed face down and top card is exposed. Object is to build on the foundation as follows:

A-2-3-4-5-6-7-8-9-10-J-Q-K
2-4-6-8-10-Q-A-3-5-7-9-J-K
3-6-9-Q-2-5-8-J-A-4-7-10-K
4-8-Q-3-7-J-2-6-10-A-5-9-K

If a faced hand card does not fit into one of the sequences, it goes onto one of four talon piles. Player may choose the talon he prefers. Cards may be played to the foundation from the talons as well as from the hand. The game ends when the hand is exhausted and, as usual, is a victory if the foundation is full.

SCORPION

This intriguing game begins with seven columns of seven cards each and a three-card *merci,* which is set aside, face down. The columns are dealt in the customary partly overlapping style. The top three cards in each of the first four columns are face down, the bottom four are exposed. All cards in the last three columns are face up.

Building is done on the cards fully exposed at the bottom of each of the columns. Any exposed card of the same suit and next lowest in rank may be used for building.

Example: If the exposed card at the bottom of one column is the

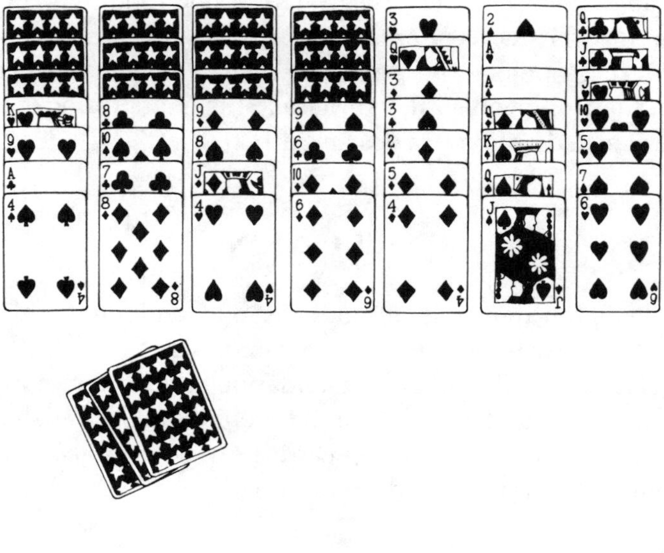

10 ♡ and the 9 ♡ lies in the middle of another column, the nine and all cards below it in its column may be moved to the ten.

When movement of cards leaves a face-down card uncovered in one of the first four columns, it may be faced up and brought into play. When a column is exhausted of cards, the space may be filled with a king (plus whatever cards happen to travel with the king).

The object, of course, is to finish with all cards arranged in four columns according to suits, from king down to ace. A good deal of time and effort can be spared by players who note impossible configurations, such as a crisscross. For example, if the 10 ♡ lies on the 3 ♠ in one column and the 4 ♠ reposes on the J ♡ in another, no way exists to unravel the pattern and win the game. A new deal is in order. If no crisscross is seen but the game stalls, the player deals the three *merci* cards face up on the first three columns. This sometimes improves the complexion of the game.

VIRGINIA REEL

Known also as Financier, this one demands considerable skill and no little concentration. Two decks are used. The player tries to transform a large tableau into a complicated array of foundations.

Before the deal, a two, three and four of different suits are arranged face up in a vertical foundation column, the two at the top and the four at the bottom. After the shuffle, seven cards go face up in a row alongside each of the foundation cards. In this display, all cards rest separately on the table, without touching.

Below the tableau, the player deals a new row of eight face-up cards. This is the talon. The remainder of the pack goes face down, serving as the hand.

The object is to build foundations in somewhat the manner of Calculation. Each of the twenty-one positions occupied by cards on the tableau must be changed into an additional foundation pile. The eight positions in the top row (which begins with the two) should develop into eight piles, each containing four cards of the same suit—2-5-8-J, with the 2 at the bottom, the 5 next, then the 8 and the J atop the pile. In the next row the suit sequence, upward from the table surface, is 3-6-9-Q. And in the third row, it is 4-7-10-K.

Play begins with exchanges of whatever twos, threes and fours are already in the tableau and can trade places with each other for proper placement as foundation cards. The next step is to see whether cards from the tableau or talon can be used to begin enlarging the new foundation piles. Naturally, after all visible twos, threes and fours have been placed, the search begins for fives, sixes and sevens of appropriate suits.

As soon as the player is stuck for a move, he deals eight new talon cards, carefully overlapping them on the original eight, which remain visible (a tactical help as the game unfolds). An unbreakable rule requires the player to *fill immediately* any vacancy on the tableau. This means that he cannot cause such a vacancy without first assuring himself that the needed two, three or four is available elsewhere on the tableau or in the fully exposed portion of the talon. He cannot create the vacancy and then deal new talon cards hoping to find the needed two, three or four among them.

The game ends after the hand is exhausted and no more plays can be found.

Note that aces are useless. When they appear in the talon they simply are borne off and replaced. If part of the tableau, they are replaced with twos, threes or fours.

SPIDER

Similar to Scorpion but much more challenging. Two decks. Ace is low, king is high. Ten piles of four cards each are dealt face down in a row. A fifth down card is added to the four piles at the left of the row. Each of the ten piles is now topped with a face-up card. The remaining fifty cards are stacked face down as the hand.

The object is to shunt cards around the tableau to develop complete single-suit sequences descending from king to ace. The rules permit preliminary building in any descending sequence, regardless of suit. But a single-suit sequence (10 ♢-9 ♢-8 ♢-7 ♢) can be moved as a unit, whereas a sequence of mixed suits (10 ♢-9 ♠-8 ♢-7 ♢) cannot, although the last two cards can be moved together, exposing the 9 ♠, which can then be moved separately.

As soon as all faced cards have been removed from a column, the down card atop the remaining pile is faced. When vacant spaces occur, they can be filled with any available card or group of cards.

When building is stalled by lack of possible moves, a new row of ten face-up cards is dealt across the top of the tableau. But a new row may not be dealt until all spaces have been filled.

As full thirteen-card suit sequences develop, they are carried off the tableau. And victory—a rare occurrence—is proclaimed when all eight suits are carried off. As experienced card players will surmise, the key to this game is getting at the face-down cards to see what they are and what can be done with them.

FORTY THIEVES

Known widely as Napoleon at St. Helena, this is a simple two-deck Solitaire with a large tableau for those with much space, time and patience. The deal creates a tableau of ten columns of four overlapping face-up cards each. The remainder of the pack is the hand.

Foundation play is the same as in Klondike. So is the tableau building except that it requires not only a descending sequence but cards of identical suit. The hand is exposed one card at a time, forming the talon. Talon cards may be spread for visibility, but only the most recently exposed one can be used. After which, of course, the most recently exposed *surviving* one can be used. Tableau vacancies may be filled at any time with any fully exposed tableau or talon card. An added feature permits movement of more than one tableau card at a time, provided that they form a self-contained sequence of one suit (*see Spider*).

After every card in the hand has been faced and further moves are stymied, the game is over. Variants use tableaus of thirty-six, thirty-two, twenty-eight or twenty-four cards simply by reducing the number of columns. In one thirty-six-card version, tableau building is exactly as in Klondike, with alternating colors rather than a single suit. In a thirty-two-card game, the builds are like those of Klondike but the aces are set out to begin the foundation as soon as they appear during the original deal of the tableau.

Other versions call for upward building rather than the customary descending sequences. And in twenty-four-card games, it often is permissible to run through the hand two or three times.

UPSIDE-DOWN PYRAMID

The curious shape of its tableau gives this two-deck Solitaire its name. After the shuffle, player deals ten columns of face-up cards. The first column consists of only one card; the second, three (overlapping for visibility and easy transfer); the third, five; the fourth, seven; the fifth, nine; the sixth, ten; the seventh, eight; the eighth, six; the ninth, four; and the tenth, two.

The remainder of the pack serves as the hand, and play is in the Klondike style.

QUEEN OF ITALY

Another two-deck Solitaire but with a couple of twists. Player deals a row of eleven face-up cards, known as *reserves*. Leaving a generous space below this row, he then faces three more cards, of which one is chosen as the foundation rank. The choice depends on the rank of the card at the extreme right end of the reserve row. Player is required to use whichever rank among the three cards will make possible the promptest transfer of the eleventh reserve card to the foundation. Foundation building is in ascending sequence and alternating colors. Thus, if the eleventh reserve were the Q ♡ or Q ◇ and one of the three cards below were a black jack, the jack would automatically become the foundation rank and would go directly below the reserves, there to form a foundation row with as many of the pack's seven other jacks as the player can locate during the remainder of the game. Lacking a black jack, the player's next choice would be a red ten or a black nine or a red eight and so on.

The foundation rank having been chosen, the remaining two cards start a third row of nine (seven being dealt from the hand). This row, below the foundation row, is the game's tableau. Building on the tableau is in descending sequence with alternating colors. Hand cards are faced one by one onto a talon pile. The top talon card is available for tableau or foundation play, as is the card at the right end of the reserves, plus any fully exposed card at the bottom of a tableau column. When all hand cards have been faced, the talon is squared off, turned down and used again as the hand. After the player has gone through the hand a second time, the game is over.

SHAH OF PERSIA

This two-deck game requires some space but offers pretty effects. All aces and kings are removed from the pack and seven of the kings are discarded. The other serves as Shah and is surrounded by the eight aces, the foundation cards.

After a shuffle, a circle of eight cards is dealt face up, one adjoining each ace. If any of these can be placed on an ace in the usual one-suit ascending sequence of a foundation pile, the move is made and the vacancy is filled from the hand. After which a third circle of eight is dealt, all possible moves are made to the foundation, and vacancies again are filled. The second and third circles are now established as *reserves* (as in Queen of Italy). Whereupon a fourth circle of eight is dealt to serve as the tableau. After foundation play and the filling of spaces, the player begins exposing cards from the hand, one at a time, trying to build in the Klondike fashion on the tableau or foundation cards. The cards in the two reserve rows may be used as if they formed a talon, but are not themselves built upon

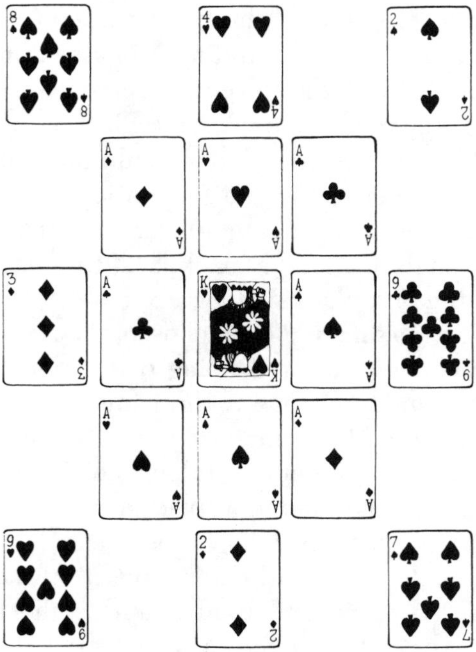

so long as they remain in their reserve positions. When the outer three cards in any row are moved, leaving only the foundation card, the two reserve positions may be filled from cards exposed on the tableau piles.

LEONI

In this intricate game, both aces and kings start foundation piles, but aces call for the usual ascending one-suit sequence, whereas cards go on the kings in descending one-suit sequence.

Before shuffling the two-deck pack, player removes an ace and a king and faces them one below the other to begin what hopefully will become foundation rows of four aces and four kings respectively.

Now things become unusual. Counting to himself, the player deals a row of six face-up cards. Whenever the card's rank corresponds to the count, it is removed and placed face down in an *exile* pile. Thus, if the fifth card in the row is a five, it heads for exile. Another card is dealt to fill its place.

After the first row of six is completed, another row is dealt, the player's mental count beginning with seven and proceeding through twelve. If a jack turns up at eleven or a queen at twelve or—for that matter—an eight at eight, the exile procedure is mandatory.

Finally, a thirteenth position is dealt face up below and to the right of position 12. And if a king materializes, it is exiled. The cycle is now repeated, with cards going into positions 1 through 13 and being exiled if their ranks correspond with the numbers of the positions. In all positions except the thirteenth, the cards are in squared-off piles. But those in the last position are spread for use as reserves.

After all cards have been dealt, play begins. The 12 positions are the tableau, from which only the top cards of each pile are playable to the foundation. Any reserve card may also be played to the foundation. As aces and kings appear, they may be moved to the top to begin the desired four foundations of each rank. But such a move can be delayed to suit the player's tactical convenience.

When no moves are possible from tableau or reserves to foundation, the exile pile becomes the hand. If a hand card is not playable to the foundation, it goes to the bottom of whatever tableau pile corresponds to its own rank. Example: A jack would go to the bottom of the pile at position 11 on the tableau. And a king would become a reserve to be played to foundation when player wished.

But when the unplayable card from the hand has been deposited in its new position, the top card of the same pile becomes playable to the bottom of whatever other pile corresponds to its own rank. This then liberates the top card of *that* pile and, unless luck is extremely bad, new cards emerge for placement on foundation.

In the foregoing situation, when the top card in a pile happens to be of a rank corresponding to the number of the pile's position, it cannot be moved to another pile, but is moved to the bottom of its own.

The player again goes to the hand after running out of moves and the process resumes. When the hand is exhausted but the game is still unfinished, one redeal is permitted. The cards from position 13 are picked up first, with those from position 12 placed under them, and so on until the entire tableau is in one unshuffled pack. The pack is turned face down and dealt as before, still without shuffling. Foundation cards remain in place.

LA NIVERNAISE

A two-deck game quite similar to Leoni, save for the appearance of its layout, plus a nice variation in foundation play.

Two columns of four exposed cards are placed on either side of a space wide enough to accommodate one foundation column of four aces and another of kings. The outer columns are called *flanks,* which may explain why the game is also known as Tourney or Tournament.

If neither flank includes an ace or a king, the game is beyond hope. Cards should be picked up for a fresh start. To avoid this nuisance, it is as well to begin by finding an ace or a king and placing it in position before shuffling and laying out flanks.

Below the flanks and the foundation spaces, player deals six columns of four overlapping face-up cards each, known as the *line.* As suitable aces and kings become exposed at the bottom of each line column, they can be placed in foundation spaces. Other cards fully exposed on the line may be used to fill vacancies on the flanks. And any flank or exposed line card can be used to build on the foundation.

In this game, unlike Leoni, it is possible to reverse the foundation sequences. Whenever an ace foundation and a king foundation are each topped with identical cards—for example a 9 ♠ on each—the player is allowed to begin building downward on the ace pile while switching to an ascending sequence on the king pile.

Whenever a line position becomes vacant, four more overlapping cards are dealt. And when play comes to a standstill, four more faced cards may be dealt to each column of the line. Finally, if no cards remain to be dealt and no moves can be made, the line cards are picked up from right to left, are turned over and, without shuffling, are dealt in rows, left to right, until six four-card columns have been formed, or until the cards run out. Two such redeals are allowed.

JAVANESE RUG

A king-size table is needed for its huge tableau, but this game has numerous addicts, and for good reason. After an ace and a king of each suit are removed from the two-deck pack, remaining cards are shuffled and dealt face up in this exotic pattern of eight columns and eight rows.

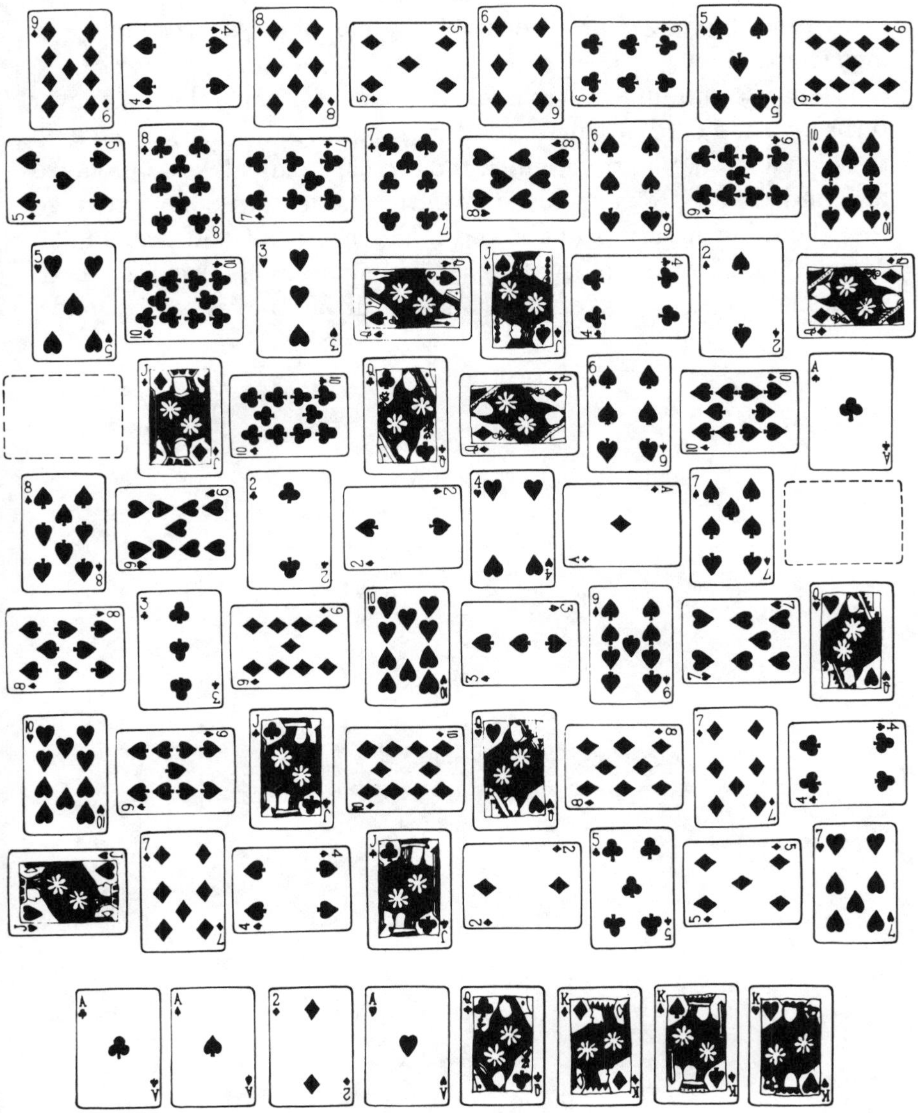

The aces and kings are placed below the tableau to begin work as the foundation. Undealt cards go face down as a hand. Foundation is built as in Leoni. Any tableau card with an exposed narrow edge can be moved to the foundation provided it is of proper rank and suit. Thus, the card at the uppermost left qualifies for placement, as does the card below it. But the card second from the left in the top row cannot be moved until removal of a neighbor exposes one of its own short edges.

When no building moves are possible from the tableau, player turns over top card of hand, and if it is unplayable, places it face up to begin a talon pile, from which the top card may always be played to foundation. Cards may also move from tableau to talon, provided that the tableau card is of the top talon card's suit and next higher or lower rank. Spaces in the tableau are never filled. The game ends when hand is exhausted of cards and no further moves can be made.

2 POKER SOLITAIRE AND MATCHING GAMES

In these Solitaires, the player tries to match cards according to suit, rank or sequence. Some offer the added attraction of numerical scoring.

POKER SOLITAIRE

Using a regular deck, the player simply turns up one card at a time, placing it wherever he pleases in what finally becomes a five-by-five square of twenty-five cards. His object is to form as many good Poker hands as possible—both horizontally and vertically. A restricted version requires that each new card be placed in a position adjoining a card previously set down (the space immediately adjacent on a diagonal is all right). Scoring follows either of two methods—American or British.

It should be noted that British scoring reflects the actual percentages of this game, whereas the American adheres to the conventional ranking of Poker hands. Strategists note that a relative high average can be maintained by playing for flushes in one direction and full houses in the other.

Hand	*Scoring* American	*Scoring* British
Royal Flush	100	30
Straight Flush	75	30
Four of a Kind	50	16
Full House	25	10
Flush	20	5
Straight	15	12
Three of a Kind	10	6
Two Pairs	5	3
One Pair	2	1

CRIBBAGE SQUARE

Whoever enjoys Cribbage will find this a pleasant game. As in Poker Solitaire, the player sets out a square of cards—in this case, four-by-four. He can place each new card wherever he chooses in the pattern. After all sixteen cards have been faced, one more serves as the starter and combines with each vertical and each horizontal hand for scoring identical to that of Cribbage (*see page 226*), even including the features of His Heels and His Nobs. A score of 61 wins.

CRIBBAGE SOLITAIRE

This time, three cards are dealt face down to the hand, two to the crib and three more to the hand. The remainder of the deck is the stock and is kept face down, with its top card faced up to serve as starter. Play proceeds exactly as in Cribbage, with hand and crib scored for the player, after which the starter card goes to the bottom of the stock, the hand and crib cards are discarded and nine more cards of the stock are used for a new hand, crib and starter. Redeals continue until stock is gone. On the last deal only four cards remain in stock and are scored as a hand, but neither His Heels nor His Nobs is counted on this final tally. A score of 121 wins, and is not easily achieved.

ACCORDION

Known also as Tower of Babel, this entertains without taxing the intelligence. A regular deck is used as the hand, from which cards are dealt one at a time in a face-up row. A dealt card of the same suit or denomination as its neighbor to the immediate left may be placed on that card. Any card may also be placed on the third card to its left provided suit or rank match. If a card to be moved already reposes on one or more other cards, the entire pile is moved. Victory consists of stacking the entire deck in one pile. Example:

The K ♣ may be placed on the 2 ♣ and then the pile of two cards can be put on the K ♡.

Among numerous variations on the Accordion theme, Striking Out Tens (or Decade) provides amusement with its challenge to discard any three successive cards whose face value totals 10, 20 or 30. Jacks, queens and kings count 10, aces 1. The row occasionally grows quite long. The goal is to end with only one card. Another variation, Marriage, begins with a queen (usually the Q ♡) as first card in the row and the king of the same suit at the bottom of the pack. Whenever cards of the same rank or suit turn up one or two cards apart, the player casts out the cards that separate the two. The object, not easily achieved, is to bring the king and queen together.

ACCORDION CRIBBAGE

A resourceful gamesman, Bill Beers, invented this one, which offers the Accordion procedure with a fine snap of Cribbage and a hint of Poker. As in Accordion, cards are dealt in a row, which can become as lengthy as fate or the player may decree.

Whenever three adjoining cards form a straight flush, three of a kind, a flush, a straight, or present a combined pip value of 15, the player scores on a Cribbage board according to the formula set forth below. When two successive cards make a pair, they also qualify for points, although the player may choose to forego those points and play a new card from the hand in hope of catching the higher score won by three-card patterns.

After a scoring combination appears and is tallied, two of the cards are brought together in a pile of their own, which remains in the row. The choice of cards for these combinations is one of the tactical delights of the game, permitting the player to form new scoring patterns —if he's lucky. As the game proceeds, not only individual cards, but piles of cards may be combined in this way.

Score adjoining cards as follows:

Straight Flush (three cards)	6
Three of a Kind	6
Flush (three cards)	3
Straight (three cards)	3
One Pair	2
15 Count (two or three cards)	2

Note: The Cribbage tradition is maintained in straights and straight flushes. For example, if 5-7-6 of two or more suits appear in that order, they are counted as a straight. If all of one suit, they form a straight flush. If the player reaches 61 points before all cards have been dealt and all moves made, he wins.

THE CLOCK

Cards are dealt face down in a circular pattern of twelve four-card piles, the position of each corresponding to a number on the face of a clock. The last four cards go face down in the center of the circle. The top card of this pile is turned up and goes to the bottom of whatever pile matches its rank. Thus, a jack belongs at the bottom of the pile at 11 o'clock, the queen at 12. And kings go under the center pile. The player then turns up the top card of the pile under which a card has just been placed and moves the new card to the bottom of the appropriately numbered pile on the clock face, then takes the top card of *that* pile, and so forth. When the pile engaging his attention contains only the four cards of its correct rank, the player moves clockwise to the adjoining pile and continues play. He wins if he manages to turn up and properly position all cards from ace through queen before the fourth king appears. But when the fourth king is faced, the game ends.

FIRING SQUAD

Player deals four cards in a face-up row, using the remainder of the deck as the hand. If two or more of the cards in the row belong to the same suit, they are removed from the game. Four more cards are now dealt, forming vertical files of overlapping cards with whatever cards remain on the original row. Once more, if any fully exposed cards belong to the same suit, they are borne off. Moreover, if any fully uncovered card has a lower denomination than a partly covered card of the same suit, the uncovered one is removed. Aces are higher than kings. As columns disappear and spaces are created, each may be filled by any fully exposed card. This helps by bringing buried cards into more active play. When all cards have been dealt and final removals made, the game is over. The object is to end with nothing but an ace in each column.

3 ADDING GAMES

Not many of these are played nowadays, which is too bad. Here are two that deserve more attention.

PYRAMID

After shuffling a regular deck, player deals a twenty-eight-card tableau like this:

The undealt cards form the hand. Its first card is faced and, if not used for immediate play, remains face up as the start of a talon. If its face value plus that of any uncovered tableau card add to 13, both cards are removed and placed on a *trash pile*, out of the game. Jacks, queens and kings count as 11, 12 and 13, others count at pip value. Whenever a king is found, it is simply added to the trash pile.

When a talon card is unplayable, the next card in the hand is faced and the game proceeds. The game usually ends when the hand is empty and all possible plays have been made. But in some versions two redeals are allowed—without reshuffling. The player wins by removing the entire tableau.

One interesting variation allows removal of tableau cards that add to 13 without use of a card from the hand. In that version, as many as three cards may be discarded from the tableau provided that one of them forms a total of 13 with each of the other two. Thus, the player might be able to cast out a 4-9-4. Some enthusiasts attempt to keep score, crediting themselves with 50 when they go out on the first deal, 35 on the second and 20 on the third. A more sophisticated tally deducts the number of remaining hand cards from the score.

BOWLING

Sid Sackson, one of the world's most gifted inventors of games, is responsible for this remarkable simulation of a great sport. Besides producing scores like those of bowling, the Sackson game requires skill and judgment.

The player uses only twenty cards—the ace through ten in both of the red or black suits. After shuffling, he deals ten of the cards face up in a bowling layout.

The remaining ten cards are dealt face down in three piles, one containing five cards, another three and the other only two. These little stacks of cards represent the bowling balls. The top card of each stack is now turned up.

The player can use whichever "ball" he chooses. If its pip value matches that of a pin card, the pin is knocked over and removed from the game. In some circumstances, to be described shortly, a ball may dispose of as many as three pins at a time. But the first ball used in any frame may never remove a pin from Row Four, and may not

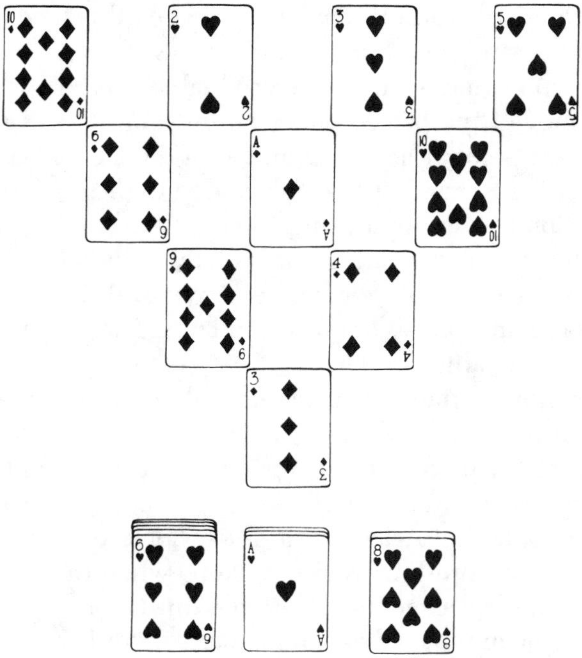

knock over the middle pin in Row Three except as part of a two- or three-pin play.

A ball card knocks out two or three pins when (a) the last digit in the sum of their pip values is identical with the last (or only) digit in the denomination of the ball card and (b) the two or three cards are adjacent in the tableau. If the "ball" is any but the very first of the frame, it can only remove a pin that is adjacent to an empty space. Or if the player is trying to knock over more than one pin with the same ball, at least one of the pins must be adjacent to an empty space.

Examples to illustrate the rules:

Using the pin pattern reproduced above, note that if the ball card is a 10, it knocks out the 9 in the second row and the 1 and 10 in the third because the sum of the three pin cards is 20, of which the last digit is 0, the same as the last digit in the denomination of the ball card.

Notice also that the rule against knocking down the middle pin in Row Three does not apply in the above case because more than one pin is going at a time. If the first ball card of the frame were a 1, it would not knock over the middle pin in the third row unless the player were sharp enough to notice that it *could* remove that pin in combination with the Number 10 pin alongside it ($10 + 1 = 11$, of which the last digit matches the number on the ball card!).

Continuing the example, after the first ball card (numbered 10) drops the 1 and 10 in the third row and the 9 in the second row, the ball card is tossed aside with the fallen pin cards and the next card on its stack is exposed. The player now chooses which of the three available ball cards to use. Another 10 would be ideal, enabling him to remove the 2, 3 and 5 in the fourth row. But he would not be permitted to knock out the pin numbered 10 in the fourth row because that pin is not adjacent to an empty space, but the pins numbered 2 and 3 are.

If all pins are knocked over, a strike is scored for the frame. When the player is unable to remove a pin with any of the three faced ball cards, the useless cards are removed to the junk pile and the next cards in the stacks are exposed. If this or a subsequent move of this kind results in all pins being removed, a spare is scored. And if all efforts result in exhaustion of the ball-card stacks without removing all pins, the number of pins already knocked out becomes the player's score in the particular frame.

Just as in real bowling, a strike in the tenth frame gives the player two more chances to score. He plays until he gets two strikes or a spare or runs out of cards and must settle for a lower count. And a spare in the tenth frame offers just one more chance to score. Either a strike or a count of less than 10 can be scored in these circumstances before the game's end.

Naturally, 300 is perfection here just as at the alleys. For optimum results, it pays to study the situation carefully. Many good combination plays are not noticeable at first glance. It also helps to keep track of the numbers of the pins and balls already removed. An alert player can have an accurate idea of what ball cards remain and can capitalize on the knowledge.

4 FOR TWO . . . OR MORE

Although Solitaire for more than one player at a time seems a contradiction in terms, it works out quite nicely.

DOUBLE KLONDIKE

Good for two, fun for three and a riot with four. Each player has his own deck, identifiable by the patterns or colors on the backs of the cards. Each deals and builds on a Klondike tableau, but only one foundation is used, and everybody plays as rapidly as possible, hoping to get his own cards onto the foundation stacks before the competitors can. Also known as Scrimble-Scramble, an apt description.

One variation is more orderly, with play in clockwise rotation, beginning with whoever displays the lowest card at the far left of his tableau. In case of a tie, play begins with the tied player nearest to the left of a player who has been appointed "caller" or referee. In yet another version, hand cards are faced as in Canfield (every third card) and may be used repeatedly. In all versions, whoever gets most cards on foundation is the winner.

MULTIPLE PATIENCE

This is simply Canfield for two or more, each using an identifiable deck of his own, building on his own tableau and attempting to place the most cards on the joint foundation. As soon as an ace appears, it must be played to the foundation, otherwise a player could reserve that key card for his own convenience.

MULTIPLE GOLF

Each player has his own deck and plays a hole of Golf (*see page 304*). Nine holes are played. The lower score on each hole gets one point or one chip. The player with the lowest total gets five.

POKER SQUARES

This is a game of skill. One player is designated *caller*. He slowly deals himself a hand of Poker Solitaire (*see page 317*), calling each card as he places it. Each other player finds the same card in his own deck and places it wherever he chooses in his own layout. After all twenty-five cards have been called and placed, individual scores are added (the British scoring system is preferable) and the winner collects the stakes. He then becomes caller on the next round.

RUSSIAN BANK

Played with a single deck, this is a less complex game than either Stung or Double-Deck Russian Bank, to be described later. Cut for deal, which gives each player a stack of twenty-six cards, face down. Dealer's opponent faces his top four cards in a row, forming half the game's tableau. He then turns up a fifth card, which plays to one of the tableau cards if it is of the same suit and adjoining rank. Thus the 4 ♠ from the hand would play to the 3 ♠ or 5 ♠, and the tableau column would then continue that ascending or descending sequence, turning the corner at 2-A-K or K-A-2. If this player's hand card is unplayable, it goes face up to begin his talon.

Dealer's first turn follows the same procedure, with his own top four hand cards completing the tableau row. He then attempts to play his fifth card and is allowed to place it on either the tableau or his opponent's talon. Beginning with his second turn, opponent has the right to play on dealer's talon. Talon building follows the same ascending or descending suit pattern as on tableau.

As spaces occur on tableau, they must be filled by the player whose moves created the vacancy. He may use either his top talon card or the fully exposed card at the foot of any tableau column. If a tableau card is chosen, the player has the privilege of reversing the sequence of the cards on its original stack. Example: If he plays the K ♠ from a tableau column, he may disclose the Q ♠ beneath it. But he may now elect to cover the K ♠ with the Q ♠ and with the J ♠ exposed by that move.

The winner is whoever gets rid of all twenty-six cards first.

STUNG

Best for two but can be played by as many as eight. Uses the regular 52-card deck, with K high, A low. Combines some of the best features of single-deck Russian Bank, Double Klondike and some pepper of its own.

Low card wins cut for deal and distributes the largest possible equal hands, which are formed into face-down packs in front of each player. Leftover cards (which are present with any number of players other than two or four) go face up to begin the four-card tableau. Tableau is best arranged in a column, for building in horizontal rows. The Klondike pattern of sequences is used, but only one card may be moved at a time.

Before tableau building is permitted, each of the four positions must be filled. And before that happens, any ace that materializes must be placed on a foundation row to begin the usual ascending suit sequences. Moreover, when the two and succeeding cards of the ace's suit appear, they must be played to the foundation before anything else can be done about the tableau.

Play begins at dealer's left. In a game for two or three, each player's first turn or two is likely to be concerned with trying to get the tableau going. Unless it is playable to the foundation, the top card of the hand goes into any vacant position on the tableau column. If unplayable on the tableau or foundation, it goes face up as the player's own talon. By which time play begins in earnest. Each player makes every legal move he can on every turn. The following order of play is mandatory:

1. Tableau to foundation.
2. One tableau row to another.
3. Tableau row to a space, permitting a foundation play.
4. Talon to foundation.
5. Talon to tableau space.
6. Talon to tableau row.
7. Talon to opponent's talon (as in Russian Bank).

Tempting though a Number 7 play may be, it must be deferred until all possible attempts have been made to find plays of higher priority. These rules make the game. Violations ruin it. To ensure observance, a player who notices a violation is allowed to declare "Stung!" Whereupon the offender gets the top card from everybody else's talon. If a player has no talon, he presents the violator with the top card from his hand. Also, the erring player must restore the tableau, foundation and other cards to the positions they occupied before his miscue.

When a player's hand is exhausted, he turns his talon face down and uses it, unshuffled, as a new hand. In most games, the winner is whoever gets rid of all his cards first. In some places, the reverse approach is taken, with the last player to have hand or talon cards being declared the loser.

DOUBLE-DECK RUSSIAN BANK

Known in some places as Crapette, this deservedly popular two-hand game enlarges the fun of Stung with numerous sophistications of its own. It uses two decks, which must be readily distinguishable from each other. From individual hands, talons and stockpiles, the players build on an eight-stack tableau and eight foundation cards. They also build on each other's stock and talon piles, often with viciously effective timing that throws the obstructed opponent into a frustrated rage.

As usual in this kind of game, the object is to get rid of all cards before the opponent can. Whoever cuts low gets choice of decks and becomes first to play after certain preliminaries have been completed. These begin when each shuffles the other's deck, returns it, and deals himself a stock of twelve cards (some prefer thirteen) in a face-down, squared-off stack situated near his right hand. Above this stockpile he places a column of four face-up cards, forming half of the tableau. The remainder of his cards are his hand. It remains face down to his left, often directly beneath the four tableau cards deployed by his opponent. This arrangement leaves plenty of room in the center for the foundation, which is started with the eight aces as these emerge during play.

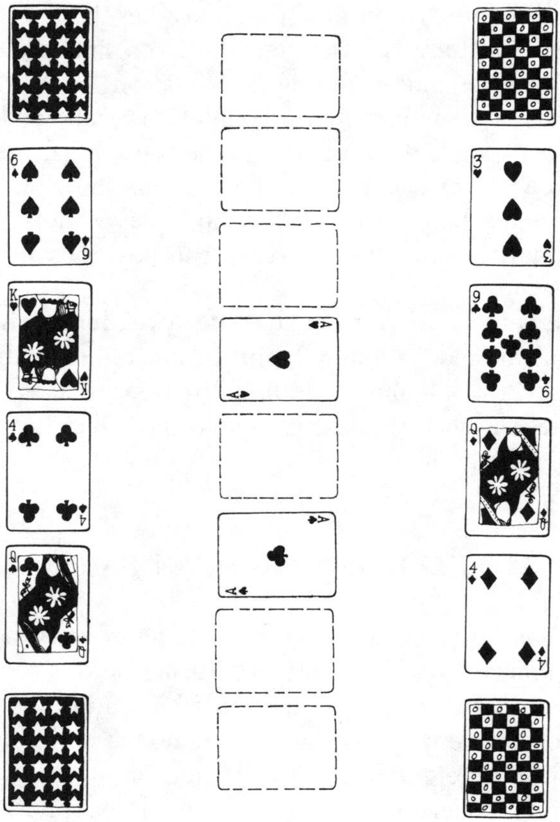

Winner of the earlier cut begins actual play, which conforms to the following priorities.

1. At his first turn, the first player begins by surveying the tableau for aces, which he moves to the center to begin the eight foundation stacks. He fills resultant tableau spaces with cards taken from the top of his stockpile. Other tableau spaces may be caused at this early stage when the player finds it possible to move one tableau card to another, building as in Stung. Again, the space is filled from stock. So are spaces brought about by shifting the two or three of a suit to a foundation ace or two.

2. When no play is found for a stock card, it goes face up atop the stockpile. The player now faces the top card of his hand, holding it while looking first for a foundation play and, failing that, a tableau play. If unable to move with the card from the hand, the player automatically concludes his turn by placing the card face up alongside the hand, beginning the talon.

3. At his first turn, the opponent makes whatever plays from tableau to foundation may have escaped his opponent's attention. He fills these and all other resultant tableau spaces from stock, the top card of which may be turned over before he begins play. With all spaces filled, he is permitted to build in either ascending or descending suit sequences on his opponent's talon and stock cards, drawing either from the top of his stock or from the tableau. When unable to use his stock card for any purpose, he is permitted to face the top card of his hand, playing first to the foundation, if possible, and then surveying the rest of the scene. His turn ends when he is out of moves and tables his hand card as first item in his talon.

4. From then on, the game proceeds by turns, with plays to the center (the foundation) continuing to take priority, and all tableau spaces filled from stock until the stock is exhausted, whereupon the hand may be used. So long as the stock has a card in it, no play may be made from the hand unless the player is unable to play the stock card. But when play of a hand card creates new opportunities for play with an exposed stock card, such play is permitted—in the usual order of priorities. Altogether logically, these new moves often reopen the possibility of traffic to opponent's stock and talon from one's own stock or hand or the tableau. The moves are permitted so long as the player continues to observe the rules governing play to foundations, the filling of tableau vacancies, and the priority of play from

stock over play from the hand. In any event, each turn ends when the player has nothing to do with a hand card but place it on his talon.

A player who notices his opponent violating priorities may say "Stop." The error must then be corrected, except if a hand or a stock card has been faced out of turn. In that case, the player calling the violation decides whether the card should be turned face down again or not. But, regardless of this, whenever a player substantiates any charge of violation, his opponent's turn ends at once. This often leaves rich opportunities for the enforcer of rules.

In some places, players yell "Stop" when an opponent so much as touches a card and then does not move it. And punishment also is levied for incorrect builds. Both these kinds of "Stop" are excessive. Persons who paw at tableau cards or others without playing them should simply be asked to discontinue the irritating practice. And incorrect builds should merely be corrected at once, without penalty.

The player who gets rid of all his stock and talon cards first is the winner. In most places this earns 30 points plus 1 more for each card in the loser's hand and talon and 2 for each card in the loser's stock.

One widely accepted variation of this game permits movement of more than one card at a time from one tableau position to another. This is achieved by departing from the conventional squared-off tableau stacks and using the kind of overlapping rows familiar in other forms of Solitaire. The player may then move any partly visible tableau card, plus all the cards built upon it, to another position on the tableau.

DESPERATION

This team game uses six regular decks, all with the same back design. Best for four or six but can be played by as few as two. Requires a lot of space.

Partnerships (if more than two persons play) may be determined by personal preference or a cut of the cards. Members of opposing teams sit in alternating positions around the table. All cut. Low card mixes all six decks and deals two twenty-one-card stacks, face down. These are the talon piles, one for each side. If odd numbers of players are involved, such as three against two, the forty-two talon cards are divided into packs of twenty-four (for the larger team) and eighteen (for the opponents).

The remaining cards are dealt in packets of five each, face down. These are the hands. To save space and provide more convenient access to the hand cards, the packets are stacked in alternating directions—the short edges of one lying parallel to the long edges of the next.

As usual, the object is to build on foundation aces—twenty-four of them in this case—and, in process, to get rid of cards. Foundation building is in ascending sequence without regard to suit or color. This combines with the game's use of numerous face-up reserve and talon cards to promote an enormous amount of activity.

The opposing player at dealer's left is called the *leader*. He takes the top five-card hand from the stack, examines the cards, and places any ace at center to begin a foundation. He keeps the remainder of his hand concealed. If nobody catches an ace on the first round of play, the leader places one of his cards before him face up on what will become four stacks of reserve cards. In turn, each player exposes one card at a time until all hands have been displayed. Naturally, the decision as to what reserve stack to choose for a card is related to the card's rank. Good players attempt to have cards of higher rank at the bottom of their reserve stacks and lower cards near the top, for ready use as the foundation grows.

After somebody's five-card hand produces the game's first ace, he turns up the top card of each talon. He then continues play to the foundation from his hand, his reserves and his team's talon (the other being exposed to help both sides plan their attacks and defenses). He also is permitted to shift cards among his four reserve stacks.

As soon as a talon card is played, the next is faced. A player's turn ends when the last card of his five-card hand is placed on a reserve stack rather than a foundation. To remain in action, he is allowed to withhold an ace from the foundation until disposing of the rest of his hand. Playing the ace (or any other card that may be last in his hand) to the foundation allows him to take another hand from the stack and continue play.

When a player neglects to move an available talon or reserve card to a foundation stack, an opponent may begin his own turn by demanding that the play be made.

The first team to empty its talon onto the foundation wins the game.

SPITE AND MALICE

Many Americans regard this as the best of all two-hand games. It combines the best elements of Russian Bank and Stung, and has replaced both at numerous tables. It is played with two decks, which must be distinguishable from each other, plus four jokers.

One deck, without jokers, is divided into two face-down packs of twenty-six cards, one per player. Each turns the top card of his pack, known as the *payoff pack* or *payoff pile*. The higher card designates the first player. In case of a tie, the packs are shuffled and new cards are exposed.

The other deck, plus the four jokers, is taken by the first player's opponent, who shuffles and deals a five-card hand, face down, to each. Remainder of the deck goes to center table as a stock.

If first player has one or more aces in his hand, he puts them in the center of the table to begin the foundation. Such play of aces and twos is mandatory throughout the game, with foundation building in ascending sequence, regardless of suit or color. Cards other than aces and twos may be reserved at player's option.

As top card of a payoff pile becomes playable to a foundation, it goes there (the object of the game), and the next payoff card is faced. When player is without foundation moves, he may play one hand card per turn to any of four discard, or talon, piles that he is permitted to start and from which he is later permitted to play to foundation cards as opportunities arise. He may not place hand cards on opponent's talon stacks. Three kinds of talon building are usually permitted—either the next lower card of the suit, or a card of identical rank and suit, or a joker substituting for a card of the same or next-lower rank. In some places, the player is also allowed to build his talons in either ascending or descending suit sequences, reversing the order at any time he pleases.

Each turn ends when a card is placed on a talon pile. Or a player may choose not to make such a play and simply end his turn by saying "Go." Before beginning his next turn, the player takes enough cards from stock to restore his five-card hand.

If stock is exhausted, all completed foundations (built from ace to king) are shuffled and placed face down as a new stock. If no foundations have been completed, all partial foundations are shuffled and become the new stock.

Jokers are usable in place of any rank except ace. Moreover, a joker can be played to the talon as one rank and thence to the foundation as another rank.

At any turn, a player may demand a count of his opponent's payoff pile, while counting his own. Inasmuch as the top cards of payoff piles are visible, and so are the talons, knowledge of the payoff count is a big assist in deciding how aggressively the rest of the game should be played.

Whoever empties his payoff pile wins. If neither player manages this, the player with fewer remaining payoff cards wins. Money settlements are usually in terms of the difference between the two final counts, with a bonus for an outright win.

The game is sometimes played by three or four, using three decks, six jokers and seventeen-card or thirteen-card hands.

PART FIVE

Cards for Children—and with 'Em

Whoever has played an afternoon of Slapjack with a convalescent minor may tend to avoid the following pages, and understandably so. In time the wounds may heal. For others, it might make sense to look up children's games such as I Doubt It and Concentration, which are not as banal as most. They provide genuine amusement for a bright child and his custodians.

SLAPJACK

Old reliable for two to eight players. Entire deck is dealt one at a time in face-down stacks. Beginning at dealer's left, successive players turn up top card and place it in a center stack. When a jack appears, first to slap it with open hand takes the entire stack, which is placed face down beneath his own. To keep the proceedings fair, cards going into play should be turned away from rather than toward the player, and slapping should be done with the hand that played the card. Whoever gets the entire deck wins. Players who run out of cards remain in the game, eligible to slap. In some places, when an enthusiast slaps a card other than a jack he must give his own top card to whoever faced the misslapped card.

BEGGAR YOUR NEIGHBOR

A nonviolent elaboration of Slapjack, favored by a slightly higher age group. Best for two players. Each gets half the deck, face down, exposing top cards in center of table by turns. When a jack, queen, king or ace appears, the opponent then faces one, two, three or four successive cards, respectively, from his own stack. If none of these is a jack, queen, king or ace, the first player takes the entire center stack and places it face down under his own. But if the second player manages to come up with one of the four key cards, the first must then do the same or lose the trick. It is not necessary to match cards, just so that one of the four presents itself. When one player has all the cards, the game ends.

ANIMALS

A Slapjack elaboration, this time with vocalizing. Best for four to six players. Deck is distributed as evenly as possible, with face-down stacks at each position. Each player elects to represent a different bird or beast. Cards are faced in turn, but kept in front of the individual players. When one player's faced card matches a card previously faced and still exposed, the first of the two to utter the opponent's animal sound wins the other's pack. For example, if the cat faces a nine, and a card of that rank stands atop the rooster's pile, the cat tries to yell "Cockadoodledoo" before the other calls "Meow!"

STEALING BUNDLES

A simplified Casino, permitting the players to exercise judgment. Best for two but can be played by three or four. Four-card hands, with four more cards face up in center and the remainder of the pack in the center as a stock. The game consists of matching the ranks of cards. Example: If a ten is in the center, the player whose turn it is can capture it with a ten from his hand. The two cards then go in a face-up stack at his place. This stack, called the *bundle,* can be captured in turn by anyone else with a ten. Occasionally a bundle gets quite large before someone able to match its top card carries it away. Players unable to capture a card or a bundle must simply place a card face up in the center. When hands are empty, new helpings of four are taken, one at a time in turn, from the stock and play resumes. Whoever ends with the largest bundle wins the game. Also known as Old Man's Bundle and Stealing the Old Man's Bundle.

OLD MAID

One queen is removed from a regular deck, which is then completely dealt, as in Slapjack. Action begins with players finding all pairs in their hands and discarding them. The remaining cards are then arranged (with elaborate precautions against being observed) in whatever order the player wants. Player at dealer's left fans his hand (if possible) and offers it face down to opponent at his own left, who must take one of the cards and put it in his own hand. If he finds himself with a new pair, he discards it and then offers his own hand to the player at his left. And so forth. Whoever gets stuck with the odd queen is the loser.

WAR

For two, with the entire deck dealt. The twenty-six-card hands are placed face down in squared-off piles. Each turns his top card and places it in front of his hand. Player of the higher card takes both and puts them under his pack, face down. If the cards are of the same rank, each counts off a number of hand cards, face up, equal to the rank. Thus, if each has faced a three, both now play three more cards, face up, and high card wins both packets. For this purpose, some play that an ace counts 1, picture cards 10 and other cards pip value. More advanced players may prefer to count ace 13, king 12, queen 11 and so forth.

A simple variation defers capture of cards until both play cards of the same suit, whereupon player of the higher card takes both packets.

Regardless of variation, and there are many, the winner is the player who ends with all the cards.

CUCKOO

Certain adults play this for money. It is not a bad game for a large group of children, but can be awful with fewer than five. Cards rank downward from king through ace. Each player has three checkers or chips and is dealt one card, face down. Player at dealer's left begins by saying "Stand" or "Change"—the first if he holds a high card and the other if he wants to try to get a card higher than the one he holds. At the word "Change," the player to his left is obliged to exchange cards with him unless that player holds a king. In such circumstances, he shows the king and the exchange is canceled. When player stands, the player to his left then declares his own wishes. After an exchange, the turn passes to the immediate left of the second player involved in the exchange. If dealer has not been forced to exchange with opponent at his right, he can stand or discard in favor of a card taken at random from the remainder of the deck. All hands are then turned up. Holder of lowest must pay a checker or chip into a pool. But if dealer drew a king on exchanging with the deck, he loses the chip—even if someone else was stuck with an ace. If two or more are tied for low, they each pay. Last player with a counter wins the pot.

AUTHORS

The object of this and related games is to collect every card of each rank. The complete set of four is called a *book*. From three to six players are usual. Complete deck is dealt, which may leave some players with an extra card but does not matter. By turns beginning at dealer's left, each player tries to complete whatever ranks are already represented in his hand. Thus, if a player holds the A ♠ and A ♡, he asks another player for the A ♣. He may not ask for a card he already holds (such as A ♠ or A ♡), but must hold a card of the desired rank. If the other player has the desired card, it changes hands and the first player's turn continues. When he holds the four cards of a rank, he displays them and puts them face down at his place. When his request for a card is mistaken—in that the other player does not have it—the turn passes to the next player. Whoever captures the most books is the winner.

PIG

An amusing pastime for three to thirteen. Deck consists of as many books (fours of a kind) as there are players. Thus, for five, all cards below the rank of ten are removed (aces are retained). After a shuffle, all the cards are dealt, producing four-card hands. At a signal from the dealer, each player pushes a card to the opponent at his left. This continues until somebody gets a book, which he announces by touching his nose with a finger. As soon as others notice this, they touch their own noses. Last to do so is the loser.

DONKEY

Much like Pig except that chips are used. Deck is stripped as before, and a number of chips one less than the number of players is placed in the center. When someone makes his book, instead of touching his nose, he takes a chip from the table. When others notice this, they do the same. The slowpoke gets no chip and loses.

MY SHIP

Instead of collecting a book, the player tries to build a seven-card flush (all cards of the same suit). Game begins with the deal of seven cards each and play consists of passing cards to the left, as in Pig and Donkey. When somebody completes a seven-card flush, he calls "My ship sails!"

GO FISH

Another watered-down Authors, this time for two to five. With more than five, seven-card hands are customary. Otherwise, five cards are best. Remainder of deck becomes a stock. In rotation beginning at dealer's left, each player asks any other for all cards of one rank. Example: "Give me your queens." If respondent has any cards of the rank, he hands them over. Otherwise, he replies, "Go fish," which requires the first player to take a card from stock, ending his turn. When a player completes a book of four cards of a rank, he shows them and then places them face down before him. In some places this ends his turn, as does the taking of a card from stock (and the possible placement of a book completed from stock). Elsewhere, the turn continues so long as the new card completes a book. The winner is whoever runs out of cards first or has the most books if the stock empties.

GO BOOM

This is a beginning exercise in the taking of tricks. Best for three to seven, with seven-card hands. Remainder of deck is a stock, face down as usual. Played in turns beginning at dealer's left. First player sets a hand card face up in the center. In turn, each succeeding player must either play a hand card of the first card's rank or suit, or must go to stock and continue drawing cards until able to play the right rank or suit. After all have played to the trick, it is taken by whoever played the high card. In case of tie, trick goes to player of the high card in the original suit. When stock becomes exhausted before a player has been able to play to a trick, the turn passes to the next player. All cards taken in play go into discard and the first player to empty his hand is the winner. Sophisticates may enjoy a scoring system under which everybody counts the cards with which they are stuck when the winner goes out. Aces count 1, picture cards 10 and the rest count at pip value. Game is usually 100 points.

In a variant called Dig, the top card of the stock is exposed and play proceeds with the effort to match the rank and suit of that card. An elaboration makes one rank (often deuces or eights) wild. Holder of a wild card may play it whenever the need or desire arises during his regular turn, and may then change the rank or suit to be played by his opponents.

I DOUBT IT

This is a deceptively simple game in which good bluffers and tots with superior memories will invariably fare best, getting rid of all their cards. Uses a regular deck for play by four or five. With six to nine, two decks are best. After shuffle, the entire pack is dealt, depositing large hands at each place and making inevitable a certain amount of uproar when cards fall to the floor during the process of picking up and arranging.

Player at dealer's left begins by placing a packet of cards (as many as four in the one-deck game and up to eight in the larger game) face down at center, announcing the number of cards and a rank: "Three aces." He is not allowed to misrepresent the number of cards, and must allege that they all belong to the rank whose turn it is, beginning with ace for the first player, and proceeding by turns downward to the two, whereupon the next player must claim to be discarding aces. Whoever has reason not to believe that the packet is as homogeneous as claimed may say "I doubt it." If exposure of the cards shows that the doubter was correct, the bluffer must take up not only the bogus packet but all other previous discards that may be on the table at the time. But if the doubter is wrong, he must pick up the cards. In case of disputes over which doubter spoke first and won the right to contest the issue, player nearest the dealer's left is given the privilege.

Nobody may pass at a turn, but must play one to four (or eight) cards and must announce the proper denomination. If anyone calls the wrong rank, the error must be corrected, but the player may not change his discards. Some kids are frighteningly shrewd about pretending to make an error in declaring the rank, which entices a victim into saying "I doubt it." The best strategists sometimes deliberately express a doubt so as to take up a huge number of cards, enabling them to monopolize one or more ranks, frustrating their opponents and manipulating the game to their own ends.

A player who expresses doubt before an opponent has actually announced his rank and played a packet is ineligible to be the doubter on that particular play.

One variant calls for three-card packets, with no sequence in the announcements of rank. In turn, each player may set down three cards and assign them any real or spurious rank he pleases.

Another game, called Cheat, involves play of one card at a time, face down. First player names any rank he pleases. Next player must call the next higher rank, placing his own card on the previous one. Whenever anyone doubts that the card is of the named rank, he howls "Cheat!" If the doubter is wrong, he gets the entire pack. If not, the cheater does. As usual, first to empty his hand is the winner.

CONCENTRATION

Excellent for two, but worthwhile for as many as six. Entire deck is set out one at a time, face down, in center of table. Some prefer neat rows and columns. Others find that a helter-skelter tableau makes a more challenging game. First player at dealer's left turns over any two cards. If they are of the same rank, he captures them and turns over two more. If they do not match, he puts them back, face down. Players with the best memories end by gobbling up all the cards. When the deck is gone, player who captured the most cards wins.

BOOK TWO

BOARD AND TABLE GAMES

PART ONE

Races and Chases

In the royal tombs of Ur, Sir Leonard Woolley unearthed elegantly crafted game boards used by Sumerians more than 5,000 years ago. Direct descendants of those prehistoric games continue to entertain millions.

The Sumerians played what are now called path (or race or chase) games. These are the most popular and, by and large, least difficult of board games. In most, the player tries to get from here to there more quickly than his opponents, usually by means involving absolutely no skill. A standard feature and leading attraction is the sudden zap, in which a player loses ground by landing on the wrong square, or because his opponent has landed on the right one.

As any veteran of Candy Land, Uncle Wiggily, Chutes and Ladders, the Game of Life or Parcheesi can testify, path games are all sisters under the skin but come in an infinite variety of disguises. The most common and least enduring are decked out in what might be called topical titles—the name of the season's most conspicuous television program, for example. Sometimes the topical games celebrate matters less fleeting, such as women's liberation or urban unrest. But path games they remain, and that ain't much.

With the exception of Backgammon, now enjoying a fashionable resurgence in North American rumpus rooms, no path game qualifies as great. Among board games of any kind, that accolade is usually reserved for Chess and Go, in which the strategy and tactics of primitive warfare become exquisite abstractions and expert play requires both extraordinary talent and monastic dedication.

No such challenges confront the player of Monopoly, which outsells all other board games in the United States and has done so for about 40 years. Because it is plainly more than just a passing fancy, Monopoly belongs in this chapter. So do other trademarked products that have earned prominent and durable popularity among adults.

And therein lies a departure for Mr. Hoyle. Ours is the first Hoyle to describe proprietary games. We do it because we want to be comprehensive. But we do not want to be ridiculous. Accordingly, no mention will be made of the short-lived topical games that come and go with each new merchandising season. Our emphasis here, as elsewhere in this work, is on the classics.

1 BACKGAMMON

This good game is the unmistakable descendant of Tabula (Table), a favorite of the Romans during the final centuries of the empire. Backgammon is also kin to Parcheesi, the staple game of India. Both must have derived from a pastime of the Sumerians that probably was ancient even then.

By the thirteenth century, the game was entrenched throughout Europe and Asia. In France it was Tric-trac. The Germans called it Puff. The Spanish variety was Tablas Reales; and the Italian, Tavole Reale. The Arabs called it Nard.

About 1750, Edmond Hoyle wrote Backgammon rules for his English constituents, which is proof positive that the game had achieved considerable importance among the nobility. Its fortunes have fluctuated ever since. During the 1920s it rode a tremendous fad in the United States, but receded by the time of the Great Depression. During World War II, it enjoyed a resurrection in Britain.

Except for continued cultivation in some of America's tonier private clubs, Backgammon lay dormant until the 1970s, when it was embraced by a U.S. contingent of the international jet set, spread quickly to college campuses and thence to the game-playing public at large. Sale of Backgammon equipment surpassed all previous records during 1972 and 1973. It seemed probable that the old game had finally achieved a permanent position in the American culture.

One comparatively new feature—doubling—has sped up Backgammon and enhanced its gambling aspects. Under this rule, a player may offer to double the stakes at any juncture. This confronts the opponent with the choice of accepting higher risk or resigning immediately.

The skill of the expert doubler does not bear comparison with that of, say, an expert Bridge player. Nevertheless, Backgammon requires a good deal of memorization, more than a little gaming sense and a higher level of general intellectual attainment than is required in most other path games. The good Backgammon player beats even a talented novice at least nine times out of ten. It is not all luck.

Players and Equipment

For two, facing each other across the board, which is divided (by the *bar*) into two rectangles. Each rectangle contains twelve elongated triangles (*points*) of alternating colors—six on each player's side—projecting toward the center of the board.

Each player has fifteen checker pieces (*stones*). The player designated as *White* uses the lighter-colored set of stones. His opponent, *Black*, uses the others. For convenience, but not by inviolable rule, it is a good idea to place the board so that White moves his stones clockwise and Black moves counterclockwise.

At the beginning, the stones and players are deployed in the positions shown in the diagram, with a white (or lighter-colored) point at White's lower left and a black (or darker-colored) point at his upper left. Regardless of the actual color of the points, those on White's side of the board are known as *White points* and those on the opposite side are *Black points*. And, although no actual numbers are inscribed on the board, each point is given a number for use in conventional notations that help in discussion of play.

Thus, the game begins with two of White's stones at B1 (Black 1), five at B12, three at W8 and five at W6.

Black's opening position corresponds, with two at W1, five at W12, three at B8 and five at B6.

Each player tries to move his pieces in such a way as to get them home (*bear off*) at his own Number One point, which is located at the edge of the *inner table* and, as we have seen, is known as B1 or W1, depending on which player we have in mind. In other path games, the inner table would be called the "home table."

The only other equipment is dice. Most sets provide two for each player, plus a cup for convenient shaking and rolling. A fifth and larger die is called the *doubling cube*. Its faces show the numbers 2, 4, 8, 16, 32 and 64. The cube is useful in showing the actual number of betting units at stake.

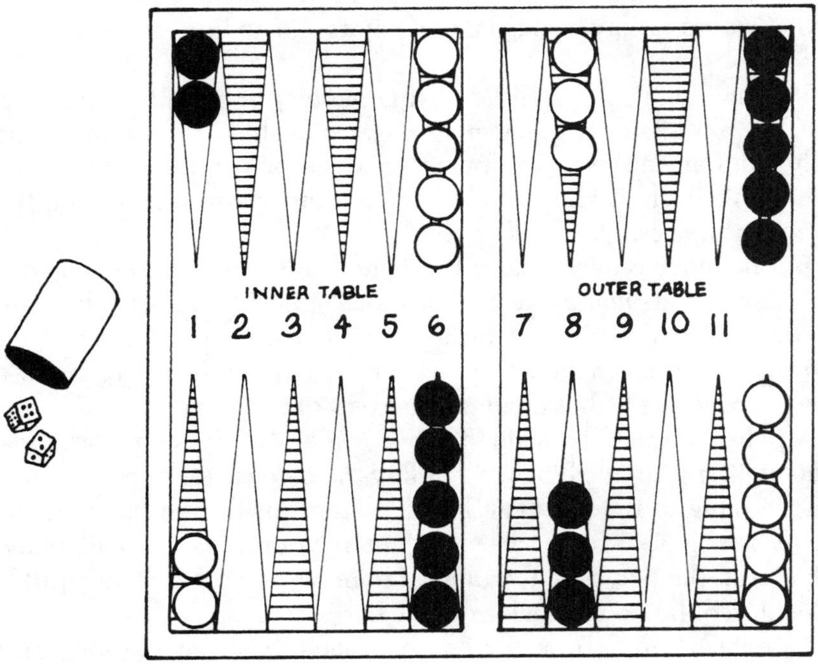

THE PLAY

Each rolls a die. High roll wins first turn. If both roll the same number, the game's stakes double automatically and players again roll for first turn. Occasionally, identical numbers again appear, and stakes redouble. In some games, automatic doubles are limited to three.

On this first roll and all succeeding ones, each die must come to rest flat. If one is *cocked* on a stone or an edge of the board, the roll is void and must be tried again.

High roller's first move is determined by the numbers he and opponent rolled in the competition for first move. At succeeding rolls, each uses two dice, and the two separate numbers govern the move in the same way. For example, if a roll produces 4 on one die and 2 on the other, the following alternatives arise:

1. One stone may be moved two points and then four more.
2. One stone may be moved four points and then two more.
3. One stone may be moved two points and another stone four.

When a double number is rolled (*doublet*), it permits four moves. Thus, a 5-5 allows the player to move one stone a total of twenty points in four moves of five points each. Or he can move four stones five points each. Or he can choose any other pattern involving four five-point moves.

But no move is ever legal if the stone *lands,* or *touches down,* on a point occupied—*made*—by two or more opposing pieces. The move is permissible if the count brings the stone to a point beyond one already occupied in that way. Making points with two or more of one's own stones is thus an important part of the game.

A point occupied by a single stone is a *blot.* Opposing stones may land on it, *hitting* the blot and sending the defenseless opposing stone off the table to the bar. The hit stone remains on the bar until the player is able to return it to play (*enter* it) on the opponent's inner table. And the player is not allowed to move any other stone until he has entered the exiled stone from the bar.

To enter a stone from the bar, the player's roll of the dice must produce a number calling for a legal move to a point on the opponent's inner table. For example, if White hits a blot after having made his own 4, 5 and 6 points, Black will have to throw a 1, 2 or 3 to enter the stone from the bar. When he fails to do so, White resumes play, continuing his own forward progress.

A player who has made all six points on his inner table enjoys a *shutout.* No opposing stone can enter from the bar. Meanwhile, the player with the shutout continues to roll the dice and move his own pieces.

After moving all fifteen of his stones to his inner table, a player begins to bear off, which is, of course, the object of the game. Example: A player with all stones on his inner table rolls a 6-2. He bears off a stone from his 6 point and another from his 2 point. If he has no stone on one or both points, he is required to bear off whatever he can—for example, a stone from the 5 or 4 point, or one from the 1 point.

Before rolling on any turn, a player may double the stakes unless the most recent double was also his. The opponent now elects either to accept the higher stake and continue play or resign.

Settling

Having won by making a double that was refused, or bearing off all fifteen of his stones before the opponent does, the victorious player collects the stakes. If the loser has borne off at least one stone, the stakes are whatever unit had been agreed on earlier, multiplied by the number shown on the doubling cube as a result of automatic doubles or challenges offered and accepted.

If the loser has failed to bear off a single stone, he is *gammoned,* and the winner gets double the entire stake (including earlier doubles already computed). If the loser not only has failed to bear off a single stone, but also has one on the bar or in the opposing inner table at game's end, the total stake is tripled.

Strategy

The earliest tactical objectives are to make points (in the sense described earlier) and to move one's two stones from opponent's inner table. Making points delays the opponent's progress by preventing him from landing where the dice might otherwise send him.

Player who wins first roll has an advantage, which good players exploit through their knowledge of the best moves for early play. Most of the recommended moves on the following table are standard—and well known by all reasonably good players. Where opinions vary, alternatives are given. The notation B12–W11 signifies the movement of a stone from Black 12 to White 11. It is assumed that White is making the moves. For Black, simply change the notation to W12–B11.

Opening Roll

(White to Move)

Roll	*Move #*	*Move*	*Alternate*
1–2	1	B12–W11	
	2	B1–B2	2 W6–W5
1–3	1	W8–W5	
	2	W6–W5	
1–4	1	B12–W9	
	2	B1–B2	2 W6–W5
1–5	1	B12–W8	
	2	B1–B2	2 W6–W5
1–6	1	B12–W7	
	2	W8–W11	
2–3	1	B12–W11	
	2	B12–W10	2 B1–B4
2–4	1	W8–W4	
	2	W6–W4	
2–5	1	B12–W11	
	2	B12–W8	
2–6	1	B1–B7	1 B12–W7
	2	B12–W11	1 or 2 B12–W5
3–4	1	B12–W9	1 B1–B5
	2	B12–W10	
3–5	1	W8–W3	1 B12–W8
	2	W6–W3	2 B12–W10
3–6	1	B1–B7	1 B1–B4
	2	B12–W10	2 B12–W7
			1 & 2 B1–B10
4–5	1	B12–W8	1 B1–B5
	2	B12–W9	1 & 2 B1–B10
4–6	1 & 2	B1–B11	1 B1–B5
			2 B12–W7
5–6	1 & 2	B1–B12	

In most games, doublets are allowed on the first roll, and the following moves are appropriate:

Roll	*Move*	*Alternate*
1–1	W8–W7 twice	
	W6–W5 twice	

2–2	B12–W11 twice W6–W4 twice	
3–3	W8–W5 twice W6–W3 twice	B12–W7 four times
4–4	B1–B5 twice B12–W9 twice	B12–W5 four times
5–5	B12–W3 twice	
6–6	B1–B7 twice B12–W7 twice	

In general, making one's own 5 point and 3 point is most desirable. Both serve important offensive and defensive purposes.

The response to the opening move is, of course, determined by the option selected by the first player. Most often, Black should hit a blot if one is left by White. Black should also avoid making a blot of his own, especially on his outer table when White splits his stones on B12. Both of White's stones would then be in position to attack the blot.

Like White, Black also tries to make points and move his back stones quickly. As the game progresses, both players should evaluate position by *counting*. The count may be made in two ways. The simpler is for the player to count 1 point for each of his stones on his own inner table, 2 for each on his outer table, 3 for each in the opponent's outer table and 4 for each on opponent's inner table.

A more precise method is to count the number of points each piece must move to bear off. Thus, a stone on your 4 point counts 4; two stones on that point count 8 (4 each); a stone on the opposing 9 point counts 16, etc. The counts for all stones are then totaled. The player with the smaller sum usually has the edge.

A count advantage of 8 or more almost always provides the basis for a profitable double. The player with the upper hand should then *break contact* (get all his pieces past the opponent's) and start a *running game*, that stage of play in which hits are no longer possible and the only consideration is the race to bear off.

Conversely, a player who counts himself behind by 8 or more should think carefully before accepting a double. With a chance to obstruct a running game it might prove wise to accept the double, since the counting advantage could easily be nullified by a hit or two. But if a hit seems unlikely, the double should be refused.

The chances of a hit drop dramatically if the distance between attacker and blot is 7 points or more. And if the opponent's made points lie between the attacker and the blot, the chance of a hit becomes even smaller.

When a stone is hit and returned to the bar, its chances of re-entry on a single roll are always better than 50–50 except when only one (or none) of the points on the opponent's inner table is open.

After hitting and re-entry are no longer factors and players have only one or two stones to bear off, doubling is imminent and counting is most important. With a total of 6 or less and no more than two stones to bear off, a player should always double. The chance of success on one roll is better than even. A double on a count of 7 is also favorable if the two remaining stones are on points 2 and 5. With any other count of 7, or any higher count, no double should be made.

The player faced with the dilemma of accepting or rejecting a double should always accept if he has one chance in three of winning. If he rejects such doubles three times he loses three units ($1 + 1 + 1 = 3$). If he accepts and wins only once, his loss is only two units (losing two units twice = four units lost; winning two units once = two units won; net loss of two units).

Recommended Reading

For more detailed and sophisticated discussion of Backgammon strategy and tactics than is possible here or, for that matter, has ever been available anywhere before, we recommend *The Backgammon Book* by Oswald Jacoby and John R. Crawford, published by Viking Press.

CHOUETTE

This is round-robin Backgammon for more than two players. Whoever cuts high card or rolls high dice becomes *man in the box* and plays alone against a team composed of everyone else. Second-high cut or roll is captain of the team and makes all plays in consultation with his teammates. Order of succession to the captaincy in succeeding games is determined by the initial roll or cut, with lowest becoming the *foot,* and last to run the team.

Captain has final say on all plays except responses to doubling. When a double is offered by either side, any member of the team may choose to resign, paying the stake to the man in the box. When the man in the box refuses a double or is beaten, he pays full stake to each member of the opposing team and then becomes its foot. The captain now becomes the man in the box and the second-ranking member of the team becomes its captain.

ACEY-DEUCEY

In this naval version of Backgammon, the stones start atop the bar and a roll of 1-2 (*acey-deucey*) entitles the player to select any doublet he chooses and also take another roll. However, he must be able to make the full 1-2 move before being allowed the doublet and the extra roll.

The game's vocabulary is more colorful than that of conventional Backgammon. The roll of a die for first turn is *piddle,* blots are *kicked* not hit, and the bar is called *fence.*

Although customs vary, a widely accepted method of settlement is one unit for every stone that the loser has failed to bear off. In some circles, a regular strategic Backgammon count is made, with one unit for each losing point. And some games regard the stakes as automatically doubled when acey-deucey is rolled. In those games, penalties for gammon and backgammon are not usually allowed.

EUROPEAN ACEY-DEUCEY

The opening position is that of regular Backgammon, but the 1-2 roll automatically doubles the stakes and gives the benefit of any doublet the player chooses, plus the *complementary doublet*—the doublet on the opposite side of the dice—plus an extra roll. Example: If the player chooses a 6-6 doublet, he makes the move and then moves 1-1, the complementary doublet. As in American Acey-Deucey, none of these benefits is permitted if the player is unable to make the original 1-2 move. Stones on a player's inner table may only be borne off. They cannot he moved to other positions on the inner table.

DUTCH BACKGAMMON

All stones begin on the bar and all fifteen must enter before any stone can be moved on the board. Also, blots may not be hit by a player who has not yet moved a stone to his inner table.

RUSSIAN BACKGAMMON

Stones begin off the board and both opponents enter on the same side. After entering at least two stones, a player is allowed to move them or enter additional stones or do both on the same roll. The full roll must be used, moving pieces already on the board if none can be entered. If a doublet is rolled, the player also uses its complement—the number computed by subtracting the doublet number from 7. Thus, rolling a 5-5, the player makes that move and follows with a 2-2. If unable to make all doublet moves (eight in all), he is allowed to take none of them.

SNAKE

This is good practice. One player places his stones in the usual opening position. The opponent (preferably the stronger player) places nine stones on the bar and two each on the adverse 1, 2 and 3 points. Play proceeds as in regular Backgammon and is a great exercise for persons interested in familiarizing themselves with the strategy known as the *back game.* This arises when a player has an unusually large number of pieces in the opponent's inner table, making and holding points there and, instead of running for his own inner table at once, playing a blocking game. Once hitting a blot, the player of the back game can sometimes prevent the opponent from moving off the bar long enough to redistribute his own forces for a homeward run. In Snake—and less often in real Backgammon—a player sometimes makes six adjoining points. This is known as a *prime.* It prevents the opponent from moving through, and sometimes prevents him from moving at all. Skillful players sometimes combine their skill with luck enough to *walk* the prime intact from the opponent's inner table to their own, where it becomes a shutout.

2 PARCHEESI

In India this game is usually played on a cloth layout with cowrie shells instead of dice. Nobody knows how old it is, but the game certainly antedates Backgammon. Closely similar games were played by the Aztecs, Mayans and other American civilizations, substantiating the theory that the Indians had migrated from Asia.

The modern North American version, familiar to all, is sold as Parcheesi, Parchesi or Pachisi, depending on the brand name selected by the manufacturer. In England, the name is Ludo. It was introduced there during the last century.

Regardless of name, this is a forebear of all modern race and chase games, and remains one of the very best.

Players and Equipment

For two to four, each with four pieces and often playing as partners. The path is the familiar cross pattern, progress along which is governed by rolls of dice.

The Play

Each starts at his own station at the end of one of the arms of the cross and tries to beat everyone else to the central goal. The first to get all four pieces home wins.

As in other path games, the relish here is *bumping*. Just when the opponent thinks he is going to win, you land your piece on a square occupied by one of his and he must return the piece to the starting position. Moreover, the bumper moves an additional twenty squares.

Variations

Among the endless multitude of games that closely resemble Parcheesi, the best are the few that permit mild exercise of judgment, as does the original. Worth mentioning in the trademarked confusion are Sorry, which uses cards instead of dice; Trouble and Globe Trotter, which use only one die; and Aggravation, which has a larger board.

Most spin-offs from Parcheesi tend to be cluttered with idiotic penalties, bonuses and other embellishments that lack enduring entertainment value because they have nothing whatever to do with judgment, much less with skill. Exempt from this blanket denunciation are the more charming of the children's path games, especially Chutes and Ladders, Candy Land and Uncle Wiggily. But for how long are we expected to remain five years of age?

3 MONOPOLY

In 1860, a Massachusetts lithographer named Milton Bradley devised a game that he called The Checkered Game of Life. It featured a board of eighty-four squares, along which pieces moved at the dictates of a teetotum—a spinner. The object was to reach the goal of "Happy Old Age" before any opponent did. En route, one hoped to avoid squares labeled "Disgrace," "Crime" and, of course, the worst luck of all, "Ruin." The virtues were all solid Puritan, the evils unredeemed, the penalties harsh. The game reflected its sweetly innocent times and became a howling success. It was the foundation on which Milton Bradley built the largest game business in the history of the world.

A few years later, young George Parker, who presently would become Bradley's leading competitor, invented something called Banking. It also reflected the times. It postulated rewards for thrift and penalties for waste.

The general idea of all this prelude is that the American public is incurably addicted to more-or-less realistic games that permit the player to simulate control over some of the problems of real life. The most successful of such games is, of course, Monopoly, which created a sensation during the Great Depression by permitting anyone to become a pretend real-estate tycoon with play money. Little if any authentic skill was involved, but rewards for greed and viciousness were abundant. Such opportunities had great appeal during the thirties. And forties, fifties, sixties and seventies.

Players and Equipment

For two to ten players who move pieces around and around a board as directed by dice, and get zapped when they land on the wrong squares. Each starts with the same amount of play money and is allowed to buy the unencumbered parcels of Atlantic City property on which he lands. Object is to monopolize certain tracts, charging exorbitant fees to players who land thereon, and finally drive 'em all bankrupt.

Strategy

Because some of the properties are offered at higher prices than others, dilemmas arise as to which are the best buys. A computer study by Irvin R. Hentzel helped settle the issue by disclosing that some of the squares were frequented more than others, meaning that the proprietors could gouge other players more often. He suggested that a player with less than $500 to spend was best off buying railroads. Someone in the $1,000–$2,000 range was well served by a monopoly on the orange-colored properties of Tennessee Avenue, St. James Place and New York Avenue or, as second choice, Boardwalk and Park Place. With more to spend, nothing could compare with the green-colored properties.

All of which is helpful when the dice happen to roll your way. But this is really not a game of skill. The luck of the roll is dominant. Stamina helps, too.

Variations

The Checkered Game of Life, which started it all, continues to be a best seller for Milton Bradley Co. It now comes in modern garb, as The Game of Life, and the goal is financial success in "Millionaire Acres" rather than a humdrum, happy old age. The modern version also has a lot to do with shrewd acquisition of insurance. Other path games of this kind abound. Among the more popular may be mentioned Easy Money, Merger, a few stock-and-bond games, Careers, Happiness, and on and on and on. The more popular ones sell by the hundreds of thousands, which means that they entertain a great many human beings. If they seem to get short shrift in these pages, no unfairness is intended. The games are so numerous, and the differences among them so insignificant, that any effort to describe them separately would waste time.

PART TWO

War Games

This group includes some of the great games of all time. Well-played Chess, Checkers and Go are more than diversions. They are confrontations as grueling as any bloodless competition yet devised by man. The board is a field of honor.

It is clear enough that our best board games reflect the martial preoccupations of the ancient cultures in which they originated. For example, about 1,500 years ago in India, the board used for a Parcheesi variant called Ashtapada was also used for Chaturanga (or Shaturanga), which was complex warfare among armies of pieces representing foot soldiers, cavalry, elephants, boatmen and rajahs. Pieces moved at the roll of a die, captures occurred, and alliances were formed and broken.

Shaturanga can be compared to Monopoly and other quasi-realistic games that divert so many persons in our century. Shaturanga gave everyone a chance to fantasize life as a rajah, including the delight of destroying the unwary—all at the roll of a die.

After Hindu law banned gambling, specifically naming Shaturanga and dice, there arose a more sophisticated and abstract game—Shatranj, which spread to Persia and thence to North Africa, the Near East and Europe. Gone was the fantasizing. The martial names of the pieces became coincidental. The game was now a pure and searching test of skill. It was the immediate forerunner of Chess.

This account, and contemporary experience, indicate rather strongly that the best board games tend to be abstract. To the degree that they attempt to reconstruct concrete problems of life, they fail as games. Yet a countermovement, unprecedented in the history of games, is now afoot and must be noted in this edition of Mr. Hoyle's work. Probability theory has made possible the fairly authentic simulation on game boards of military, sports, economic and social problems. Some of the resultant products call for scholarship and skill to rival those demanded by Chess. They have a chapter of their own, later on. I mention them here only because their most notable examples include games of war.

1 CHESS

Chess achieved its present form during the fifteenth century and has discouraged modification ever since. It needs no tinkering. It is an apparently inexhaustible resource in which the inquiring mind can always find fresh challenges.

Which is not to say that only geniuses enjoy this game. Like Bridge or, for that matter, Tennis, Chess rewards persons who may lack talent for the game but enjoy concentrating and have taken the trouble to learn the basic moves.

Our function here is to offer the most elementary introduction to the rules and procedures of this marvelous game.

Players and Equipment

Two players face each other across a board of sixty-four squares—eight squares in each of eight columns (*files*) and eight in each of eight rows (*ranks*). Squares are of alternate and contrasting color, customarily referred to as White (the lighter) and Black (the darker). Pieces for each player are also of contrasting colors and are called White and Black.

The board is positioned with a white space at the lower-right-hand corner on each player's side (*see illustration below*).

Because White always makes the first move, it is customary in non-tournament play for one player to conceal a White pawn in one hand and extend both closed fists to his opponent. If the opponent guesses the location of the pawn, he gets the White pieces for the first game. If he guesses wrong, he plays the Black.

Each player has sixteen pieces:

King (K)
Queen (Q)
Two rooks (R)
Two bishops (B)
Two knights (Kt)
Eight pawns (P)

The game starts with the pieces in the following positions.

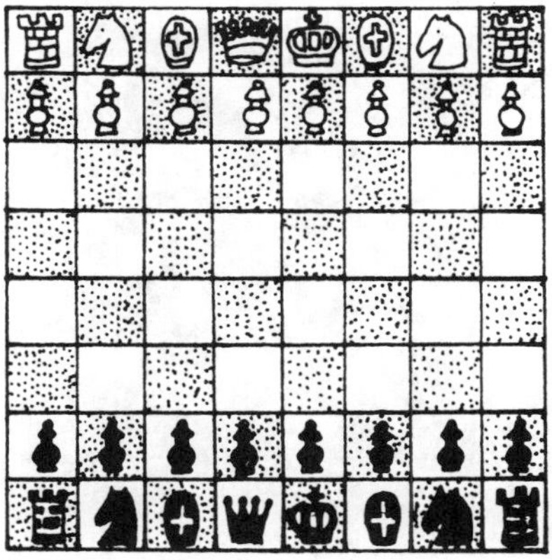

Note that the queen always begins on a square of its own color—White queen on a white square, Black queen on a black.

The Moves

Each piece has distinct abilities.

King: Moves one square at a time in any direction, but not to a square that can be reached on the next move by an opposing piece.

Queen: Moves any distance along any rank, file or diagonal, but may not turn a corner or jump over a piece in its path.

Rook: Moves any distance along any rank or file, but may not move diagonally or jump an obstructing piece.

Bishop: Moves any distance along any diagonal, but may not jump.

Knight: Turns a corner on each move. Thus, may move one square along its rank or file and then complete the move by turning at right angles and going two more squares. In process, the knight can jump over other pieces. Note that the knight may also move *two* squares along its rank or file, turning at right angles and completing the maneuver by proceeding *one* square.

BLACK

WHITE

Pawn: Its first move may be one or two squares forward along its own file, at the option of the player. Subsequently, it advances one square at a time, still on its own file, except when capturing, as explained below.

Note that in Chess discussions it is customary to differentiate between pawns and pieces—with the humble pawn the only nonpiece on the board.

Castling

If neither the king nor one of its rooks has moved during the game, nothing stands between them on their rank, and the king is not *in check* (defined below), the player is allowed to *castle.* This consists of moving the king two squares toward the rook and then jumping the rook to the square on the other side of the king.

Castling "Short" or on the King's Side

BEFORE CASTLING

AFTER CASTLING

Castling "Long" or on the Queen's Side

BEFORE CASTLING

AFTER CASTLING

Captures

All pieces and pawns capture by landing on a square occupied by an enemy piece or pawn. However, the pawn may not capture by making its normal forward move. It captures in special ways:

1. By advancing diagonally one square, onto a square occupied by an opposing piece or pawn.
2. *En passant,* when positioned on the fifth rank and the opposing pawn on an adjacent file moves two squares (in its first move of the game). The capture is made by moving behind the enemy pawn and removing it from the board.

BLACK

WHITE

Black pawn, which is in its starting position, has opted to move two squares, bypassing the white pawn on QB5. White may now capture the black pawn on Black's Q3 square, as though Black had moved the pawn only one square instead of two. However, this capture must be made immediately by White or else White loses the option to capture *en passant.*

Queening

When a pawn reaches the eighth rank—as far as it can proceed along a file—it can be *promoted* to whatever status the player chooses (except that of a king). He usually chooses that it become a queen, although he can make it a rook, bishop or knight.

Winning

The game is won by placing the opposing king in such straits that it cannot avoid capture on the next move. When a move attacks the square occupied by the king, the attacking player announces "Check." The opponent then avoids defeat by moving the king, interposing a piece between the king and the attacking piece or capturing the attacking piece. If none of these alternatives exist, the game is lost, which is signified by the victor saying "Checkmate" or "Mate." Many games do not proceed that far, but end with the resignation of the player who finds defeat unavoidable.

Draws

A draw may be declared and play terminated if any of the following situations arise.

Stalemate: Although not in check, a player is unable to make a legal move of any kind.

Perpetual Check: A player may claim a draw if able to check the opponent's king on every subsequent move, regardless of inability to produce mate.

Repeated Position: If a player finds himself about to move with the position of all pieces exactly the same as they have been on two previous occasions at his turn, he may claim a draw.

Fifty-Move Rule: If the players have contrived to move fifty times without moving a pawn or committing some other irreversible act such as castling or capturing, either of them can demand a draw.

The opponent must accede unless able to prove that his victory is inevitable.

Mutual Consent: At any stage after Black has made his thirteenth move, the players can agree to a draw.

Insufficient Force: A player with nothing left but his king can claim a draw if his opponent has only king and bishop or king and knight or king and both knights. Mate is impossible in these circumstances.

Errors and Penalties

The International Federation of Chess is the official arbiter of tournament play. Its rules are admirably lucid. Those most likely to concern the present reader are:

1. It is not proper to touch a piece without actually moving it. If the player wants simply to adjust its position on its square, he should announce "I adjust." In serious play, if he fails to make this announcement, he must move the piece he touches.
2. If a player feels the need to touch an opposing piece but does not wish to capture it, he must ask permission. Failing to do so, he must capture the piece, if possible.
3. When a legal move is made, it may not be withdrawn.
4. When an illegal move is made, the pieces are returned to their original position and a legal move is made.
5. A player may not make distracting comments or accept advice from onlookers.
6. In tournament play, it is customary to require the players to complete at least thirty moves in two hours and forty-five in three hours. In some circumstances, twenty moves an hour may be required. And *rapid transit* means a move every ten seconds.

Notation

In the English-speaking world, most Chess literature describes and analyzes games by means of a notation system that identifies each square on the board by two different abbreviations. One set of abbreviations refers to the position of the square as seen from White's side. The other set identifies the squares as seen by Black.

Thus, the white square at the lower-right-hand corner of White's side of the board is KR1—king's rook's square on the first rank. From Black's vantage, the same square is KR8—the square on the eighth rank of his king's rook's file. And White's Q1—first rank, queen's file—is Black's Q8.

The opening moves in a game might be reported as follows:

	White	*Black*
1	P-K4	P-K4
2	Kt-KB3	Kt-QB3
3	B-Kt5	P-Q3

In each column of notations, the letter before the hyphen identifies the piece moved and the abbreviation after the hyphen indicates the square to which the piece moved. In the foregoing sequence, White opened by moving his king's pawn two ranks to his K4 square. And Black responded by moving *his* king's pawn two ranks to his own K4 square. The reader should observe that it was not necessary to designate these pawns as king's pawns. The only pawns capable of moving to K4 at this stage of the action are the king's pawns, which makes the abbreviation "P" entirely satisfactory for notation purposes.

After the three moves recorded above, the position of the pieces is this:

BLACK

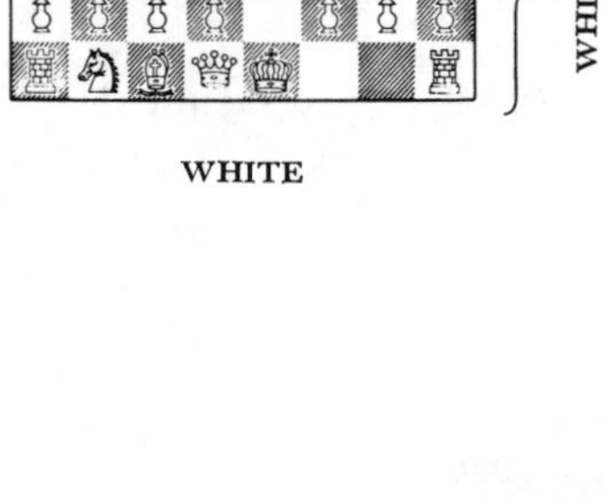

WHITE

When reporting a capture, the notes replace the hyphen with an "x." BxKt means that the only bishop in position to capture a knight has done so. If more than one bishop was situated to make such a capture, the note would be QBxKt or KBxKt, or B(3)xKt, indicating that the bishop on the third rank captured the knight.

Other abbreviations:

ch	check
!	best move possible
?	bad or questionable move
O-O	King-side castle
O-O-O	Queen-side castle

An algebraic style of notation is more popular elsewhere in the world and is used by many British and American experts in their own communications. It assigns one designation to each square: a8 means the square at White's farthest left, on the farthest rank. The same designation is used for Black, who simply regards a8 as the square on the nearest rank in the farthest right-hand file.

The game described above in the so-called English notation would be reported by algebraic notation in this way.

	White	*Black*
1	d2-d4	d7-d5
2	g1-f3	b8-c6
3	f1-b5	d7-d6

Strategy

Chess games are customarily analyzed in three stages—the *opening*, the *middle game* and the *end game*. Most opening moves attempt to distribute each side's forces in ways that have been established by Chess literature as best calculated to carry out one or another conventional strategy. Inasmuch as countering tactics have also been established during centuries of play, weaknesses—real or potential—soon appear in either or both formations, and the middle game may be regarded as the effort to exploit and/or repair such weaknesses. The end game is the attempt to deliver the *coup de grace* after developing dominance in the middle game.

During each stage, the strategic elements of *time, space* and *force* are paramount, with time and space of greater urgency in the opening, and force being unleashed afterward.

Time (or *tempo*) refers to the number of moves needed to mount or counter an attack. It is an especially crucial factor in the early stages, when economy of time in developing an effective attack is often the difference between victory and defeat.

To avoid slow development, a single piece should seldom move more than once during the opening stages. Good players have sufficient grasp of the established opening patterns to concentrate on the effort to achieve a useful formation in minimum time. They move a piece twice during this phase only when (a) surprised by an opponent's own moves and (b) hoping to enforce a comparable loss of time on the opponent.

The important task of quick development is regarded as complete when the rooks are *connected*—no longer separated by intervening pieces on their rank. Castling is a useful means of connecting the rooks.

Control of space is almost as important as time during the opening. Of all space, the center squares are most essential. Good players do not necessarily try to occupy Q4, Q5, K4 and K5, but place their pieces in such patterns as to threaten capture of any opposing piece that moves onto one of those vital center squares. To control the center is to prepare for divisive thrusts with pieces from either the king or queen side of one's own formation.

Established opening sequences that offer even competition for time and space are:

Ruy Lopez

	White	*Black*
1	P-K4	P-K4
2	Kt-KB3	Kt-QB3
3	B-Kt5	P-QR3 or P-Q3 or Kt-KB3

Giuoco Piano

	White	*Black*
1	P-K4	P-K4
2	Kt-KB3	Kt-KB3
3	B-B4	B-B4

Evans Gambit

White	*Black*
1 P-K4	P-K4
2 Kt-KB3	Kt-QB3
3 B-B4	B-B4
4 P-QKt4	

Two Knights' Defense

White	*Black*
1 P-K4	P-K4
2 Kt-KB3	Kt-QB3
3 B-B4	Kt-B3

Four Knights' Game

White	*Black*
1 P-K4	P-K4
2 Kt-KB3	Kt-QB3
3 Kt-B3	Kt-B3

King's Gambit

White	*Black*
1 P-K4	P-K4
2 P-KB4	PxP

King's Gambit Declined

White	*Black*
1 P-K4	P-K4
2 P-KB4	B-B4

Sicilian Defense

White	*Black*
1 P-K4	P-QB4
2 Kt-KB3	P-Q3
3 P-Q4	PxP

Alekhine's Defense

	White	*Black*
1	P-K4	Kt-KB3
2	P-K5	Kt-Q4

French Defense

	White	*Black*
1	P-K4	P-K3
2	P-Q4	P-Q4

Queen's Gambit

	White	*Black*
1	P-Q4	P-Q4
2	P-QB4	PxP

Queen's Gambit Declined

	White	*Black*
1	P-Q4	P-Q4
2	P-QB4	P-K3
3	Kt-QB3	Kt-KB3

Queen's Indian

	White	*Black*
1	P-Q4	Kt-KB3
2	P-B4	P-K3
3	Kt-KB3	P-QKt3

King's Indian

	White	*Black*
1	P-Q4	Kt-KB3
2	P-B4	P-KKt3

Nimzo-Indian Defense

	White	*Black*
1	P-Q4	Kt-KB3
2	P-B4	P-K3
3	Kt-QB3	B-Kt5

The P-K4 and P-Q4 openings are referred to as regular, while those beginning with other moves are considered irregular. Many so-called irregular openings are diversionary attempts to attain positions reached more directly by regular means.

When opening positions are established and development is well under way, consideration of force assumes importance equal to that of space and time. Force refers to the power of the pieces. For convenience in appraising force, the pieces are assigned approximate values:

P = 1 Kt = 3 B = 3 R = 5 Q = 9

Force is more than simply arithmetical. Moreover, it cannot be isolated from other tactical considerations. Good players often sacrifice valuable pieces to gain time and space. That, of course, is the primary purpose of the *gambits* noted in some of the openings, where a player exposes a pawn to capture and hopes to penalize the opponent who captures it.

Among other elementary tactics, more of which are used during middle play than in the openings, these should be mentioned.

Attack: A threat to capture an opposing piece on the next move.

Counterattack: With one of his own pieces under attack, the player mounts an attack of his own against an opposing piece of equal or greater value.

Guard: An attacked piece is defended by another one that threatens to respond by taking the capturing piece. Note that guarding does not work if the attacking piece (such as a bishop) is of less value than the piece under attack. To bring up a knight to guard the attacked queen is useless, inasmuch as the opponent will happily trade his bishop for the queen.

Withdrawal: If unable to guard an attacked piece effectively, as in the above example, the player may decide to move it out of harm's way.

Obstruction: To frustrate attack on an important piece by an opposing queen, rook or bishop, a player might interpose a piece of his own on a square guarded by another of his own.

Pin: A pretty maneuver that ties down an opposing piece. If the opposing piece is moved, it exposes its king to check.

BLACK

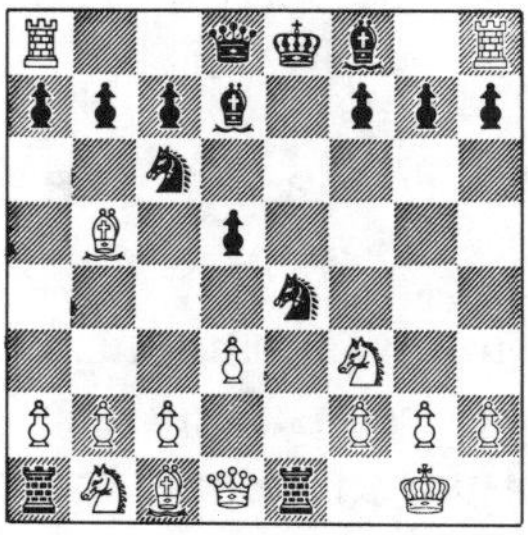

WHITE

Fork: A piece attacks two or more opposing pieces at once.

Discovered Check:

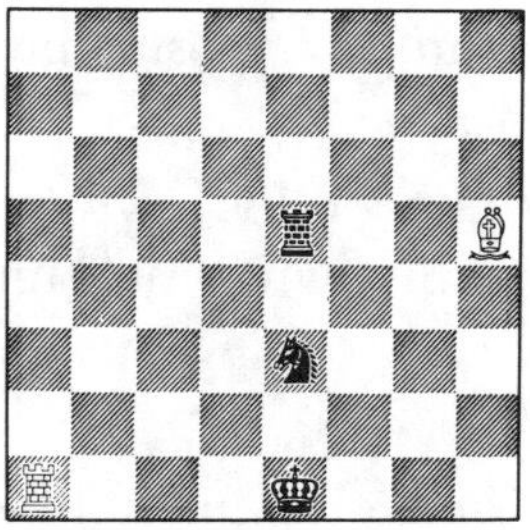

When Black moves his knight to KKt5, the White king is under check by the Black rook. The knight is immune to capture by the White bishop because White must attend to the check. Note that a move of the knight to QB7 creates another tactical advantage, *double check* (check by two pieces, in this case the Black rook and Black knight). It also produces a fork on the White rook and White king. Since the king can escape double check only by moving, the White rook is doomed.

Some familiar end-game situations require the player to promote a pawn or two and may involve the tactic of *opposition.* Favorable opposition is the ability of a king to drive the opponent's king aside, as in the following position:

BLACK

WHITE

If White is to move in this position, Black has the opposition because the White king must step aside. Similarly, if this position occurs immediately before Black's move, the advantageous opposition is White's.

Assuming that White has the move and takes his king to KB1, Black presses the advantage by advancing his king to Q7. This paves the way for promotion of the Black pawn to a queen and the inevitable checkmate.

Example Game

Paul Morphy was one of this country's first great masters. He won the following game at the age of 12, playing blindfolded.

	Morphy	*E. Morphy*
1	P-K4	P-K4
2	Kt-KB3	Kt-QB3
3	B-B4	B-B4
4	P-B3	P-Q3
5	O-O	Kt-B3
6	P-Q4	PxP
7	PxP	B-Kt3
8	P-KR3	P-KR3
9	Kt-B3	O-O
10	B-K3	R-K1

11	P-Q5	BxB
12	PxKt	B-Kt3
13	P-K5	PxP
14	Q-Kt3	R-K2
15	BxPch	RxB
16	KtxP	Q-K1
17	PxP	BxP
18	QR-K1	B-R3
19	Kt-Kt6	Q-Q1
20	R-K7	Resigns

Recommended Reading

Those with a new taste for Chess should seek information beyond the mere sip possible here. Chess literature is enormous and much of it is excellent. The best include:

John Collins, *Modern Chess Openings*, rev. by Larry Evans (Pitman).
Larry Evans, *New Ideas in Chess* (Cornerstone Library).
I. A. Horowitz, *Chess Openings, Theory and Practice* (Simon and Schuster).
———, *How to Win in the Chess Openings* (Cornerstone Library).
———, *Modern Ideas in the Chess Openings* (Cornerstone Library).

HANDICAP CHESS

If players are unequal, various handicaps help make their game more interesting. Examples:

1. Count any draw as a victory for the weaker player.
2. *Pawn and Move.* The stronger takes Black and begins by removing his king's bishop's pawn.
3. *Pawn and Two.* As above, but play begins with White taking two moves. White usually is forbidden to move beyond his fourth rank on these moves.
4. *Knight.* Stronger takes White, without the queen's knight.
5. *Rook.* Stronger takes White, without the queen's rook but usually placing the queen's rook's pawn on QR3 to protect it.

6. *Rook, Pawn and Move.* Stronger takes Black, without the queen's rook and king's bishop's pawn.

7. *Rook and Knight.* Stronger takes White, without queen's rook and king's knight.

8. *Queen.* Stronger takes White, without a queen.

9. *Capped Pawn.* Stronger takes White and must mate with his unpromoted king's bishop's pawn or lose.

10. *Unequal Time.* Stronger plays rapid transit, allowing weaker to take five minutes a move.

KRIEGSPIEL

Each player has his own board and pieces out of sight of his opponent. A third party serves as referee, keeping track of the proceedings on a board of his own.

When White moves, the referee says only "White has moved." When either player attempts an illegal or impossible move, the referee says "No" and the player tries another. When a player deliberately attempts a series of illegal moves for purposes of deception, the referee announces "Impossible," alerting the opponent to what has been happening.

When capture occurs, the referee names the square on which it happened. He does not identify the involved pieces, unless the capture was *en passant,* which the referee simply names as such.

When a player moves a piece into a position that brings the opponent's king into check, the referee announces the check and its direction, which may be "On the file," "On the rank," "On the long diagonal," "On the short diagonal" or "By the knight." The long diagonal is simply the longer of the two diagonals (toward the opponent's side) that extend from each square on the board.

Besides what they glean from the referee's announcements, players can piece together pictures of the opposing position by asking "Any?" The referee is then required to say "Try" if any of the player's pawns are in position to capture an opposing man. The player then moves whatever pawn he pleases. If it captures an opposing piece, that ends his move. If not, he is allowed to withdraw the move and try others until he captures an opponent or, frustrated, abandons the process for a move with another piece.

THE LITTLE GAME

Pieces are positioned as shown.

BLACK

WHITE

White should win this end-game study, having the advantage of first move. Inexperienced players will find the exercise rewarding.

PEASANT'S REVOLT

BLACK

WHITE

Analysis shows that Black (with a pawn and four knights) should win, but careful play is needed.

STRATEGO

From a Chinese variant of Chess there arose the Jungle Game, antecedent of this trademarked game of pure strategy that is becoming quite popular in North America. Each player deploys and maneuvers an army of forty pieces, all of the same size and shape, with identification of individual rank concealed from the opponent. Except for Bombs and Flag, which are stationary, all pieces are movable one square at a time forward, sideways or backward. The object is to capture the enemy Flag, the position of which is deduced by the positions of its protective Bombs. There are many ingenious features, such as the ability of the Marshal to destroy any lesser piece except the Spy, which destroys him. A good game.

FEUDAL

Another relatively new proprietary game. Pieces representing medieval characters are secretly positioned before the opposing formations are revealed and the action starts. As in Chess and Stratego, some pieces have more power than others. Wise use of these forces, plus a "terrain" factor, gives this game considerable appeal.

2 CHECKERS (DRAUGHTS)

In recent years this descendant of prehistoric path games has been hailed by various experts, who declare that it is much more worthwhile than the public had been led to believe. Although no large likelihood of an all-out resurgence is discernible, there is no doubt that Checkers has been unfairly downgraded in the past.

Players and Equipment

For two, with a Chess board placed so that a white square stands at the lower-right-hand corner on each player's side.

The pieces—or men, or checkers—are of contrasting colors (usually black and red) but are referred to in most game analyses as Black and White. Each player has twelve, which are arranged for the beginning of play in the familiar pattern shown in the illustration. Such illustrations traditionally show the pieces on white squares for better visibility. But the game itself is played on dark squares.

The Play

By tradition, Black moves first, although some decide first move by drawing lots or flipping coins. Pieces move forward diagonally

one space at a time to unoccupied black squares. If the square is occupied by an opposing piece and the square beyond is unoccupied, a jump and capture may be made.

Captured pieces are removed from the board. Multiple captures sometimes occur at a single turn.

BLACK

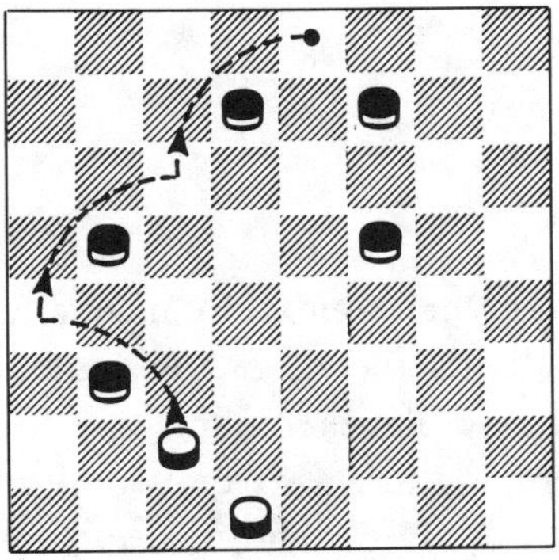

WHITE

If a piece can capture an opponent, it must do so. If multiple capture is possible, it must be completed. If a player can capture with more than one of his men, he is allowed to choose which capture to make at the particular turn. But a capturing move *always* is made in preference to a noncapturing one.

When a checker reaches the last row (*king row*) on the opposite side of the board, it is *crowned,* or *kinged.* Opponent places a checker of the same color on it. It now is a *king* and may move backward as well as forward, and may even combine forward and backward motion on the same maneuver when multiple capture is involved. However, when a checker arrives at the king row and is crowned, its move ends at once. It may not capture an opposing piece until the next turn.

BLACK

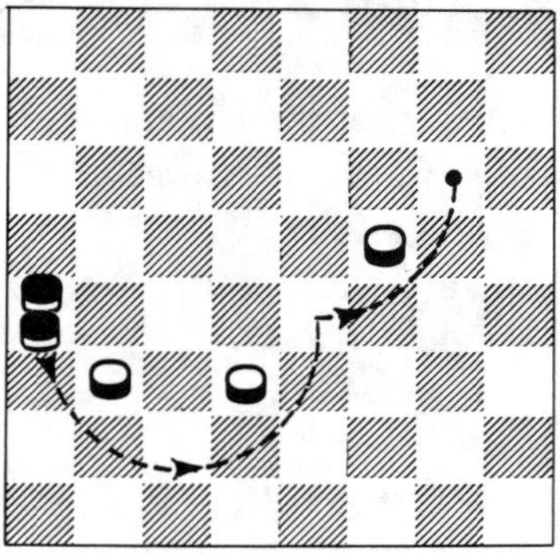

WHITE

Winning

A player is defeated when unable to make a legal move on his turn. He may have lost all his pieces or, as sometimes occurs, may be unable to move whatever pieces remain.

By mutual consent, games also may end as draws. If a player proposes a draw, an opponent who refuses must show an increased advantage within forty additional moves or the game is drawn.

Notation

Because only thirty-two of the board's squares are used, notation is simple. Each black square is numbered, beginning at White's upper left and Black's lower right.

BLACK

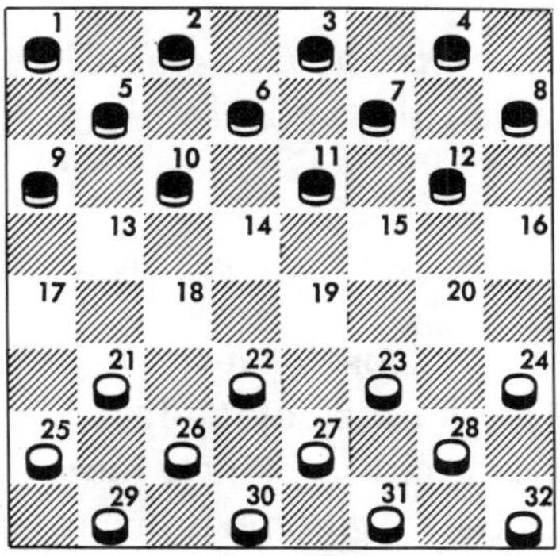

WHITE

A move noted as 10-6 means that the player lifted the piece on square 10 and moved it to square 6. When the numerical difference between the squares is larger than 5, it means that the move involved at least one capture. And a notation that includes an asterisk signifies the game's winning move.

Errors and Penalties

Having touched one of his men, the player must move it. He may not adjust the position of an opponent's piece, or touch it for any other reason, without permission.

Under tournament rules promulgated by the American Checkers Association, the player must make his move in six minutes, unless it involves a capture and is the only capture available to him. In that circumstance he must move in one minute. Violation of the time limit means forfeit.

Restrictions

Experts have long since exhausted the possibilities of *free-style* or *go-as-you-please* play, in which Black chooses his own opening moves. In tournaments, the *three-move restriction* is standard. A card is drawn at random from 137 on each of which one permissible three-move opening pattern is described. Play then proceeds along the prescribed three-move opening line. The match consists of two games with the same opening, the players alternating as Black and White.

Earlier, a *two-move restriction* was used, but it fell into discard after the experts mastered all its possibilities.

Strategy

Good Checkers players look for a draw because victories are infrequent. They play cautiously, hoping for an error by the opponent. Their game is much like old-fashioned football, in which scoreless ties were common and the long bomb unheard of.

Some of the more popular openings:

Alma

Black	*White*
1. 11–15	2. 23–19
3. 8–11	4. 22–17
5. 3–8	

Glasgow

Black	*White*
1. 11–15	2. 23–19
3. 8–11	4. 22–17
5. 11–16	

Laird and Lady

Black	*White*
1. 11–15	2. 23–19
3. 8–11	4. 22–17
5. 9–13	6. 17–14
7. 10–17	8. 21–14

Old Fourteenth

Black	*White*
1. 11–15	2. 23–19
3. 8–11	4. 22–17
5. 4–8	

Fife

Black	*White*
1. 11–15	2. 23–19
3. 9–14	4. 22–17
5. 5–9	

Souter

Black	*White*
1. 11–15	2. 23–19
3. 9–14	4. 22–17
5. 6–9	

Whilter

Black	*White*
1. 11–15	2. 23–19
3. 9–14	4. 22–17
5. 7–11	

Defiance

Black	*White*
1. 11–15	2. 23–19
3. 9–14	4. 27–23

Will o' the Wisp

Black	*White*
1. 11–15	2. 23–19
3. 9–13	4. 22–18

Dyke

Black	*White*
1. 11–15	2. 22–17
3. 15–19	

Cross

Black	*White*
1. 11–15	2. 23–18

Double Corner

Black	*White*
1. 9–14	2. 22–18

Most free-style games begin with 11–15 or 9–14. Other openings allow White to gain the upper hand (usually by 22–18, 24–20 or 21–17).

The opening phase generally gives way to a middle-game war of attrition when each player has lost from two to four men. A key position for the middle game is the *bridge*. For Black, this means men at 1 and 3. For White the positions are 30 and 32. The bridge prevents opposing pieces from crowning. In expert play it is maintained as long as possible, and usually is subjected to heavy attack.

Another familiar tactic is the *shot*—sacrifice of one man for the capture of two or more opposing ones.

Mastery of the middle game depends less on bridges and shots, however, than on the expert's memory of fixed formations or patterns, the permutations of which are too vast for intelligible discussion here. Casual players do quite well by learning some of the better openings and the fundamental end-game positions.

In the end game, the pieces may be reduced to three kings against two, or four against three. The principle is to exchange pieces until facing only one opposing king with two of one's own, or even matching one against one in proper position.

Black wins as follows:

Black	*White*
16–19	27–31
20–24	32–27
28–32	27–20
19–24	20–27
32–23	

If White chooses to respond to the first move in the sequence with 27–24 instead of 27–31, Black wins with 20–27, to which White must reply 32–16, paving the way for Black's 28–24. White can now only retreat until pinned against the edge of the board.

Most end games duplicate or resemble various classic patterns identified and analyzed long ago. One of the most important is known, fittingly enough, as *first position* and was elucidated by William Payne in the eighteenth century.

Black wins as follows:

	Black	*White*
	11–16	32–28
	16–20	28–32
	20–24	32–28
	24–27	28–32
	19–23	32–28
	27–32	28–24
	32–28	24–20
(a)	23–19	20–24
	19–15	24–27
	15–18	4–8
	18–15	27–23
	28–32	8–12
	32–28	23–27
	15–18	12–16
	28–32	27–24
	18–15	24–28
(b)	15–11	16–19
	32–27	28–32
	27–31	19–23
	11–15	32–28
(c)	15–19	

(a) Black prevents the White king from reaching the single corner.
(b) If Black plays 15–18 instead of 15–11, White earns a draw with 16–19, 32–27, 19–23.
(c) White must now lose a piece, giving Black decisive advantage.

William Payne also analyzed the familiar *second position,* in which the player who is to move can always defeat an opponent even though each has one king and two uncrowned men.

Recommended Reading

The principal openings and end-game positions are well explained in *The Complete Guide to Checkers* by Tom Wiswell (Collier Books). Wiswell's *Secrets of Checkerboard Strategy* (Simon and Schuster) is also recommended.

LOSING CHECKERS

Checkers in reverse. The object is to lose all pieces, or position them so that none can move.

SPANISH CHECKERS

The board is rotated so that a white corner stands at each player's lower left. A king's moves are identical with those of the bishop in Chess. It can move any distance along any diagonal and captures by jumping the captured piece and coming to rest on the diagonally adjacent vacant square. Also, where a player of American Checkers is permitted to choose between two or more capturing moves, in this game, he must make the move that involves the more immediate captures.

ITALIAN CHECKERS

With the board positioned as in Spanish Checkers, American rules apply until a king is crowned. A king may be captured only by another king. Also, where it is possible to make capturing moves with both a king and a single piece, the king move is required. Finally, when faced with opportunity for more than one capturing move, it is compulsory to capture the piece or pieces of higher value. Thus, capture of a king and an uncrowned piece would be required, even though an alternate move to capture two single pieces might lead to a better playing position.

GERMAN CHECKERS

The king is called a queen (*Damen*). It moves diagonally, as in Spanish Checkers, but when capturing may land on any space along the diagonal beyond the position of the captured piece. Moreover, with a choice of places to land, the player is compelled to go to a square that permits continued captures, until no more captures are possible. Uncrowned pieces move one square forward, as in American Checkers, but may capture backward as well as forward. When one lands on the crowning row, it is not crowned unless its move ends there. If it can capture another piece by moving backward, it must do so. This defers its crowning until it returns to the crowning row on a subsequent move.

3 GO

This infinitely subtle game of encirclement originated about 4,000 years ago in China, where it is called Wei-Ch'i. It was introduced to Japan around 500 A.D. and presently became that country's national game. By the sixteenth century the Japanese were so obsessed with Go that a state-supported school was established for the study of what had by then transcended diversion and become an actual art form.

Persons who know both games assure us that Go is as taxing as Chess. More to the point may be Go's reflection of unique cultural values unfamiliar in the West. For that reason, the game remains something of a curiosity here. Not many North Americans are likely to immerse themselves sufficiently to become expert. The quality of Western Go is a far cry from the Oriental and probably will stay that way for a long time. For example, we tend to make the game shorter and easier than the original. Our rules vary according to locality.

Players and Equipment

For two, facing each other across a board crosshatched by nineteen vertical and nineteen horizontal lines. The 361 intersections, or *points,* are positions for placement of the *stones,* which are disk-shaped playing pieces. Most games are played with 181 black and 180 white stones. One player is Black, the other White.

The diagramed intersections marked by dark dots are called *handicap points.* The letters and numbers are for purposes of game notation and do not appear on actual playing boards.

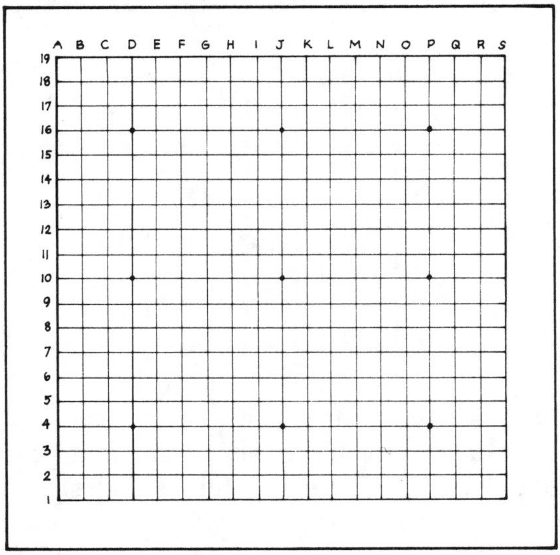

The Play

Beginning with Black, players alternate in placing one stone at a time on intersections. Each tries to surround as many vacant intersections as possible.

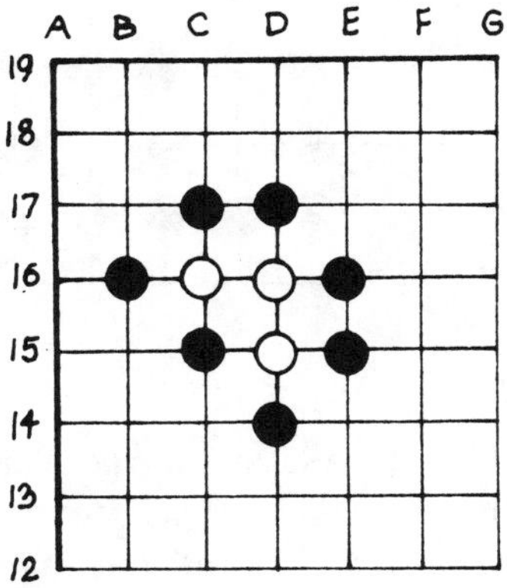

When two or more stones of like color occupy adjacent points on a vertical or horizontal line, they are *connected* and may be captured when surrounded by opposing stones. The unit is said to *live* when one of its members adjoins a vacant point. And if completely encircled the entire unit *dies*.

In the illustration, three white stones are captured by Black. They will be removed from the board and held by the captor until the game ends.

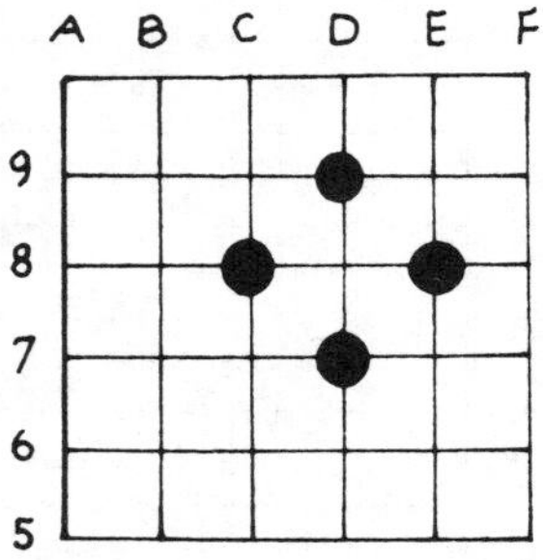

Here Black has created a strong formation called an *eye*. White may not play to D8 because his stone would be a prisoner and removed immediately. Such a deliberately self-destructive move is illegal. The only way to capture this eye is to surround it at D10, C9, E9, B8, F8, C7, D6 and E7 and then commandeer D8.

A stronger formation is the *double eye*, as shown below. It is completely invulnerable to capture, because either D9 or F9 are always vacant, keeping the unit alive.

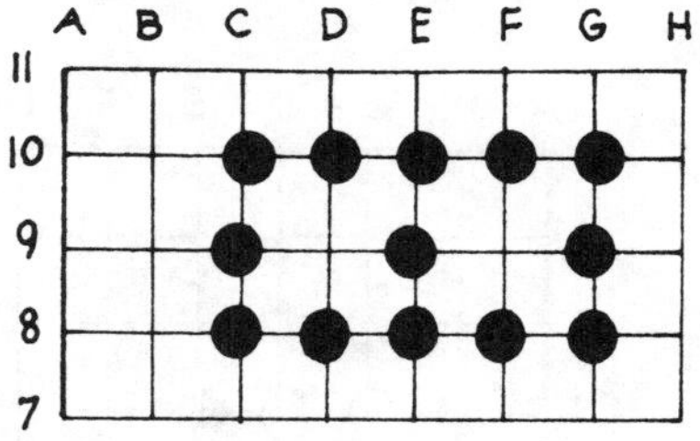

Winning

The game ends when the players agree that all possible territory has been taken. Each then removes whatever dead opposing stones may not yet have been formally captured. Next, each uses captured enemy stones to fill vacant points encircled by the opponent. Points surrounded by a mix of black and white stones are simply filled with unused stones of either color. Each player's score now becomes the number of points (a) encircled by his own forces and (b) still vacant after opponent has used all captured stones to fill such vacancies.

The same effect is achieved by less traditional means—counting vacant points encircled by one's own stones and subtracting the number of stones lost through capture.

Strategy

The most effective opening techniques concentrate on the corners and proceed to the sides. Such positions are easier to defend than those toward center.

The most common openings, with Black making the first move, are C4 or D3 (or C16 or D17; Q4 or P3; Q16 or P17). More daring are D5 or E4 and their counterparts elsewhere on the board. A typical example:

Black	*White*
1. C4	2. E3
3. G3	4. C3
5. B3	6. D4
7. C5	8. C2
9. D7	10. B2

White's plays of E3, C3 and D4 in response to Black's first three moves created a *tiger mouth*—a versatile formation which is easily protected and threatens development in three directions. Yet Black has the advantage.

A more even game unfolds after the following start:

Black	*White*
1. C4	2. E3
3. H3	4. D5
5. C5	6. D6
7. C7	8. C6
9. B6	10. B7
11. B8	12. D7
13. C8	14. B5

15. A7 (capture)	16. C3
17. B4	18. B3
19. D4	20. E14

Black has captured a point, but White has staked strong claims to the corners. As play progresses, both sides will try to expand their units by *extension*—creating a smaller number of large units rather than depending on a larger number of small ones. Bigger units are harder to attack.

Care is taken to avoid *false eyes:*

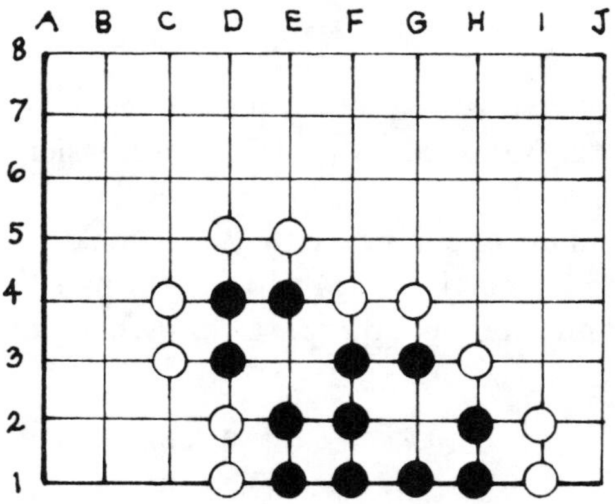

In the illustrated position, Black is not as impregnable as he might seem. He does not have the double eye, but two distinct units. When White plays E3, he captures the black stones at D3, D4 and E4.

Misplay of the following position can produce a *ladder* formation, and disaster.

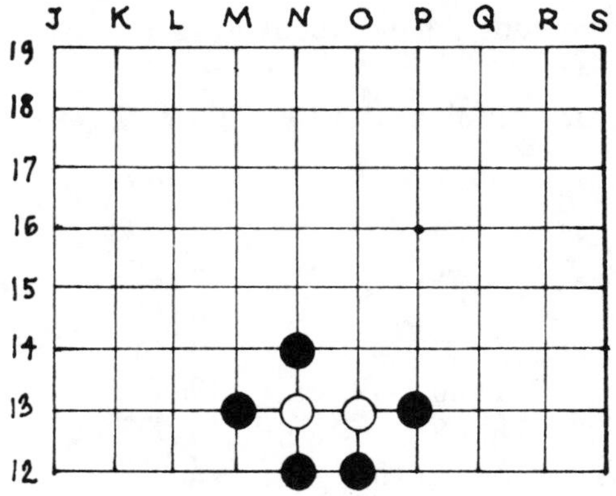

If White tries to escape capture with 014, Black counters with 015, leaving White only one way out . . . P14. Play then proceeds as follows:

Black	*White*
O15	P14
Q14	P15
P16	Q15
R15	Q16
Q17	R16
S16	R17
R18	S17
S18	

This leads to the position below:

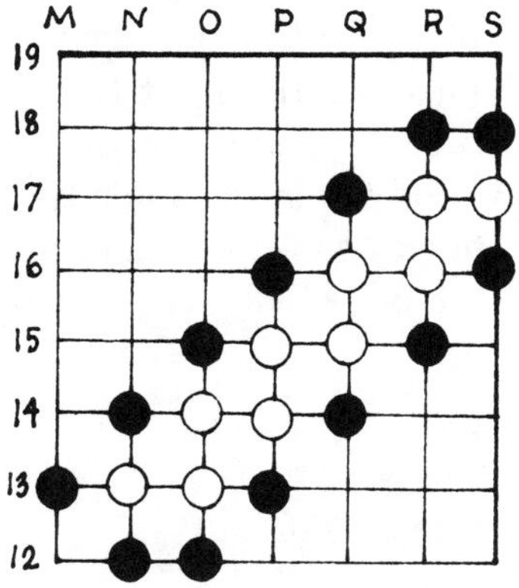

White is run to the edge of the board and loses 10 stones. If he had abandoned the original formation, White would have lost only two stones, a dramatic illustration of what happens when the heedless throw good stones after bad.

Enclosed territories invite attack. Defense hinges upon protection inside and outside the formation perimeter. A bungled defense may result in a *seki,* an impasse in which neither player can effectively lay claim to the territory.

A unit is secure against attack only when it encloses at least three points which are divided into two or more distinct groups (as with eyes) by *partition.* Partition of three points is accomplished by placement of a stone on the middle one of the three, the partition point. A player with four points on a line may use either of the middle two as partition points. If an opponent occupies either, the defender takes the remaining one immediately, thus protecting the unit. Four vacant points in the shape of a *T* are also easily defended by partitioning on the middle point atop the *T*. However, if the four points are in a square they cannot be secured. If the player puts a stone on any of the four points, attacker need only play his stone on the diagonal for a successful invasion.

The principle of partition into equal or almost equal groups of points aims at preventing attacker from establishing a living unit inside occupied territory. The principle applies to territories of all sizes.

Throughout the game, a player attempts to apply constant pressure against adverse territory. At the same time, he tries to stay out of precarious positions himself. The player who doesn't fear attack is free to threaten capture and enclose points. This player has the *sente,* or initiative. He carries the fight to his opponent, who is too busy defending himself to mount an offensive of his own.

If one player is too good for his opponent, a *handicap* is used. The weaker player takes Black (goes first) and may also place stones on the handicap points (*see page* 397). Handicaps are graded from two to nine points:

1. D4, P16
2. D4, P16, P4
3. D4, P16, P4, D16
4. D4, P16, P4, D16, J10
5. D4, P16, P4, D16, D10, P10
6. D4, P16, P4, D16, D10, P10, J4
7. D4, P16, P4, D16, D10, P10, J4, J16
8. D4, P16, P4, D16, D10, P10, J4, J16, J10

GO BANG

Also known as Go Maku, its Japanese name, this simplification of Go can be played on a chessboard, a Go board or with pencils and an eighteen-square-by-eighteen-square piece of graph paper. The object is to be first to place five—but not six or more—of one's stones in an uninterrupted straight line, vertically, horizontally or diagonally. In the paper-and-pencil game, one player marks his position with crosses, the other with naughts. And with a chessboard, players frequently are limited to twelve stones each, using the squares rather than the intersecting lines. Versions have been marketed as Peggity, Spoil Five and Pegfive.

BOXES

This good old paper-and-pencil game resembles the Go family in that the goal is to capture territory by surrounding it. A rectangular pattern of dots is used—usually ten or twelve rows of eight or ten dots each.

By turns, each of the two players draws horizontal or vertical lines joining two dots—one line per turn. Whoever draws the fourth line that completes a box has captured that box and marks it with his initial.

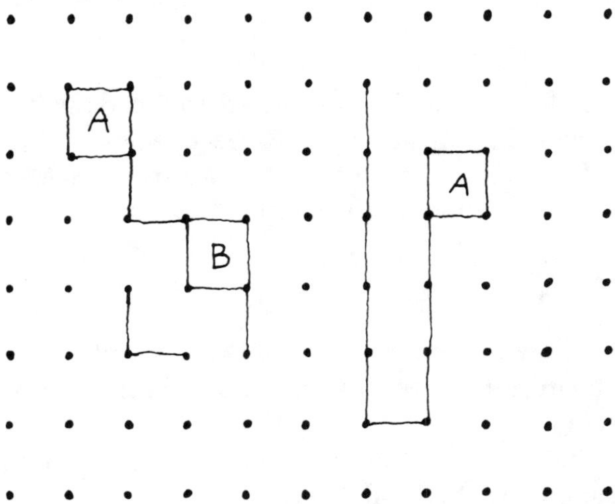

After winning a box, the player takes a second turn, whether he wants to or not. In some localities, it is compulsory to use one's move to win a box if it can be done in the turn. But the game is more interesting without that requirement. Winning tactics consist mainly of avoiding a situation like the one illustrated at the right side of the above diagram. The opponent can win the entire area at his next turn. The winner is the one who captures the larger number of squares.

4 THE MILL

This cousin of Tic-tac-toe is also related to Go Bang and has been traced to ancient Egypt, Rome and Greece. Known alternatively as Nine-Man Morris, Three Men's Morris, Morris and Mill Race, the game was greatly popular in Elizabethan England.

Players and Equipment

For two, each with nine pieces of contrasting color. Depending on the type of board, the pieces may resemble checkers or may be pegs for insertion in holes.

The numbers in the illustration are for explanatory purposes. They do not appear on an actual Mill board.

The Play

The primary object is to form *mills*—three pieces in vertical or horizontal rows. These are impregnable to attack but permit removal of enemy pieces. Because diagonal mills do not count, diagonal lines are often not inscribed on modern boards.

Play begins with players taking turns positioning one piece at a time. No point may be occupied by more than one piece. Until all

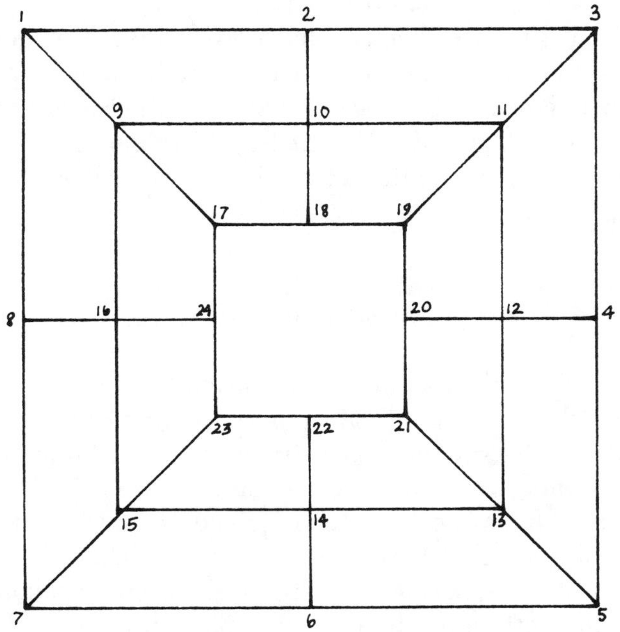

eighteen pieces have been deployed, no piece may be moved from its original position. But afterward, pieces may be moved, one space at a turn, vertically or horizontally, along lines to vacant points.

When a move completes a mill (such as 1-2-3 or 1-8-7), the player is permitted to remove any opposing piece that is not itself part of a mill.

In some games, a player with only three remaining pieces is permitted to move any distance to any vacant point.

Winning

The game ends when a player has only two men, or cannot move.

Strategy

Good players usually have difficulty beating each other. The typical game ends in a draw. But the innocent newcomer is a sure loser.

The most important tactical points are 10, 12, 14 and 16, which offer greatest latitude for mill formation.

Good players strive for the *double mill.* For example, with men on 3, 4, 5, 11 and 13, the player makes a new mill each time he moves the piece from 4 to 12 or back again. A lesser advantage comes from a formation such as 1, 2 and 3, with 4 vacant. To move a piece back and forth between 3 and 4 is to form a new mill at every other turn.

A position like 9, 10 and 17, with 1 and 11 open, is called a *fork*. It resembles the Chess tactic in that the opponent's next move cannot prevent a mill.

SCORE FOUR

A proprietary game that adds a dimension to The Mill. The board is a square with sixteen spindles in a four-by-four pattern. The players place beads on the spindles, each trying to situate four beads in a row, or a column, or a diagonal or—entering the third dimension—any angle that finds the four beads joined by a straight line. For example, a player might have one of his beads at the bottom of the stack on one spindle, second from the bottom on an adjoining one, third from the bottom on the next one, and fourth from the bottom on the fourth. A simpler version is played on a three-level board, each level resembling an ordinary three-by-three Tic-tac-toe layout. The result is a three-dimensional Tic-tac-toe, marketed under various names.

TWIXT

With elements of Go and The Mill, this proprietary game involves attempts to build a fence from the player's side of the board all the way to his opponent's. Meanwhile, the opponent is trying to do the same thing. A somewhat more elaborate version is Boundary, which uses pegs and an elastic string that can be stretched to make captures.

5 CHINESE CHECKERS

This used to be called Halma, which is Greek for "jump." But it is neither Greek nor Chinese, nor does it much resemble Checkers. It was developed and marketed in England about fifteen years before the turn of the century. It is one of the extremely few patented games to achieve any longevity.

Modern American versions offer a board patterned like a six-pointed star with cups to accommodate marbles, or holes to receive pegs. Each of two to six players is equipped with from ten to fifteen pieces (marbles or pegs, depending on the manufacturer). At the start, each player's pieces are positioned in the point of the star facing the player. The object is to move all pieces to the star point directly opposite. This is done by moving one piece per turn, one hole at a time. It is done more rapidly by means of Checkers-type jumps. Pieces may jump any intervening piece, but no captures are made. Skill consists largely of trying to form a string, or *ladder,* of one's own pieces right across the board, preparatory to jumping them one at a time into the goal. An entertaining game.

6 BATTLESHIP

This good old pencil-and-paper game, known by some as Salvo, is also available in board form. Do-it-yourselfers make their battle zones by marking graph paper into boxes of ten squares by ten or by drawing such grids themselves on any old paper. Each prepares two grids, one representing his own battle zone and the other the enemy's. To facilitate play, each zone is marked alphabetically across the top—A through J—and vertically along the left side—1 through 10. One now can identify any individual box by its coordinates, A-1 being the uppermost left and J-10 the lowest right.

Without allowing the opponent to see what's going on, each positions his fleet of four ships. The battleship is represented by five squares which the player encircles. Naturally, the squares must be adjacent and in a straight line (diagonals if the player chooses). The fleet also includes a cruiser (three squares) and two destroyers (two squares each). At least one square must separate the members of a fleet.

First to play fires a salvo of seven shots, naming the seven squares under bombardment. As he does so, he inscribes a "1" in the corresponding squares on the grid that represents the opponent's zone. Similarly, the opponent records this first cannonade with a "1" in each bombarded square of his own zone. After the salvo, the attacked party announces whether any of his vessels has been hit. He names the type of ship and how many times it was struck. But he does not reveal the coordinates of the hit squares.

When all squares of a vessel are hit, the ship is sunk and the player's own fire power is reduced. Loss of the battleship lowers the player's shots per salvo by three. Loss of a cruiser costs two and a destroyer one.

Most players quickly learn to concentrate their fire for maximum destruction and more rapid disclosure of where the enemy forces lie. The game ends after the loser's last ship goes down.

SUB SEARCH

This is a three-dimensional version in which a surface fleet tries to sink enemy submarines. Coordinates include depth (at three possible levels) as well as the usual surface grid. The submarine fleet has counterattacking fire power of its own, such as torpedoes.

7 RISK

One cut above the usual path or chase game is the kind that requires a bit of thought but does not submerge the element of luck. In recent years the market has been congested with these trademarked products, most of which permit the winner a sense of vast, even global, power. In this example, which is one of the best, the winner rules the world. The board is a map on which two to six players position their armies for battles settled by rolls of dice. As players win battles and accumulate territory, they add to their armies and become harder to defeat. At a comparable level are competitive products such as Dogfight, Broadside, Ploy and Battle-Cry. Broadside seems to require more strategy than the others, but all have the virtue of entertaining an adult without overtaxing a reasonably competent child.

PART THREE

Dice Games

The rolling of bones dates from the caves, when real knuckle bones were regarded as dependable fortune tellers. Efforts to predict the future are only a short step from those other transactions with fate known as gambling. So bones are undoubtedly man's oldest gaming equipment.

For thousands of years, dice have been six-sided cubes, each face bearing its own number and the numbers on opposite faces always adding to seven. In North America, the favorite dice game is Craps, of which the most equitable variation is the kind played under correct rules in private homes or other noncommercial surroundings. In old England, Craps was called Hazard, a good name for it. For information about the kind of Craps played in gambling casinos, see Book Three.

1 CRAPS

Players and Equipment

For any number, using two dice. On proper dice, not only do numbers on opposite faces add to seven, but when the ⚃ faces up, it should be possible to turn the dice so that the ⚁ faces the player, the ⚀ is at his right and the ⚅ at his left.

The Play

Players form a circle on the floor or, in luxurious settings, around a gaming table. Either by mutual consent or high roll of the dice, one player becomes the *shooter.*

Shooter announces the size of his bet and deposits the full amount in the center. In some games a minimum bet is established. Other players *fade* any part of shooter's bet (bet against him) by making their own announcements and putting their own bets in front of them. When shooter's entire bet is faded, he rolls the dice. If part of his bet is not faded, he takes that part back before rolling.

The first roll often decides the outcome of the bet. If shooter throws a 7 or 11, the roll is a *natural* and he wins the bets. If he rolls 2, 3 or 12—*craps*—he loses.

It is customary and proper to throw the dice so that they bounce off a wall or some other backstop before coming to rest. Where this is not possible, prudent tradition requires a thorough shake of the dice and the farthest practicable toss.

If the dice come up 4, 5, 6, 8, 9 or 10 on the first roll, the particular number becomes shooter's *point.* He must roll again and continue rolling until the dice either come up with a 7 or the point. The 7 is a *miss* and the shooter loses. But if the point is made before a 7, the shooter *passes* and collects the money. Having won, the shooter may continue to roll or may choose to pass the dice to the player at his left. The same applies after tossing Craps on a first roll. But after a player misses his point by throwing a 7, he is obliged to relinquish the dice.

Note that the shooter passes if his roll equals the point. But the dice may show two different faces than they did when the point was established. For example, if shooter's first roll produces ⚂ and ⚂, he also wins with ⚄ and ⚀ or ⚁ and ⚃ –provided they turn up before a 7.

Besides the main bets, *side* bets are customary. In these, any player may offer to bet that the shooter will make his point or that he will not. And a *come* bet is a wager to the effect that the shooter will produce a winning sequence beginning with the next roll. A *don't come* bet backs the opposite forecast. In the come and don't come bets, the shooter's point, if any, is disregarded and, for purposes of settling the particular bet, the next roll is treated as if it were the first.

At any juncture between rolls, a player may decide that the shooter is going to win and may offer a *right* bet–"Five bucks he's right." A player of opposite mind offers a *wrong* bet.

And *hard-way* bets are also frequent. These proffer odds on the proposition that the shooter will make his point by rolling a double. This necessitates that the point be 4, 6, 8 or 10, in which case hard way means ⚁ ⚁, ⚂ ⚂, ⚃ ⚃ or ⚄ ⚄.

Finally, sharp Craps players sometimes invite bets on whether an upcoming roll will be a 6 or 8 or a 5 or 9 or a 4 or 10. The correct odds on such propositions can be found in the section on Strategy, below, and should be committed to mind by anyone planning to brave a Craps session with sophisticated players.

Errors and Penalties

A throw is void if either die does not lie perfectly flat when it comes to rest. This is known as *cocked dice.*

Arguments as to which players acted first in fading a shooter's bets are resolved in favor of the player who faded the entire amount. If two or more did so, the argument is won by the disputant who lost most recently as shooter. Where none faded the entire bet, the preference goes to the player who faded the largest amount or, failing that, lost most recently as shooter.

Strategy

Whether playing the so-called "sociable" game or trying one's luck in a casino, strategy requires knowledge of the correct odds against the various rolls. In casinos, as we shall see in Book Three, the player bets against the house rather than against other players, and the odds are fixed to give the house the advantage it needs to stay in business. In sociable games, the only fair odds are those that give each bettor an equal chance and leave the outcome entirely to luck. Unfortunately, civilization is befouled with folks who see a Craps game as an opportunity to swindle the unwary. They offer unfair odds on various side bets. This is not sporting. Indeed, it is morally indistinguishable from supplying loaded dice. The best defense against such swine is to leave immediately.

Here are proper odds.

Point	*Odds Against*
6 or 8	6–5
5 or 9	3–2
4 or 10	2–1
4 hard way	8–1
6 hard way	10–1
8 hard way	10–1
10 hard way	8–1

In the more basic part of the game—the even-money right-way and wrong-way bets and those that fade the shooter—the shooter or anyone else who bets that he will pass is playing at a slight disadvantage. In a representative series of such bets, the right-way loses about $1.40 on every wagered $100. Which means that it pays to fade and make wrong-way bets.

Exotic propositions sometimes offer seemingly large odds against a particular sequence of numbers occurring in a given number of rolls. Such bets should be avoided except by mathematicians capable of figuring and memorizing their complicated percentages. Suffice to say that anyone offering such a bet has almost certainly done his arithmetic in advance and is probably looking for suckers.

2 POKER DICE

As the name implies, this is Poker played with dice. Five regular dice can be used, with the ⚀ counting as an ace and ranking above the ⚅ . Special Poker dice have faces showing actual A, K, Q, J, 10 and 9 instead of pips. The game is best for five or fewer, each with a set of dice.

A turn consists of three rolls in an effort to produce the best hand. In most places, the player is allowed to set aside whatever dice turn up favorably, hoping that the remaining dice will fill out the desired hand on the next roll or two. Elsewhere, the player must decide whether to stand with the hand produced by the first roll or whether to roll all the dice a second and, perhaps, a third time. After all have had a turn, high hand wins. Hands rank exactly as in Poker played with a wild card—from five of a kind downward, but without flushes. In some games, the ace can be placed either at the top or bottom of a straight and in others it is used as a wild card.

LIAR DICE

The several versions of this game come closer to Poker than Poker Dice does, mainly because they permit bluffing. In one variant, the two players are separated by a screen behind which they conceal their rolls. In another, no screen is used, two or more can play, and the dice are hidden by shaking them in cups and depositing them on the table behind the player's sheltering hand.

In all versions, the opponent to the player's immediate left is the *caller*, or *doubter*, with special privileges. After the player rolls and looks at his concealed hand, he may decide to stay with one or more of the dice, rolling the others a second and/or third time. Having finally stayed, he then announces a complete holding—"Fives and threes with a deuce." He is not required to tell the truth. Having heard the announcement, caller can decide whether to try to beat the hand or simply call the bluff. In the two-hand version, the bluff is called by lifting the screen that separates the two sides and inspecting the shooter's hand. If the hand is as represented, the caller loses. But if he catches the shooter bluffing, he wins.

In two-hand Liar Dice, it is customary for both players to shoot at once. This speeds up the game in case doubter decides to compete rather than call a bluff. In games with more than two, each player starts with three to five chips representing that many betting units. One player shoots at a time, and losses go into a pot. Play proceeds until all but one player has been wiped out. The survivor takes the pot.

All variations are best when doubter is required to adhere to his first decision—competing or calling. Having refrained from calling, he may decide to try another roll or two in hope of improving his own hand. Having failed to do so, he must still engage in a showdown rather than changing his mind and calling a bluff.

OTHER VARIANTS

Poker Dice and numerous modifications thereof are played with great enthusiasm in North American bars and, where law permits, at the counters of cigar stores and billiard emporiums. Such variations are covered in Book Four.

3 YAHTZEE

Sales of this trademarked dice game approach those of Monopoly and Scrabble. Actually, Yahtzee is a proprietary version of a classic called Yacht, which has been around for years. The games are almost identical, although Yahtzee jazzes up the proceedings with special bonuses on certain rolls.

Any number can play. As in Poker Dice, five dice are used, with as many as three rolls per turn. A tally sheet itemizes the thirteen different kinds of rolls that produce scores. These range from *yahtzee* (five of a kind) through full houses to pairs. After he has entered a tally for one of the thirteen hands, the player cannot score again for that kind of hand. Thus, as play progresses, players have fewer options. After everybody has had thirteen turns, or after the options are exhausted, scores are added and highest wins.

TRIPLE YAHTZEE

This offers extra bonuses and requires a bit of thought in choosing the kinds of bonuses to seek.

YACHT

As in Yahtzee, the player retains whatever dice please him on the first roll and tosses the others again in hope of improving the hand. *Yacht* (five of a kind) is worth 50. Straights are worth 30. Four of a kind earns the total number of pips shown on all five dice. So do full house and *choice* (any five dice). Pairs (or singles 1 through 6) count only the number of pips on the scoring dice—for example, 6 for one 6, 12 for two, etc. Two pairs are not permitted. Each player has twelve turns and, as in Yahtzee, may not score in a category in which he has already scored. The categories are yacht, six-high straight (*big*), five-high straight (*little*), four of a kind, full house, choice and the six different pairs.

CRAG

Like Yacht, with only three dice and two rolls per turn. A score sheet includes the game's thirteen possibilities, the highest being *crag* (when a pair plus the third die total exactly 13), which is worth 50. When three dice, not including a pair, total 13, the tally is 26. Three of a kind counts 25. Four different straights are recognized and each is worth 20. They are *high* (4-5-6), *low* (1-2-3), *odd* (1-3-5) and *even* (2-4-6). Pairs are tallied as in Yacht.

DOUBLE CAMEROON

This version uses ten dice, three rolls per turn and ten scoring categories. After completing his rolls, the player divides the dice into two groups of five, attempting to score with each. Ones through sixes and full houses score the total of the five dice in the hand that fits the selected category. Five of a kind scores 50. *Large Cameroon* (a six-high straight) earns 30. *Little Cameroon* (five-high straight) gets 21.

4 HELP YOUR NEIGHBOR

This fast game for two, three or six players uses three dice. Each player has his own point or points, from 1 through 6. All numbers on a die are assigned, so that in the two-player game, first roller has points 1 through 3 and opponent has the rest. With three players, each gets two points. Turns proceed clockwise, one roll at a time. Players whose numbers appear on the rolled dice place one chip in the center for each such appearance. Thus, if someone rolls 2-2-3, the player with the 2 deposits two chips in the center and player with 3 adds a chip of his own. First player to get rid of all his chips (it is customary to start each game with three chips each) is the winner.

VARIATIONS

Innumerable changes are possible in Help Your Neighbor. Using one to three dice, players sometimes get rid of a chip only when they roll a number in exact rotation. Thus, until somebody rolls a 1, nobody can score, and afterward, only a 2 scores, followed by a 3, and so on. In other versions, players are permitted to add or subtract the three rolled numbers to produce whatever digit suits immediate needs. Attractive equipment for this type of game is sold under various trade names.

PART FOUR

Tile Games

1 DOMINOES

It is assumed with some logic that dominoes are the offspring of dice. The markings on dominoes are the same as those on dice. And dominoes are known as *bones*.

These flat, rectangular gaming pieces may have originated in India. They were well established in ancient China and are thought to have been brought to Europe by some mercantile pioneer of the magnitude of Marco Polo. By the eighteenth century, Dominoes was immensely popular in most of the Western world. It remains so, and deservedly.

The Draw Game

Anyone with a good card memory and common sense can play acceptable Dominoes. Here is one of the fundamental versions.

Players and Equipment

Best when played by two, but adaptable to three or four. Uses the basic *double-six* set of tiles consisting of twenty-eight bones.

The six bones with double numbers are called *doublets*. A doublet belongs to only one *suit*—the one identified by its number. Other

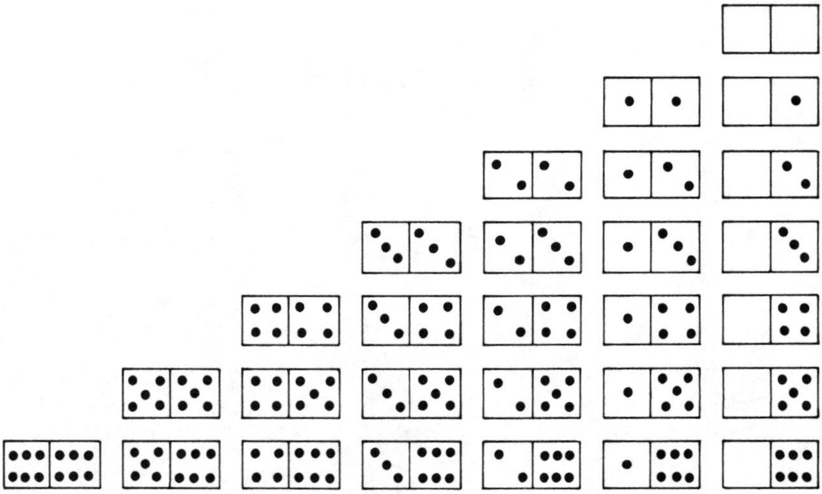

bones belong to two suits because they bear two numbers each. Some games are played with larger assortments, known as *double-nine* and *double-twelve*, but the double-six is in wider use.

THE PLAY

All bones are mixed face down at center table. Players then take one at a time until—in the two-hand game—each has seven. When three or four play, each takes five. The denominations are concealed either by holding the tiles in a hand or standing them on edge so that only their backs are visible to the opponents.

Undistributed tiles are set aside, still face down, in a *boneyard.*

In some games, the first bone exposed for play (the *set*) is the highest doublet that has been drawn. In a livelier version, first to play is designated by a previous draw for higher (*heavier*) bone, and the set can be any tile that suits the player's strategy.

Second player in the clockwise rotation must match one end of the set with a tile of his own. That is, if the set is 5-5, the second player must follow with a tile that bears a 5. If unable to do this, he draws from the boneyard until he gets a playable bone. He must play such a bone at either side of the set, and immediately—without hunting for another, more advantageous bone.

Assuming that the second player responds to the set with a 5-3, the next player has the choice of playing a 5 or a 3. And thus play proceeds, with each player permitted to play at either end of the tile structure. Doublets are placed perpendicular to other tiles. In some games, the doublet used as the set is not placed perpendicularly, but this makes little difference. A typical conformation arising from the plays described above:

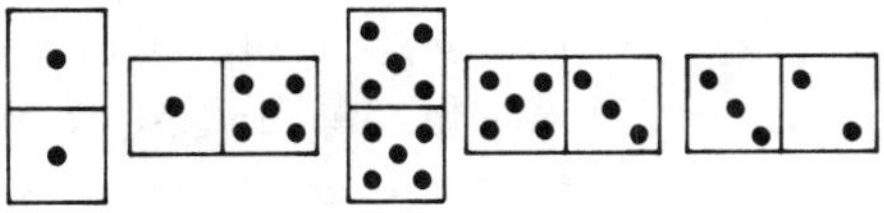

Note that the long sides of a doublet are *open*—the surfaces against which subsequent plays are made. But only the short ends of other dominoes are open.

Winning

The first to get rid of all his bones is the winner, which some announce by calling "Domino." Winner gets 1 point for each dot held by his opponents. Settlement may come after each such round, or game may be set at 50 or 100 points. Where neither player can play and each is stuck with bones, the winner is the player with the lowest total of dots. His margin over the loser or losers is computed by subtraction.

Errors and Penalties

If a player takes too many bones at the start, he must keep any of the extra ones that he has seen. A player who takes too few bones must correct the error as soon as it is discovered.

When a player exposes a bone while drawing from the boneyard, he must keep it.

When an incorrect play is made and noticed, it is withdrawn, unless the next player has already taken his turn, whereupon the erroneous play stands.

Strategy

Aside from understanding that the entire shooting match involves only twenty-eight bones, the denominations of which should be memorized and kept in mind, good players try to leave themselves maximum options. For example, if a 5 can be played, someone with a holding of 2-4, 3-5 and 4-5 would probably prefer to play the 4-5, which would leave a 2, 3, 4, and 5 for later use.

By the same reasoning, doublets usually are played as early as possible, since they offer only single possibilities for later play.

One cherished tactic is the *block*, which is brought about by playing so that both ends of the layout belong to the same suit at a time when no more bones of that suit are to be had. The unfortunate opponent must then exhaust the boneyard and pay.

MUGGINS

Known also as All Fives and Sniff, this is one of the most challenging variations. Whoever draws heavier bone plays first, a privilege that rotates in subsequent games. The first doublet played is *sniff*. It need not be the set, which can be any bone first player prefers. The sniff is open on all four edges, which means that the layout can branch off in four directions.

Whenever a play results in all open ends showing a pip count that totals five or a multiple thereof, the player scores *muggins* points equal to that total.

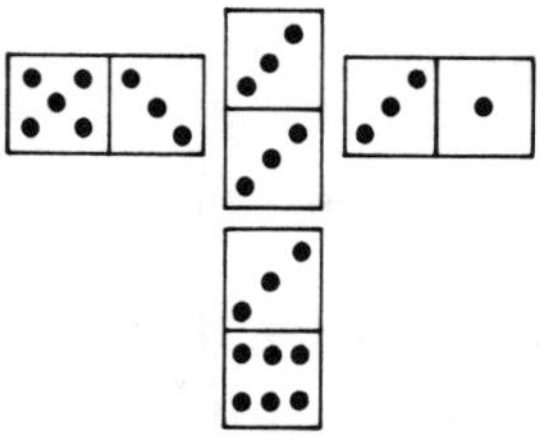

In the illustration, the 3-3 sniff was played alongside the 5-3 set. The next play was the 3-1, after which a player scored 15 points by placing the 6-3. Note that the total of the open ends is 15.

In some circles, if a player fails to credit himself with his muggins points, an opponent can preempt the points by calling "Muggins!"

Because playing for muggins points is preferable to concentrating on going domino, many good players believe that no more than one trip to the boneyard should be allowed on any turn. This prevents shrewd operators from hunting for bones with which to make extra muggins points.

Settlements can be made in numerous ways, as in Draw.

ALL THREES

Muggins, but counting 3's and multiples thereof, instead of 5's.

BERGEN

The highest doublet held at the beginning is the set in this game, which resembles Draw except as follows. A bonus of 2 goes to the player whose bone creates a *double-header*—the same suit at each end of the layout. And a *triple-header,* worth 3, is when the doublet of a suit is at one end and a bone of that suit open at the other. The player going domino earns an extra point, as does the player with low score in a blocked game. A total of 15 wins.

MATADOR

This is Draw, but bones are placed against each other only when their dots total 7. The task is facilitated by four *matadors*—wild bones that may be used at any time. These are the 6-1, 5-2, 4-3 and 0-0. Either end of a matador may be placed on the layout. The 0-0 partially blocks the layout because only another matador may be placed alongside it.

BLOCK GAME

The Draw Game for two to five players, each on his own. No boneyard is used. A player unable to act simply passes that turn.

POOL

This is the Block Game for three to five. With three players, each gets seven bones. With four players, each gets five, and with five players, each gets four. The winner is the first to score 100 points, although accounts are sometimes settled after each game. In blocked games, each loser pays the full difference between his count and the winner's.

FORTRESS

Also called Sebastopol, this is Block for four—each with seven tiles. The player with the doublet 6 plays set. The set is open on all four edges, and nothing but 6's can be played until all four have been covered. Play then proceeds as in Draw.

TIDDLY-WINK

For six to nine players, each with three bones. Highest doublet sets. Plays are made only at one end of the layout, and no draws are made from the boneyard. A doublet allows its player an extra turn. Usually stakes are placed in a kitty before play starts and winner takes all.

FORTY-TWO

A partnership game for four, using dominoes as if they were the cards in a game of Pitch. The three bones whose ends total 5 (5-0, 4-1, 3-2) are *counters* worth 5 extra points each in the final tally. The 5-5 and 6-4 are 10-point counters.

Partners sit opposite each other, as in cards. Each draws seven bones. Player with the 1-0 bids first and may pass or offer any bid from 30 to 42, or one of two special bids—84 and 168. After the auction, highest bidder names the trump suit and *pitches* a bone that bears the suit.

Winner of each trick leads to the next. All players must follow suit if able, but may play any other suit if unable to follow. Heaviest trump played wins the trick, unless no trump was played, whereupon heaviest bone of the led suit wins. In tallying, each of the seven tricks counts 1 point, and the counters score 35 for the total of 42.

If high bidder's side reaches or surpasses its contract, both sides tally their own totals. If the contract is not met, the high-bidding side scores zero and opponents register the amount of the contract plus whatever points they scored. Bids of 84 or 168 are contracts to take all 42 points. If fulfilled, those contracts earn only 42 points. Otherwise, opponents get the entire bid of 84 or 168, plus their own points. In most games 250 wins.

Among several variations of Forty-Two is one in which doublets are regarded as a suit of their own, along with the 0 through 6.

QUINTO

This proprietary game resembles Muggins, but the tiles bear actual numerals instead of dots.

2 MAH-JONGG

Here is the chop suey of table games. It sounds Chinese and looks Chinese and indeed once was Chinese, but it has been considerably Westernized. At bottom, it is Rummy played with tiles and an exotic vocabulary. Compare it with Canasta. Both enjoyed tremendous vogues in North America, although not even Canasta caught on as quickly or spread as rapidly as Mah-Jongg did during its boom a half century ago.

Players and Equipment

During its period of proliferation, the game was modified by local custom and no successful effort has ever been made to bring uniformity to its rules. What we shall do here, therefore, is confine ourselves to the basics, which apply to play in most places.

The standard game is for four, each playing alone. The equipment includes 144 tiles, a pair of dice and a supply of sticks or chips for use in keeping score. Also supplied is one rack per player, for holding tiles so that only the player can see them.

Of the 144 tiles, 108 are *suit* tiles, 28 *honor* tiles and 8 *flowers* (or *seasons*).

Suits: Three suits contain thirty-six tiles—four of each denomination from 1 through 9. The suits are *bamboos* (or *sticks* or *bams* or *boos*), *circles* (or *dots* or *balls*) and *characters* (or *cracks* or *actors*). Suit tiles numbered 1 and 9 usually are given higher point values than others. They are called *terminals,* whereas 2 through 8 are *simples.*

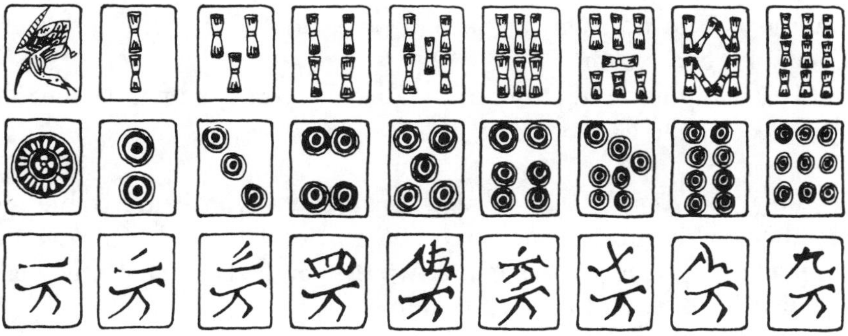

Honors: Four each of seven honor tiles—*red, green* and *white dragons* and *east, north, west* and *south winds.*

Flowers: Eight, usually in two sets of four, numbered from 1 through 4. In some variations, these tiles may appear as only one set of eight, each of a different color. Sometimes these are called seasons.

The Play

A roll of the dice establishes who plays East. Others take the other places at the table and are designated by the other cardinal compass points, as in Bridge. The importance of the East position is that its wins or losses are automatically doubled.

Each *round* consists of four *hands,* or *deals,* with East retaining that position for each new hand only if he has won the previous. When East loses, the compass points rotate clockwise, and the former South becomes East, with all the privileges and problems of that seat.

The compass points also are used in designating the *prevailing wind* of each of the round's four deals. On the first, East *prevails*—which means bonus points for a player who gets a set of the prevailing wind's tiles. On the second deal, South prevails, and thereafter West and North.

After completion of a round, the dice are thrown again to see who shall occupy the East position.

The Wall: At the start, all tiles go face down at center table and are thoroughly mixed. Each player then builds a *wall* face down at his place—eighteen tiles long and two tiles high. The completed walls are pushed together to form a square.

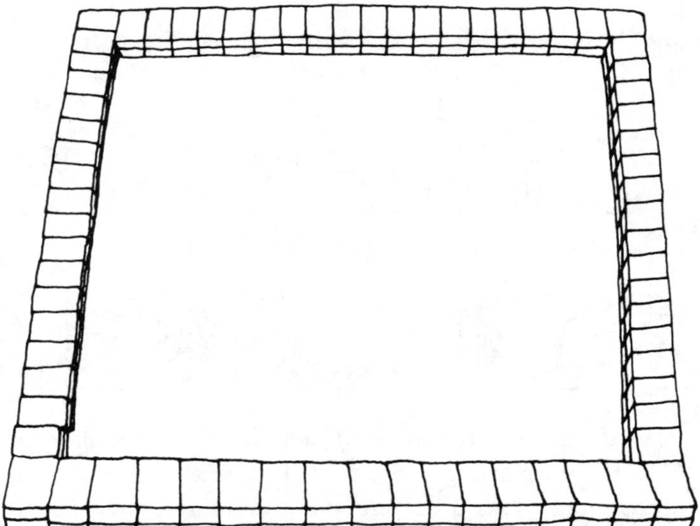

After these preparations, East rolls the dice and counts off their total, beginning at his own position and continuing clockwise around the compass. The player at whose place the count ends must now *break the wall.* The simplest way is a dice roll by the designated player, who adds the rolled number to the total of East's previous throw. He then counts out this tally on his own wall, beginning with the stack at his far right and continuing stack by stack toward the left. If the total count exceeds eighteen, the player continues around the corner onto the wall at his left. The stack at which the count ends is lifted out. The bottom tile of the lifted pair goes face down atop the stack immediately to the right of the break in the wall. And the other lifted tile also goes face down on the adjoining stack at the right. This maneuver creates the *garden.* The two tiles in the garden are *loose.* Whenever both have been drawn into hands (*see below*), a new stack from the right side of the break replenishes the garden by promotion to the top of the wall as before.

Drawing Hands: East takes two stacks (four tiles) from the immediate left of the break and places them on his rack, which usually is of a different color than the other three. In clockwise turns this continues until each has twelve tiles. On the next turn each takes a thirteenth and East concludes this phase by taking an extra one.

When a player gets a flower, either during the hand-drawing stage or later, he *grounds* it face up between his rack and the wall, replacing it with a loose tile from the garden. As this demonstrates, the playing hands contain only suits and honors.

Object: As in Rummy, each tries to develop a *complete hand* containing sets of identical tiles or numerical sequences or both. A numerical sequence of three tiles is a *chow.* Three tiles of identical denomination and suit or wind or dragon form a *pung.* And a pung augmented by a fourth identical tile is a *kong.* When a player has four sets plus a pair (a *pillow*), he wins (*woo* or *mah-jongg*).

During play, the hand contains exactly thirteen tiles, not counting flowers or the fourth tiles of kongs. Because fourteen tiles are required for woo, the final chow, pung, kong or pillow is formed with a tile drawn from the wall, the garden, the discards or an opponent's kong, as will be explained.

Grounding and Discarding: East begins play by discarding a tile face up in the center. This reduces his hand to the required thirteen. Turns then proceed counterclockwise, via North. Each turn begins with a draw and ends with a discard, except that no discard is made when a player goes woo.

A player may draw a discard if he can use it to ground a chow, pung or kong. Otherwise, he draws from the wall at the immediate left of the break. Draws of loose tiles from the garden occur only when the hand must be replenished after grounding a flower or a kong.

A chow, pung or kong formed by drawing a discard is said to be *exposed.* Inasmuch as discards are not taken except to form an exposed set, the set is grounded immediately, face up.

But a set formed by drawing a tile from the wall or garden is *concealed,* and for tactical reasons need not be grounded at once. Concealed sets earn higher scores than the others, but to earn the bonuses they must be grounded before an opponent goes woo.

For example, a concealed kong not grounded counts only as a concealed pung when someone woos.

A player with a grounded concealed pung may convert it to a kong by adding a tile drawn from the wall or garden. But a discard may not be taken for use on a grounded pung.

To distinguish concealed from exposed sets, the end tiles of concealed kongs are grounded face downward, as are the middle tiles of concealed pungs.

If an opponent adds to a grounded pung a fourth tile that a player needs for woo, the player may immediately *rob the kong,* take the tile and declare woo.

Discards may also be taken out of turn as soon as they appear—provided, of course, that player who takes the discard is able to use it immediately in grounding a set. In case two players want the same discard, priority is awarded, in order, to the player who needs the tile for woo, and then for a kong, a pung and, finally, a chow. If the claimants each want the tile for a set of the same rank, the tile goes to the one whose normal turn would occur first. After a player takes and uses a discard out of turn, the turn passes to the player at his right. Thus, players between the discarder and the out-of-turn grounder lose their turns.

Even if nobody has gone woo, the game ends when only fourteen tiles remain on the wall and no more discards can be used.

Scoring

Beginning with the player who completes a hand for woo, scores are awarded to each hand. If nobody has gone woo, scoring begins with East. First, points are totaled to compute the *count.* The count is then multiplied according to the bonus tiles contained in the hand. Note that in most systems of scoring, chows do not contribute to the count.

Set Points

	Exposed	*Concealed*
Pung of Simples (2 through 8)	2	4
Pung of Terminals (1 or 9)	4	8
Honor Pung (Winds or Dragons)	4	8
Kong of Simples	8	16
Kong of Terminals	16	32
Kong of Honors	16	32

Extra Points

Woo (Mah-Jongg)	20
Each Flower	4
Pair of Terminals	2
Pair of Honors	2
Pair of Player's Own Wind (If Prevailing)	4
Drawing Winning Tile from Wall	2

Multipliers

	Multiply By
Pung or Kong of Honors	2
Pung or Kong of Prevailing Wind	2
Pung or Kong of Own Wind	2
Own Flower	2
Go Woo with Garden Tile	2
Go Woo with Last Tile from Wall	2
Woo with Hand Entirely Concealed	2
Clean Hand (Winning Hand of One Suit)	2
Pure Hand (Clean Hand, No Honors)	8
Bouquet of All Four Flowers	8
All Chows and a Worthless Pillow	2
No Chows	2
All Terminals, With Honors	2
All Terminals, No Honors	Limit

Note that these bonus multipliers are distinct from one another. Thus someone holding a *bouquet* multiplies by 16—by 8 for the four flowers and by 2 for his own flower.

The *limit* is usually 500 points. Variations in scoring are almost as abundant as in play.

Strategy

After mastering the nomenclature, a good Rummy player has absolutely no trouble here.

PART FIVE

Mancala Games

These fascinating, elegantly simple games are beginning to captivate Americans after thousands of years as popular attributes of many African and Indian cultures. According to legend, the principles were disseminated by early followers of Mohammed. Slaves brought Mancala games with them to the Western world. And hand-carved burnished wood Mancala boards now adorn numerous North American living rooms.

KALAH

This is the Syrian name for the basic Mancala and has been adopted by the American manufacturer of one trademarked version. In Egypt, the same game is Mankala'h. The Tamil of southern India call it Pallanguli. Barely changed, it is played in Ghana as Wari and in the Caribbean as Awari.

The nicest and most decorative boards are handmade, but the game is perfectly enjoyable on industrial plastic. The Kalah board, and most others, looks like this.

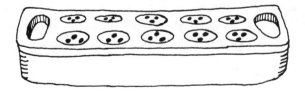

The two larger pits are the *mancalas* or *kalahs*—the scoring pits. The game begins with three pebbles, seeds or other small tokens in each of the smaller pits. The two players face each other across the board. In turn, each lifts all seeds from a pit on his own side and distributes them, one seed per hole, in a counterclockwise direction, beginning with the pit immediately adjacent to the one from which the seeds are taken. The player's own kalah is included in this distribution if the count brings the player to it. But no seed is placed in the opponent's kalah.

For example, player "A" might take the three seeds from A2 and sow them in A1, Kalah A and B6. The tactic is to sow the last seed of each batch in one of the player's own empty pits. When that happens, the successful player is allowed to take all seeds from the opponent's pit directly opposite and place them in his own kalah. The seed used to complete the successful maneuver also goes into the kalah.

Play ends when all six pits on one side are empty. Seeds remaining in opposing pits then go into the kalah of the player who cleared his own side. The winner is the player who ends with more pebbles in his own kalah.

VARIATIONS

No count exists of the versions available to experienced Mancala players. Among the simplest is the practice of permitting an extra turn to a player who contrives to sow the last pebble of a batch in his own mancala. Another greatly complicates strategy by awarding all pebbles on his own side of the board to the player whose opponent has gone out. Therefore, the primary object is to avoid going out until most pebbles have already been distributed favorably.

In Oh-War-Ree, a U.S.-manufactured version, as many as four players are accommodated at a circular board. Capture of pits, rather than pebbles, is one way of playing.

A full-dress treatise on these games is long overdue. As even a novice can tell, the possible subtleties and elegances are at least equal to those of Backgammon.

PART SIX

Games of Logic

Any sedentary game worth the name requires logical thought, but a new category of game actually explores the realm of logic and manages to do so entertainingly. The games are so instructive that some are used in schools. Their growing popularity attests hopefully that large numbers of our young remain amenable to mental exercise.

1 WFF 'N PROOF

This is not one but twenty-one games based on the logical laws of propositional calculus. The first game of the series is quite simple, but the others are complex enough to challenge anyone. Persons out of the habit of using their brains can count on severe headaches.

All the games are played with a set of specially lettered dice. Voluminous instructions guide the player from each elaboration to the next. Six-year-olds often master the simplest, called Shake-A-WFF, in which each player has eight dice, three of which he rolls in an attempt to produce a Well-Formed Formula (*WFF*, pronounced "Woof"). A WFF (just to give you the general idea of the kind of thing that six-year-olds can do and the kind of thing that I can't) is authentic "if and only if it is a 'p,' 'q,' 'r,' or 's'; or it is a two-unit expression in which the first unit is an 'N' and the second unit is a WFF; or it is a three-unit expression in which the first unit is a 'C,' 'A,' 'K,' or 'E' and the second and third units are WFF's."

The object is to form the longest possible WFF's, adhering to those rules. And, supercilious kidding aside, few games are more worthwhile. Players who master Shake-A-WFF proceed to Count-A-WFF and beyond, becoming familiar with rules such as conjunction-in, conjunction-out, implication-in, and so on.

2 QUERIES 'N THEORIES

A game for two or more from the makers of WFF 'n Proof. Here players try to discover the rules governing sentence formation in a mythical language. The result is nothing less than a drill in the scientific method, and is thoroughly engrossing.

One player, designated as the *Native,* creates his own language with letter sequences such as *YB, BY, YBB,* which represent full sentences. He also fixes on a replacement rule or rules that might prescribe that any *Y* is replaceable by a *G.* Thus the sentence *YB* could also be *GB* and *BY* could be *BG.*

Having decided on his language, the Native sets forth colored chips—for example, a yellow one representing *Y,* a blue being *B* and a green standing for *G.* The other players then ask questions by placing chips of their own on cards. By placement of these chips, the questioner may inquire if, for instance, any sentences in the language begin with *G* or end with *Y* or have a *G* in the second position. Through trial and error, induction and other well-established forms of organized thought, a capable questioner eventually can speak the language.

3 CLUE

This is a path game in which the element of the race takes a back seat to logical thinking. The object is to deduce the solution of a murder.

Special cards include one for each possible murderer, each possible murder weapon, and each room in which the foul deed might have been committed. One card from each category is chosen at random and goes unseen into an envelope. The remaining cards are then dealt to as many as six players.

At the roll of a die, players move tokens around the board from room to room. Having landed in a room, the player may suggest that the murder was committed there, by a suspect he names, using a particular weapon. If the opponent at the player's immediate left holds one or more of the corresponding cards, he shows only one of them to the player who has made the guess. Nobody else sees the card. The player now knows that the particular room, suspect or weapon is not implicated—because it is not in the envelope.

While direct revelation of that kind is the surest information obtainable, it is far from the entire story. By listening to other players' suggestions and noting whether cards are shown to them, an alert thinker can make substantial inferences.

4 MATHEMATICAL VARIATIONS

Among better games that provide mathematical recreation are Tuf and Equations. Tuf provides up to four players with dice bearing numerals and mathematical symbols. The object is to form the longest possible true equations. Equations is more sophisticated, with a playing board as well as dice, and rules that permit alert players to obstruct each other's developing equations.

PART SEVEN

Word Games

Everybody has played Ghosts, Hangman, Anagrams and Scrabble. But how many have explored the possibilities of Dictionary, in which fraud is essential? Word games fascinate millions. Here are the best.

1 SCRABBLE

One of the most successful proprietary games in the history of the industry, this variation of Anagrams uses lettered tiles marked with scoring values. The tiles are placed face down and the two to four players take up seven tiles each and place them on racks where they cannot be seen by the opponents. By turns, players form words by placing tiles on the vacant squares of the Scrabble board. A crossword pattern develops, with the object being to place tiles of the highest values on squares that provide the largest point bonuses, such as double and triple scores. After each turn, the player replenishes his store of tiles. The game ends when the stock is exhausted and someone forms a word with his last tile, or everybody is unable to form a new word. Among variants is RSVP, in which the tiles are lettered on both sides and are played onto a vertical rack. Another, RPM, features a revolving board and requires quicker thinking.

BALI

A splendid Solitaire word game adaptable to competitive play by two, three or four. Uses lettered cards in a Klondike pattern of seven columns. Cards are moved to form vertical words, which are then removed from the board. As vacancies occur atop the columns they are filled from the deck, from which plays also are made to the columns when no word-building shifts are possible. The consonant cards are numbered, and the player uses these values in computing the score earned by the words he forms.

PERQUACKEY

For two or more, using lettered dice. While a three-minute egg timer operates, the player makes as many words as possible from letters turned up by one roll of the ten dice. No more than five words are permitted to contain the same number of letters. Scores are awarded in each size category. After scoring 2,000, the player becomes vulnerable, gets three extra dice and must then make not less than 500 points per turn or be penalized 500. First to score 5,000 wins. Ad Lib is among several similar games.

2 JOTTO

This excellent trademarked game for two provides each with a pad on which to (a) write a five-letter word, (b) record the opponent's attempts to guess the word and (c) record his own attempts to guess the opponent's word. By turns, each player calls out a five-letter word and is told which of its letters appear in the opponent's secret word. First to guess an opponent's word gets points, depending on how many attempts were required.

3 DICTIONARY

The more the merrier in this one. One player takes a dictionary (preferably unabridged) and looks for a word that the others cannot define. He announces it and spells it. He then writes its dictionary meaning on a piece of paper that he folds and sets aside. Meanwhile, the others concoct their own fraudulent definitions and hand the folded papers to the holder of the dictionary. After all returns are in, the ringmaster reads each, including the true definition of the word. Votes are taken. Each vote for a player's phony definition wins him 3 points. A player's vote for the true definition is worth 1 point. Whoever gets the most points on a round gets the dictionary for the next round. Naturally, this game requires talent in synthesizing definitions that sound real. If anyone really knows the meaning of the test word, a new one should be chosen.

4 ANAGRAMS

The good old stand-by still has many adherents. Best for five or six, using Anagram cards or tiles. Under governance of an egg timer or the like, each player turns up a card or a tile from the center stock and tries to make a word that combines it with other exposed letters. Whoever makes five (or ten) words first wins.

5 GHOSTS

For any number, without pencils, paper or other equipment. First player calls out a letter and opponents each follow with a letter that follows the previously called letters in the spelling of a word. But the object is to avoid completing a word. If a player doubts that the previously called letter can form part of a word with the other letters, he may challenge. The challenged player then names the word, which must be locatable in a standard dictionary. Proper names are not permitted. The best variation permits each player to specify whether his letter belongs before or after the sequence of letters previously called.

6 CROSSWORDS

Each player draws a five-by-five crossword box. In turn each calls a letter that each places wherever he pleases in one of his own twenty-five squares. At the end, each vertical or horizontal five-letter word counts 5, and each smaller word down to those of two letters counts as many points as they contain letters.

C	O	V	E	Y	5
O	V	E	N	E	4
M	E	T	A	L	5
M	R	A	P	L	3
A	G	A	I	N	5
5	4	3	3	4	

7 HANGMAN

One player (the *hangman*) draws dashes representing the letters in a word. The opponent has nine chances to guess it. Each time a wrong letter or wrong word is guessed, the hangman draws another element of this fateful picture.

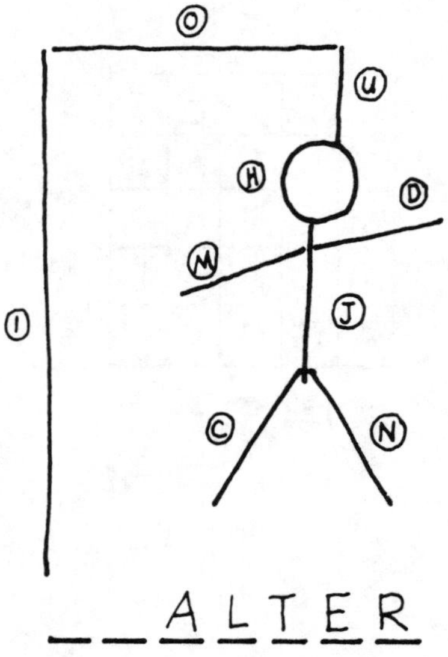

8 GUGGENHEIM

This is not exclusively a word game, but requires knowledge of a wider character. Known also as Categories, it can be played by almost any number, each with pencil and paper. Each player names a category—animals, flowers, occupations, authors, etc. These are listed vertically by all. And then a five- or six-letter word is taken at random from a dictionary and is written horizontally at the top of the paper, with plenty of space between the letters.

The word should contain no ridiculously difficult letters, such as *x*, and should not include any letter more than once. The game then consists of each player trying to write a suitable word or name in each category, forming columns in which each word begins with the appropriate letter.

	L	*O*	*V*	*E*	*R*
Animals:	Lion	Otter	Vixen	Elephant	Rhino

Time should be limited to not more than twelve minutes—assuming four players and four categories. The limit can be extended by three minutes per additional category. A player whose word is unmatched by any others gets 1 point for each opponent. Each match deducts 1 point from that maximum score. At the end of each round, the player with the most points is winner.

PART EIGHT

Games of Simulation

A school child sits at a computer keyboard and pretends to be the absolute monarch of a prehistoric land with an agricultural economy, a drought problem and a looming famine. What shall he do? Shall he raise prices? Or would the country be better off with rationing?

The computer program is ready for any choice he is likely to make. It responds quickly to his orders, showing the young ruler the consequences, large and small, of each decision, and presenting new dilemmas.

By any definition, this classroom activity is a game. That it simulates a more-or-less real situation does not disqualify it as a game—as any player of Monopoly would be quick to confirm. That it also instructs in logic, sociology, anthropology, social psychology, political science, mathematics, history and economics, and does so under conditions that find the student highly receptive, is scarcely beside the point.

And so, schoolroom games have graduated from the Musical Chairs and Mulberry Bush routine of kindergarten. With the computers on which they depend, games of immense sophistication are now found at schools and universities throughout the country. And cousins of these games have been reduced to the compass of the lithographed playing board and have appeared in stores, where they are gobbled up by a small but growing cult of enthusiasts.

Because they derive from the actual probabilities of finite situations (past, present or theoretical), and otherwise simulate reality in explicit terms, the new games offer vicarious pleasures like those of Monopoly and its kin. However, the subject matter inclines toward a grander scale. One now commands the victorious forces at Gettysburg, or tries to upgrade the performance of the losers at Normandy, or sees whether Ralph Branca can finally keep the ball low and away from Bobby Thomson on a historic afternoon at the old Polo Grounds.

The player is both participant and spectator at the same time. And the probabilities of failure or success are bounded by the batting averages, the speed afoot, the fire power, or other material limitations of the actual team or army that one pretends to command. Which is why this kind of game may not afford pleasures of quite the magnitude offered by Chess, in which the player depends entirely on his own resources. And can't blame Ralph Branca. Or Hitler.

1 GETTYSBURG

One of the earliest and best of the realistic war games, Gettysburg is an excellent introduction. It is played on a gridded topographical map. Square playing pieces, or counters, represent military units that were actually in the battle. Each is marked with its authentic name plus a numerical *battle factor* and *movement factor*. The battle factor relates to the unit's actual fighting strength and the movement factor to its mobility. Thus, divisions have larger battle factors than do regiments. And cavalry units move farther on a single turn than infantry can.

The game begins on June 30, 1863. Each unit enters play at the exact point on the map and the exact time it entered on that fateful day. The time factor is recorded by turns, each complete turn representing an hour.

On each turn, the player brings in the units prescribed by history for that particular hour, and may then move any, all or none of his other units already on the board. When Union and Confederate units occupy adjacent squares, a skirmish results. Its outcome is determined by a table stating the results of conflict between two such units occupying terrain of the particular kind (tops or bottoms of ridges, and so forth).

If both have their wits about them, the make-believe Meade must inevitably defeat the pretend Lee, but the ebb and flow of tactics is so delicious to addicts that inevitability is no deterrent.

D-DAY

This is more demanding than is Gettysburg. The commander of Allied forces selects one of seven possible invasion sites—not necessarily Normandy. The opponent, commanding the German forces, must guess where the invaders will try to land. If ten or more Allied divisions cross Europe into Germany within fifty weeks (one week per turn), the good guys win.

MIDWAY

Still more difficult, with planes and ships secretly deployed, and requiring a good bit of deductive skill.

BLITZKRIEG

This best seller is the pinnacle of battle-simulation games. It involves almost 400 military units of eight distinct varieties, and the terrain is enormously varied—including forests, mountains, deserts, cities and fields.

2 SPORT SIMULATION

Tens of thousands of statistically oriented, spectator-sport-minded Americans belong to sedentary leagues engaged in ferocious competition that employs one or another type of simulation game. Although manufacturers such as Strat-O-Matic and APBA continue unknown to the public at large, they thrive on the custom of these dedicated gamesters. The activities of the various leagues are solemnly chronicled in newsletters. World Series and Super Bowls are numerous and, what with one thing and another, it can be said that we have here many little worlds serving as sanctuaries from the larger, crueler world outside.

Some of the football and baseball games are quite elaborate. Each seeks verisimilitude by permitting the player all tactical options available to a professional manager or coach. Plus, of course, the possibility of using Babe Ruth, Hank Aaron and Ted Williams in the same lineup. No matter what the lineup, the statistical probabilities of the particular sport are embodied in each play, along with the range of likelihoods involved in a confrontation between Ruth and Seaver—or Nagurski and the Miami Dolphins' defensive line.

Generally, the play involves as much deception as real athletic contests do. The amount of ground gained on a particular play from scrimmage is bounded first by the relationship between the offensive and defensive formations, and secondarily by the roll of dice, spin of a pointer, turn of a special card, or combination thereof. Knowledge of each sport always prevails over ignorance or indifference.

Among the baseball games, APBA and Strat-O-Matic were the most exhaustively realistic when these words were written. The best of the football games—Pro Quarterback—was no longer available, its manufacturer having gone out of business. His difficulty may have been that his product was a test of sheer tactical skill between the two human beings playing it. In this field, popularity seems to depend on equipping each player with make-believe rosters of present or former professional players, and imposing fewer tactical burdens. Among games of that kind, Football Strategy and Pro-Football are worth examining.

3 MONOPOLY PLUS

A simulation game called Executive Decision anoints each of five or six players as competing corporate managements. Each must decide what raw materials to buy and how much to pay. The prices fluctuate according to rising or falling supplies affected by the players' demands.

Each starts with an equal amount of capital and secretly writes a list of the materials he wants, in what quantity and at what price. All purchase orders are revealed simultaneously, changing the available prices and supplies. The player who makes a poor choice may be unable to obtain raw material for the next phase—manufacturing. Which is followed by sales.

The statistical history of the stock market is built into The Stock Market Game. Here again, play is a matter of trying to buy cheap and sell dear without positive knowledge of whether the next minute is going to bring a bullish, bearish or mixed trend. Preferred stocks, blue chips, warrants and bonds are all involved. So is a faithful simulation of the 1929 crash.

In The Cities Game, one player (or team) is Government, another is Business, a third is Agitator, and a fourth is Slum Dweller. Business and Government begin with 90 percent of the money and the least interest in (a) social disturbance or (b) fundamental change. Each phase of play is influenced by the exposure of an *Issue Card,* which may define the proceedings as centering on slum clearance, police brutality, recreational facilities, etc. Negotiations ensue. Slum Dwellers and Agitators often threaten riots which, if carried off, cost every player half his capital. Double crosses abound. However, as play proceeds and the former underdogs begin acquiring money of their own, the urge to riot diminishes. Sometimes, an enlightened balance is achieved in which all parties vote to cooperate, the double crosses end, and a condition called *Future City* is achieved.

This sort of thing achieves a global character in Diplomacy, in which uneasy alliances drive home the point that nobody should make the mistake of trusting anybody else. The game is best for six or seven and takes hours, with long periods of secret negotiation, attempts to capture supply centers, wretchedly dishonest breaches of trust, and covert movements of land and naval forces.

The possibilities are so vast, and the joys of prevarication so profound, that a whole cult has arisen. The most effective opening moves are published in printed bulletins, along with scholarly debate about ensuing tactics. In fact, Diplomacy is a proving ground for persons interested in the abstract theory of games. This is nothing for folks with short attention spans.

BOOK THREE

GAMBLING-CASINO GAMES

Although customers win money in gambling houses every day, such good luck is exceptional. And it seldom endures. Whoever persists at the gaming tables eventually loses whatever money he has allocated to that pastime.

Which is not necessarily bad. A casino is, after all, a place of business. Like most other businesses, its function is to enrich its proprietors, not its customers. It does that by selling recreation of a particularly exhilarating kind. Its revenues derive from the "house percentage" embodied in the odds offered on every bet.

For example, the actual odds against *pass* at the Craps table are 251 to 244. But the house pays the pass bettor only even money. The difference is the house's edge. It amounts to 7/495 of every dollar wagered on pass—or 1.4 percent. On the other hand, if the bettor prefers to put his money on the contrary outcome—*don't pass*—the house edge remains at almost exactly the same percentage. This is achieved by treating a roll of 2 (in some places 12) as if it were a tie. The money just lies there, awaiting the shooter's fate on his next attempt to pass. Thus, the house remains properly impartial. It could not care less how you bet on the next roll, or whether you win it or lose it. Its own long-range prosperity is built into every move that you and your gambling companions make.

The attitude in these pages is that intermittent flings at casino gambling are great fun and worth the expense—provided that the gambler's mental hygiene permits him to bet intelligently and minimize loss. Some games are unfit for play. And in the more reasonable games, some bets are much more unfavorable than others.

In the final reckoning, the only skill allowed a casino gambler is knowledge of (a) which bets are least unfavorable and (b) when to go home. The point deserves emphasis.

A gambler is not allowed to exercise the kinds of skill open to players of other games. He is supposed to bet only on events whose outcome he can neither influence nor foresee.

If he can influence the outcome and does so, he bets on sure things, which makes him not a gambler but a crook.

Or, if special knowledge enables him to predict the outcome often enough to overcome the element of chance, he no longer is a gambler but a shark. When a shark is discovered working for the house, the cops come. And when a shark is found camouflaged as a respectable customer, he either gets the bum's rush or the casino changes the rules of the game to obstruct his skill.

Although news of crooked casinos has been rare of late, much publicity has been given to persons able to convert casino Blackjack from a gambling pastime into a sure thing. These talented players keep close track of the fall of the cards. Accordingly, they know when the composition of the dwindling deck warrants heavy bets. They profess high moral dudgeon when casinos change the rules to restore the house's percentage.

It's an interesting controversy in which this customer-oriented book is squarely on the side of the casinos. To convert gambling into a sure thing—by card-counting or other means—is as reprehensible when a customer does it as when a casino does it.

Books on casino gambling that purport to teach card-counting Blackjack systems might be likened to restaurant guides that contained chapters on ways and means of ripping off knives, forks and spoons. I have never been able to figure out what the authors of the Blackjack books are so all-fired proud of. And, furthermore, not one reader in 10,000 can learn to count cards well enough to make Blackjack into the coveted sure thing. Especially now that the casinos protect themselves by dealing from as many as four decks at a time and shuffling frequently.

On the other hand, knowledge of the proper way to play basic Blackjack is a perfectly honorable way of increasing the fun of the game while cutting the house edge to a minimum.

In Blackjack as in other games, we assume that our reader does not crave absolute professional mastery (toward which goal excellent help is available in other books). Therefore, we shall simply describe and explain some of the better bets and some of the worst pitfalls, and avoid the supersophistications. To set the stage, we shall begin with the most important attribute of the intelligent gambler—money management.

1 BASIC PRINCIPLES

The house percentage is implacable. Efforts to systematize wagering and overcome those unfavorable odds must eventually fail. That some betting systems defer the inevitable is worth knowing. Prospects are brightest for the recreational gambler who declines to remain in the casino long enough to confront the inevitable.

Some useful principles:

Limit Losses: Play to win, but expect to lose. Never allow the day's (or night's) losses to exceed a comfortable, predetermined sum. Make no attempt to recoup during the session in which the loss limit is reached. Do not resume gambling until the next visit—be it a day or a year later.

Limit Risks: Mathematics shows that one's best chance of doubling the betting capital is to place it all on an even-money Craps or Baccarat bet. If the bet wins, the bankroll is doubled. If it loses, a great deal of time has been saved. But most persons want to spend more time at their gambling. And few really need to double their gambling capital. A prudent way to buy time is to use a good system on a relatively good series of bets, with a betting unit of not more than 2 percent of capital. Thus, a $20 Craps player should have $1,000 to back it up.

Limit Winnings: Just as the smart gambler does not enter the casino without knowing the maximum he will allow himself to lose, he also imposes a maximum on his winnings. The aforementioned proprietor of a $1,000 bankroll may be prepared to lose $500 of it on each of his two nights at the resort. His chances of paying for the vacation out of winnings are enhanced if he also resolves to quit for the night after winning $250 or $300. This advice seeks to counter the lunacy of gambling fever, which is full of nonsense about riding hot streaks, turning on the old "extrasensory perception," and so forth. Our advice also abandons the schoolroom formulas of mathematicians who are constantly comparing the chances of doubling one's betting capital with the chances of being ruined. Why should those be the only alternatives?

Common sense (*and* probability mathematics) shows that a $20 bettor trying to win $400 is not quite as prudent as one trying to win only $200. For one obvious example, the $400 man may be ahead by as much as $350 before hitting a downdraft and getting wiped out. If he had been content with $200, he'd have been home free. It happens all the time.

Luck: The person who confines himself to the least unfavorable bets, using a good betting system and a sensible percentage of his capital, will probably have better luck than might otherwise befall. Beyond that, the subject is moot. Mathematics teaches that common conceptions of the law of averages are totally erroneous. Each turn of the wheel or toss of the dice is an independent event. The probability of its occurrence is identical at all times. Although a number may not have turned up in the last forty-eight throws, it is not "due." The likelihood of its appearance on the next roll is neither larger nor smaller than before. Persons who believe otherwise embrace the gambler's fallacy, or, as the professors term it, the Doctrine of the Maturity of Chances. It's a sure way to lose.

On the other hand, it is equally fallacious to believe in the inevitability of decisive winning or losing streaks. In any representative sample of casino occurrences, every possible pattern of wins and losses will be found—none of them sufficiently predictable to assure a profit to the customer.

2 BETTING SYSTEMS

Most betting systems fail because they are based on notions about the maturity of chances. If the player loses a bet, he increases the size of the next bet on the theory that a win is "due." After a few successive losses, he either is out of money or is required to make a bet larger than the casino will accept. All casinos have house limits, which vary from table to table and place to place.

A few superior systems attempt to maneuver the betting pattern so that somewhat more money is at stake on a winning roll than on a losing one. To promote logical thought, we shall begin the review of betting systems with the poorest and proceed to the best.

DOUBLING UP

This procedure is known as the *martingale* and is applied to even-money bets such as red or black or odd or even or pass or don't pass. Believing firmly in the gambler's fallacy, the player wagers that the so-called law of averages will overtake him in time to produce a profit. After every losing bet (on, for example, red), he doubles the stakes.

If the first bet is $1, and loses, the second is $2 and, during the prolonged streaks of one kind or another that occur frequently (if unpredictably) at all gaming tables, the ninth bet is $256. By that time the martingale fancier has lost $255. If the $256 bet wins, he is $1 ahead and can begin again. Alas, he inevitably encounters the house limit, which ends the betting progression in deep red ink.

Persons unconvinced of the inevitabilities sometimes try to achieve quicker profits than a successful martingale affords. Instead of merely doubling the stakes after each loss, they add a fixed sum to the doubled amount. For example, a $10 bettor might add $2 each time, making his second bet $22, his third $46, and so on. Inasmuch as losing streaks occur at random, without regard to the system player's grand designs, the house limit is reached sooner and losses are heavier.

TREND REVERSAL

The player lurks at the table waiting for three or four passes in succession, after which he places one betting unit on don't pass (or red or odd or whatever even-money bet has not paid off in the last three or four plays). He may even combine this procedure with a martingale of some kind.

He must lose because he has tied himself to the gambler's fallacy. No law of nature makes the next roll of the dice more likely to be don't pass when the previous three or five or twelve have come up pass.

We have already mentioned that and repeat it here only for emphasis. But here's something else. The notion that 1,000,000,000 turns at the table should yield about 500,000,000 passes and 500,000,000 craps, or busts, is simply not true. For example, it would be well within the realm of probability if 49.9 percent—or 499,000,000—of the turns were craps, or busts, and 50.1 percent—or 501,000,000—were passes. The difference would be 2,000,000 passes. By that time, the guy who hung around waiting for three passes in a row so that he could bet the other way would have been ruined repeatedly, if he lived so long.

Trend reversal is no better than the martingale.

HOT TRENDS

Casinos keep their roulette wheels in good repair. When one gets out of balance sufficiently to produce conspicuously biased results. it is decommissioned and fixed. Nevertheless, a school of thought holds that no wheel is absolutely *perfect*. Scholarly types chart the results, looking for the recurrence of certain numbers or groups of numbers. Having spotted a trend, they try to ride it. Unfortunately, such short-range trends are bound to occur even with a perfectly balanced wheel because random results *must* eventually include patterns of all kinds. Where faith in the hot trend is combined with a martingale, rapid disaster waits.

PYRAMID

Known also as *up-and-down* or *D'Alembert,* this implementation of the gambler's fallacy prolongs the action considerably and is especially helpful to someone (a) willing to accept a moderate loss and go home before things become really desperate or (b) willing to settle for an even more moderate profit and go home when it is achieved.

After each losing bet, the stake is increased by one betting unit. After each winning bet, it is reduced by one unit. The first bet in the series is for one unit, and if it wins, the next bet is treated as the first of a new series. But if it loses, a longer series begins in which (hopefully) each pair of bets (one win and one loss) shows a profit of one unit.

Because the bet increases one unit after each loss and decreases one unit after each win, it can be seen that more money is involved in the winning bets than in the losses. This often compensates for the predictably larger number of losing bets than winning ones.

Unfortunately, and very much as usual, the player who persists along this line without a reasonable stop-loss limit or stop-profit limit is absolutely sure to hit the protracted losing streak that ends in collision with the house's betting limit.

CANCELLATION

This also has something to recommend it when the player uses a sensibly small wagering unit, severely limits his evening's losses and is willing to leave with a small profit (if lucky enough to accumulate one). Indeed, the system produces a profit on red or black or pass or don't pass or similar bets even when the player loses as many as two of every three attempts.

To play cancellation, the player writes a string of numbers, such as 1-2-3-4. The amount of each bet is the sum of the numbers at the ends of the string. In this case, the first bet is five units. If it loses, the string becomes 1-2-3-4-5. And the next bet is six units. If the first bet is a winning bet, the two end numbers are crossed out and the string becomes ~~1~~-2-3-4-~~5~~. And the next bet is six units (2+4).

If all numbers on the string are crossed out, the player is ahead by an amount equal to the sum of the original string of numbers—in this example, 1+2+3+4=10.

The player determined to break the bank must eventually reach the house limit while experiencing a perfectly normal losing streak. But someone willing to settle for moderate wins or losses can do quite well. Comparatively speaking, that is.

THE GRIND

This system buys maximum action with a minimum bankroll and, in the hands of a player free of irrational greed, can produce pleasant victories more often than not.

The object of each betting sequence is to win one unit. If the first bet (one unit) wins, the profit is pocketed and a new sequence is begun. If the first bet loses, the next bet is also one unit. Having fallen behind, the player follows each *losing* bet with another of the same size. While still behind, each *winning* bet means that the next bet will be larger by one unit.

Thus, if during a particular sequence the player is six units behind and is betting two units and loses, he now is eight behind and bets two. If he wins, he is again six behind and now bets three. If that wins he is three behind. His next bet is four. If it wins, he is one ahead and the sequence is over. His next bet is therefore one unit.

No bet is ever larger than necessary to yield the desired profit of one unit. In the foregoing example, if the winning bet of three units had left the player only two behind, his next bet would also have been three—to produce the desired profit of one.

When playing Craps, Roulette or Blackjack, the player finds it easy to compute the bets mentally. When a sequence ends, the chip or chips that represent the profit should be put in a separate pocket.

A reasonable approach for a player with a $100 loss limit would be to fix his betting unit at $2 and resolve to walk away after winning $50. If this sounds chintzy to the big movers in the audience, let them consider a $1,000 loss limit, a $20 betting unit and a maximum evening's profit of $500.

Large bettors must beware of encountering the house's betting limit and suffering an evening's loss. Both they and smaller bettors often do well to terminate a losing sequence long before it gets serious. For example, if the player's maximum loss is fixed at fifty units for the evening, it often pays to quit a sequence when its loss exceeds twenty units. Go have a cup of coffee. Then start over again. It often is possible to wipe out the twenty-unit loss and proceed to the maximum profit.

But not always.

3 BANK CRAPS

Although he may harbor a generally high level of self-esteem, the newcomer to casino gambling is likely to be intimidated by the Craps table. Clustered there beneath billows of tobacco smoke are men and women who know all the moves. Their faces are taut with the controlled hysteria of the veteran high roller. They emit occult sounds. Their hands and chips fly too quickly for the unpracticed eye.

But stay around. Craps is a good game. It should be tried. With even slight familiarity (a state readily achieved by reviewing pages 413–416 plus what follows here), the newcomer discovers that most of the apparent high rollers are not high rollers at all. And even if they are, they almost invariably suffer from a disastrous ignorance of the game. Compounded by a curious refusal to learn it.

In any case, the stickmen, dealers and other casino functionaries at or near the table are customarily willing to help. One soon feels comfortable enough to take a fling.

From the percentage standpoint, Craps is the best of casino games. Or can be, for an intelligent bettor. No skill is needed beyond rudimentary knowledge of the proper odds on the best bets.

The Layout

This is a typical Nevada Craps layout. Variations occur throughout the state and elsewhere, but seldom matter unless they involve modifications of the odds. Of that, more later.

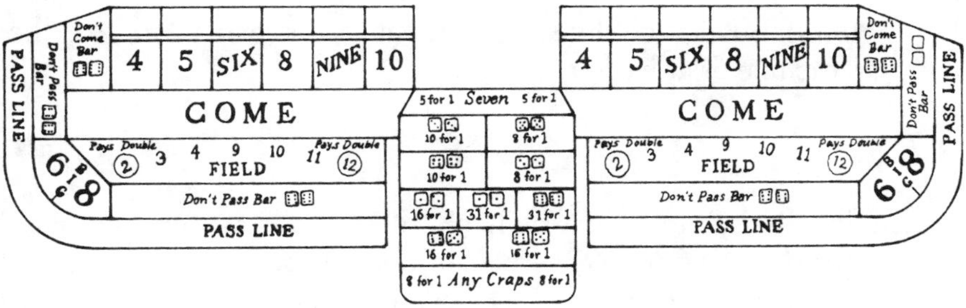

The beginner's attention is directed to the *pass line* (known plausibly as *front line*). That is where the shooter bets that he will win, and where other like-minded players also bet on the shooter's luck. Persons interested in betting that the shooter will fail can patronize the *back line*—the smaller portion of the layout labeled "Don't Pass." The word "Bar" means a stand-off or tie. Nobody wins or loses. Chips placed on that part of the layout remain there, uncollected by the house but not returned to the bettor if the shooter throws a 2 (or in some places, a 12).

We shall refer to other parts of the layout in connection with the specialized bets that apply to them.

Procedures

One reason the game seems so hectic is that the rules invite separate bets on each toss of the dice. Therefore, chips are removed from the layout after each throw and many new bets are made before the stickman then pushes the dice to the shooter for the next toss.

The shooter is required to throw the dice to the farther end of the table, preferably bouncing them off the amply padded backboard so that nobody will suspect him of trying to cheat.

Players able to get space against the table find grooves in which to place their chips. Otherwise, it is no great hardship to hold them.

Care must be taken to get bets down in time. If unable to reach the appropriate part of the layout, simply put the chips down and tell one of the dealers what the bet is. The chips will then be put where they belong. And although the hustle and bustle is considerable, efficiency runs high.

It is important to understand that nobody is required to roll the dice. If a player's turn comes and he prefers to abstain or to continue betting on the back line, he simply directs the stickman to give the cubes to the player at his left.

Best Bets

The fledgling Craps player is likely to be most comfortable playing *the grind* (*see page 478*) on pass or don't pass.

The house edge on pass is 1.414 percent. And on don't pass it is 1.402. These are among the least unfavorable bets available in casinos.

When more at ease and hungry for additional activity, the player might want to extend his betting to come or don't come. Players who play both pass and come (or the contrary back-line bets) usually lose their evening's allotment more quickly because of the extra action. But on lucky nights, they win considerably more quickly.

The house percentages on come and don't come are identical with those on straight front- and back-line betting.

A come bet is made at any time after the shooter's first toss (the *come-out*). It bets that the next number to appear will be a *natural* (7 or 11) or a point that the shooter will subsequently make. In effect, the come bet initiates a private game-within-a-game between player and house. If the shooter survives for a dozen throws or more before *sevening out* (losing), a come player may make repeated bets of that kind and have money at stake on several points. And when the shooter finally throws the fatal 7, the come bettor's losses on his remaining numbers are partly defrayed by the 7 which—for him—is a natural.

The don't come bettor is similarly situated, betting on the back line that the next throw will be a craps, or that if the shooter produces a point, it will not be made. Here again, the player may find himself with multiple bets involving numerous points.

Many persons love such action, but not many are able to keep accurate track of what's going on. Over the long run, a simple front- or back-line grind produces a large proportion of profitable sessions.

Advanced Play

Preferable to pass or don't pass and much less confusing than come or don't come is a combination of front- or back-line betting with what are known as *free bets* (or *free odds* or *front-* or *back-line odds*).

Almost all casinos allow a player who has bet on pass to make an additional bet of the same size on the shooter's point. Such a bet is made at the actual odds that the point will be made. Repeat: *Actual odds!*

In offering the correct odds, without a house percentage, the casino is fully entitled to call such bets "free."

The odds:

6–5 on a 6 or 8
3–2 on a 5 or 9
2–1 on a 4 or 10

A don't pass bettor is allowed to make the corresponding free bet on the back line—laying the odds in a wager that finds the house betting that the shooter will make the point.

This generous acquiescence to the true percentages of the game reduces the house edge to less than 1 percent! When the player bets pass and takes the odds on the point, the house edge on the total transaction becomes .848 percent. And the don't pass bettor who lays the odds is at a disadvantage of only .832 percent.

No more favorable terms are offered at any game in any American casino. In the past, some houses occasionally presented slightly better opportunities, allowing the player to double his bet when taking or laying the odds. This reduced the house edge to 6/10 of 1 percent. With the inevitable legalization of casino gambling in states other than Nevada, enlivened competition will probably reincarnate double odds, and may also give rise to other inducements of the same character.

In the meantime, players able to keep wits intact at a Craps table will do well to play a grind on pass while making every possible free bet. Or, if the spirit moves, play the whole thing negatively on the back line.

In some places, if the player's pass or don't pass bet is not of an amount that permits a rounded payoff when a free bet is made, the casino allows the player to increase the free bet by the necessary amount. For example, if betting $4 on pass, the player is permitted to make a free bet of $5 in hope of collecting the 6–5 odds on the 6 or 8 tossed by the shooter on his come-out.

In some casinos, which should be shunned, the player whose line bet is not of an appropriate amount is allowed to increase it all he wants—but not at the proper odds.

For that reason, it is essential to memorize the odds.

It is equally essential to remain awake and alert when doing all this business at a Craps table. As already remarked, the proceedings are hectic. A player unable to keep mental pace should retreat at once to straight line betting, preferably with a grind.

Bad Bets

The worst possible bets are the ones made in casinos that pay substandard odds. For example, some places bar not only the 2 or 12 on the back line but sometimes smuggle in the 3. Inasmuch as a 3 occurs twice as frequently as a 2 or 12, it increases the house percentage to more than 4 percent. Unless, as the old joke puts it, this casino has the only game in town, and you are not going to be able to gamble again for the rest of your life, why patronize such a table?

As to the other bad bets at Bank Craps, they are numerous. For purposes of this book, the most expeditious approach is a blanket one: If the bet was not covered in the foregoing pages, it should be avoided because it allows the casino an exorbitant edge.

To offer an example, some players are enamored of *field bets,* in which they put money on the proposition that a 2, 3, 4, 9, 10, 11 or 12 will appear on the next throw. Such a bet looks reasonable, inasmuch as it pays even money and the chances of one of those seven numbers turning up seem better than the chances of 5, 6, 7 or 8. Alas, the four losing numbers can be rolled in a total of twenty different combinations of the dice. But the seven field numbers account for only sixteen of the possible combinations. This, combined with the house odds of even money, gives the establishment an edge of more than 11 percent on every field bet.

Some of the *hard-way bets* extract more than that—as much as 22 percent in some casinos!

With line and free bets available, it seems a waste of energy to learn the rest of the game.

4 BLACKJACK

Alone among casino games, Blackjack metes out rewards in direct ratio to the player's skill. Anyone motivated to master some rather complicated tactics can reduce the house edge to a level approximately equal to that of Craps. But considerable study and experience are required.

Layout and Procedures

The usual setup provides seats for six or seven players. During slack periods, a single player is allowed as many hands per deal as he may please, and as may be available.

In most casinos, the dealer uses from two to four decks of cards, dispensing one card at a time counterclockwise from a special box (*shoe*). To frustrate the minuscule percentage of players able to case the deck and tell what cards remain in it at the end, the practice of dealing from a single deck is being abandoned. Moreover, dealing procedures include the precaution of reshuffling the combined decks after about three-quarters of the cards have been dealt.

The game resembles parlor Blackjack (*review pages 284–287*) except that (a) the house now does all the dealing, (b) the dealer

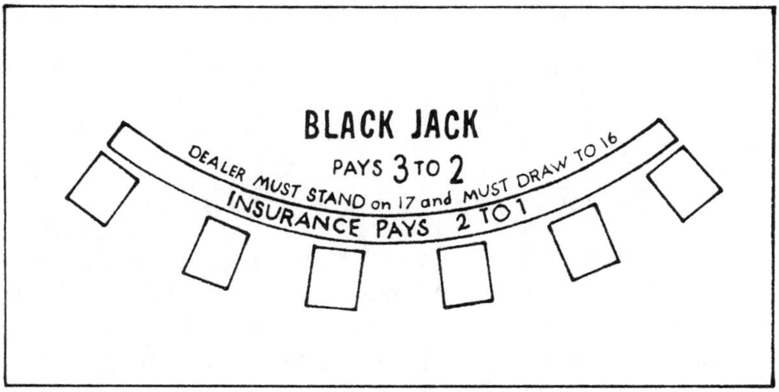

must stand on a count of 17 and (c) the player who busts loses his bet, even though the dealer may also bust.

In that last rule lies the casino's main advantage. Each player is required to complete his own draw before the dealer does. As players bust, their bets are collected and they are out of action, regardless of how the dealer may fare at his own turn.

Depending on local policies, players may get one or both of the first cards face up. The practice of dealing both face up seems to be spreading and makes sense. In any case, no cards are dealt until all bets are made.

The dealer always takes one card up and one down, usually in that order.

Basic Tactics

Hard Hands: A hand in which there are no aces, or if there are, the player exercises his option of counting each ace as 1 point. The following tactics are effective.

Dealer's Exposed Card	*Player Should Draw When Holding*
2 or 3	12 or less
4, 5 or 6	11 or less
7 or higher	16 or less

OTHERWISE STAND PAT

Soft Hands: When counting an ace as 11:

Dealer's Exposed Card	*Player Should Draw When Holding*
A to 8	17 or less
9 or higher	18 or less

Doubling Down: Casinos vary in their permissiveness toward this play. Some allow it on any combination of the first two cards. Others allow it only on a count of 11, or of 10 or 11. Depending on the house rules, the best approach is to double the bet whenever holding 11. If holding 10 and the dealer shows neither a 10-count card nor an ace, double. With 9, double only if dealer shows 6 or less.

Splitting Pairs: Some houses allow only a one-card draw to a split pair. Regardless, aces and eights should always be split. And fives and tens should never be split. When to split other pairs is a question too complex for the casual player. Interested parties should consult Recommended Reading, below.

Insurance: If the dealer shows an ace, many casinos solicit insurance bets, on which they pay 2–1 in the event that the dealer actually holds a natural blackjack count of 21. This is a miserably stupid bet to make except for someone who has counted the preceding cards and is reasonably sure that the dealer has the natural. Otherwise, the 2–1 odds give the house a large edge.

Betting Technique

A player who follows a tactical pattern such as the one described above can do quite nicely using a grind system (*see page 478*) at the Blackjack table. The betting unit should be a multiple of two so that the player's own natural blackjack hands will be paid promptly at the full odds of 3–2.

Recommended Reading—Advanced Tactics

In 1962, Dr. Edward O. Thorp, an exuberant mathematician, revealed that he had figured out the game and had been taking casinos to the cleaners. Moreover, he published his strategies, which included tactics much more refined than those set forth above. Chief among the Thorpian sophistications were techniques for keeping track of the high-count cards and undermining the house percentage.

Thorp's disclosures precipitated guerrilla conflict between the casinos and "casedown" players able to count the cards. Whenever the houses revised their dealing procedures and other rules to stay ahead of the card-counters, increasingly elaborate offensive techniques were proposed in book after book. As suggested earlier, the entire saga has its unseemly aspects and, besides, extremely few players are sufficiently motivated or sufficiently talented to learn these techniques.

Nevertheless, readers who feel equal to tactics more complicated than the basic ones described in these pages should read Thorp's *Beat the Dealer*. Besides refining the instructions on what to hit and when to stand, the professor offers various card-counting systems, a general grasp of which may improve the reader's game without provoking difficulties with casino managements.

5 ROULETTE

By common consent, this comparatively leisurely game forms the boundary between casino games worth bothering with and casino games designed exclusively for suckers. With its high house advantage of slightly more than 5¼ percent on all but one of the numerous bets it offers (at most North American tables), the game is not nearly as reasonable as Craps, competent Blackjack or Baccarat. But it requires little thought, except for players of money-management systems, and purveys a kind of *continentale* elegance that many tourists find diverting.

The Layout

The U.S. roulette wheel contains thirty-eight slots, of which two are the 0 and 00 and the rest are numbered 1 through 36. The odds against any particular number turning up are therefore 1 in 38—or 37–1, but the house does not pay the full odds. It pays 35–1 on a single number, for an edge of 5.26 percent. If the player chooses to play the *red* (the color of eighteen of the numbers), the house pays even money instead of 10–9 (that is, 20–18). The house edge therefore remains at 5.26 percent, as on *black* or *odd* or *even* or any of the other possible bets except on a five-number *line* bet, when the edge leaps to just under 7.9 percent.

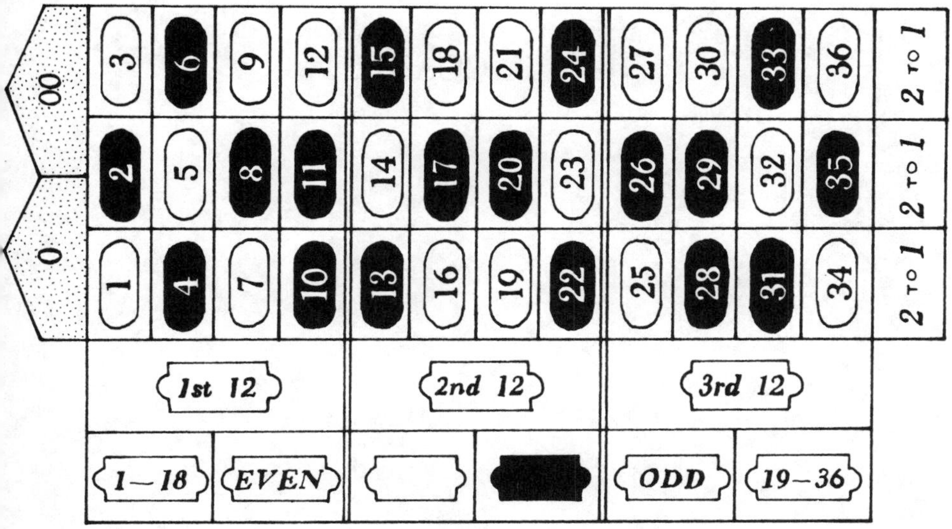

Most European and a very few American wheels have only one 0. This reduces the house edge to 2.7 percent. At Monte Carlo, the house does not collect on the 0 but lets all bets stand until the next turn of the wheel. This pares the edge still further, to about 1.4 percent, making Monte Carlo Roulette a comparatively worthwhile game. On the other hand, occasional casinos in the Western Hemisphere have experimented with wheels containing 0, 00 and 000 –for an exorbitant edge of 7.69 percent.

Tactics

The house advantage of more than five cents per wagered dollar is extremely difficult to withstand. The larger the number of bets (à la the big swingers who seem to cover the entire table with their chips), the greater the house profit on every spin. To get the best run for the money, try a *grind* (*see page 478*) on black or red, or odd or even. For slightly more excitement, try a *cancellation* (*see page 478*) on one of the columns or one of the twelves. Chances at the U.S. Roulette table are never bright, but are best for the player who is thoroughly prepared to lose, and not only imposes a severe limit on losses but goes home as soon as his winnings (if any) exceed a nightly minimum.

6 BACCARAT

As played in the United States, this ritualized card game demands nothing of the participant except his money. His only choices are whether to bet on the *bank* or on the *player,* and how much. Every other move is dictated by the rules, copies of which are distributed to all comers.

Layout and Procedures

The table usually accommodates ten or twelve customers and a house dealer. The layout is clearly marked for bets from each seating position on either of the only two alternatives—bank and player. Beginning at Seat 1, each customer serves in turn as *banker*—a symbolic role, inasmuch as everyone plays against the house, including those who choose to bet on the bank. Banker slides four cards face down to the dealer from a *shoe* that holds as many as six shuffled decks. The dealer slides the first pair to the customer chosen to act the part of player. Ordinarily, this honor goes to whoever has made the largest bet on player. The other pair goes back to the banker. After dealer flips player's pair and announces their value, banker exposes his own pair and dealer calls their value.

Subsequent action is dictated by the printed rules, with the winner

PLAYER
HAVING

1·2·3·4·5·10	DRAWS A CARD	
6·7	STANDS	
8·9	NATURAL Banker Cannot Draw	

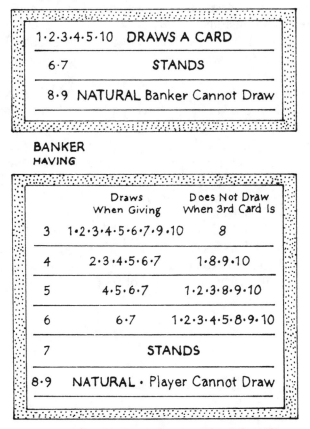

BANKER
HAVING

	Draws When Giving	Does Not Draw When 3rd Card Is
3	1·2·3·4·5·6·7·9·10	8
4	2·3·4·5·6·7	1·8·9·10
5	4·5·6·7	1·2·3·8·9·10
6	6·7	1·2·3·4·5·8·9·10
7	STANDS	
8·9	NATURAL · Player Cannot Draw	

PICTURES AND TENS DO NOT COUNT

IF PLAYER TAKES NO CARD
BANKER STANDS ON 6

the hand that equals or comes closest to a total count of 9. Picture cards and tens are not counted in the addition.

All bets are paid at even money. When banker wins, so do the customers who bet on the bank. And when player wins, so do those who bet on him.

The house collects 5 percent of all winning bets made on the bank. This produces a house advantage of 1.06 percent on such bets. The edge on bets that back the player is 1.23 percent, and the average house take at Baccarat is a modest 1.15 percent.

TACTICS

Because the game is completely mechanical and permits absolutely no judgment, the customer's only problem is to avoid losing more than he can afford. The low house edge should encourage use of a *grind* or *cancellation* (*see pages 478–479*) approach to money management.

Rules vary somewhat from place to place, which need cause no concern. The house takes care of everything, relieving the player of responsibility for his own actions.

In Chemin de Fer and other European variations seldom played in North America, the customer has more options. One is the celebrated call of "*Banco*," which means that the caller has decided to bet against the house for the entire amount in the bank.

Baccarat and its permutations are much quieter than Craps, much fairer than Roulette and immeasurably easier than Blackjack. It is ideal for persons who seek a comparatively square shake and do not care to exert themselves too much. The only drawback is that betting minimums usually are higher than at other casino games.

7 OTHER DIVERSIONS

The following casino games are included simply for the record. Some of them are fun, but all entail outrageously high house percentages. Craps, Blackjack, Roulette and Baccarat are every bit as much fun and give the player a better shake.

CHUCK-A-LUCK

Known also as birdcage. Three dice are enclosed in a device (*chuck cage*) resembling a wire hourglass. The house man flips the cage, the dice drop to the bottom and bounce around. The player has bet on any number from 1 through 6. If his number appears once, he is paid off at even money. If the number appears twice, he collects 2–1, and a triple gets him 3–1. Three dice can fall 216 different ways. Of these, 91 are winners for the player. In combination with the standard payoffs, these relatively few winners produce a house edge of just under 8 percent.

KENO

A fancied-up Bingo or lottery wherein the player gets a card with eighty numbers on it and marks from one to fifteen of them. If those he chooses turn up in twenty numbers produced by one or another mechanical device, the player wins. Indeed, he can win thousands of dollars for a bet of less than a dollar. A seduction, but the house edge is in the vicinity of 20 percent.

WHEEL OF FORTUNE

Where she stops nobody knows and the house gets 14.5 percent of the money. Variants such as Money Wheels and Big Six Wheels yield even larger profits to the operators.

SLOT MACHINES

These are only nominally games. They have a hypnotic effect on some folks, who would rather feed coins into them than stand at crowded gaming tables. They seldom extract a house percentage of less than 10 percent and sometimes go as high as 50 percent.

BOOK FOUR

GAMES FOR CLUB CAR AND TAVERN

As if drinking were not sufficient diversion, man has developed innumerable supplementary entertainments for the long hours spent in bars. The most popular of these are Shuffleboard, Bumper Pool, Darts, Ski Ball, and other forms of scaled-down, usually mechanized athletics familiar throughout North America.

Somewhat scarcer and considerably less far-flung are sedentary pastimes with which two or more conscientious drinkers can beguile themselves without (a) risking prolonged conversation or (b) putting coins in slots or (c) expending precious energy.

Once in a great while, something like The Match Game captures the fancy of an in-group, is publicized and spreads. But not often. Which is why the reader may be appalled to discover that the dice game played at bars and other counters in his neighborhood is unmentioned here. No slight is intended. The game has simply not spread. Few do.

Among those that have, here are the best.

1 MATCH GAME

More than one fashionable member of the New York literary set was reputed to carry his own set of solid-gold matches for use in what surely has been—and to a small extent remains—the most soigné bar game of all time.

Can be played by two to six, but is best with at least four and not more than six. Each player has three matches (which need not be made of precious metal). Each extends a closed fist containing, at individual tactical option, from one to three matches or no matches at all. Whoever guesses the combined total wins the round.

Procedure

Because the last player to guess the total in a game for three or four has the advantage of making deductions based on his opponents' calls, it is necessary to determine who shall call first and what the order of succession shall be. This is done simply by playing a preliminary round in which one of the players goes first by mutual consent and the others follow clockwise. Here, as in the game itself, nobody may repeat a number already called. The player who comes closest to guessing the true total of matches concealed in extended fists wins the right to go last on the first official round. The player with the second-most-accurate call goes next to last, and so forth. After each round, the disadvantage of calling first rotates clockwise, as does the advantage of calling last. As we shall see, this advantage tends to diminish when more than four play.

In the usual game for three or more players, the object generally is to avoid losing (and having to pay for drinks). Therefore, the winner of a round simply drops out and remains out until a final round determines the loser.

In a two-hand game, victory usually goes to the first to win two rounds.

In all versions, a round can be won only by guessing the exact total of matches. If nobody does so, the round is a stand-off and is replayed.

Tactics

This is a game of genuine skill, in which a good Poker player will defeat a mediocre gamesman almost every time. For a hint of the ramifications, consider a two-hand game in which player A extends an empty fist and his opponent holds two. Player A then calls "None." His opponent promptly wins by calling "Two." The first player has made it too easy by calling "None" and revealing that he was holding no matches.

Similarly (and still in the two-hand game), a call of "Five" must mean a holding of two or three, and "Six" must mean three, and "One" must mean none or one.

Because logic is so powerful a factor, good players solve the two-hand problem by trying to escape unharmed from the disadvantage of going first. They do this by deliberately misrepresenting the situation. For example, holding none, the first player might call "Four"—a patent impossibility known as *miscall* or *bluff* or *overcall.* If the opponent, holding two, responds "Three," the round is a tie. The bluffer has reached his goal. He has lost nothing and on the next round it is his turn to call last.

Needless to say, a playing pattern of unvaried bluffs is as self-defeating as any other too-predictable tactic.

In games for three or more, where the rule against repeating an opponent's call serves to decrease the advantage of going last, the best tactics are based not only on psychological readings of opponents' patterns but on knowledge of the game's simple averages. Mathematically, if not actually, the average player holds one and a half matches. Without other evidence to go on, the best call is one's own holding plus a match and a half per opponent.

Needless to say, all Match Game players know the averages and take them into account when bluffing.

FINGERS

This ancient European predecessor of The Match Game requires no equipment except a full set of fingers on one hand. Best for two, each of whom extends a hand on signal, simultaneously calling the total number of fingers to be displayed by both. It is permitted to extend a closed fist (no fingers) or any number of fingers from one to five. To win a round, one of the players must be exactly right. Ties do not count. First to win five or ten rounds wins the money or the drinks or both. When three or more play, it is best to continue on the one-versus-one basis, with others waiting to play the winner.

2 DOLLAR POKER

One day recently in the bar of New York's Regency Hotel, nobody was playing The Match Game, but a jolly group was hard at Dollar Poker, known also as Liar's Poker.

The equipment consists of a dollar bill per player. The best game is for five or six, although two can manage.

Referring to the serial number on his own bill, each player tries to predict the best Poker hand possible by using the best of his numbers in combination with those on the unseen bills of his opponents. Numbers rank downward from zero through one.

The game begins with an auction, in which each player may bid or pass. A pass simply defers bidding until one's turn comes up again. Each bid must surpass the previous. For example, five eights is a higher bid than five sevens. After bidding ends with a full round of passes, the bills are displayed. If bidder can form the bid hand from the serial numbers, he wins. Otherwise, he pays everybody.

For protection against sharpers who use favorite bills with especially potent combinations of numbers, some groups start with three to five bills from each player. A dealer shuffles and deals the bills. In some circles, each player gets only one bill per round. In others, he gets three or four or five and can choose the one he prefers for each round. And in some games competition involves not Poker hands but the number of times a digit appears on all bills involved in the game. In this version, the auction is won by the person whose bid names the largest amount of the highest digit.

Winner collects the losing bills.

Tactics consist of realizing that dollar bills have eight-digit serial numbers. In the two-hand game, when one player calls a pair, an opponent holding two of the same number can usually win by bidding four.

3 DICE GAMES

Poker Dice, Liar Dice and Help Your Neighbor appear in various forms as favorite bar, counter and club-car diversions. We have discussed them on pages 417–418 and 421. Other good dice games are beyond number.

Games to Avoid

In general, any dice game in which the bartender or shopkeeper serves as banker is likely to be a high-edge proposition for the house. Even less fair are tavern "games" that actually are not games at all but sure-thing stunts, tricks or gags. For example, all public libraries contain literature explaining how to make money by, for example, offering somebody 2–1 that he can't name three of the numbers contained in the serial number on your dollar bill. The proper odds are more than 5–1. That's not a game but a swindle.

INDIAN DICE

For any number, using five dice. The object is to roll the highest Poker hand, with the 1 wild. Straights do not count. Each player has three throws and is permitted to set aside any number or numbers he likes on either of the first two.

TWENTY-SIX

Storekeepers used to augment their incomes with this one, which produces a house edge of about 20 percent when played unfairly. However, it makes a good head-to-head game. Each player chooses a point from 1 through 6 and throws ten dice thirteen times. Whoever produces his point the most times in the thirteen rolls wins the money. In some places, a total of twenty-six or more calls for a double payoff.

BUCK DICE

With three dice, each player continues rolling as long as each roll produces his point at least once—earning a score of one point per appearance. The point is established in advance by rolling a single die. After a roll fails to turn up the point, the next player tries. Fifteen points is *buck,* and means that the player drops out, a sure winner. Three of a kind of the point number is *big buck,* worth an immediate 15. Three of any other kind is *little buck,* worth 5. Loser is only player who has not made 15. In some places, when the score reaches 13, the player rolls only two dice. With 14, only one die is used.

YANKEE GRAB

A three-dice game, played for whatever stakes suit the group. Each player has three tosses and must set aside the highest die of the first two rolls (only one if there is a tie). The player's score is the sum of the first two dice set aside plus whatever he throws on his third try. High score wins.

BARBOODI

This is a two-dice competition between two players, known as *fader* and *shooter,* with other players wagering on the outcome.

Fader begins by announcing the size of his bet with shooter (up to whatever maximum the group has established). Shooter and fader then alternate throws of the dice with 3-3, 5-5, 6-6 or 6-5 winning and 1-1, 1-2, 2-2, and 4-4 losing. No other rolls count. When shooter throws 1-2 and loses or fader wins with 6-5, shooter keeps the dice. Otherwise, they go to fader, who becomes the next shooter. The player at his right becomes fader.

Index